PEACEKEEPING

Pergamon Titles of Related Interest

Harkavy GREAT POWER COMPETITION FOR OVERSEAS BASES:
The Geopolitics of Access Diplomacy
Mroz BEYOND SECURITY: Private Perceptions Among
Arabs and Israelis
Mroz INFLUENCE IN CONFLICT: The Impact of Third Parties on the
Arab-Israeli Dispute Since 1973
Nicol PATHS TO PEACE
Wiseman/Taylor FROM RHODESIA TO ZIMBABWE:
The Politics of Transition

Related Journals*

INTERNATIONAL JOURNAL OF INTERCULTURAL RELATIONS
WORLD DEVELOPMENT

*Free specimen copies available upon request.

PEACEKEEPING
Appraisals & Proposals

EDITED BY
HENRY WISEMAN
PUBLISHED FOR THE
INTERNATIONAL PEACE ACADEMY

PERGAMON PRESS
New York Oxford Toronto Paris Frankfurt Sydney Tokyo

Pergamon Press Offices:

U.S.A.   Pergamon Press Inc., Maxwell House, Fairview Park,
                     Elmsford, New York 10523, U.S.A.

U.K.   Pergamon Press Ltd., Headington Hill Hall,
                     Oxford OX3 0BW, England

CANADA   Pergamon Press Canada Ltd., Suite 104, 150 Consumers Road,
                     Willowdale, Ontario M2J 1P9, Canada

AUSTRALIA   Pergamon Press (Aust.) Pty. Ltd., P.O. Box 544,
                     Potts Point, NSW 2011, Australia

FRANCE   Pergamon Press SARL, 24 rue des Ecoles,
                     75240 Paris, Cedex 05, France

**FEDERAL REPUBLIC   Pergamon Press GmbH, Hammerweg 6,
OF GERMANY**   D-6242 Kronberg-Taunus, Federal Republic of Germany

Copyright © 1983 International Peace Academy

Library of Congress Cataloging in Publication Data

Main entry under title:

Peacekeeping, appraisals and proposals.

(International Peace Academy series)
"Published for the International Peace Academy."
Includes index.
1. United Nations--Armed Forces. I. Wiseman,
Henry. II. Series.
JX1981.P7P39   1983   341.5′8   82-22575
ISBN 0-08-027554-0

Printed in the United States of America

To Marcus, brother and life-long friend,

and to the memory of our father, Sam.

Acknowledgments

The initial ideas for this volume emerged several years ago from a small group of practitioners and scholars invited by Arnold Simoni to deliberate on the future of peacekeeping at his summer home in Orillia, Ontario. Some of the ideas then generated have served as basic themes and integrative guides to the design of this volume. I am grateful to him for this seminal endeavor. I also extend my considerable and special thanks to the contributors of this volume who, though pressured by the demands of active and prominent professional careers, agreed to devote the time, thought, and work in accepting invitations to write articles dealing with specific sectors of peacekeeping, and for the diligence and patience with which they responded to my pleas for minor modification and editorial revisions.

I am also indebted to Angela Clark of Pergamon Press for guidance throughout and acceptance of several revisions and additions to the original manuscript, and to Florence Musaffi, who, with competence and without complaint, scrutinized, corrected, and shepherded the manuscript through her typewriter from beginning to completion.

Overall, my deepest appreciation is extended to General Indar Jit Rikhye and the many members of the Academy for the inspiration, willing assistance, and friendship proffered since our first meeting at the International Seminar conducted by the Academy in Vienna in 1970. Beyond this, no acknowledgement could be complete without due recognition to the creative and devoted work of those diplomats and soldiers from some 55 nations, and members of the UN secretariat, who have given reality to the concept of peacekeeping and who have built the foundation upon which new structures of peacekeeping and conflict resolution may be created in the future.

Contents

Foreword
Indar Jit Rikhye

United Nations peacekeeping has gone through periods of innovation, creative development and expansion, coupled at times with periods of difficulty, failure, and disillusionment. The International Peace Academy (IPA) was formed in 1969–70 during a hiatus, when troublesome images of past and then current operations over-shadowed any optimism about the future. But optimism remained in the minds of many who were most experienced and knowledgeable. They had shared in shepherding the formation of mandates through the Security Council and the General Assembly and had contributed much to their political and operational success, as well as to coping with the difficulties and failures. It was they, with the optimism born of experience and necessity, together with friends with faith in the future, who decided to form the IPA to conduct research and international training in the field of peacekeeping.

Their faith and conviction were well founded. In the 1970s, a resurgence in the practice of UN peacekeeping and commensurate developments in regional and other forms of non-UN peacekeeping took place. During those years the research and practical training provided by the IPA for diplomats and military officers, the constructive dialogue between practitioners and academics, and the "off-the-record" meetings on crisis issues where the application of peacekeeping seemed promising and propitious, all contributed to practical political developments.

In the 1980s, the UN and regional organizations and governments face distressing strategic, political, economic and humanitarian issues that generate grave and threatening conflicts at an unrelenting and devastating rate. There is greater need now than ever before to improve existing models and develop new procedures of conflict management.

In international politics, the IPA seeks to contribute through research, publication and dialogue, a means of assisting in the development and utilization of effective procedures for conflict management. To this end, it has launched new programs in the fields of multilateral negotiation and of inquiry into the crucial relationships between the provision of security and disarmament. Its primary focus, however, remains in the field of peacekeeping, which has evolved to new international levels of legitimacy with diverse means of application. This, then, is the time for a careful assessment of the past along with a critical look into present developments. It has seldom been more important to draw on the lessons of history for application with constructive imagination to the future.

The editor, Henry Wiseman, who has been associated with the IPA since the first international seminar held in 1970 in Vienna, was recently IPA's Director of Peacekeeping Programs, and has published extensively on peacekeeping. Many of the contributors are well-known and seasoned diplomatic and military practitioners with vast and diverse experience. They offer here their wisdom and scholarly analysis from many perspectives. Others, recognized academic authorities in the field, offer the benefit of detached critique. Together they present a knowledgeable and profitable synthesis of theory and practice with reasoned assessments of future possibilities.

The IPA is therefore very pleased to sponsor this new volume of analytical and original articles at a time when great efforts are necessary to cope with and contain the numerous and dangerous conflicts that shatter the peace in so many regions of the world, and which threaten to escalate into disastrous international military confrontation.

Major General Indar Jit Rikhye (Ret.)
President, International Peace Academy
New York, New York

December 1982

Introduction
Henry Wiseman

The tension and struggle between the forces for change and the forces for the maintenance of the status quo are constant and dynamic features of the international system. This struggle is manifested in the frequent occurrence of ferocious and intractable conflict. By contrast, but by no means as persistent and powerful as the systemic propensity to conflict, are the creation and utilization of international structures, instruments, and procedures for the containment and resolution of these conflicts by political means. The attempts to superimpose peaceful regulatory systems upon the disordered world are extremely hazardous and difficult. The national political propensities to make war are far more powerful than the international processes to maintain peace. Nonetheless, the will, determination, and imagination of peoples and states persist in the quest to make order out of chaos and prescribe peaceful measures for progressive social change.

Peacekeeping is one such measure initiated by the United Nations as part of the overall process for the management of conflict. As a nonenforcement procedure, it began its life in 1946 as a relatively simple means of international observation of the manner with which parties in conflict complied with UN resolutions to cease hostilities. Since that time, peacekeeping has evolved in size, complexity, legitimacy, and effectiveness, though frequent practice has also demonstrated weaknesses and limitations. Both success and failure have given rise to controversy. Peacekeeping has been evaluated and judged, however, not only upon its own level of achievements and upon its legal, political, and structural capabilities, but predominantly against the background of the lackluster performance of the United Nations in its primary responsibility for the maintenance of international peace and security. The consequence of this approach is that operations have been analyzed

and judged on a case by case basis; there being a close
correlation between the ad hoc character of each operation and
the generally segmented evaluation by its critics. While fundamental, such analysis is no longer adequate.

There are two basic reasons to substantiate this assertion. The first is that these fractured modes of analysis fail
to provide an historical perspective of the development of UN
peacekeeping itself; and secondly, they also fail to perceive
peacekeeping in relation to the many profound changes and
events that have and are occurring in the international system, especially the shift from a bipolar to a polycentric system, the growth and problems of development of the Third
World, the failure of detente, and the evident need to either
revitalize detente or find new ways to relax international
tensions, contain and resolve conflict, and bring a halt to the
conventional and nuclear arms race.

In the present era, political analysts, theoreticians, and
statesmen are giving increased attention to the nature of
conflicts and crises. We are just at the beginning of our
endeavors to understand them and to search for new and
effective means of management, which range from anticipation
and prevention to peaceful means of resolution before as well
as after problems have erupted into open conflict. Peacekeeping has already proven to be a flexible and adaptable
instrument that can be usefully applied by itself as a stopgap
measure or, more comprehensively, as part of an overall
process of peacemaking. The perception and analysis of
peacekeeping should be released from the isolation of its
historical confinement so that its inherent and potential utility
can be better and more fully understood - with the reasonable
expectation that it would be more effectively and frequently
applied by the UN and as well by regional organizations such
as the OAS and the OAU, by other special ad hoc measures as
were innovatively employed to replace the UN Emergency Force
on the Sinai after the Security Council failed to renew its
mandate in 1979, or by the Commonwealth in association with
the United Kingdom in Rhodesia in 1980. The literature on
peacekeeping is largely retrospective. A fuller appreciation
of the realities of peacekeeping - of what it can and cannot
accomplish - as well as imaginative considerations of possible
future applications should be entertained alike by scholars,
diplomats, and military analysts. The potentially productive
relationship between peacekeeping and humanitarian assistance
to areas of natural, political, or military disaster; the provision of security as a necessary counterpart to arms control
and disarmament; and the relationship between peacekeeping
and development are matters which have already been raised in
international forums and are just beginning to be explored in
the academic community. All this is welcome, yet much more
still needs to be done in the exploration of new approaches to
the prevention, containment, and resolution of conflict.

The human and electronic networks of communications at the UN and just about every other diplomatic forum are clogged with pleas for nations to demonstrate the "political will" to resolve the many pressing international problems, though at the present time there appears little sign that such "political will" is sufficiently widespread to bring immediate results. The least that can be done, however, is to demonstrate constructive procedures, proposals, and models to guide or even inspire their deliberations when the political will is forthcoming. Perhaps it is not too much to hope that some of the ideas and analyses herein may encourage them to do so.

This line of argument is not meant to ignore or downgrade the many problems which confront sponsoring organizations, contributing states, and host countries, or the reasons why many states are indifferent or oppose the practice of peacekeeping. These are amply delineated and discussed in this volume. While looking to the future, the authors have been urged to be as critical as required by careful analysis of past and ongoing experience. And this they have done with the care and insight that their considerable individual experience and knowledge bring to bear on the subjects under consideration, with the result that many controversial issues are exposed and discussed from a variety of perspectives.

A critical analysis of past experience as a realistic and imaginative guide to the future have guided the substance and perspectives of the chapters which follow. All the chapters were expressly written for this volume. They deal with the historical analysis of operations, the characteristics of contemporary practice, current trends, and probable and desirable futures. With necessary lead time to put together a volume of this nature, it is difficult to keep up with the new active engagements, new approaches, and the innovative ideas that are flowing into the field from a variety of sources. Therefore, those readers who would like a volume of this kind to offer a full analytical update of current operations together with the litany of new proposals and also a tour de horizon of new concepts, will, I hope, be satisfied with demarches in all three areas that may not match all these expectations. Events are happening too fast for the scholar or the practitioner to be historically up to date and futuristically precognitive, the latter a difficult feat under any circumstances. Nonetheless, the reader will find herein substantive, articulate, and cogent analyses by eminent scholars and practitioners.

The chapters are gathered according to subject area in five parts: "Historical Review and Analysis"; "National Perspectives"; "Operational Considerations: Political and Military"; "Regional Peacekeeping"; and "Peace, Law, and the Future." For convenience, a short descriptive review is placed at the beginning of each part.

PEACEKEEPING

I
Historical Review and Analysis

Introduction to Part I

These articles present an historical overview of United Nations peacekeeping from its tentative beginning as a small observer group in the Balkans in 1946 to the large and complex peacekeeping operation launched in Lebanon in 1978. Rikhye casts the practice of UN peacekeeping within the larger picture of the Charter and the general political characteristics of the UN, the context of East/West relations and the emergence of the Third World. His personal military and political experience with the formation, operational command, and political implications of peacekeeping provide valuable insights into the complexities, problems, achievements, and the nature of the often weak relationship between the dual processes of peacekeeping and peacemaking. His critique is based on analyses of individual cases; UN, regional, and unique ad hoc arrangements; as well as the provisional UN arrangements for Namibia. Comparative analysis presents at one and the same time an in-depth understanding of the practice of peacekeeping and a comprehensive appreciation of its evolution in a world which bears little resemblance to postwar expectations. For the very reason of the failure of the superpowers and the UN to maintain peace, peacekeeping stands out as an impressive accomplishment. He concludes that many of the analyses of peacekeeping "were only partly accurate, and have failed to take account of the developmental, flexible, innovative and versatile manner in which peacekeeping has been used from its very inception."

Wiseman's article presents a chronological examination of all UN operations, dealing with the characteristics of each conflict, the political negotiations leading to the decisions to call for cessation of hostilities and the formation of observer and/or peacekeeping forces, the nature of their mandates and operational modalities of the forces placed in the field, and the ultimate disposition of each operation.

3

This thematic format serves as a basis for comparative analysis of each aspect over time, demonstrating, among other matters, changes in the political forces which sponsor or acquiesce in the establishment of peacekeeping operations and incremental growth and complexity of the operations themselves. Wiseman also elaborates on the controversies over the very concepts, principles, and operational modalities of peace-keeping, showing to what extent many of these matters have been more or less resolved in practice and how many states in the Third World (and in specific cases the USSR and France) have shifted from positions of opposition to support. The description and analysis contained in this chapter furnish the evidence and argumentation for his second chapter, "Peace-keeping: The Dynamics of Future Development." Part I offers a framework and substantive background information for a profitable appreciation of the chapters that follow.

1
Peacekeeping and Peacemaking
Indar Jit Rikhye

The leaders of the Grand Alliance, who led their nations to victory in World War II, agreed to establish the United Nations to maintain international peace and security. Procedures to resolve conflicts peacefully were included in the charter; and, if this failed, the Security Council (unlike the League of Nations) was established to enforce peace if necessary. It was not long after the signing of the United Nations charter in San Francisco that the cold war between the East and West grew in intensity and so clouded the issues that the potential of the United Nations in the maintenance of peace and security could not be fully activated. The mutual suspicions and rival interests of the two sides prevented the employment of arrangements to enforce peace when needed. With the exception of the United Nations operation in Korea, which was made possible due to a Soviet walkout from the Security Council when it refused to invite the representative of the People's Republic of China to participate in the debate, the Council never agreed to enforce peace.(1)

The evolution of peacekeeping, not originally envisaged in the charter, has occurred mostly in response to the failure of the Security Council to make sufficiently effective use of pacific measures to resolve conflicts and/or to enforce peace, and of the failure of the world organization to agree on an effective means for limiting the arms race. In facing the challenges to make peacemaking efforts more effective, the United Nations' peacekeeping system was first developed to observe, monitor, supervise, and report on agreements to end hostilities or accomplish cease-fires. Initially, as in the Balkans, Palestine, and Indonesia, military observers were provided by governments represented on United Nations commissions in the areas concerned. It was not until the establishment of specific United Nations military observers for

5

truce supervision in Palestine and for the observation of the
cease-fire in Kashmir, that observers were no longer responsible to the representatives of their governments, but directly
to the United Nations. In fact, from then on, military observers were not necessarily drawn from the nations represented
on peace missions.

The term "peacekeeping" not to be found anywhere in the
charter, was first used when the United Nations General
Assembly,(2) under a Uniting for Peace resolution,(3) established the United Nations Emergency Force (UNEF) consisting
of military units and aircraft to take over the Suez Canal area
which had been earlier occupied by Anglo-French forces. The
peacekeepers were required to supervise the withdrawal of
foreign forces from Egyptian territory, to provide security for
the canal clearance operations, and to interpose themselves
between the Egyptian and Israeli forces during the latter's
phased withdrawal. On completion of these tasks, UNEF was
deployed between the Egyptians and the Israelis along the
armistice demarcation line in the Gaza Strip and along the
international frontier in the Sinai. Furthermore, UNEF was
made responsible to ensure the freedom of shipping through
the Straits of Tiran.

All these functions carried out by UNEF were within the
scope of typical military operations. There were, however,
also differences in the establishment and the introduction of
the United Nations force from that of normal military operations, i.e., the troops were equipped with light arms for
self-defense only, the host country was consulted in the choice
of national contingents, and they received the consent of the
host country to enter their territory. Above all, their
functions and objectives were to be effected by their very
presence and not by fighting. They had no enemy. The
experience of UNEF became the basis for all subsequent United
Nations peacekeeping operations.

The term "peacekeeping" has, over time, acquired connotations that apply to many variable methods in the treatment of
conflict, and has come in usage for various types of non-
United Nations missions by military and paramilitary groups.
A distinction needs, therefore, to be drawn between these
kinds of activities and United Nations' peacekeeping. Non-
United Nations peacekeeping has come to mean whatever those
applying it have wished it to mean, from total suppressive
action to the use of minimum military force in the control of
violence. In United Nations' peacekeeping, however, enforcement plays no part. It is a concept of peaceful action, not of
persuasion by force. The fundamental principles are those of
objectivity and nonalignment with the parties to the dispute,
ideally to the extent of total impartiality from the controversial
issues at stake. The "weapons" used by the peacekeeper in
achieving his objectives are those of negotiation, mediation,

quiet diplomacy, tact, and the patience of Job - not the self-loading rifle.(4) Thus, United Nations peacekeeping is designed to end hostilities through peaceful means, thereby creating a climate within which the peacemaking process may be successfully applied. Peacekeeping is, therefore, not the culmination of conflict, but only a beginning of a new stage of the process in the peaceful resolution of conflict. It is the use of nonenforcement military measures for the continuation of diplomacy.

The experience of peacekeeping in its various forms over the last thirty-five years indicates that it is not a panacea to be applied to all conflict situations. In fact, its usage has been limited, and it has varied degrees of success. Broadly speaking, peacekeeping has been applied on an ad hoc basis to meet emergency situations. It is only in the case of Namibia that a peacekeeping operation for the transfer of power has been preplanned, and this exception has yet to be applied and to prove its usefulness. However, in almost every case, peacekeeping has been applied to areas beyond the dominance of the superpowers.

The superpowers with their respective blocs have prevented another global conflict by the maintenance of approximate balance of forces, including the nuclear deterrent. This has brought peace to Europe for more than three decades (hitherto unknown in its history). However, "soft areas" remain on the fringes of the East-West defense alliances, and the ability to project their military power wanes on the extremities of their respective zones of influence. It is in these "soft areas" (e.g., the Balkans, Cyprus, Lebanon, and Yemen) and the "extremities" of power zones (e.g., Korea, West Irian, and Rhodesia (Zimbabwe) that the use of peacekeeping forces has proved suitable. A second characteristic of peacekeeping is its association with the process of decolonization. The rising demand for self-determination after World War II could no longer be resisted by the war-weakened European colonial empires. The sudden withdrawal of colonial authority left power vacuums, exposing ethnic, geographic, ideological, historic, and religious rivalries, of which Cyprus, India-Pakistan, Indonesia, and Palestine are examples. Peacekeeping evolved as a useful tool to assist in the peaceful transfer of power, and enabled the Western powers to limit, if not altogether isolate, struggles for national liberation from the cold war that had begun to pervade almost every aspect of international relations. A third characteristic of peacekeeping resulted when the leaders of newly independent and unstable regimes, lacking the means to restore law and order or to provide security, invited, or readily accepted, United Nations intervention. The United Nations operations in the Congo and Cyprus fall under this category.

A review of the United Nations peacekeeping experience also demonstrates that there have been notable instances where peacekeeping could not be applied. In superpower confrontation situations, as in Berlin and the Cuban missile crisis, the United Nations played only a peripheral role. Also, in areas where the superpower interests are directly involved - e.g., the Czechoslovakian and Hungarian crises in the Soviet bloc, and conflicts in Latin America, which are within the sphere of influence of the United States - the United Nations has been called upon to play a marginal or nominal role.

Nor have the Western European nations tolerated any third-party intervention in dealing with disputes within their own areas of jurisdiction, as in the case of the civil war in Northern Ireland or the conflict between the United Kingdom and Iceland over fishing rights. There are other examples of the exclusion of the United Nations machinery for peacemaking and peacekeeping. These are the India-China border war, the Chinese occupation of Tibet, the Sino-Soviet border conflict, the war in Indochina, the invasion of Kampuchea by Vietnam, the Chinese "punishment" action against Vietnam, and the war in the Horn of Africa.

Furthermore, the application or nonapplication of peacekeeping to certain types of conflict situations have been subject to unique considerations. In the first instance, the United States was able to successfully rely on this system as an extension of its foreign policy in dealing with conflicts as in the Balkans, the Congo, Cyprus, Lebanon, and West Irian, where it desired to exclude Soviet influence. This was possible because the United States enjoyed a dominant influence over the United Nations General Assembly through the 1960s. Successive United States administrations and the Congress also found it a more acceptable means to achieve decolonization, which they supported, and to help allied European powers in this process. Notwithstanding Soviet objections, the United States emerged with augmented influence in those areas where peacekeeping was applied.

Since the infusion of many new African and mini-states to the United Nations and the consequent loss of an automatic majority in the General Assembly, the situation has significantly altered. Yet, in spite of United States' disappointment at the emergence of bloc voting contrary to its wishes, and the labeling of these actions by some United States leaders as "the tyranny by the majority," as on issues relating to apartheid in South Africa and self-determination for the Palestinians, the United States has, nevertheless, rallied majority support in the General Assembly on a number of occasions, including serious situations of the American hostages in Iran and the Soviet military intervention in Afghanistan. However, neither of these two instances has proved suitable for the application of peacekeeping as part of the process of conflict resolution, though peacekeeping is still suggested as a useful measure to establish a favorable environment for the resolution of the Afghan crisis.

It has been stated earlier that, before the establishment of UNEF, the United Nations relied on commissions and military observers for peace observation to facilitate the peacemaking process. The first example of the use of a fact-finding and reporting mission arose on a Greek complaint that Albania, Bulgaria, and Yugoslavia were actively supporting the guerrillas operating in the northern part of Greece. In April 1947 the Security Council formed a commission which found evidence confirming the Greek complaint, but a minority report by Poland and the Soviet Union contested this. The Council, unable to adopt any resolutions to resolve this question, removed the item from its agenda, thereby enabling the General Assembly to deal with the matter, which it did in September 1947. The Assembly called upon Albania, Bulgaria, and Yugoslavia to stop aid to the guerrillas. It established a United Nations Special Committee on the Balkans (UNSCOB). The military attaches from the embassies and consulates of the member states of the committee in the region acted as military observers. During its four years of existence, UNSCOB submitted regular reports to the General Assembly, which led to the adoption of several resolutions, resulting in the termination of external assistance to the guerrillas.

Other examples of observer missions are the United Nations Military Observer Group in India and Pakistan (UNMOGIP), to supervise the cease-fire line in Kashmir; and the United Nations Truce Supervision Organization (UNTSO), to supervise the armistice lines between Israel and neighboring Arab states, which were established over thirty years ago and are still in operation. Although, since their establishment, there have been three wars in each region - between India and Pakistan, and between the Arabs and Israelis - these observer missions continue to perform useful functions in the international efforts to resolve these continuing disputes. UNMOGIP, even in its present reduced form, provides a United Nations presence in an area where a serious conflict remains unresolved. This presence is a deterrent, and helps normalize conditions along the cease-fire line. What is even more important is that it is in a position to provide early warning in the event relations between Pakistan and India deteriorate and the opposing armies move toward a military confrontation. Such an early warning should enable the Security Council, or the powers that wield influence on the parties, to take preventive measures.

Similarly, UNTSO continues to perform an important role in the Middle East. It keeps the Security Council informed of incidents and other developments that threaten peace. It is able to conduct low-level diplomacy to diffuse and prevent

escalation of minor crises, and, to a limited extent, it provides
a deterrent to open hostilities. The importance of UNTSO is
highlighted by the unique nature of its mandate, which makes
it the only peacekeeping mission in the area that may continue
unless specifically terminated by the Security Council; an
unlikely possibility as long as its presence is needed. All
other peacekeeping forces require periodic renewal. UNEF II,
an important ingredient to the Camp David accord, was terminated in the face of a Soviet veto threat, making it
necessary for the parties to the Camp David accord to
establish a peacekeeping operation outside the framework of
the United Nations to monitor, among other matters, the
border between Egypt and Israel following the latter's
withdrawal from the Sinai in April 1982.

In Indonesia, fighting broke out between the Dutch
colonial authority and Indonesian nationalists in July 1947 when
the two sides failed to agree on the implementation of the
November 1946 agreement for the independence of the Indonesian archipelago. The Security Council, despite the objection
of the Soviet Union, asked the five Western consuls in Batavia
to observe the cease-fire that the Council had called for. The
consuls, in turn, recommended that military assistants, to be
provided by the nominated states, should carry out observer
responsibilities on the ground. This was accepted by the
Council. A Good Offices Commission (GOC) was also appointed
by the Council, consisting of military advisors of three member
states of the Council, which established a United Nations
presence in the area. These military advisors helped supervise the cease-fire, delineated demilitarized zones and
cease-fire lines, and performed many other functions which led
to the cessation of hostilities. When the Dutch, citing
increasing violations by the Indonesians, abrogated the truce
in December 1948 and launched a "police action," the Security
Council reconstituted the GOC as the United Nations Commission for Indonesia (UNCI). The military observers were
increased in number to supervise the new cease-fire, and all
hostilities ended by 15 August 1949. UNCI supervised the
withdrawal of the Royal Netherlands forces and helped to deal
with the question of the future of the Royal Netherlands
Indonesian Army. Having assisted in establishing a satisfactory environment for Dutch and Indonesian renegotiations, a
final settlement was reached. An instrument for the transfer
of sovereignty was signed in 1950; and UNCI was disbanded in
the early part of 1951.

These examples clearly demonstrate the usefulness of
peacekeeping as an important tool in diplomacy. Similarly, the
United Nations has utilized military observers to great advan-
tage on many other occasions, e.g., in Yemen during 1963-64
(UNYOM), in Lebanon in 1958 (UNOGIL), and in the Dominican
Republic in 1965 (UNDOMREP). Each of these missions played

a useful, though varied role in furthering the process of peaceful resolution of those conflicts. However, the use of peacekeeping forces, starting with UNEF, also made it possible for the United Nations to meet greater and more complex challenges.

Without going into the details of the events that led to the Suez War in 1956, it was the nationalization of the Canal by President Nasser that brought the crisis to a head. Impatient and dissatisfied with the diplomatic efforts to resolve the crisis, France and the United Kingdom decided to seize the Canal by force. Israel, already looking for a way to end the fedayeen raids from the Gaza Strip, became a willing partner to this decision. In finding a solution to this complex problem, the United Nations had to consider a number of factors. The Anglo-French invasion was intended to internationalize the control of and security arrangements for the Canal. The Israelis wished to eliminate fedayeen bases. All three were determined to punish Nasser, and nothing would have pleased them more than his downfall. On the other hand, Nasser wished to be rid of foreign troops on Egyptian soil and to retain sovereignty over the Canal.

The conception and implementation of UNEF provided most of the answers to satisfy all the parties. Lester Pearson, the Canadian Secretary of State for External Affairs, was the first to suggest the creation of an international force to replace the Anglo-French and Israeli forces, and it was Dag Hammarskjold who gave UNEF its final shape, which became a model for the future. With the establishment of UNEF, the evolution of its operational role, and the status of the forces' agreement with the host country, almost all demands of the parties to the conflict and the needs of the international community were met. UNEF proved a perfect solution for a complex problem. The British, French, and Israeli forces were persuaded to withdraw only on the basis that an international force would replace them. After much pressure from the United States, the Israelis agreed to withdraw from the Sinai provided UNEF patrolled the frontier. Later, the Israelis also agreed to vacate the Gaza Strip when UNEF replaced them and assured discontinuation of fedayeen activity. Finally, the Sharm el Sheikh was turned over to UNEF with the guarantees that the Egyptians would be excluded from the area and freedom of navigation through the navigable channel of the Straits of Tiran would be assured, an assurance supplemented by American commitments. UNEF was not a panacea to all the problems related to the Arab-Israeli conflict, but it did establish an environment for negotiations to continue. As described earlier, no fruitful discussions followed, and a status quo was maintained for the next ten and a half years.

However, though created to meet an emergency, UNEF remained much longer in the area than had been anticipated.

During its tenure, it kept peace and quiet along the armistice demarcation line in the Gaza Strip and the international frontier between Egypt and Israel, and kept the shipping lane through the Straits of Tiran free from interference. The Arabs, Israelis, and the international community, lulled by this long period of relative peace, did little to deal with basic and serious issues that divided the Arabs and the Israelis. All concerned were troubled and disappointed by the inaction. But the Palestinians, who suffered most from the Arab-Israeli conflict, decided in the mid-1960s to resort to violence, thereby opening another chapter in the long struggle between the Arabs and Israelis. The subsequent withdrawal of UNEF in May 1967 was followed by the Six-Day War in June 1967, which left the Arabs defeated and humiliated and Israel in occupation of large parts of Arab territories.

The withdrawal of UNEF was a disappointment to many who had hoped that this novel instrument would be sharpened for future use. Some others felt that peacekeeping only served to maintain a status quo where a solution was not possible or perhaps not desired. The fact was that the Americans and the Soviets, with rival interests, could not reconcile their differences and let matters rest. It was the withdrawal of UNEF that led to war. Had the Security Council responded and the superpowers agreed, UNEF could have continued in the area as a basic condition for the renewal of the negotiations.

But once again (after the Six-Day War), the parties to the conflict, the international community, notably two superpowers, missed favorable political opportunities to deal with this conflict. In November 1967, the Security Council adopted Resolution 242 as the best compromise, but left the main issues to be resolved. Unable to tolerate the insult of occupation of the Sinai and the loss of revenue by the closure of the Canal, Nasser resorted to a war of attrition. When Nasser died, his successor, President Sadat, vowed revenge and launched another war in October 1973. The negotiations to end this war led once again to a United Nations peacekeeping operation, UNEF II, which was a central factor in the series of negotiations, conducted by the United States Secretary of State, Henry Kissinger, to first disengage the Egyptian-Israeli forces in the Sinai. Subsequent negotiations between Israel and Syria resulted in a further peacekeeping operation on the Golan Heights, the United Nations Disengagement Observer Force (UNDOF). This revival of peacekeeping as an essential element of the diplomatic process in the Middle East was decided by the Security Council on the initiative of its nonpermanent members, after the initial United States-Soviet-sponsored call for a cease-fire went unheeded. It did not take Kissinger long to learn that peacekeeping was the perfect instrument for his step-by-step diplomacy to resolve the

Arab-Israeli conflict. UNEF II was established to separate the Egyptians from the Israelis east of the Canal and to enable the latter to withdraw beyond the strategic passes in the Sinai. A United States-Sinai mission, equipped with electronic surveillance equipment, was added to observe the disengagement, to provide early warning, to enhance credibility of UNEF II, and to manifest the American commitment to peace.

The introduction of UNDOF on the Golan Heights enabled Kissinger to negotiate an Israeli-Syrian disengagement of their forces. Personnel from the United Nations Truce Supervision Organization in Palestine (UNTSO), established in the area in 1948-49, were added to UNDOF and, as well, to the United Nations Interim Force in Lebanon (UNIFIL) in 1979 to supervise the withdrawal of Israeli forces which had occupied the territory from the Israeli border to the Litani River and to maintain the area as a buffer zone, all to provide experience and continuity. The Soviet Union, realizing the importance of UNEF II, insisted that Poland contribute a logistics contingent, and, in a rare show of cooperation, the Americans and Soviets sent military observers to join UNTSO.

Further negotiations on the Arab-Israeli conflict faced strong opposition from the Israelis to the participation of the PLO, whereas the Soviets espoused the Palestinian cause and backed Syria and other hard-line Arab states. In the hard realities of American politics, it also suited the United States to exclude the Soviets from future negotiations. This limited the negotiations to Egypt, Israel, and the United States, which culminated in the Camp David accords, bringing peace between Egypt and Israel. But there is little progress in the resolution of the future of Palestinians. Additionally, the Soviet threat of veto in the Security Council caused the discontinuation of UNEF II, which created difficulties in the formation of arrangements for the final phase of withdrawal of the Israelis from the Sinai, leading to plans for an "independent" peacekeeping operation headed by the United States. At least some other form of peacekeeping would be required in the Sinai.

The presence of UNDOF on the Golan continues to be vital. It provides a safety valve to Israelis and Syrians alike, permitting Syria to undertake large-scale peacekeeping in Lebanon and look to protecting its eastern flank from Iraq, with whom its relations seem to sour periodically. Similarly, the presence of the United Nations Interim Force in Lebanon (UNIFIL) curtails, with varied degrees of success, the escalation of PLO raids into Israeli and further Israeli retaliation, while itself subject to attack and casualties. Nevertheless, its presence is still valuable even though it is at the center of a political and military quagmire and Israeli-supported Christian troops control strategic approaches from South Lebanon to Israel. Removal of UNIFIL would undoubtedly cause alarm in Israel and might well oblige them to reoccupy the area south of the River Littani with serious international consequences. The presence of UNIFIL also serves Syrian interests. Syrian forces are widely dispersed. Besides the Golan Heights and Lebanon, they are also involved in maintaining law and order in Northern Syria. The presence of UNIFIL is an assurance against possible Israeli or Israeli-encouraged activity from the Bekaa Valley.

Despite the importance of continuing peacekeeping in the Middle East, the lessons of UNEF I must not be forgotten, i.e., that peacekeeping is only a means to an end and not an end in itself.

There are notable applications of peacekeeping by the United Nations that were an essential prerequisite to a peace-making process. When fighting broke out between the Dutch and the Indonesians in West Irian in 1962, it was immediately followed by negotiations to end hostilities. A group of United Nations military observers implemented the cease-fire and also had the difficult task of collecting Indonesian infiltrators dropped and landed haphazardly all over the remote island. The United Nations then assumed temporary administration of the territory through the United Nations Security Force in West New Guinea-West Irian (UNTEA). Later, a United Nations-supervised referendum was held to decide its future. UNTEA was also responsible for the maintenance of law and order during the interim period of administration by the United Nations. After six months, there was a peaceful transfer of authority to the Indonesians.

The United Nations operation of the Congo (ONUC) of 1960-64 faced challenges of a kind hitherto unknown to peace-keeping operations. In the initial phase, it had to assist the new government in restoring law and order. This task was made extremely difficult by a mutiny of the Armee Nationale Conglais (ANC) soon after the Congo became independent with the immediate removal of all the white officers and noncommis-sioned officers. Therefore, instead of assisting the ANC, the United Nations force frequently found itself having to restore order among the ranks of the ANC security forces themselves, and having to assume responsibility for maintaining law and order, and facilitate normal working of governmental, social, and economic institutions. The ineffectiveness of the central Congolese authority and the coup d'etat that followed led to the splintering of the young nation. The province of Katanga had already declared secession a few days after independence was achieved. Subsequently, the provinces of Oriental and Bakwanga followed suit. Only ONUC succeeded in maintaining a semblance of authority of the central government over the country, and it was ONUC that facilitated the work of the United Nations Conciliation Commission, the reconvention of parliament, and the subsequent restoration of the authority of the newly appointed government over the country, except for Katanga.

The mineral-rich province of Katanga, strongly supported by foreign economic interests, maintained its secession for a much longer period by means of international lobbying and a well-equipped Katanga gendarmerie, led by Belgians and white mercenaries. After two unsuccessful attempts to deal with the problem of foreign military personnel and political negotiations to end the secession, a hesitant Security Council authorized ONUC to use force in the last resort in order to reunify the country and restore law and order in Katanga. The caution advised by the Western bloc led to more negotiations and delay. In the meanwhile, the Katangese increased their pressure on ONUC troops, sealing off their camps and installations, blocking roads and access to the airport at Elizabethville, assaulting United Nations persons, and so on. Shooting incidents increased until the situation became intolerable for the United Nations. And, because of a lack of discipline among the mercenaries, danger to the mining installations became so threatening that the members of the Security Council unanimously decided that ONUC should act. In a brilliantly conducted military operation and acting in self-defense, ONUC ended the secession of Katanga and secured life and property. The introduction of massive United Nations and United Nations-channeled aid during the early life of the young nation was also made possible by ONUC. There is little doubt that the Congo, now called Zaire, has remained a unified nation largely through the efforts of ONUC.

The Congo experience proved useful to the United Nations when it was called upon to deal with fighting between the Greek majority and the Turkish minority in Cyprus, which occurred in 1964 a few months after the acquisition of independence. The United Nations established the Peacekeeping Force in Cyprus (UNFICYP) which, besides separating the adversary forces, was required to protect both communities, assist in civil police duties in the areas of conflict, and provide emergency economic assistance in areas of scarcity.

But the practice of peacekeeping does not end with the United Nations. Regional organizations have evolved their own systems of conflict management and peacekeeping. Both the Organization of American States (OAS) and the Organization of African Unity (OAU) have effectively used military observers to report on specific outbreaks of conflict and to monitor cease-fires. As in the case of the United Nations, these regional organizations have found observation and monitoring effective systems in support of diplomatic measures to manage conflict. However, there is only one example of the OAS employing a peacekeeping force, i.e., to deal with the civil war in the Dominican Republic in 1965. The OAU attempted in 1978 to introduce a peacekeeping force to end the civil war in Chad. But, in that case, only Nigerian troops under the aegis of the OAU arrived in Ndjamena. Finding the situation too complex to be dealt with by a single nation, Nigerian troops were withdrawn some four months later. The OAU has continued its efforts to deal with the fighting in Chad and with the later intervention by Libya in 1980, through diplomatic means and through the creation of another but unsuccessful peacekeeping operation. There was also a call for assistance from the United Nations in some form of cooperative peacekeeping to no avail. The OAU renewed its efforts to introduce a new peacekeeping force toward the end of the year with troops from Senegal, Zaire, and a small contingent from Nigeria. The force faced difficulties achieving effective strength and carrying out its mandate and resulted, eventually, in failure.

The application of peacekeeping by OAS in the Dominican Republic in 1965, in spite of some political difficulties in the earlier phases, was more than justified by the end results. The causes of the conflict were political, social, and economic. When General Trujillo, the strongman who had harshly ruled over the Dominicans for almost 30 years, was killed, his assassins chose democracy. Juan A. Bosch, an historian, mild in character but popular with the masses, was elected president. But the established military and economic elites of the Dominican Republic soon tired of Bosch's economic and social policies, removed him from office, and installed a junta. Donald Reid-Cabrel, a businessman, emerged as the new strongman. However, when he failed to improve the economy, these same elites urged a return to democracy. Reid-Cabrel agreed, but when his actions indicated that he had little desire to give up power, a pro-Bosch group of officers staged a coup, resulting in a civil war. OAS then established the Inter-American Peace Force (IAPF), which was mandated to end the fighting, control the rival armed civilian and military factions, protect human life and property, and create conditions to enable an OAS committee, which was established to deal with the political crisis, to start negotiations. The factions first agreed to a provisional government, which was to pave the way for new elections. This was made possible by IAPF through its vigilance in keeping incidents of individual or small factional fighting from escalating, and in generally maintaining law and order. This phase was successfully accomplished, and a duly elected government was installed. IAPF remained long enough to help integrate and reorganize the Dominican Security Forces.

The Commonwealth has also been actively considering the use of peacekeeping. During the war in Nigeria in 1967-70, the Commonwealth considered the introduction of a peacekeeping force to end the fighting and help resolve the conflict. But the Nigerians, like most Africans at that time, were suspicious of peacekeeping because they feared that it might work against them, as they believed it did when the

Lumumba government, which they supported, was overthrown in the early stages of ONUC. For this and other reasons, no peacekeeping operation was established. However, in the case of the Rhodesian crisis, the Lancaster House conference in London of 1980 did agree on a Commonwealth monitoring force to monitor the cease-fire during the transition phase when elections were held. Additionally, the presence of the Commonwealth electoral observers helped enormously in the peaceful transfer of power from a white minority to a black majority rule in Rhodesia, now called Zimbabwe.

What of the future? Extensive negotiations have resulted in detailed United Nations preparations to supervise a cease-fire and the election of a constituent assembly for Namibia. But these plans to bring about the independence of Namibia have been cast into grave doubt by the actions of South Africa and the Reagan administration in the United States. Yet there can be little doubt that some form of third party peacekeeping operations will take place. As 1981 draws to a close, it takes little imagination to envisage the utilization of peacekeeping in the resolution of the many grave conflicts which threaten regional security and international peace.

It is not our intent here to speculate on what specific cases may occur in the future, but to emphasize that, despite serious disagreements, the overall international political climate is both conducive and supportive to the use of peacekeeping as a conflict control mechanism both by the United Nations and by regional organizations. There can be no doubt that the growing frequency and intensity of conflict in many regions of the world require this form of third party intervention. The world is too explosive a place to allow the fires of conflict to rage without concerted effort to dampen and extinguish them.

Different exigencies will require different remedies. Can peacekeeping fulfill the many and different functions that will be required in the future? The development and practice of peacekeeping as here described demonstrates the versatility and adaptability of the process. Furthermore, there is increasing evidence of a confluence of peacekeeping and peace-making, blending these two elements into a more effective instrument of conflict resolution, as demonstrated in a very unique way under trying conditions in the Congo and in an innovative and integrated way in Rhodesia. Plans and pro-posals for Namibia are also of this type. It may well be that the Camp David accords, effective in the peaceful resolution of conflict for Egypt and Israel, may also prove to be a funda-mental stage in larger and more complex arrangements for a fuller settlement of the increasing problem of self-determination for the Palestinians.

Until recently, peacekeeping has been regarded as a narrow and specific activity associated with the United Nations and the process of decolonization; as subject to many weaknesses and deficiencies; and, after the forced withdrawal of UNEF I in 1967, as terminal.   Too often, the weaknesses were stressed; it was viewed as confined to the era of decolonization and as inflexible in purpose and performance. In retrospect, these analyses of peacekeeping were only partly accurate, and have failed to take account of the developmental, flexible, innovative, and versatile manner in which peace-keeping has been used from its very inception.

NOTES

1. During the UN Congo operations, the Security Council Resolution S/5002 did authorize the UN force "to take vigorous action, including the use of requisite measure of force, if necessary. . . ."

2. United Nations General Assembly Resolution 1000 (I ¦-1) of November 5, 1956.

3. United Nations General Assembly Resolution 377 (v).

4. See Indar Jit Rikhye, Michael Harbottle, and Bjorn Egge, The Thin Blue Line (New Haven: Yale University Press, 1974), chap. 2.

2
United Nations Peacekeeping:
An Historical Overview
Henry Wiseman

INTRODUCTION

United Nations peacekeeping had a remarkable beginning in 1956 with the establishment of the first United Nations Emergency Force (UNEF I) in the Middle East which followed the invasion of Egypt by Israel, France, and the United Kingdom. This was a dramatically innovative venture charged with the task of supervising the withdrawal of the invading forces from Egyptian territory and the subsequent monitoring of the armistice lines. UNEF I was followed by two further large-scale operations: the United Nations Force in the Congo (ONUC), called upon to ensure the withdrawal of foreign military elements which had entered the newly independent country and to ensure its territorial integrity against secessionist movements; and the United Nations Forces in Cyprus (UNFICYP) in 1964 to prevent a recurrence of fighting between the Greek and Turkish communities and to contribute to the maintenance of law and order and the restoration of normalcy.

Between 1956 and 1964, the UN thereby firmly embarked on a new and important modality of conflict resolution in the interests of international peace and security. Peacekeeping manifested achievements and promise and, as well, problems and limitations. On the Sinai, UNEF I maintained effective interposition between Egypt and Israel for more than ten years. In the Congo, for four years, ONUC accomplished and ensured, under extensive and protracted difficulties and at great political and financial cost, the sovereign integrity of the state. In Cyprus, UNFICYP was an effective interposition between Greek and Turkish communities which drastically minimized the degree of local conflict, but has been prolonged

much beyond its original mandate and international expectation
because of the failure of the parties and of the efforts of the
UN to achieve a political settlement.

The founders of the UN foresaw the need to provide and
utilize means to avert, contain, and/or resolve conflicts in
order to protect humankind from the scourge of war; the
primary responsibility being to promote and maintain international peace and security. Chapter VII of the Charter
entrusted the basic authority and responsibility to the Security
Council. The means prescribed was the Military Staff Committee, which, it was anticipated, would command a large military
force by land, sea, and air to prevent or repel aggression
from any quarter, excepting the permanent members of the
Security Council.

East-West talks on the size and organization of a UN
military force produced grandiose proposals, but concluded in
total failure. The frigid winds of the cold war chilled the
diplomatic corridors and assembly halls of the UN and the
Military Staff Committee lapsed into dormancy. History, notwithstanding these efforts to redirect it into peaceful paths,
unfolded in the eruption of frequent and violent conflicts
threatening and disrupting regional and international peace and
security. Thus challenged, and without any ready mechanism
to cope with such situations, the UN resorted to the innovative
and ad hoc measures of peacekeeping; innovative because it
was entirely unplanned and unforeseen, and ad hoc because it
was necessary to devise new political and structural procedures for the administration and direction of peacekeeping
forces. But peacekeeping, though it employs the use of
military forces to supervise the cessation of hostilities and the
maintenance of cease-fires, is not an enforcement measure as
might be understood to be within the scope of Chapter VII of
the Charter, although there are some gray areas subject to
varying interpretation.

The ad hoc nature of the first operations has characteristically persisted in all later ones. And although many of the
practices and procedures have become institutionalized, efforts
to formalize the source of authority and guidelines for financing and administrating peacekeeping forces have, so far,
failed. The Special Committee on Peacekeeping Operations
(Committee of 33), established in 1965, continues with its
deliberations without final agreement. Consensus on several
aspects have, however, been adopted in practice, and each
successive operation, as elaborated in later pages, draws on
previous experience and provides a firmer base for the future.

There have been progressive developments and many
accomplishments, which, unfortunately, have been often over-
shadowed by controversy. The Soviet Union opposed UNEF I
on the grounds that the General Assembly did not have the
constitutional competence to mandate a peacekeeping operation,

despite the fact that the Security Council authorized the issue to be moved from its agenda to the General Assembly. The Soviets were additionally angered because the invaders of Egypt went unpunished and Soviet influence was partially excluded from the area by the introduction of UNEF I. The Soviets opposed the Congo operation because the UN sided with "pro-Western" President Joseph Kasavubu, and rejected Soviet-supported Prime Minister Patrice Lumumba, curtailing Soviet intervention on his behalf. France, for its own reasons of colonial management in Africa, also opposed both UNEF I and ONUC. And problems have abounded. The peace, ably maintained by UNFICYP, was shattered by the Turkish invasion of Cyprus in 1974, to be restored once again after a considerable shift in the relative situations of the Greek and Turkish communities. The United Nations Interim Force in Lebanon (UNIFIL), since its inception in 1978, has been plagued with violations of the terms of its mandate by the parties concerned and has been subject to military attack, suffering many casualties. A constant problem is the danger in each operation that, as in Cyprus, a peacekeeping operation may itself become a critical factor in maintaining the status quo and retard the process of political settlement.

Moreover, France and, in particular, the Soviet Union refused to pay their assessments for UNEF I and for ONUC. American reaction was so severe that for a year (1964) the UN was paralyzed over the issue. In conceptual and political terms, peacekeeping was regarded from different political perspectives: as a phenomenon attendant to the process of decolonization; as neocolonialist by many African states; as an ad hoc UN instrumentality without basis in the UN charter; as too subject to the discretion of the secretary-general for its implementation; and as a point of dispute between those states which perceived the UN, as described in the words of Dag Hammarskjold:

> primarily as a dynamic instrument of governments through which they, jointly and for the same purpose, should seek such reconciliation but through which they should also try to develop forms of executive action, undertaken on behalf of all Members, and aiming at forestalling conflicts and resolving them, once they have arisen, by appropriate diplomatic or political means, in a spirit of objectivity and in implementation of the principles and purposes of the Charter;(1)

and those states which claimed the UN to be no more than an organizational structure for state consultation and action only when, in accordance with the Charter, states agree to do so; but that the organization itself is without political or legal competence of its own.

With these and other real and conceptual controversies continuously hindering the practice of peacekeeping and eroding its support and legitimacy, there can be little wonder that, after the debacle in 1967, the doomsayers seemed to be right that the practice of peacekeeping had come to an end.(2) It was then that UNEF I was withdrawn at the request of Egypt and by the decision of then Secretary-General U Thant under the guns of the Six-Day War, without formal consideration of the question by the General Assembly which had mandated the operation.

We now know that the doomsayers were wrong. Since 1973, three more UN operations have been launched in the Middle East, the UN plan for Namibia is still very much on the agenda, there has been the unique but very successful "Commonwealth" operation in Rhodesia/Zimbabwe, the Organization of African Unity (OAU) has mounted a complex operation in Chad, and several proposals are afloat for peacekeeping and crisis management in such difficult and diverse situations as the conflicts between Kampuchea and Thailand, between Iran and Iraq, and in El Salvador. The nature of the international system has changed considerably from the time UNEF I was established in 1956. The functions of peacekeeping have evolved in complexity; regional organizations are more actively engaged; and, with conflict endemic in the international system, many statesmen have come to regard peacekeeping as the major accomplishment of the UN. They view peacekeeping and conflict resolution as the necessary prerequisites to meaningful disarmament and the social and economic development of the Third World. Peacekeeping will appear frequently on the international agenda in the 1980s and beyond.

That is the subject of the last section of this volume. Here I will present an overview of the evolutionary process, showing that there are four distinct historical periods, and demonstrating the functional growth, political maturation, and institutionalization of the process. The four periods are the nascent period, 1946-1956; the assertive period, 1956-67; the dormant period, 1967-73; and the resurgent period which started in 1973.

THE NASCENT PERIOD: 1946-56

Once the UN embarked on peacekeeping as a novel mode of conflict abatement in 1956 and thereafter, a reexamination of previous similar UN actions revealed them to be generic antecedents. There were the United Nations Special Committee on the Balkans (UNSCOB) of 1946 to investigate the Greek allegations of illegal infiltration from Albania, Bulgaria, and Yugoslavia in support of insurrection in Greece; the establishment in 1947 of special commissions to supervise the cease-fire leading to the independence of Indonesia; the Truce Commission for the Middle East in 1948, which later became the United Nations Truce Supervisory Organization (UNTSO) and is still in existence; and the United Nations Military Observer Group in India and Pakistan (UNMOGIP) along the border within Kashmir which separated the forces of India and Pakistan, and which is also still in existence. In retrospect, these operations, functionally focused on observation, fact-finding, and reporting, and each requiring limited numbers of personnel, were derivative of World War II situations and the process of decolonization.

United Nations Special Committee on the Balkans (UNSCOB), 1946-49

Greece, in the aftermath of World War II, was faced with violent guerrilla war by leftist insurgents in the northern part of the country and military provocations between itself and its northern neighbors, with each accusing the other of instigation and aggression. Consequently, in response to "disturbed conditions" in northern Greece along the frontiers between Greece on the one hand and Albania, Bulgaria, and Yugoslavia on the other, the Security Council on 19 December 1946 unanimously adopted a resolution which established a "Commission of Investigation to ascertain the facts relating to the alleged border violations along the frontiers."(3) These countries were called upon to assist in the work of the commission, and the commission itself was to report on its findings and was invited "to make any proposals it may deem necessary to rectify the situation."(4) The commission was composed of diplomatic representatives of all eleven members of the Security Council, which included the Soviet Union and Poland.

The central questions were whether Greece's northern neighbors were supporting the guerrilla movement in Greece, and the counterclaim that Greece itself was responsible for the civil war on its own territory and was conducting a provocative and expansionist policy toward its neighbors; both questions were manifestations of the emerging East-West struggle.

As a result, the commission found it difficult to ascertain the facts. A second Security Council resolution, over the objections of the Soviet Union and Poland, authorized the formation of a subsidiary group to work directly in the affected areas.(5) Albania, Bulgaria, and Yugoslavia refused to cooperate, denying the commission the essential component of the consent of the parties in the performance of its duties. Nonetheless, the commission did establish nine investigating teams and submitted a massive report of 767 pages of its findings and recommendations. The Western members of the Security Council subscribed to the conclusions of the report that the three countries were supporting guerrilla warfare in Greece. These findings were rejected by the Soviet Union and Poland, which held Greece responsible for repressive measures and claimed that its neighbors merely provided humanitarian assistance to political refugees. France abstained from either view and from the Security Council establishment of a new commission or commissioners to provide continuous observation of violations in the border areas and to assist in resolving complaints and controversy. As before, controversy and lack of cooperation in the field blocked further Council action. By a procedural vote initiated by the United States, the matter was dropped from the agenda and shifted to the General Assembly.

Over the objection of the Soviet Union and like-minded states, the Assembly adopted a resolution which called upon the parties "to establish normal diplomatic relations," cooperate in the "pacific settlement of frontier incidents and disputes," and of "refugee problems" and the "transfer of minorities." To observe compliance of these matters, the resolution also established a Special Committee on the Balkans (UNSCOB).(6) The membership, as designated by the Assembly, was made up of representatives from Australia, Brazil, China, France, Mexico, the Netherlands, Pakistan, the United Kingdom, and the United States, with seats held open for Poland and the USSR which were never occupied.

UNSCOB divided itself into three committees to (1) function as observer groups, (2) deal with political problems, and (3) deal with refugees and minorities. But it did not receive the required cooperation from Yugoslavia, Albania, and Bulgaria; in fact, three of its observers with a Greek liaison officer were fired on from the Albanian border.(7)

The basic functions of UNSCOB were those of observation and conciliation. It filed reports and made recommendations on avoidance of border violations, movement of refugees, etc., but had marginal impact on the situation. A separate Conciliation Commission was set up by the General Assembly in 1949(8) and UNSCOB itself was disbanded by resolution of the Assembly on 7 December 1949. In its place, on the basis of the Uniting for Peace Resolution, a Balkan subcommission was created to monitor the situation as required.(9) This latter commission functioned on a low level. By 1953, the situation became relatively stable and Greece recommended that the military observers be reduced to three and that the commission be entirely disbanded by July 1954. It made no further reports to the General Assembly.

UNSCOB, created to assist in the observation and resolution of serious civil conflict exacerbated by border violations

between Greece and its neighbors, was modest in size, protracted, and very limited in effectiveness because it had the
support of only one of the parties and its supporters in the
Security Council. Of some note was that the finances, which
were projected to be $611,440 to 1948 alone, were accepted as
a general budgetary item - over the objections of Poland and
the USSR.

Indonesia

In the immediate aftermath of Japan's surrender to allied
forces, Indonesia declared its independence on 17 August 1945.
The Netherlands, the former colonial power of Indonesia,
refused to accept the fait accompli. Political and military
action ensued which destabilized the entire situation. The
issue came before the Security Council which, on 1 August
1947, "called upon the parties (a) to cease hostilities forthwith, and (b) to settle their disputes by arbitration or other
peaceful means."(10) On 25 August, the Security Council
requested its members with career consular representatives in
Batavia to "cover the observance of the 'cease-fire' orders and
the conditions prevailing in areas under military occupation."(11) The Consular Commission was thereupon composed
of members from Australia, Belgium, France, the United
Kingdom, and the United States.

The was the first time the Security Council called for the
establishment of a cease-fire between belligerents, and the
resolution of 25 August, was the first time it established any
body specifically "to cover the observance" of a cease-fire,
though the personnel assigned to the task functioned basically
as members of their own governments with the attachment of
military officers.

The Indonesian situation evolved in a very fluid manner,
politically and militarily, moving toward agreements not fully
implemented and without clear disposition of forces and cease-
fire lines. The actual tasks of good offices and negotiations
were undertaken by a Committee of Good Offices established
by the Security Council by resolution, also of 25 August,
which was later reconstituted as the United Nations Commission
for Indonesia (UNCI). When large-scale hostilities were
resumed, the Security Council again called for a cease-fire on
24 December 1948,(12) and on 28 January called upon the consular commission "to facilitate the work of the United Nations
Commission of Indonesia by providing military observers
[Milobs, with an executive staff called Milex] and other staff
and facilities to enable the Commission to carry out its
duties."(13)

Additional military advisors were made up of personnel
from Australia, Belgium, China, France, the United Kingdom,

and the United States, their number not at any time exceeding
63. Their functions, stemming from the initial call to cover
the observance of the cease-fire, were manifold and complex
spanning a vast territory within Java and Sumatra. They
included, over time, the demarcation and observation of
cease-fire lines, supervision of the withdrawal of troops,
checking on infiltration between the lines, reporting on guerrilla activities, investigating violations reported by various
parties, inspecting rubber estates to determine the extent of
destruction inflicted by terrorist action, and a host of related
activities as detailed throughout Alastair Taylor's comprehensive study, Indonesian Independence and the United
Nations.(14)

The literature on peacekeeping makes infrequent reference
to the Indonesian experience,(15) and United Nations historical
documentation of peacekeeping ignores it. (It has never been
referred to in the documentation of UN peacekeeping operations
by the Special Committee on Peacekeeping Operations since its
inception in 1965.) The main reasons are probably that the
Milex, while reporting to the Security Council, functioned
under the aegis of their respective national diplomatic missions
and that the UN secretariat played a minimal role. There is
no doubt, however, that their functions were very similar to
those performed by any other peacekeeping observer mission of
the UN.

As Taylor points out, if the rights and duties, military
organization, deployment, and procedures had been clearly
defined, their tasks would have been greatly facilitated. In
fact, Milex and the parties did prepare the "Netherlands-
Indonesian Manual" of military definitions and rules.(16)
Functionally, the tasks of the military observers came well
within the definition of peacekeeping as the practice is now
understood, and played a key role in guiding events to the
ultimate transfer of sovereignty of the territory to Indonesia in
December 1949.

United Nations Truce Supervision Organization in Palestine
(UNTSO), 1948

It was, therefore, not without precedent that the Truce
Commission first established by the Security Council in
Palestine was also composed of members of the Security Council
which had career officers in the territory in question. But
that anticipates the development of UNTSO which became the
progenitor of six other UN peacekeeping operations in the
Middle East.

The United Kingdom, as the mandatory power over
Palestine, was faced with mounting political pressures, violence
and military activity between the Arabs and Israelis, and its

own forces were subject to harassment and attack. Unable and apparently unwilling to negotiate or impose a settlement acccpt-able to the parties with respect to the establishment of a single Palestinian or separate Israeli and Palestinian states, and anxious to be relieved of the burden, the United Kingdom asked that the question be placed before the General As-sembly. On 15 May 1947, the General Assembly adopted a resolution creating a special committee (UNSCOP) "to prepare a report on the question of Palestine," and granted it "the widest powers to ascertain and record facts, and to investigate all questions and issues relevant to the problem of Pales-tine . . . [and] submit such proposals as it may consider appropriate for the solution of the problem of Palestine."(17)

The inquiry and deliberations of UNSCOP led to a further General Assembly resolution of November 1947 calling for the creation of a commission of five members elected by the General Assembly to be charged with the responsibility of assuming the mandatory powers from the United Kingdom, and of carrying out the partitioning of Palestine and the inter-nationalization of Jerusalem.(18) The Arabs (wanting a unitary state) opposed the partition plan; the Jewish agency accepted, with misgivings; and the United Kingdom, declaring its unwillingness to uphold a plan not acceptable to both parties, announced its decision to withdraw on 15 May 1948.

The situation from that point on deteriorated very rapid-ly, making the General Assembly plan inoperable. Thereupon, the Security Council again took on the issue and twice called for an end to violence and military and paramilitary activity. And then, on 23 April 1948, it called "upon all parties concerned to comply with specific terms for a truce in Palestine . . . [and established] a truce commission for Palestine composed of those members of the Security Council which have career consular officers in Jerusalem,"(19) which, in effect, were those of Belgium, France, and the United States.

The General Assembly took parallel action on 14 May 1948 by terminating the Palestine Commission it established in November 1947, and creating the office of a United Nations mediator in Palestine with instructions to cooperate with the truce commission created by the Security Council.(20) The following day, the United Kingdom withdrew its forces, Israel was proclaimed a state, and was immediately invaded by its Arab neighbors; full-scale war broke out.

Faced with a new though not entirely unanticipated situation, the Security Council, on 22 May, in stronger language than theretofore, called for a cease-fire within 36 hours and for the truce commission to report on compli-ance.(21) The truce commission asked for military advisors to enable it to fulfill its responsibilities. This was authorized in a further Security Council resolution of 29 May wherein it

instructed "the United Nations mediator for Palestine in concert
with the truce commission to supervise the observance of the
above provisions [those detailing the terms of a cease-fire for
a period of four weeks agreed to by the parties] . . . and
decides that they shall be provided with a sufficient number of
military observers."(22)   The mediator thereupon appointed
military observers from Belgium, France, and the United
States, all members of the Security Council and of the truce
commission, with five additional Swedish army officers as
personal representatives of the mediator, Count Bernadotte.
As war resumed, the number of military observers grew to 572
and then became known by the acronym, UNTSO. It is noteworthy that, though emanating from a Security Council
resolution, the observers were placed under the authority of
the office of the Mediator created by the General Assembly.
UNTSO was at its inception, and continues to this day, a
hybrid peacekeeping operation. It was the creature of astute
pragmatism.   Created inferentially by a Security Council
resolution and attached to the mediator established by the
General Assembly, it lacked a precise structural mandate.
This, in turn, gave it great flexibility, allowing it to be
adapted to special circumstances, though its basic function has
consistently been the supervision of cease-fires. It was, for
example, operationally linked with UNEF I in 1956 and assisted
in securing and monitoring the cease-fire along the Suez after
the war of 1967 and again in 1973. This was accomplished
with the consensual agreement of the Security Council and the
consent of the parties. But the process was initiated and
executed by the secretary-general who has been able to
exercise relatively wide discretion in the administration of
UNTSO.

        Another feature of UNTSO was the creation, on the
initiative of the parties, of Mixed Armistice Commissions
(MACs) which, while setting their own rules of procedure,
assisted in such matters as prisoner exchanges and supervision
of demilitarized zones in accordance with the several armistice
agreements. The composition of UNTSO, never larger than
572, was originally comprised of members from Sweden,
Belgium, and France and was at later stages expanded to
include members from the United States and the Soviet Union,
the latter included in 1973 when it matched the United States
complement of 35 observers (see Appendix). Nevertheless,
the permanent members were generally excluded from later
peacekeeping operations, it being the common political view
that peacekeeping is best performed by the middle and smaller
powers.

        Like UNSCOB, the truce commission from which UNTSO
evolved was composed of career consulars of national governments.   Though in the early stage they were required to
report to the Security Council, they were far more indepen-

dent than the military command of their chief of staff who was directly responsible to the secretary-general. Of equal importance is the fact that UNTSO has its origins as an associate instrument responsible to the mediator. Later practice structurally disassociated the functions, i.e., the separation of peacekeeping and peacemaking, though the division of function and authority was sometimes blurred and gave rise to confusion and conflict, as between the chief of staff and the secretary-general's special representative in the Congo.

UN Military Observer Group in India and Pakistan (UNMOGIP), 1948

As in the case of UNTSO, the creation of UNMOGIP evolved from a prior commission of the Security Council established "to investigate the facts" and "to exercise . . . mediatory influence"(23) between Pakistan and India which had gone to war over the disputed territories of Jammu and Kashmir. The disposition of the disputed territory had not been determined by the British plan of partition. The Security Council, when the issue was first brought before it in January 1948, called upon the parties to "take immediate measures within their power . . . calculated to improve the situation."(24) The hostilities continued and the Security Council established the United Nations Commission on India and Pakistan (UNCIP), consisting of three members: one selected by India, a second by Pakistan, and a third designated by both parties. This was later expanded to five including representatives of Czechoslovakia, Argentina, the United States, Belgium, and Colombia. The Soviet Union argued, without success, that UNCIP be directly represented by members of the Security Council.

UNCIP was instructed to proceed to the area in dispute, put its good offices at the disposal of the parties, and order the holding of a plebiscite. The same resolution also enabled UNCIP to establish "such observers as it may require."(25) By 1 January 1949, UNCIP negotiated a cease-fire and dispatched military observers to the field by the 24th of the month, to become known as the UN Military Observers Group in India and Pakistan (UNMOGIP). However, the cease-fire itself was detailed only on 27 July, by virtue of the Karachi Agreement, which also belatedly provided that UNCIP station observers wherever it deemed necessary.

The functions of UNMOGIP were related strictly to the cease-fire and kept separate from the political tasks of the UN representative created by the Security Council resolution of 14 March 1950.(26) Its functions comprised the control of the withdrawal of troops from the lines of demarcation, observation

of the cease-fire line, and the determination of violations along
the 500-mile frontier between Pakistan and the states of Jammu
and Kashmir.   At the outset, the composition of UNMOGIP
numbered approximately 40 observers from Belgium, Canada,
Norway, Mexico, and the United States, the total number
never exceeding 102.   United States personnel remained until
March 1954 when the Prime Minister of India asked that they
be removed from participating in UNMOGIP.   (See Appendix
for further information on composition.)   UNMOGIP has been
financed as part of the regular UN budget without major
controversy.

The nature of the mandate and its execution placed the
primary responsibility for the direction of the operation with
the secretary general who was given relatively wide latitude.
This became clearly evident in 1965 when hostilities between
India and Pakistan were renewed on a large scale on the
Kashmir front and along the entire border between the two
countries.   Two thousand complaints to UNMOGIP in the first
five months of 1965 was evidence of the gravity of the
situation and the enormity of the task of some 45 UN observers.   The Security Council issued a cease-fire order on 20
September and called upon India and Pakistan "to co-operate
fully with the United Nations Military Observer Group in India
and Pakistan . . . in its task of supervising the observance of
the cease-fire."(27)   Thus, an additional operation was put
into place to deal with a major outbreak of war.   Nevertheless,
UNMOGIP has proved to be a most valuable international observer presence to restrain conflict along the border between
India and Pakistan while the jurisdiction of the contiguous
areas remains in dispute.

Summary

The first of the four cases of this nascent period, UNSCOB,
arose out of a civil war and attendant border violations.   It
was immediately a cold war issue and the observers did not
receive cooperation from all the parties.   The other three
cases all arose from colonial situations.   Only two of the cases,
UNSCOB and Indonesia, resulted in lasting settlements, with
UNTSO and UNMOGIP still functioning.

They share a number of common characteristics and
features which arise in later observer type and larger scale
peacekeeping operations.   Among the common characteristics
are: a) each emerged from an inquiry or good offices commission, b) with the exception of UNMOGIP, personnel were
drawn from national diplomatic missions in the region and later
augmented by military officers chosen on the same basis; c)
each involved observation and reporting of military activities,
with Indonesia the first case specifically required to monitor a

cease-fire line; d) consent of the parties was a necessary factor in each case, and where several of the parties (i.e., in the case of UNSCOB) withheld consent, the operation was severely limited; e) contrary to the norm of later practice, major powers either participated or were invited to participate; f) whereas the Security Council was the initial source of all four operations, in two cases, UNSCOB and UNTSO, the General Assembly also participated in the definition or elaboration of mandates, indicative of what happened later in the Congo and of the dispute over the question of a residual authority of the Assembly in matters of peacekeeping; g) the secretary-general played an important support role and coordinating function; and h) the financing, while nowhere near as large as in later operations, was accepted as a regular budgetary item under some objection forthrightly manifested by the USSR in 1962 in its refusal to pay its assessment for UNEF I.

There were two features which were unique at the time: the invocation by the General Assembly of the Uniting for Peace Resolution in the case of UNSCOB, and the fact that UNTSO owes its existence to action taken by the secretary-general in the interpretation of the will of the Security Council.

This was a slow growth period largely concentrated in the early years of the UN before the failure of the U.S.-Soviet negotiations for the creation of a large-scale UN military force to repel aggression and maintain international peace and security under the direction of the Security Council became fully evident. Furthermore, the four operations of this period were modest and lacked the drama associated with later operations; particularly UNEF I, which was born in the heat of a grave crisis requiring astute innovative diplomacy to launch a pacific military operation by an international force of close to 6,000 men. UNEF I exemplified a quantum leap from its predecessors but, nonetheless, in direct linear descendency.

THE ASSERTIVE PERIOD, 1956-1967

United Nations Emergency Force I (UNEF), 1956-1967

Seized with the volatile crisis resulting from the Israeli, British, and French invasion of Egypt to overcome fedayeen raids into Israel and to impose a settlement on Egypt in regard to the Suez Canal which Egypt had nationalized, the Security Council was deeply divided on the issue. On the one hand, the Soviet Union charged the Western members with aggression; and, on the other, there was a major rift between Israel, the United Kingdom and France, and the United States which condemned this action. With the Council deadlocked, and on Yugoslavia's iniative on the basis of the Uniting For Peace Resolution the second time it was invoked, the item was removed from the Council agenda and placed before the General Assembly. Following a period of intense and creative diplomacy, the Assembly, in emergency session, passed four resolutions between 2 and 5 November 1956, the last of which established "a United Nations Command for an emergency international force to secure and supervise the cessation of hostilities."(28) The modalities of the operation were set out in a report of the secretary-general submitted at the request of the General Assembly.

In accordance with these resolutions, the parties which had invaded Egypt were required to adhere to an immediate cease-fire, to withdraw all Israeli forces behind armistice lines as per the agreement between Egypt and Israel of February 1949, and to implement the total withdrawal of all British and French forces.

According to its mandate, UNEF I carried out the following functions: primarily securing but not enforcing the cease-fire, supervising the armistice lines and the withdrawal of forces (which required the maintenance of a safety cordon around embarkation ports for the British and French forces), keeping peace among the civilian population, monitoring key areas in the Sinai (particularly Sharm el Sheikh overlooking the Straits of Tiran), and manifold functions related to the maintenance of order and stability of the Gaza Strip.(29) In order to carry out these and related activities, which it did for ten and a half years, the size of the force ranged from 3,000 to 6,000 contributed by 10 countries with the original complement drawn from UNTSO.

The differences between UNEF I and its predecessors are numerous in consequence of the gravity of the situation which seriously threatened international peace and security. Its interpository role was at a level well beyond that of Indonesia or of UNMOGIP where the operative word was to "observe" the cease-fire in contrast to "secure" the cease-fire in the case of UNEF I. The very large difference in size is indicative of the qualitative difference in function. The secretary-general, in the execution and administration of UNEF I, assumed responsibilities far greater than on any previous occasion, a matter of bitter East-West controversy. Much of this responsibility fell to Ralph Bunche who had been active in the work of UNTSO and in Middle East affairs generally. During the rigors of the cold war, in 1953, Secretary-General Dag Hammarskjold appointed two under-secretaries general, one Russian and one American. Ralph Bunche, with whom he could consult on critical issues, filled a new post, thus bypassing the under-secretary general for Security Council affairs, a post that, by agreement, is held by a Russian. It was a national outgrowth

of these events that the office of the under-secretary general
for special political affairs was subsequently established to
manage all peacekeeping operations, and that Bunche became
the first incumbent of the office.

Though it was a nonenforcement action, and despite the
fact that the General Assembly had acted before in the cases
of UNSCOB and UNTSO, this time the size and complexity of
the operation illicited seriously conflicting views on the
competence of the General Assembly to conduct such action
even when the Security Council is deadlocked.   Because of
size and unanticipated duration, the cost of UNEF I amounted
to $220 million. The General Assembly decided at the outset,
as in previous cases, that the expenses should be borne by
the organization in apportionment with the regular budgetary
scale of assessments. This, in conjunction with ONUC, became
a matter of divisive controversy that all but immobilized the
UN.   UNEF II was created purely as a peacekeeping operation,
and was not an outgrowth of or adjunct to commissions of good
offices as occurred in previous cases.   Lastly, the magnitude
of the crisis, which was global in context, the creative diplomacy, and the size and innovative character of UNEF I for the
first time, excepting Korea, affirmed the competence of the UN
to fulfill its foremost responsibility of the maintenance of
international peace and security.

UNEF I became a model for several later UN peacekeeping
operations, despite the manner of its inglorious demise by the
secretary-general at the insistent request of Egypt.   Under
the pressures of Egyptian re-entry into the Sinai, which put
UNEF I in a politically sensitive and militarily dangerous
situation, the secretary-general withdrew the force without
calling a special session of the General Assembly to consider
the situation. Presumably the untenable situation and the
principle of consent were adequate justification for this decision. Because of this, the provocative and persistent question
remains unanswered: had the Assembly been able to effectively
reaffirm the mandate of UNEF I and convince Egypt to hold
back its reoccupation of the Sinai, could the 1967 war have
been averted? Had this been the case, there would not have
been Israeli occupation of the Gaza and the West Bank, the
1973 war may not have taken place, and the Middle East might
not be as volatile and such a constant threat to international
peace and security as it is today. Supposition as well as the
actualities of history need occasionally to be analyzed to comprehend the full potential of peacekeeping capability in the
management of conflict.

United Nations Observation Group in Lebanon (UNOGIL),
1958

Within two years of the formation of UNEF, Lebanon brought a
complaint before the Security Council that the United Arab
Republic (UAR), the Union of Egypt, and Syria were subvert-
ing the government of Lebanon and infiltrating arms and men
across its borders.(30)   The situation was further complicated
by civil strife in Lebanon itself, partly because of the decision
of the pro-Western President Chamoun to seek an unconstitutional second term in office.   As in previous cases, the
Security Council was divided on East-West lines, with the West
supporting the Lebanese complaint and the Soviet Union
opposed.
        However, a resolution was passed, 10 for and only the
Soviet Union abstaining, "to dispatch an observation group to
proceed to Lebanon so as to ensure that there is no illegal
infiltration of personnel or supply of arms.... across the
Lebanese border."(31)   The resolution also authorized "the
Secretary-General to take the necessary steps to that end."
The functions of UNOGIL were thereby strictly limited to those
of observation without ancillary tasks related to good offices or
mediation.
        The situation in Lebanon, however, deteriorated.   There
was a violent pro-Soviet coup in Iraq, and Jordan feared its
own destabilization.   The United States responded by sending
troops to Lebanon, and the United Kingdom followed suit in
sending troops to Jordan.   In the meantime, UNOGIL reported
that it failed to uncover any major infiltration into Lebanon.
The problem then became whether UNOGIL could serve to
deflate the crisis and, if so, how.   Several resolutions were
placed before the Security Council, but none gained adequate
support.   Once more, as in UNSCOB, UNTSO, and UNEF I,
the matter was turned over to the General Assembly.
        The Arab states there put forward a resolution, which
was adopted, requesting the secretary-general to make "such
practical arrangements as would adequately help in upholding
the purposes and principles of the Charter in relation to
Lebanon and Jordan . . . and thereby facilitate the early
withdrawal of foreign troops."(32)   The functions of UNOGIL
remained substantially the same but considerably enlarged at
the discretion of the secretary-general.   Further, UNOGIL
provided the diplomatic backdrop for the withdrawal of American and British forces, in a manner somewhat similar to UNEF
I and the withdrawal of British and French forces from Egypt
in 1956.   By 9 December 1958, UNOGIL was disbanded.
        The size of UNOGIL was approximately 600, its function
limited to observation and reporting, and its presence in
Lebanon a pacific contribution to the resolution of the
Lebanese and broader political crises in the area.   As such,

it belongs clearly in the observer category of peacekeeping.
Twenty small and middle powers participated. The total cost
of $3,697,742 was, as in previous cases, apportioned in the
regular budget. There are, however, several other matters of
note: wide discretion was granted to the secretary-general by
resolution of the General Assembly, a procedure opposed by
the Soviet Union: the Soviet Union moderated its opposition
because of the support of Arab States for the operation; and
lastly the short duration of UNOGIL.

United Nations Operation in the Congo (ONUC), 1960

ONUC was the most complex of all UN peacekeeping operations.
However, only the briefest analytical account can be presented
here. The Republic of the Congo achieved its sovereign
independence from Belgium on June 30, 1960. Within days
there was a mutiny in the army. The mineral rich province of
Katanga declared independence and Belgian troops returned,
ostensibly for the protection of Belgian lives and property.
The president of the republic appealed to the secretary-
general for assistance. Acting under the authority of article
99, he requested a meeting of the Security Council.

The Council promptly called upon Belgium to withdraw its
troops and for the secretary-general "to provide the government [of the Congo] with such military assistance as may be
necessary, until . . . the national security forces may be able,
in the opinion of the Government, to meet fully their
tasks".(33) This was the founding mandate for the formation
of ONUC which expanded to a force of almost 20,000, lasted
for four years, was the continuous source of virulent controversy, cost approximately $400 million, and so divided the
UN that its very existence was threatened.

The basic elements of controversy were Belgian procrastination in the withdrawal of all its military personnel; the
split between the Soviet-backed prime minister and the
Western-supported president of the Congo; the persistence of
secessionist movements; the almost total breakdown of civil
authority; and, as a result of all this and more, the core
question of the level of authority and degree of force to be
employed by ONUC to safeguard the territorial integrity and
political independence of the Congo. Because of these almost
intractable complications, there were five basic Security
Council and General Assembly resolutions necessary to clarify
and amplify the mandate and specify the functions. The key
elements were, as quoted above, and that of the Assembly
resolution, which "requests the Secretary-General to take
vigorous action to assist the Central Government of the Congo
in the restoration and maintenance of law and order . . . and
to safeguard its territorial integrity and political inde-

pendence,"(34) by the Security Council which "urges the
United Nations to prevent the occurrence of civil war;"(35)
and later "authorizes the Secretary-General to take vigorous
action, including the use of requisite measures of force" for
the apprehension and retention of all foreign military and
paramilitary personnel which, in effect, authorized ONUC to
overcome the secession of Katanga.(36)   It was on a peace
mission to Katanga Province that Secretary-General Dag
Hammarskjöld lost his life in a plane crash.
     The special and unique aspects of ONUC are numerous.
It arose out of a classical colonial situation and operated within
the scope of the internal affairs of the Congo; the resolution
of the Assembly clearly implied use of force; and the Assembly
assumed the legal competence to take such action.   The Council was more explicit in its resolution on the use of force.
Both are evidence that· ONUC was inextricably involved in the
internal affairs of the Congo which, in addition to the above,
included operational control of elements of the Congolese army
and the pressure put upon the various political factions to
form a viable national government.   The resolutions also
provided fuel to the growing controversy of just what is the
residual authority of the General Assembly in matters of
peacekeeping, especially since the Charter makes no reference
to and did not anticipate the practice of peacekeeping.
     Other elements of note are the direct relationship between
decolonization and peacekeeping; the wide discretionary latitude of the secretary-general in the conduct of the operation,
vigorously attacked by the Soviet Union; the threat by Ghana
and other African countries to withdraw their contingents
because of opposition to political decisions taken by the
Assembly and the secretary-general; the Soviet refusal to pay
its share of the costs of ONUC which were, nonetheless,
considered normal "expenses" of the organization;(37) and, in
the end, United States reaction to this Soviet refusal to pay
for ONUC and also its assessment for UNEF I which virtually
paralyzed the UN during 1964, though France had also refused
to pay its assessments for these operations.   The $400 million
cost of ONUC almost bankrupted the organization, and the
United States threatened a resolution to deny the Soviet Union
its voting rights in the General Assembly if it did not pay.
Ultimately, a compromise was found in a vague Soviet statement
about possible payment and the creation of the Special Committee on Peacekeeping Operations to seek guidelines on the three
crucial problems of financing; the authority, if any, of the
General Assembly to mandate peacekeeping operations; and the
range of discretionary authority of the secretary-general
vis-à-vis the Security Council in the direction of peacekeeping
operations.
     In 1964, ONUC appeared to be a disaster for the UN.
Yet, in retrospect, the Congo (now Zaire) maintained its

territorial integrity, the UN survived, and a great deal of peacekeeping experience was gained in the process of conducting such a large and complex operation - experience which was called into play very shortly thereafter in Cyprus. But because of the diverse and persistent controversies it engendered, including the charge of neocolonialism, all UN peacekeeping came to be regarded as a phenomenon attendant to the process of decolonization and would, therefore, come to an end when and as soon as decolonization had run its course. The fact that the UN mounted yet another major operation in Cyprus stemming from the withdrawal of colonial power of the United Kingdom further demonstrates this relationship. But ONUC, notwithstanding the magnitude, controversy, and costs which almost exhausted the UN, also demonstrated the inherent validity of peacekeeping as an instrument for the containment of conflict.

UN Security Force in West New Guinea (West Irian), 1962-63

In sharp contrast to the overwhelming problems which befell the UN in the decolonization of the Congo, the "decolonization" of West Irian under the trusteeship of the UN was a well planned and smoothly implemented operation. The great irony is that the United Nations Temporary Executive Authority (UNTEA) and the UN Security Force (UNSF) were authorized during the height of the controversy over UN peacekeeping in the Congo, and actions which generated opposition in respect to ONUC were not disputed in the West Irian operations.

When the Netherlands withdrew from Indonesia in 1949 under the supervision of UN military observers, the dispute over the Dutch-held territory of West Irian, claimed by Indonesia, was not resolved. It was not until 1961 that the Netherlands declared its readiness "to terminate its sovereignty over Netherland's New Guinea [West Irian] . . . [and] is prepared to bring the administration and the development of the Territory under the active supervision of the United Nations and is prepared to accept a decision of the General Assembly which clearly guarantees the right of self-determination of the populace."(38)

This proposal was rejected by Indonesia which insisted on the validity of its own claim to the territory; and, to assert its claim, it took military action leading to a naval clash and infiltration of the territory in January 1962. Subsequent negotiations and consultations with the secretary-general and a mediator, Ellsworth Bunker of the United States, culminated in an agreement based on the Dutch proposal of 1961, except that UN authority would be of a temporary nature to facilitate the ultimate transfer of the territory to Indonesia.

The details of the agreement acknowledged the role conferred upon the secretary-general "and authorizes him to carry
out the tasks entrusted to him; and, among other matters the
Secretary-General will provide UNTEA with such security
forces as the United Nations Administration deems necessary;
such forces will primarily supplement existing Papuan [West
Irianese] police in the task of maintaining law and order."(39)
Other articles provided the UN administrator with discretion to
transfer UNTEA's authority to Indonesia. A further Memorandum of Understanding provided for a cease-fire, no reinforcement of forces by the parties, and for the secretary general
"to assign UN personnel i) to observe the implementation of
this agreement and ii) in particular to take necessary steps for
the prevention of any acts endangering the security forces of
both parties."(40)

Subsequent to this agreement, the General Assembly
authorized "the Secretary-General to carry out the tasks
entrusted to him in the agreement."(41) Financing of the
operation was assumed by the parties. The vote on this
resolution was 89 - 0 - 14 with the Soviet Union in favor and
only France and members of the French community of states in
opposition. Within two weeks of the vote, UNTEA and UNSF
took up their duties in the exercise of temporary UN sovereignty over the territory. The secretary-general took full
charge of the operation leading to a phasing in of Indonesian
sovereignty by May 1963. It was left to Indonesia, in
accordance with an agreement of August 1962, to ensure the
right of the populace to express their wishes as to their
future.

Functionally, the basic tasks of the military observers of
UNTEA were the observation of the cease-fire, protection of
the security of the Dutch and Indonesian forces, and the
restoration of the situation in the event of breaches of the
cease-fire. That of UNSF was the maintainance of law and
order which, it must be assumed, would entail the use of force
if necessary. Twenty-one military observers from six countries were attached to UNTEA, plus 1,608 officers and men
from UNEF, ONUC, and UNSF, of which 1,537 were from
Pakistan.

Coming at a time when the repercussions of ONUC were
undermining the UN, it is somewhat surprising that the West
Irian "peacekeeping" operation received such extensive support
from the General Assembly, including that of the Soviet Union.
Of course, there were vast differences in scale and divisiveness. Nonetheless, the secretary-general, under attack for
exceeding his authority and discretionary action in ONUC, was
given wide jurisdiction over the negotiation and management of
UNTEA and UNSF.(42) Furthermore, the very innovative and
unprecedented assumption of temporary authority over a
territory (tantamount to the assumption of sovereign author-

ity) and the related functions of maintaining law and order could easily have raised profound questions of jurisdiction between the Security Council, the General Assembly, and the secretary-general. But this did not happen - the secretary-general and the Assembly assumed the dominant roles.

Apart from these and related issues, the fundamental difference was that ONUC was established to overcome a crisis, which deepened as events unfolded and required political decisions bound to displease one party or another, whereas UNTEA and UNSF were brought into the situation, as in the case of UNMOGIP based upon the Karachi agreement, after the parties had agreed to terms for resolution of the issue. All this suggests that, when there are fundamental constitutional differences about the practice of peacekeeping, it is frequently the political effects of a situation that generate conflict which then becomes focused on the legitimacy of peacekeeping rather than on its consequences.

UN Yemen Observation Mission (UNYOM), 1963-64

At the same time the West Irian conflict was pacifically resolved under the authority of the UN, Yemen was torn by civil strife exacerbated by external support of the United Arab Republic (Egypt and Syria) for the rebellious Sallal faction and of Saudi Arabia for the loyalist Badr faction. Through the intervention of Ralph Bunche (on behalf of the secretary-general) and the United States mediator, Ellsworth Bunker (who had also been instrumental in the West Irian issue), all the parties agreed to a military disengagement and to the presence of a UN observer mission. The nature of events unfolded in a very similar manner to its predecessor in West Irian. Presumably, it appears that the secretary-general, once again at the request and with the concurrence of all parties, would be within his competence to send an observer mission to monitor a disengagement.

But the Soviet Union raised objections, taking the position that it was a matter of international peace and security and, therefore, solely within the competence of the Security Council.(43) But because none of the parties wished to engage in a public debate that could be counterproductive, a Council resolution sponsored by Ghana and Morocco was adopted without debate with a Soviet abstention. It noted "with satisfaction the initiative of the Secretary-General," and acceptance by the parties directly concerned "of identical terms of disengagement," as well as the agreement of "Saudi Arabia and the United Arab Republic to defray expenses" and requested "the Secretary-General to establish the observation operation as defined by him . . . [and] to report to the Council on the implementation of the decision."

Such was the unique manner in which an observer mission was launched. Morocco emphasized that it was not to be considered as a precedent, but as later events show in respect of the UN India-Pakistan Observer Mission (UNIPOM) of 1965, the secretary-general was again primarily instrumental in establishing a peacekeeping operation with the consent of the parties under a broadly worded resolution of the Council. In the initial stage, some officers and men were drawn from UNTSO, with the total complement not exceeding 189. UNYOM was stationed in a demilitarized zone extending 20 kilometers on the Saudi-Yemen border. Its functions were limited to observing, certifying, and reporting on the compliance of the parties to the terms of the disengagement. The effectiveness of the force, however, was hampered because the fundamental requisite, namely, full adherence of the parties to the disengagement, was violated. Mediation by the secretary-general's special representative was attempted but with minimal success. The situation reached a stalemate and, by 4 September 1964, the operation was terminated.

Despite its limited success, the operation is noteworthy in that the secretary-general again played a critical role throughout the affair; and that the Soviet Union, though opposed, permitted the operation to proceed because it was the will of the parties concerned. The nature of the situation leading to the operation was, in some respects, similar to that of UNSCOB in the Balkans and UNOGIL in Lebanon; and, with them, UNYOM is clearly classified as an observer mission. It is also an instance where the will and prior agreement of the parties became the staging platform for a peacekeeping operation.

UN Peacekeeping Force in Cyprus (UNFICYP), 1964

It is a seeming paradox that UNFICYP was established by the Security Council in March 1964, at a time when the General Assembly was all but paralyzed over the East-West dispute over the financing and direction of ONUC and UNEF I. The UN was in a state of near exhaustion over the consequences of peacekeeping, yet it found it necessary to establish a new and what proved to be an extensive and prolonged operation. Since, however, the initial mandate was for three months only, it is reasonable to assume that at the time no one could foresee that it would last well into the 1980s.

In 1960, the United Kingdom, in agreement with Greece and Turkey, established a federal-type constitutional system for an independent Cyprus that would carefully balance the rights of the Greek (80 percent) and Turkish (20 percent) populations on the island. It was inherently unstable and intercommunal violence occurred in December 1962 and escalated in 1964. Two alternate means of managing the crisis were the joint intervention by the three guarantor powers – the United Kingdom, Greece, and Turkey – or the establishment of a NATO peacekeeping force on the island. But neither was politically feasible so the issue was placed before the Security Council.

On 4 March 1964, the Council called upon the parties to take all "measures necessary to stop the violence" that threatened international peace and security, and created a UN peaceforce "to use its best efforts to prevent a recurrence of fighting and, as necessary, to contribute to the maintenance and restoration of law and order and a return to normal conditions."(44) Once again, the secretary-general was required to organize and manage the force; but, this time, the financial problem was avoided by requesting the contributing countries, as possible, to pay their own costs with the balance to be covered by voluntary contributions.

The basic function of UNFICYP was interposition along the buffer zone between the Greek and Turkish communities, with freedom of movement throughout the island. The initial size of the force was approximately 6,500 drawn from Western and Scandinavian countries, with the largest number from the United Kingdom for reasons of direct interest and presence. This was the first time a major power participated so extensively in a peacekeeping mission. Over time, the functions of UNFICYP expanded from direct interposition along the dividing line to resolving various clashes between the two communities, the adjudicating of local disputes, and in general maintaining "law and order" – by then a characteristic phrase to cover a multitude of undefined tasks to defuse and stabilize the situation. For that purpose, a special civilian police force (UNCIPOL) was created.

The resolution which established UNFICYP also provided for a mediator, designated by the secretary-general, to seek a political resolution to the problem. However, the deep-seated antagonism between the communities persisted as before. Archbishop Makarios, the president and leader of the Greek community, found the status quo established by the presence of UN troops supportive of his own position. The situation was further complicated by policies and actions of both Greece and Turkey. As a result, continuous efforts at mediation were fruitless and the mandate became subject to automatic renewal every six months. UNFICYP is a clear case where effective peacekeeping is denied final completion of its mandate because of the failure of the peacemaking process.

Though the political situation was volatile and complicated by movements to unite Cyprus with Greece and alternate proposals to divide the island, the overall peace was maintained by UNFICYP. But that peace was dramatically shattered by the Turkish invasion of the island in 1974 which

engaged UNFICYP in a fire fight as Turkey sought to extend
its hold over UN bases. The fighting was fierce and the UN
suffered casualties. The crisis was placed before the Security
Council with a further round of resolutions and unsuccessful
attempts at mediation. But the major change was a shift in
the status quo after 1974 from one which favored the Greek
community to one which favored the Turkish community, with
the army of Turkey occupying the eastern part of the island.

UNFICYP has very capably fulfilled its mandate, even
during the Turkish invasion of 1974. But it suffers from the
failure to achieve a political solution, and has become identified
as a causal factor in the maintenance of the status quo.
However that may be, there can be no question that it contributes to the peace in the eastern Mediterranean, an area
adjacent to the already volatile Middle East. Still, the problem
of perpetuation is a difficult one, seriously trying the patience
and the resources of the participant countries. Though they
reduced the size of their contingents to less than 2,500 in
1982, UNFICYP remains in place because of the greater danger
that would result from its withdrawal. However, it does
weaken the commitment and the capability of the participant
states to make troops available for other peacekeeping operations.

It seems that states that are willing to spend huge sums
on military establishments to deter war and aggression become
impatient when far more modest resources are allocated for
peacekeeping. However, looking at peacekeeping as a developmental process, UNFICYP marks the closest occurrence to the
heartland of either East or West; and, for all its problems, has
not become a major point of issue between them. The Soviet
Union has raised no objections to the periodic renewal of the
mandate. There can be no doubt that it is also a factor in the
maintenance of international peace and security, a matter of
equal or even greater importance than persistence of communal
strife on the island of Cyprus.

Mission of the Representative of the Secretary-General
in the Dominican Republic (DOMREP), 1965

DOMREP, which was composed of General Indar Jit Rikhye and
two military observers, is certainly the smallest of all UN
observer missions. President Juan Bosch, the reformist
candidate of the Dominican Revolutionary Party, was elected
president of the Dominican Republic in December 1962, after 30
years of the Trujillo dynasty; but he, in turn, was ousted by
a military coup in September 1963. By April 1965, there was
again a military uprising by Juan Bosch, with others, in an
attempt to oust the military junta installed in 1963. Rioting
and insurrection were widespread, culminating in a state of

civil war. On 25 April, the United States decided to intervene, ostensibly to protect U.S. citizens and property. But the intervention rapidly escalated to a force of 22,500 officers and men with the clear and ultimate objective of preventing the return of the "radical" Juan Bosch to power.

The Organization of American States (OAS) legitimized the U.S. intervention, after the fact, through a resolution of 6 May to establish an Inter-American Peace Force to maintain the security of the inhabitants, the protection of human rights, and "the establishment of an atmosphere of peace and conciliation that will permit the functioning of democratic institutions."(45)

Though regarded by the OAS as a regional matter, the question of United States intervention was raised by the Soviet Union in the Security Council. The debate was enjoined as to whether or not OAS-U.S. intervention of such a scale was, in fact, an enforcement action. Despite U.S. resistance, the Council passed a resolution on 14 May which called for a cease-fire and insisted that the secretary-general "send as an urgent measure, a representative to the Dominican Republic for the purpose of reporting to the Security Council on the present situation."(46) Once more, the secretary-general was placed in the position of having to conduct an observer mission under conditions of political controversy between the United States and the Soviet Union. Politically, the secretary-general's special representative, General Rikhye, tried to bring about a cease-fire, while the sole function of the military observers was to observe and report.

However, because of opposition from the United States and other parties, the conditions of observation were made exceedingly difficult, and General Rikhye, on arrival, was denied access to the parties. The UN in size and in effect, therefore, played only a minor role in the affair. For the first time, however, a UN observer mission functioned in South America within the jurisdiction of the OAS - a matter pushed vigorously by the Soviet Union. There were many problems as to just what role the UN actually served other than the sanction of a UN presence. DOMREP remains to this day an aberration in the pattern of UN peacekeeping and clearly demonstrates that UN peacekeeping, at least to date and in the likely future, is viable only outside the regional orbits of the superpowers. Neither has there been any subsequent "cooperation" or overlapping of peacekeeping/observer operations by the UN and a regional organization. Under very different circumstances, the Organization of African Unity (OAU) requested UN cooperation in 1981 in the establishment of a peacekeeping operation in Chad, but without result. DOMREP, therefore, remains a unique event in the annals of UN peacekeeping experience.

UN India-Pakistan Observation Mission (UNIPOM), 1965-66

The last operation established in the Assertive Period was
UNIPOM in 1965. As noted earlier, war broke out between
India and Pakistan in Kashmir along the line patrolled by
UNMOGIP and along the length of the West Pakistan-India
border. A Security Council meeting called upon both sides to
take forthwith all steps for an immediate cease-fire,(47) which
went unheeded. A further resolution two days later again
called for a cease-fire and requested the secretary-general "to
take all measures possible to strengthen the United Nations
Military Observer Group in India Pakistan."(48) The
secretary-general proceeded immediately to the war area and
made arrangements to increase the size and effectiveness of
UNMOGIP. Yet hostilities persisted, and a further Council
resolution demanded "that a cease-fire should take effect . . .
[and that] the Secretary-General provide the necessary
assistance to ensure supervision of the cease-fire and the
withdrawal of all military personnel."(49) On the basis of this
and preceding resolutions, the secretary-general decided to
separate UN supervision of Kashmir (which was patrolled by
UNMOGIP) from the Western front where he set up a separate
India-Pakistan Observer Mission (UNIPOM), though coordinated
with UNMOGIP.

Proceeding on the assumption that the parties would
accede to the cease-fire which came fully into effect by 22
October, UNIPOM was fully deployed by 14 October. The
commander was drawn from UNFICYP, about 30 observers were
temporarily deployed from UNMOGIP and UNTSO, and the
balance of the complement of approximately 100 were contributed by 10 member states.

Thus, assertive action by the secretary-general brought
into being a new UN peacekeeping operation based solely on a
Council request for assistance. As Roslyn Higgins has written, "To a degree greater than usual, the Security Council
has in effect delegated its authority to the Secretary-
General."(50) The Soviet Union, which had voted in favor of
the respective council resolutions, strongly objected to the
unilateral action of the secretary-general.

The functions of UNIPOM were as those of UNMOGIP -
observation of the cease-fire lines and withdrawals of troops -
but they lacked the clear definition as specified by both India
and Pakistan in the Karachi Agreement upon which UNMOGIP
was based. UNIPOM's finances were, as with UNMOGIP,
apportioned as part of the regular budget of the UN, which
was a matter of controversy in the Council, though the Soviet
Union, in this case, paid the assessments for 1965 and 1966.
These were remarkable events to occur after paralysis of the
UN in 1964 over the broad discretionary role assumed by the
secretary-general in the administration of peacekeeping oper-

ations and over the question of financing. Equally noteworthy, and perhaps the reason for Soviet payment of its
assessments, was its instrumental role as the successful
mediator between India and Pakistan which gave rise to the
Tashkent Agreement of January 1966 and the complete withdrawal of the forces of both sides to agreed positions on the
western border by 25 February 1966. UNIPOM was thereupon
disbanded and UNMOGIP left to maintain its vigil of the cease-
fire lines in Kashmir.

Summary

The Assertive Period, which began with such great promise in
1956 with the establishment of UNEF I, ended in disillusionment
with its withdrawal under fire in 1967. It was an incredible
decade with the launching of three major operations (UNEF I,
ONUC, and UNFICYP), of the singularly unique UNTEA, and
the observer operations of UNYOM, DOMREP, and UNIPOM.
Seemingly, the UN had come of age. It proved itself able to
take bold and assertive action in the pursuit of international
peace and security, notwithstanding the severe enfeebling
effects of the destructive and persistent cold war during this
period. But its very assertiveness was also the cause of great
controversy, marked especially by the article 19 debate of
1964. Ironically, its lack of assertiveness in allowing the
withdrawal of UNEF I in 1967 was also the cause of controversy and disillusionment.

After 1967, the great accomplishments of peacekeeping
receded into history, but the problems and controversies it
engendered lingered on. UNMOGIP carried on without fanfare,
and UNFICYP continued, as it then was seen, as living testimony that peacekeeping was only a half measure; that without
attendant and successful peacemaking, it could be only a
limited instrument in the management of conflict. Furthermore,
the Special Committee on Peacekeeping (Committee of 33) had
made no substantive progress in its deliberations since its
inception in 1965, and the fact that peacekeeping was also
concomitant with decolonization reinforced the view that,
because the process of decolonization was close to completion,
the utility of peacekeeping would be terminated. And so it
was that, in 1967, peacekeeping entered into a new phase of
dormancy.

THE DORMANT PERIOD, 1967-73

The Dormant Period lasted for approximately six years, during
which time no new operations were authorized or implemented.

After 1967, functions of UNTSO were shifted to the patrol of the Golan Heights and the Suez Canal where it was caught in the war of attrition launched by Egypt against the Israeli forces encamped along the Bar Lev line. UNTSO was unable to do more than observe and report and/or limit the intensity of the ongoing hostilities. This, and the continuing status quo in Cyprus were, at that time, all too indicative of the weaknesses of peacekeeping and the growing disenchantment of contributing states. About the only indication of any positive nature was that the negotiations of the Committee of 33 produced in 1969, at the urging of Canada and the Third World members, a model format for an ultimate agreement on the establishment, direction and control, legal and financial arrangements, and operational procedures for "United Nations military observers established or authorized by the Security Council for observation purposes pursuant to Security Council resolutions."(51) For a time, this generated optimism that some of the key issues dividing East and West could be resolved with favorable consequences for the future of peace-keeping. But even this advance could not overcome the general attitude that the heyday of peacekeeping had come to an end. Not all, however, succumbed to the mood of pessi-mism. It was in 1969 that the International Peace Academy was created with the encouragement of then Secretary-General U Thant and which has since contributed so much to worldwide research, training, and enhancement of the practicality and legitimacy of peacekeeping.

THE RESURGENT PERIOD, 1973

There is nothing like a crisis to shatter preconceived notions and alter the course of events. The Egyptian and Syrian attack on Israel in October 1973 was one such event that produced unanticipated consequences which, within the context of this chapter, were the establishment of new peacekeeping operations on the Sinai and the Golan Heights. It was also in the Middle East, following the Israeli attack on Lebanon as far as the Litani River in 1978, that the third operation of the resurgent period occurred to supervise the withdrawal of Israeli forces and the return of Lebanese forces to the area. In conceptual and practical terms, notwithstanding criticisms, limitations, and disenchantment, these operations mark a further extension and elaboration of UN peacekeeping, demon-strating once again its utility and flexibility in times of grave crises.

United Nations Emergency Force II (UNEF II), 1973-79

The October war of 1973, which began with the attack upon
Israel by Egypt and Syria, with other Arab support, was even
more intense and dangerous to the parties and to international
peace and security than those of 1967 and 1956. This time
there was the threat of direct Soviet intervention and the
critical United States response of a military alert. At first
Egypt and then Syria made far-reaching advances into Israeli-
held territory, followed by dramatic and successful Israeli
counterattacks. Under the circumstances, the most readily
appropriate neutral ground to devise action to halt hostilities
and avoid their unknown consequences was the Security
Council. Debate was marked by anger and accusation; but,
nonetheless, there was swift enactment of three successive
resolutions of 22, 23, and 25 October with mutual support of
the Soviet Union and the United States by a vote of 14-0,
China abstaining.(52) Three resolutions were necessary before
a cessation of hostilities was achieved. It is noteworthy that
the last resolution was sponsored by eight nonpermanent
members: Guinea, India, Indonesia, Kenya, Panama, Peru,
Sudan, and Yugoslavia.

The first resolution called for a cease-fire, the second
also called for a cease-fire and requested the secretary-general
to dispatch observers to supervise it, and the third again
called for the parties to honor the cease-fire and established a
UN Emergency Force: "to be composed of personnel drawn from
State Members except the permanent members [this despite the
adverse view of France and the Soviet Union] . . . and
requests the Secretary-General to report within 24 hours on
the steps taken to this effect."(53) This report was provided
within the 24 hours and was far more comprehensive than any
similar report until that time. In setting out the structure
and functions of UNEF II, the secretary-general was careful to
respond to the import of the Security Council resolution of 25
October which called for the setting up of a force "under its
authority." In recognition of the predominant authority of the
Council and wishing to avoid ambiguity or disagreements on
the administrative role of the secretary-general, he carefully
delineated the functions and organizations of UNEF II and the
relationship between himself and the Council:

The Force will use its best efforts to prevent a
recurrence of fighting: and having in mind past
experience, I would suggest the following guidelines
for the proposed Force:

The Force will be under the command of the
United Nations, vested in the Secretary-General,
under the authority of the Security Council. The

command in the field will be exercised by a Force
Commander appointed by the Secretary-General with
the consent of the Security Council. The Commander will be responsible to the Secretary-General.

The Secretary-General shall keep the Security
Council fully informed of developments relating to
the functioning of the Force. All matters which may
affect the nature or the continued effective functioning of the Force will be referred to the Council
for its decision.

His report also enunciated the importance of "freedom of
movement"; that the force be provided with "weapons of a
defensive character only"; that "it shall not use force except
in self-defense"; that the size of the force be on the order of
7,000; and that the cost, estimated at $30 million for the first
six months, "be considered as expenses of the Organization to
be borne by Members in accordance with Article 17, paragraph
2 of the Charter."(54) These matters were accepted without
dissent, though China, opposed to the resolution, refrained
from voting because of the prevailing broad support.   In
approving the report, the Council also decided that, after the
initial period of six months, the force "shall continue in
operation thereafter, if required, provided the Security
Council so decides."(55) Considering the withdrawal of UNEF
I in 1967 at the request of Egypt in conformity with the
principle of consent without further consideration by the UN,
this time the Council made certain that it would be consulted
and that it would decide the question of termination.   The
mode of financing was later elaborated by the General Assembly in terms of a specially scaled assessment and adopted by a
vote of 108 in favor, 3 absentees, and 1 objection, with the
Soviet assertion that this was an ad hoc arrangement and
therefore not to be regarded as a precedent.(56)
     In terms of its organization and operational procedures,
the only major politically divisive issue was the matter of
participation.   The Soviet Union insisted on "equitable geographic composition," and after much negotiation Poland was
included to share the logistic responsibilites with Canada.
There was full agreement on the central interpository functions
of the force, as stated in the resolutions, to supervise the
implementation and maintenance of the cease-fire and the
return of the parties to the positions of 22 October.   Subsequently, arrangements were concluded for a sizeable
disengagement or buffer zone controlled exclusively by the UN
force, with UN-monitored limited armament zones of each party
on each side.   These arrangements offered far better assurance against infiltration and surprise attack than provided
under previous operations by the narrow cease-fire lines as in

the cases of UNMOGIP in Jammu and Kashmir, or UNTSO along the Suez line after the 1967 war; thereby exemplifying the crucial difference between the "observation" of a cease-fire and "maintenance" of a cease-fire.

Overall, the UN played a prominent role in negotiating the modalities of disengagement and their execution. A command structure drawn from UNTSO with contingents from UNFICYP enabled the UN to become operationally effective within a matter of approximately 48 hours of the decision, demonstrating that, though there are no formal agreements or guidelines for peacekeeping operations, institutionalized practice and competent administration are very effective, perhaps more effective than they would be were the Committee of 33 to define the regulations and procedures.(57)

One of the most productive aspects of UNEF II was that it provided a support base and functional participation to the process of peacemaking by assisting in the negotiations at kilometer 101 for the supply and redeployment of the Egyptian Third Army encircled by Israeli forces, and the interim agreement of September 1975 for the partial withdrawal of Israeli forces from the Sinai. The latter included the very novel arrangement of the early warning U.S.-Sinai Field Mission for the tactical surveillance of the Mitla and Giddi passes as an added measure of security to the military patrols conducted by UN forces. The Agreement of 1979 entailed an additional withdrawal of Israeli forces from the Sinai and the commensurate redeployment of UNEF II. Finally, the complete withdrawal of Israeli forces from the Sinai by April 1982 was to be accompanied by the installation of a new UN or other multinational peacekeeping force to monitor the borders and other designated areas.

But because of Soviet and Arab opposition to the peace agreement between Israel and Egypt, the Council would not authorize a new peacekeeping operation. Therefore, steps were taken by the parties and the United States to make arrangements for a non-UN multinational peacekeeping force to be installed in April 1982. UNEF II was terminated in 1979 by the simple expedient of nonrenewal of its mandate. Nevertheless, UNEF II was one of the most extensive, sophisticated, and successful UN operations to the present time.

United Nations Disengagement Observer Force (UNDOF), 1974

The war of 1973 was fought on two fronts: Egypt/Israel and Syria/Israel. The Security Council on 22 October had called upon all parties to terminate immediately all military activity. By the end of October, all military action on the Egyptian front had ceased. But on the Syrian front, though the front lines remained stable, military action persisted well into 1974 under the watchful eye of UNTSO observers. It was not until 31 May that an agreement on disengagement between Syrian and Israeli forces was signed at Geneva. This set the stage for the Security Council adoption of a resolution (sponsored by the Soviet Union and the United States) "to set up immediately under its authority a United Nations Disengagement Observer Force" and requesting the secretary-general to take the necessary steps to this effect. It was passed by a vote of 13 to 0; China and Iraq did not participate in the vote.(58)

The principal structure and composition of UNDOF are the same as for UNEF II, with UN control of a neutral zone between the parties and UN supervision of limited armament zones on either side, and the establishment of an Israel-Syria Mixed Armistice Commission. Initial personnel were drawn from UNEF II and from UNTSO and the total size was about 1,250. By the end of June, under the supervision of UNDOF, all forces were redeployed in accordance with agreed arrangements.

Because of the many similarities with UNEF II, further elaboration of UNDOF would be redundant. There are, however, several notable factors that deserve emphasis. The first is that the terms of the peacekeeping operation were fully negotiated by the UN and the parties before the Council resolution which authorized its establishment; the second is that, whereas the Israeli-Egyptian dispute has been resolved by a peace treaty, that of Israel-Syria has not. The state of belligerence and tension continues. The presence of UNDOF is, therefore, extremely critical to peace in the area. This was particularly true during the Israeli invasion of Lebanon in 1978 when there was danger of escalation, and again in 1981 when Syria and Israel exchanged threats over Syrian missiles in the Bekaa Valley. At the height of the danger, Syria and Israel quietly requested, through UNDOF, inspection of each other's zones of limited arms to ascertain whether either was conducting secret mobilization in the area. The fact that no such mobilization was evident offered some assurance that no imminent action was intended. In an area so dangerous and volatile, the value of peacekeeping in contributing to the peace, however tenuous, cannot be overestimated. UNDOF will likely remain in place for some time to come.

UN Interim Force in Lebanon (UNIFIL), 1978

In sharp contrast to UNDOF, which was negotiated over a period of months by the parties, by members of the Security Council, and by the UN secretariat, UNIFIL was established within four days of the Israeli invasion of Lebanon to the Litani River on 15 March 1978, an action taken in response to

Palestinian raids into Israel over the Lebanese border.   The
Security Council called:

> for strict respect for the territorial integrity, sover-
> eignty and political independence of Lebanon . . .
> upon Israel immediately to cease its military action
> against Lebanese territorial integrity and withdraw
> forthwith its forces from all Lebanese territory . . .
> [and decided] to establish immediately . . . a United
> Nations force for Southern Lebanon for the purpose
> of confirming the withdrawal of Israeli forces,
> restoring international peace and security and
> assisting the Government of Lebanon in ensuring the
> return of its effective authority in the area.(59)

The resolution was carried by a vote of 12 in favor with the
abstentions of Czechoslovakia and the Soviet Union.   The
latter opposed but did not veto the resolution because of the
support of Lebanon and other Arab states.   China did not
participate in the vote.
    On the same day as this resolution, the secretary-general
submitted a report detailing the principles and parameters of
the UNIFIL operation.(60)   Its authorized strength was established as 4,000.   It was financed on the basis of the same ad
hoc formula as UNEF II and UNDOF (later confirmed by General Assembly resolution of 21 April).   The first elements were
drawn from UNTSO, UNDOF, and UNEF II.   In an effort to
achieve "balanced composition," several East European states
were invited to participate, but declined.   In an unusual
move, France, with historic interests in the area, offered to
participate.   It did so when no objection was raised by
members of the Council.   In most general aspects, the organization of UNIFIL is like its two immediate predecessors, and
it operates with its own command but under coordination of the
chief coordinator of all the UN peacekeeping forces in the
Middle East.   The secretary-general's report was adopted
immediately by the Council.   The UN had responded to yet
another Middle East crisis in great haste.
    The guiding principles of UNEF II were again adopted,
but there the similarity of organization is sharply contrasted
with dissimilarity in the situation and its consequences.   While
preparing the secretary-general's report and the first steps of
implementation, members of the office of the under secretary-
general for political affairs did so with misgivings.   They knew
that it was the necessary course of action; at the same time,
they sensed the enormous complexity and anticipated difficulties UNIFIL would have to face.   They were correct in their
assessment.
    The mandate involved international and domestic elements
including both state and nonstate actors subject to erratic and

volatile behavior. UNIFIL ran into direct resistance from PLO and Lebanese Christian Militia de facto forces, and Israel withdrew only after heavy international pressure. But even then, not entirely, having left the Christian Militia to act as its surrogate in areas contiguous with the Israeli border. Moreover, Lebanese forces on several occasions were forcibly prevented by de facto forces from entering the area in accordance with the mandate.

This, the last UN peacekeeping force to be established to date, was caught in a situation which resembles, in several respects, the most difficult aspects of UNTSO, ONUC, and UNFICYP. As a result, it was responsible for maintaining order in an area it does not fully control; it was meant to prevent infiltration, cater to the needs of the civilian population (in the initial stage it had to provide for 47,000 families), be in continuous liaison with all political elements, and keep in sight the ultimate objectives of its primary mandate. As with all peacekeeping operations, it was prohibited from using force except in self-defense - but, even so, UNIFIL was involved in numerous engagements; suffered many casualties; and, on several occasions and subject to varied interpretation, took the military initiative to forestall or prevent action by one party or another.

These were not the only problems. Because of the necessity of quick response, UNIFIL lacked adequate personnel, staff organization was uncertain, there was lack of transport and other related functions, and uncertainty about the choice of headquarters. Naqoura was finally selected, but proved to be badly exposed to hostile action and, on several occasions, came under bombardment from the tanks and artillery of the Christian Militia. The problems were so severe that by April 1978 the Council found it necessary to increase the size of the force from 4,000 to 6,000.(61)

The costs were also high, from its inception in March 1978 to June 1982 amounting to $449,889,727. To compound the difficulties, some 20 states including the Soviet Union have refused to pay their assessments, making it necessary to call for voluntary contributions. These and other related problems were the subject of frequent reports by the secretary-general.(62)

The stubborn resistance to the fulfillment of UNIFIL's mandate marred it from the very beginning. It was, therefore, constantly engaged in liaison with both governmental and de facto forces with respect to the cessation of hostile action among the parties and against UNIFIL itself. At the time, UNIFIL existed in a sea of instability with more than 50 military factions controlling and fighting over the territory in and around Beirut, with 30,000 Syrian troops in partial occupation of Lebanon, and the constant danger of Israeli threats to attack Syrian SAM 6 emplacements in the Bekaa Valley as well as actual strikes against PLO forces both inside and beyond the UNIFIL area. These conditions caused dismay among the participant states which have suffered casualties and complained vigorously about the lack of cooperation of the parties. But none withdrew, save Canada which at the outset set a terminal date for its participation.

The gravity of the situation persisted, requiring the maintenance of UNIFIL in the area to do its utmost, even under the difficult circumstances to hold the peace, and in general, fulfill its mandate. In April of 1979, Lebanese forces entered the area and were incorporated into UNIFIL, under its command. But the overall situation remained critical. Peace-keeping as a non-enforcement action was strained to the limit, confirming the misgivings expressed by members of the office of the under secretary-general for political affairs.

On June 1982, Israel launched its second invasion deep into Lebanese territory, forcing UNIFIL to stand aside, as Israeli forces advanced. Up to that time, UNIFIL had been essential in preventing uncontrolled escalation of fighting in the area. It could not have been expected to do so in the face of Israeli actions, nor did its mandate include provisions for such an eventuality. UNIFIL served its purpose from 1978 to June 1982. Ensuing events will influence any further assessment of the situation and whether UNIFIL, still in the area, will have a role to play pending the Lebanon Israel negotiations.

HISTORICAL APPRAISAL

This historical overview of the development of peacekeeping covers the entire postwar period, 1946 to 1981, and is itself a mirror of the evolution of the UN in the area of its primary responsibility for the maintenance of international peace and security. It is, therefore, also inextricably related to the patterns of East-West relations, the onset of the cold war, and the consequent failure to make use of the enforcement authority of the Security Council as prescribed in Chapter VII of the Charter. After the Cuban missile crisis of 1962, the cold war moderated with movement toward detente but has since reverted to the cold war posture. Over this period of 35 years, the process of decolonization has brought many new nations of the Third World into the UN and the power configuration of the world has shifted markedly from a bipolar to a multipolar system. The practice of peacekeeping, without attempting to determine a measurable extent of the correlations, has been unavoidably affected by these and related factors which influenced its pattern of development and its utility.

In the first two years of the Nascent Period, 1946-56, there occurred four observer-type peacekeeping operations. Of these, UNSCOB was directly entwined with the East-West strategic and ideological struggle in the Balkans. The other three - Indonesia, UNTSO, and UNMOGIP - were all manifestations of the process of decolonization. Both the Security Council and the General Assembly were involved in establishing mandates. All of the operations evolved out of committees of good offices or inquiry that required military observers to monitor the situation. UNSCOB and Indonesia utilized diplomatic representatives resident in the affected areas, whereas the observers for UNTSO were named from designated countries by the mediator in concert with the Truce Commission, and the same occurred in the case of UNMOGIP by the parties to the Tashkent Agreement. The secretary-general assisted in the first two cases and was instrumental in the latter two cases, indicative of later operations. With the exception of UNTSO, which numbered just less than 600, the size of each of the other three was less than 100. The principle of consent was inherent in each operation except for Albania, Bulgaria, and Yugoslavia's refusal to cooperate with UNSCOB. Countries participating excluded the Soviet Union and its allies, though in the case of UNSCOB they were invited and refused. The United States participated in UNTSO and in the early years of UNMOGIP. But these were exceptions, the common practice being the selection of participant states from the middle and smaller powers. Overall, the Nascent Period is one in which the fundamental characteristics and problems become apparent that reappeared in later operations.

During the Assertive Period, as already noted, peacekeeping emerged in full form, e.g., UNEF I "to secure and supervise the cessation of hostilities"; ONUC, "to provide the government with such military assistance as may be necessary" and "take vigorous action to assist the . . . government in the restoration of law and order"; and UNFICYP, "to use its best efforts to prevent a recurrence of fighting and, as necessary, to contribute to the restoration of law and order." UNTEA was entirely unique in the sense that it became the sovereign authority during the period of sovereignty of West Irian from the Netherlands to Indonesia. In sharp contrast to the Nascent Period, the size of the operations numbered in the thousands with vastly larger responsibility, complex organization, and financial burdens. The other three operations in this period - UNYOM, DOMREP, and UNIPOM - are of the observer type similar in characteristics to UNMOGIP.(63) In most cases, the process of decolonization was a basic causal factor, but war resulting from military aggression also brought about a peacekeeping operation (UNEF). Throughout this period, the factors of consent, the nonuse of force except in self-defense, and the participation only by middle and small powers (the United Kingdom in UNFICYP being the exception) evolve as fundamental principles.

Whereas in the Nascent Period East-West antagonism is a complicating issue, it emerges full blown in respect to UNEF and ONUC. In both cases, there were grave disagreements over the extent, if any, of General Assembly competence to mandate peacekeeping operations, a deep division over the authority and discretion of the secretary-general in conducting the operations, and disagreement over the mode of financing. The severity of these matters all but paralyzed the General Assembly in 1964, though, it must be noted, UNFICYP and to a large degree UNTEA enjoyed general support, and DOMREP, the first and only incursion of peacekeeping at a level of observation, occurred in the sphere of influence of one of the superpowers.

For the above reasons, and those discussed in the body of this chapter, the Assertive Period is followed by six years of dormancy; then to be succeeded by a period of resurgence of three major peacekeeping operations. And here we find a number of remarkable features. There is no role played by the General Assembly, neither the Soviet Union or the United States propose or wish it; the relationship between the Security Council and the secretary-general is clarified and resolved; and the modes of financing are agreed upon, excepting the difficulties in respect to UNIFIL. The principle of consent is still operative, but diminished in at least two respects: the first on the matter of composition where Israel had to give way on the participation of Poland; and the second in respect to the matter of termination where, in contrast to UNEF I, the mandate of UNEF II clearly enunciates the authority of the Security Council in that regard. Another change occurred in the matter of composition namely, the participation of a Soviet-sponsored communist state and that of the permanent members of the Security Council, i.e., the Soviet Union in UNTSO after 1973 and France in UNIFIL, which may be indicative of a developing trend. There are three other features that deserve reiteration: (1) joint Soviet-U.S. sponsorship of UNDOF; (2) the important supportive role of the nonpermanent Third World members, as in the sponsorship of the resolution on UNEF II; and (3) the innovative use of a non-UN remote sensing unit, i.e., the Sinai Field Mission.

Looking back over the 15 operations considered from 1946 to 1981, the evidence is clear that the nature of the crises giving rise to UN peacekeeping have become more varied and the functional tasks mandated to these operations are also more numerous and more complex. The circumstances evoking peacekeeping derive from colonialism, state to state hostilities, territorial disputes, domestic instability, and the activity of nongovernmental de facto forces. The resultant tasks vary widely including observation of special situations, such as infiltration in UNYOM; the supervision and ensurance of cease-fires; the exclusive control of demilitarized zones; the maintenance of law and order; and the assumption of temporary sovereignty. Some of these functions have required large numbers of personnel and the provision and use of more sophisticated levels of armament, as in UNFICYP and UNIFIL. Without diminishing the many and serious problems of UN peacekeeping, many of which are mentioned in the body of this chapter, the historical evidence indicates a progression to higher levels of complexity and sophistication. It is for this reason that the format of this presentation is chronological rather then topographical.

At they very least, peacekeeping has not only survived the inherent problems and damaging effects of the cold war and, as well, the many changes in the international system, it has over time gained legitimacy and strength as a utilitarian and competent instrument in the limited arsenal of UN capability in the management of conflict.

NOTES

1. "Two Differing Views of the United Nations Assayed," The Strategy of World Order, vol. III, ed. Richard A. Falk and Saul H. Mendelovitz (New York: World Law Fund, 1966).

2. For a discussion of this matter see H. Wiseman, "Peacekeeping: Debut or Denouement?" C.I.I.A., Behind the Headlines, vol. XXXI, nos. 1-2, February 1972.

3. SC Res. 339, 19 December 1946.

4. Ibid.

5. YUN 1946-47, p. 364.

6. GA Res. 109 (ii), 21 October 1947.

7. YUN 1948-49, p. 252.

8. Ibid., p. 294.

9. GIA 508 A & B (VI), 7 December 1951.

10. SC Res. 459, 1 Aug. 1947.

11. SC Res. 525 (1), 25 August 1947.

12. S/1150, 24 December 1948.

13. SC Res. 1134, 28 January 1949.

14. (London: Stevens and Sons Limited, 1960), p. 103.

15. See Rosalyn Higgins, United Nations Peacekeeping 1946-1967, vol. 2, Asia, for a succinct account. (London: Oxford University Press, 1970).

16. Alastair M. Taylor, Indonesian Independence and the
United Nations. London: Stevens & Sons, 1960, p. 435.

17. GA Res. 106 (S-1), 15 May 1947.

18. GA Res. 181 (11) A, 29 November 1947.

19. SC Res. 727, 23 April 1948.

20. GA Res. 186 (ES-1), 14 May 1948.

21. SC Res. 773, 22 May 1948.

22. SC Res. 801, 29 May 1948.

23. SC Res. 654, 20 January 1948.

24. SC Res. 651, 17 January 1948.

25. SC Res. 726, 21 April 1948.

26. SC Res. 1461, 14 March 1950.

27. SC Res. 211, 20 September 1965.

28. GA Res. 1000 (ES-1), 5 November 1956.

29. A/3694 and add. 1, Report of the Secretary General, 9
October 1957. See Higgins, United Nations Peacekeeping. pp.
259-60.

30. See Higgins, Asia, vol. 1, p. 536.

31. SC Res. 4022, 11 June 1958.

32. GA Res. 1237 (ES-11), 21 August 1958.

33. S/4387, 14 July 1960. See B.W. Bowett, United Nations
Forces (New York: Praeger, 1964), p. 154.

34. GA Res. 1474/Rev. 1 (ES-10), 20 September 1960.

35. SC Res. 4741, 21 February 1961.

36. SC Res. 5002, 24 November 1961.

37. GA Res. 1583, 20 December 1960.

38. GAOR 16th sess. 1054 plenary meeting, p. 640.

39. Agreement between The Republic of Indonesia and the
Kingdom of the Netherlands concerning West New Guinea (West
Irian), as cited in Higgins, Asia, vol. 2, p. 101.

40. Ibid. p. 112.

41. GA Res. 1752, 12 September 1962.

42. See Higgins, Asia, vol. 2, p. 119.

43. See David Wainhouse, International Peacekeeping At The
Crossroads (Baltimore: Johns Hopkins University Press, 1973),
pp. 164-65.

44. SC Res. 5575, 4 March 1964.

45. Wainhouse, International Peacekeeping, p. 472.

46. SC Res. 203, 14 May 1965.

47. SC Res. 209, 4 September 1965.

48. SC Res. 210, 6 September 1965.

49. SC Res. 211, 20 September 1965.

50. Higgins, Asia, vol. 2, p. 352.

51. A/7742 appendix. See also H. Wiseman, "Peacekeeping: Debut or Denouement?"

52. SC Res. 338, 22 October; SC Res. 339, 23 October; and SC Res. 340, 25 October 1973.

53. Ibid.

54. S/11052 and Rev. 1, 27 October 1973, "Report of the Secretary-General on the Implementation of Security Council Resolution 340."

55. SC Res. 341, 27 October 1973.

56. GA Res. 3101, 11 December 1973.

57. See chapters 7 and 8 in this volume by Brian Urquhart and J.D. Murray, respectively, for a detailed discussion of this question.

58. SC Res. 350, 31 May 1974.

59. SC Res. 425, 19 March 1978.

60. S/12611, 19 March 1978.

61. SC Res. 427, 3 May 1978.

62. For example, see S/13258, 19 April 1979, "Interim Report of the Secretary-General."

63. For a lucid analysis of observer missions and peace-keeping operations as distinct types, see Indar Jit Rikhye, Michael Harbottle, and Bjorn Egge, The Thin Blue Line (New Haven: Yale University Press, 1974).

II
National Perspectives

Introduction to Part II

Following the general scope of the preceding chapters, Part II focuses directly on the national policies of key state action. It assesses the practice of UN peacekeeping from the perspective of parties in conflict, i.e., host state considerations, and the policy motivations and issues confronting states that contribute forces to UN operations.

Only a representative sample of parties in conflict agreeing to peacekeeping operations could be presented here, i.e., the considerations of Egypt and Israel. But these are states with prolonged, direct, and varied experience, as in the manifestation of Canadian peacekeeping policy spanning contributions to all UN operations from 1949-1979.

Elaraby, in thorough fashion, deals with the conditions of the fundamental aspects of consent, the nature of the mandates, and the requisite functions of the force in the field. Special consideration is given to the conditions of the withdrawal of UNEF I in 1967, asserting the right of Egypt to call for the withdrawal and the legal authority of the secretary-general to so decide. These elements are again examined in respect to the changed conditions of UNEF II and the novel functions of the disengagement arrangements, buffer zones, the phased withdrawal of Israeli forces from the Sinai, and the final termination of the operation. "The Egyptian Experience" is a careful political and legal appreciation of host state considerations and of Egypt's positive affirmation of peacekeeping.

"The Israeli Experience" covers the entire range of Israeli involvement in peacekeeping since 1948. The political aspects and functional performance of peacekeeping operations, including the work of mixed armistice commissions, the ability of the peacekeeping efforts to prevent terrorist infiltration, the status of forces, duration and withdrawal, composition and political control are all examined in depth. Of these, the last three issues are of considerable contention as to principle and practice. On the matter of host country considerations (none of the peacekeeping forces patroled within Israeli borders), the argument is put forward that "national sovereignty becomes irrelevant"; and, on the matter of UN political control of operations, it is argued that impartiality and apolitical control prevail up to the level of the secretary-general, beyond that, pro-Arab partiality prevails in the Security Council. Emphasis is also placed on the necessary relationship between peace-keeping and peacemaking which, it is argued, is blurred and inconclusive. The chapters by Elaraby and Comay together provide incisive analyses of the major peacekeeping operations in the Middle East, clearly revealing points of differences, disagreement, and accommodation.

Contributing country policies and the assessment of the advantages and disadvantages of such participation are the subjects of the next two chapters. In "Canadian Attitudes toward Peacekeeping," Pearson deals primarily with the broad scope of Canadian foreign policy and the emphasis Canada has placed on the United Nations from its very inception. Con-sideration is given to Canada as a middle power seeking to maximize its influence in world affairs. Regarding the Canadian role in the Suez crisis of 1956, it "had the effect of galvanizing what had been a dormant impulse to clothe the UN with real authority and give meaning to the commitment to earmark forces for UN service," which Canada had done as early as 1950. Canadian peacekeeping policy was seriously affected by the events of 1967, yet it continued to enjoy a sufficient and continuing base of support for direct parti-cipation in all later UN peacekeeping operations, and to play a political role in the UN Special Committee on Peacekeeping Operations in the search for agreed constitutional and practical guidelines for the establishment and implementation of future operations.

In partial contrast, Byers in "Peacekeeping and Canadian Defense Policy: Ambivalence and Uncertainty" recognizes that "peacekeeping has been acknowledged as a cornerstone of Canadian foreign and defense policy" since 1950. He cautions, however, that the policy "has been fraught with uncertainty, ambivalence, and difficulty." The full range of Canadian peacekeeping experience, including the non-UN Indochina operations, is examined in the light of the frequent differences in view between the formulators of foreign policy and of defense policy, and the comparative assessment of advantages and disadvantages. The priority of the defense commitment to peacekeeping in relation to the major alliance commitments and the defense of Canada receives particular attention, showing the strain on defense resources, as well as fluctuating support and, at times, direct opposition to participation in peace-keeping operations.

Together, the chapters by Pearson and Byers cover the wide range of concerns and numerous factors that are taken into account by a major contributor to UN peacekeeping, thereby posing many of the questions that current and potential contributors face in making these decisions.

3
UN Peacekeeping:
The Egyptian Experience
Nabil A. Elaraby *

INTRODUCTION - BASIC CONCEPTS

The ability of states to settle their disputes peacefully and the ability of the international community to undertake the requisite collective action whenever peace is threatened have not yet materialized in our contemporary world. The United Nations was created essentially as a universal organization dedicated to the maintenance of world peace. The Charter entrusted the Security Council with vast and wideranging powers to enforce its decisions in order to maintain international peace and security. When confronted with the realities of the post-World War II era, the system proved inoperable. Member states were forced to seek new concepts and devise new methods to cope with their quest for maintaining international peace and security. The concept of a peacekeeping operation, which is not a collective enforcement measure, was gradually devised to undertake certain functions. Views on the reasons behind the inapplicability of implementing the elaborate collective security system outlined in the Charter have differed. The consideration of these views are, however, beyond the scope of this chapter. What is of direct relevance is that the recourse to UN military personnel became more frequent whenever armed hostilities erupted.

Observers were dispatched, in the 1940s, to the Balkans, Palestine, and Kashmir in order to provide the Security Council with accurate and impartial information on developments pertaining to the maintenance of peace. What started with a handful of unarmed observers, developed, in less than ten

---

*The views expressed by the author do not necessarily reflect the policies of the government of the Arab Republic of Egypt.

years, into regular armed units comprising thousands of men. Likewise, the tasks assigned to the peacekeepers underwent considerable developments, from a simple mandate to observe and report on cease-fire violations to complicated responsibilities relating to policing areas, manning checkpoints, and patrolling borders with a right to defend their assigned positions with armed force, as an extension of their right to self-defense.

Peacekeeping, with the acceptance and consent of the concerned states, gradually developed into an ever-increasing aspect of UN activities. The Egyptian experience with UN peacekeeping is varied and rich. Egypt has served as host country to two important peacekeeping operations. Egypt has also been involved since 1949 with UN observers. UNEF I was, indeed, a pilot project originally envisaged and launced to meet the requirements of the 1956 Suez crisis. It was later developed and its mandate expanded to enable it to undertake long-range responsibilities. Its considerable success paved the way for the general acceptability of this newly devised method. UNEF II was also, in more than one sense, a pilot project. From its inception it was entrusted with sensitive and varied tasks.

The scope of this chapter will be confined to the examination of the establishment, stationing, functioning, termination, and other relevant issues of the two major UN peacekeeping forces that were created following the 1967 and 1973 armed conflicts, respectively.

UNEF I(1)

The Establishment of UNEF I

The United Nations Emergency Force (UNEF I) was established by General Assembly resolution 1000 (ES-1) dated 5 November 1956 with a specific mandate "to secure and supervise the cessation of hostilities in accordance with all the terms of General Assembly Resolution 997 (ES-1) of 2 November 1956."

There were no precedents in the annals of the United Nations to follow. There were, moreover, no Charter provisions which the United Nations and the host country could rely upon for guidance. It should be acknowledged that, due to the vision, patience, perseverance, and courage of Secretary-General Dag Hammarskjöld, the United Nations was able to overcome the inherent difficulties in composing, stationing, and operating in a relatively short time a pilot project which proved to be of great value.

Egypt's Acceptance of the General Assembly's Resolutions Concerning the Establishment of UNEF

Although the Egyptian government abstained on Resolution 1000
(ES-1), which established the United Nations Command,(2) the
secretary-general received, a few hours later, a cable from
Egypt's foreign minister stating that his government had
accepted that resolution.(3) It could, therefore, be stated
that Egypt "had accepted the Force in principle by formally
accepting the resolution 1000 (ES-1) establishing a United
Nations Command."(4)

The Egyptian Government's Negotiation with the Secretary-
General and the Good Faith Accord.
        Despite the acceptance of resolution 1000 (ES-1), Egypt
was of the opinion that, as the host country, its sovereignty
and territorial integrity could be affected by the presence of
foreign troops.   It wished to get from the secretary-general
certain assurances and clarifications before the actual arrival
of the force in Egypt.   In his "Summary Study," Hammarskjöld stated that he:

> had, therefore, given interpretations of the relevant
> General Assembly resolutions to the Government of
> Egypt, reporting in full to the Advisory Committee on
> the interpretations given. The Advisory Committee
> had approved these interpretations and recommended
> that the Secretary-General should start at once the
> transfer of the Force to Egypt, an action to which
> the Government of Egypt had consented on the basis
> of the interpretations given by the Secretary-
> General.(5)

In a previous report, Mr. Hammarskjöld had made the same
point, stating to the General Assembly that

> before consenting to the arrival of the Force, the
> Government of Egypt wished to have certain points
> in the resolution of the General Assembly clarified.
> An exchange of views took place between the
> Secretary-General and the Government of Egypt in
> which the Secretary-General, in reply to questions
> addressed to him by the Government of Egypt, gave
> his interpretations of the relevant General Assembly
> resolutions, in respect of the character and func-
> tions of the Force . . . [and that] on the basis of
> resolutions, as interpreted by the Secretary-General,
> the Government of Egypt consented to the arrival of
> the United Nations Force in Egypt.(6)

Thus, it should be borne in mind that the secretary-general's interpretations and negotiations with Egypt had, in fact, a dual function which highly increased their importance. First, the Egyptian consent to the entry, presence, and functioning of the force, which was embodied in the good-faith accord and the 8 February 1957 agreement with Egypt, was a direct result of the interpretations given by and the negotiations concluded with Mr. Hammarskjöld. Second, the General Assembly's approval of the secretary-general's interpretations rendered them binding on the United Nations as an official understanding of UNEF's presence, including the duration and functioning in Egypt.

The essence of the exchanges between the secretary-general and the Egyptian government centered on the latter's anxiety to clarify its position with regard to the duration of UNEF's stay on its territory. Egypt wanted to know how long it was anticipated that the force would remain. The secretary-general is reported to have responded that, "while a definite reply was impossible, the emergency character of the Force linked it to the liquidation of the crisis."(7) He is further reported to have told the advisory committee that he explained to Egypt that UNEF would stay on its territory until the "liquidation" of the "immediate crisis."(8) Moreover, he reportedly said that "[if] different views should arise as to the ending of the crisis, the question would have to be negotiated with the parties."(9)

Egypt, however, was not satisfied, and addressed a memorandum dated 11 November 1956 to the secretary-general, noting that, since it was agreed that Egyptian consent was indispensable for the entry and presence of the UN forces on its territory, "if such consent no longer persists, these forces shall withdraw."(10) Mr. Hammarskjöld's answer was to remind Egypt that the considerations motivating its consent were the same as those to which the General Assembly had directed the tasks of the force. Accordingly, "so long as the task, thus prescribed, was not completed, the reasons for the consent of the Government remain valid, hence withdrawal of consent prior to completion of the task would run counter to the acceptance by Egypt of the decision of the General Assembly."(11)

Again, this interpretation proved to be inadequate to allay the fears and apprehensions of the Egyptian government, which advised the secretary-general on 13 November of its refusal to subscribe to his interpretation. The secretary-general's reaction was embodied in a message to Egypt which emphasized that: "if arrangements were permitted to break down over the principle that the troops must remain until completion of their task, he could 'not avoid going to the General Assembly' for a decision as to what could or could not be accepted as an understanding."(12) Egypt thereupon

allowed the UN force to enter its territory. Thus, it may be
assumed that Egypt implicitly accepted the secretary-general's
position on the link between the duration of the force and the
completion of the task.(13)
          Notwithstanding Egypt's tacit acceptance, the secretary-
general felt it imperative that he fly to Cairo and clarify
Egypt's exact position with the highest authorities. His
objective is reported to have been "to induce that government
to limit its freedom of action by agreeing to make a request for
withdrawal of troops conditional upon the completion of their
task. Whether or not the task was in fact completed would be
a question which would have to be submitted to interpretation
by the Assembly."(14)
          The result of his negotiations in Cairo was summarized in
an "aide-memoire on the basis for the presence and functioning
of the UNEF in Egypt,"(15) which the General Assembly
approved on 24 November 1956,(16) transforming the note into
a binding understanding between the UN and Egypt. Mr.
Hammarskjöld considered it as laying another foundation for
the presence and functioning of the force and for the continued cooperation with the Egyptian authorities.(17)   The
aide-memoire contained the following basic points:

1.   The government of Egypt declares that, when
       exercising its sovereign rights on any matter
       concerning the presence and functioning of
       UNEF, it will be guided, in good faith, by its
       acceptance of General Assembly resolution 1000
       (ES-1) of 5 November 1956.

2.   The United Nations takes note of this declara-
       tion of the government of Egypt and declares
       that the activities of UNEF will be guided, in
       good faith, by the task established for the
       force in the aforementioned resolutions; in
       particular the United Nations, understanding
       this to correspond to the wishes of the Govern-
       ment of Egypt, reaffirms its willingness to
       maintain UNEF until its task is completed.

3.   The Government of Egypt and the Secretary-
       General declare that it is their intention to
       proceed forthwith, in the light of points 1 and
       2 above, to explore jointly concrete aspects of
       the functioning of UNEF, including its station-
       ing and the question of its lines of communica-
       tion and supply; the Government of Egypt,
       confirming   its   intention   to   facilitate   the
       functioning of UNEF, and the United Nations
       are agreed to expedite in cooperation the imple-
       mentation of guiding principles arrived at as a
       result of that joint exploration on the basis of
       the resolutions of the General Assembly.(18)

Thus, the aide-memoire, without specifying the necessary details for the stationing and functioning of the force, envisaged future concrete arrangements between Egypt and the secretary-general on the status of the force. These arrangements were reached on 8 February 1957.(19)

An analysis of the task of the force

In analyzing the "task" assigned to the force, it is appropriate to recall that General Assembly resolution 1000 (ES-1), which established UNEF, assigned to it a specific mandate "to secure and supervise the cessation of hostilities in accordance with all the terms of resolution 997 (ES-1) of 2 November 1956."(20) It follows that, when Egypt conveyed its acceptance to the secretary-general, its consent was given on the basis of the task contained in the aforementioned resolution. The clarifications requested by Egypt were made by the secretary-general and approved by the advisory committee and, eventually, by the General Assembly.

Arguments have been advanced, by jurists as well as politicians, contending that by allowing UNEF to enter and operate on its territory, Egypt voluntarily curtailed its sovereignty and limited its future freedom of action. It was precisely in anticipation of such arguments that Egypt's foreign minister placed on record his country's position regarding the presence and functioning of UNEF:

Distinctly erroneous interpretations were given by a few speakers - just a few - of the position taken by the General Assembly in relation to the present crisis. We still believe, however, together with the overwhelming majority of the Members of the Assembly that, among other things, it has been and remains clearly the intention of the Assembly to secure, without any condition whatsoever, the withdrawal from Egypt of the invading armed forces of France, the United Kingdom and Israel, and fully to respect Egypt's sovereignty.

We still believe that the General Assembly resolution 997, 2 November 1956, still stands, together with its endorsement of the principle that the General Assembly could not request the United Nations Emergency Force to be stationed or to operate on the territory of a given country without the consent of the Government of the country. This is the proper basis on which we believe, together with the overwhelming majority of this Assembly, that the United Nations Emergency Force could be stationed or could operate in Egypt. It is the only basis on which

Egypt has given its consent in this respect. Furthermore, it is important to leave no place for any
equivocation, not only regarding the basis on which
this Force is stationed or operates in Egypt, but
also regarding what its functions are and what they
are not.

Our clear understanding - and I am sure it is the
clear understanding of the Assembly - is that the
Force is in Egypt only in relation to the present
attack against Egypt by the United Kingdom, France
and Israel, and for the purposes directly connected
with the incursion of the invading forces into
Egyptian territory. The United Nations Emergency
Force is in Egypt, not as an occupation force, not
as a replacement for the invaders, not to clear the
Canal of obstructions, not to resolve any question or
settle any problem, be it in relation to the Suez
Canal, to Palestine or to any other matter; it is not
there to infringe upon Egyptian sovereignty in any
fashion or to any extent, but, on the contrary, to
give expression to the determination of the United
Nations to put an end to the aggression committed
against Egypt and to the presence of the invading
forces in Egyptian territory.

In other words, as must be abundantly clear, this
Force has gone to Egypt to help Egypt, with Egypt's
consent; and no one here or elsewhere can reasonably or fairly say that a fire brigade, after putting
out a fire would be entitled or expected to claim the
right of deciding not to leave the house. I would
like to submit, in this connection, that we are in the
process of creating quite an important precedent.
This being the first time that such a force as the
present one has been established by the United
Nations, it is essential that we establish and carefully observe right principles as a basis for its work
and relationships. Otherwise, we would, from the
very beginning, be casting serious doubts on the
whole process and damaging the prospects of continuing in this direction.(21)

In the light of the clarifications advanced by Egypt's foreign
minister, it seems appropriate to conclude that Egypt did not
consider that it had relinquished any of its prerogatives as a
sovereign state with respect to the duration of UNEF being
stationed on its territory. It should, however, be taken into
consideration that, by its acquiescence and tacit acceptance of
the secretary-general's interpretation of the relevant resolu-

tions, and on the basis of its good-faith commitment, Egypt
was under an obligation to abide by the General Assembly's
determination of whether the task had been completed. What
should be emphasized is that the task referred to here is
confined to the original mandate of the force as contained in
resolution 1000 (ES-1).

In a report by the secretary-general dated 24 January
1957,(22) it was suggested that, following the withdrawal of
Israeli forces from Egypt, it would be essential to scrupulously
observe the provisions of the 1949 General Armistice Agreement. The General Assembly took note of the report and
called upon Egypt and Israel to respect the General Armistice
Agreement.(23) The Assembly, moreover, considered inter alia
that "the scrupulous maintenance of the Armistice Agreement
requires the placing of UNEF on the Egyptian-Israeli armistice
demarcation line and the implementation of other measures as
proposed in the Secretary-General's report."(24)   Thus, the
General Assembly apparently expanded the original functions
assigned to UNEF, but did not clarify whether the "task" of
the force would encompass its continued deployment on the
armistice demarcation line and whether Egypt's acceptance of
the previously defined "task" would automatically be extended
to cover the newly acquired functions assigned to UNEF by
General Assembly resolution 1125 (XI).   It could well be
argued that, during a grave crisis, no attempts are usually
made to answer all aspects of the relevant questions.   The
Assembly did endorse, in general terms, the secretary-
general's report and opted throughout the 1956-1957 episode to
leave to him the sensitive task of interpreting the intent of its
resolutions.   This procedure was welcomed and even encouraged by Mr. Hammarskjöld.   As the interpreter and
administrator of the political pronouncements of the United
Nations deliberative organs, the secretary-general's political
role was greatly enhanced.   In point of fact, it soon became
evident that the secretary-general's office had developed real
political clout through the provisions of article 98, more than
what was originally envisaged when the Charter was
drafted.(25)

Israel never accepted UNEF deployment on its side of the
demarcation line.   Though Egypt accepted UNEF to patrol its
side of the Egyptian-Palestinian border, it never entered into
new agreements with the secretary-general which could be
interpreted as qualifying its right to ask for the withdrawal of
the force.

In a later report to the General Assembly, the secretary-
general confirmed:

> The consequence of such a bilateral declaration is
> that, were either side to act unilaterally in refusing
> continued presence or deciding on withdrawal, and

were the other side to find that such action was contrary to a good-faith interpretation of the purposes of the operation, an exchange of views would be called for towards harmonizing the positions. This does not imply any infringement of the sovereign right of the host Government, nor any restriction on the right of the United Nations to decide on the termination of its own operation whenever it might see fit to do so. But it does mean a mutual recognition of the fact that the operation, being based on collaboration between the host Government and the United Nations, should be carried on in forms natural to such collaboration, and especially so with regard to the questions of presence and maintenance.(26)

The Withdrawal of UNEF I

The events that developed in May 1967 are relevant to this chapter from the viewpoint of the secretary-general's legal authority to accept Egypt's request without prior explicit endorsement from the General Assembly.

The secretary-general ordered the withdrawal of UNEF only after discussing his intended decision with the advisory committee. The committee was thus informed that the secretary-general's reply, to be handed shortly to the Egyptian permanent representative, would mean an end of UNEF I. Yet, to use U Thant's words, "(T)he Committee did not move as it was its right to do under the terms of paragraph 9 of General Assembly Resolution 1001 (ES-1) to request the convening of the General Assembly on the situation which had arisen."(27)

It has been argued that the General Assembly should have been consulted before the withdrawal of the force. The secretary-general, however, took a different position on this matter. He considered it sufficient to inform the advisory committee, which was comprised of the countries providing contingents as well as the permanent members in the Security Council, before making his decision. He justified his decision by citing a host of practical, legal, and constitutional issues which in his judgment dictated the options available to him and the course he finally adopted.(28)

The secretary-general's decision was, nevertheless, widely criticized. U Thant himself stated in a report to the Assembly that "(T)he decision to withdraw UNEF has been frequently characterized in various quarters as 'hasty' and 'precipitous'."(29)

After the decision was taken, it was only natural that the force could no longer exercise its functions properly since,

among other factors, it was expected to disintegrate due to the
desire of some of the contributing countries to withdraw their
contingents immediately.(30)   In retrospect, it is relevant to
examine here the extent of the secretary-general's legal
authority to decide on the withdrawal.   Was it within the
secretary-general's consitutional authority to take that historic
decision without prior endorsement from the General Assembly?

It must be pointed out that the secretary-general and the
Egyptian government, as parties to the agreements regarding
UNEF I, were under legal obligation to act in good faith and to
negotiate with a view to reconciling their disagreements.   In
case of unresolved issues between the two parties, the Assembly would be the competent organ to decide the outcome of the
dispute.   However, if no disagreement exists, if the wishes of
one party could be accommodated by the other, within the
general guidelines previously endorsed by the Assembly, then
clearly no legal obligation falls on either party to resort to the
Assembly.

Part of the problem would be to consider to what extent
Egypt was entitled to decide unilaterally that the task of the
force had been completed and to request its withdrawal.   The
secretary-general's considered opinion was that Egypt never
qualified its right to ask for the withdrawal.   Its right to
request the withdrawal of UNEF I was an integral part of the
exercise of its sovereignty on its territory.   The secretary-
general also believed that the good-faith agreement did not
apply to the task envisaged in resolution 1125 (XI) but related
only to the original task.(31)   Although no state or group of
states decided to take the matter to the Assembly before the
decision was reached, U Thant was severely attacked.

An aide-memoire, supposedly written by Mr. Hammarskjöld, that was cited by Ernest Gross in a letter to the editor
of the New York Times, on 25 May 1967, contributed to increasing the vehemence of the attacks on the secretary-
general's decision.(32) U Thant said that this aide-memoire was
not in any official record of the UN nor was it in any of the
UN official files.(33)   Moreover, the General Assembly, the
advisory committee on UNEF I, and the Egyptian government
were not informed of its contents or even its existence.   U
Thant concluded his characterization by stating that "(T)his
paper, therefore, cannot affect in any way the basis for the
presence of UNEF on the soil of Egypt as set out in the
official documents, much less supersede those documents."(34)
Though its authenticity has not been doubted, one is inclined
in all objectivity to accept the secretary-general's argument
regarding the private nature of the aide-memoire.   However,
its very existence, coupled with the conflicting positions taken
by the members of the advisory committee, might cloud the
question of why the secretary-general opted to decide on the
withdrawal without the Assembly's consideration of his
decision.

It is submitted that the interpretation of the relevant
documents would assert his legal authority with regard to the
decision to withdraw the force.   The legal consitutional
elements involved would, however, dictate a certain process
which must be followed.   He was obliged, in any event, to
seek the advice of the advisory committee before ordering the
withdrawal, a course which he followed.   He was also obliged
to inform the General Assembly and the Security Council,
which he did.   It has been proposed that the secretary-
general should have warned the Egyptian government that
withdrawal would not be acceptable until the Assembly or the
Council had given the matter due consideration.(35)   Such an
argument, as stated earlier, is not substantiated by an
objective perusal of the relevant documents.   To this must be
added that the contributing countries and, more important, the
members of the advisory committee did not adopt a unified
stand or even a majority stand against the decision to withdraw.   Some of those states were members of the Security
Council and could have easily asked for an urgent meeting of
the Council and moved to forestall the conveyance of the
secretary-general's decision to Egypt.   This did not take
place, and all the states with prior knowledge of the decision
either approved or acquiesced.

It is significant that the question of the secretary-
general's authority concerning his relation with the General
Assembly had been discussed ten years earlier and the views
advanced by Mr. Hammarskjöld on the matter, though contested by Israel, had been approved by the Assembly.   On 25
February 1957, Israel put forward the following question:
"Would the Secretary-General give notice to the General
Assembly of the United Nations before UNEF would be withdrawn from the area, with or without Egyptian insistence, or
before the Secretary-General would agree to its withdrawal?"(36)   The Secretary-General's response was as follows:
"An indicated procedure would be for the Secretary-General to
inform the Advisory Committee on the United Nations
Emergency Force, which would determine whether the matter
should be brought to the attention of the Assembly."(37)

Thus it might be inferred that, when the General
Assembly accepted the views of the secretary-general in
February 1957, it had in fact inadvertently laid down the
procedure which was followed ten years later.   It should also
be pointed out that, had the Assembly considered the Egyptian
request in an emotional and tense political atmosphere, the
result might have been detrimental to the prestige of the UN
itself.   It also could have undermined the usefulness of future
UN peacekeeping operations.   Moreover, UNEF I was not
envisaged as a fighting force and was not equipped to stop the
eruption of fighting.   Therefore, it would have been a helpless
target.   Whatever position one might take on the merits of

U Thant's decision, the lesson to be drawn from this episode undoubtedly stresses the importance of a United Nations presence in certain troubled areas. It should be added that, in any future UN peacekeeping operation, it will always be desirable to cover all possible contingencies in advance in order to reduce future disagreements that are likely to arise regarding such matters as the presence and the withdrawal of a given peacekeeping force.

UNEF II

The cessation of the October 1973 hostilities required that the Security Council establish UNEF II. It was obvious that tension was rapidly escalating and that the region, as well as the whole world, was fraught with imminent and grave dangers if fighting were to continue any further. Controversial issues pertaining to the constitutional aspects of peacekeeping were quietly sidestepped.

When the General Assembly established UNEF I in 1956, many were skeptical and harbored serious doubts. Criticism and apprehension were, moreover, loudly voiced in 1967 when the withdrawal of the forces unleashed a chain of events that culminated with the Israeli armed attack. The wealth of experience acquired by the UN in peacekeeping operations proved, however, to be a prescription for future success. And, in retrospect, it could even be stated that UNEF II was not conceived in an atmosphere shrouded with any uncertainty about its viability. It is suggested to consider the life span of UNEF II by examining the following issues.

The Establishment of the Force

When fighting erupted on 6 October 1973 on both the Egyptian-Israeli and the Syrian-Israeli fronts, no UN peacekeeping forces were stationed in the region. Following the adoption of Security Council resolution 338 on 22 October 1973, it became evident that Israel was not observing the cease-fire in pursuit of its military objectives. The Security Council adopted a second resolution on 23 October which requested the secretary-general to take measures for immediate dispatch of UN observers to supervise the observance of the cease-fire.(38) The UN military observers were not able to discharge this task, and the Council was faced with repeated Israeli disregard of the cease-fire. Tension escalated rapidly between the two superpowers as they exchanged implied threats. It thus became imperative to defuse the pending crisis. A UN peacekeeping force was considered convenient for this purpose. On 25 October, the Security Council adopted resolution 340 which called for the increase of the UN military observers as well as the immediate setting up, under its authority, of a United Nations Emergency Force (UNEF II).(39)

The Role of the Secretary-General

As a direct consequence of the criticism addressed to U Thant's decision to withdraw UNEF I in 1967, the secretary-general's role in the establishment of UNEF II was slightly altered in 1973 with a view to ensuring tighter supervision by the Security Council. Some salient points which reflect on the role of the secretary-general should, at this stage, be emphasized:

1. UNEF was being established by the Security Council with the blessing of the two superpowers, and not by the General Assembly as had its predecessor. Thus, the functions assigned to the secretary-general could be carried out in closer consultation with the limited number of members of the Council. By way of illustration, when Waldheim was instructed in resolution 340 (1973) "to report within 24 hours on the steps taken," he informed the president of the Council that he would deliver the requested report within the time-limit and proposed, as an urgent measure, certain interim arrangements. On the same evening, he obtained the approval of the members of the Security Council and was able to proceed with the proposed interim arrangements. Such close relationships could not have existed with the General Assembly and its much larger, and less orderly, membership. As a corollary, the secretary-general's mandate was, in fact, executed under the direct supervision of the Security Council. In his report on the establishment of UNEF II, the secretary-general stated clearly that "All matters which may affect the nature or the continued effective functioning of the Force will be referred to the Council for its decision."(40)

By contrast, the General Assembly in 1956 delegated wideranging powers to the secretary-general when UNEF I was created. It even established an advisory committee under the secretary-general's chairmanship to, inter alia, assist the secretary-general in the responsibilities falling to him "under the relevant resolutions."(41) The Assembly also decided that the advisory committee should be "empowered to request . . . the convening of the General Assembly and to report to the Assembly whenever matters arise which, in its opinion, are of such urgency and importance as to require consideration by the General Assembly itself."(42) Consequently, the Assembly did not require or assert its direct authority and supervision on the functioning of UNEF I. The extent of the secretary-general's freedom to act without prior Assembly approval could

clearly be detected by recalling the views expressed by
Hammarskjöld in his report to the Assembly when he stated:

> The Secretary-General had, therefore, given inter-
> pretations of the relevant General Assembly
> resolutions to the Government of Egypt, reporting in
> full to the Advisory Committee on the interpretations
> given. The Advisory Committee had approved these
> interpretations and recommended that the Secretary-
> General should start at once the transfer of the
> Force to Egypt, an action to which the Government
> of Egypt had consented on the basis of the inter-
> pretations given by the Secretary-General.(43)

2.   As a consequence of the UNEF I withdrawal, UNEF II
was established with a fixed time-limit of six months. It was
also decided "that it shall continue in operation thereafter, if
required, provided the Security Council so decided."(44)
Egypt did not insist on any assurance about the duration of
UNEF II on its territory. No doubt, its decision was influenced by the fixed time-limit contained in resolution 341
(1973). On the other hand, it should be noted that, when the
Security Council issued the cease-fire injunctions on 22 October 1973, it was one part of a package. Resolution 338
(1973) contained two more very significant demands. It called
upon the parties to start immediately "the implementation of
resolution 242 (1967) in all its parts."(45) It also decided
that, immediately and concurrently with the cease-fire,
negotiations shall start "under appropriate auspices aimed at
establishing a just and durable peace in the Middle East."(46)
With the exception of the period that immediately followed
Israel's violations of the 22 October cease-fire lines, it could
be generally stated that an atmosphere of rising expectations
seemed finally, albeit reluctantly, to be dawning on the Middle
East.

The Consent of the Host Country

It is an established fact that a United Nations peacekeeping
operation is not an enforcement measure. Consequently, a
competent UN organ, whether Council or Assembly, may decide
to establish a peacekeeping operation without, or before,
obtaining the consent of the host country. It is, however,
inconceivable to dispatch a peacekeeping force to any given
country without its consent. Only after the determination by
the Security Council that a threat to international peace and
security exists can the Council decide to coerce a state and
infringe on its sovereign territory. The Assembly does not
have such powers. Hammarskjöld realized that the element of

consent is indispensible and wrote in his report to the General
Assembly on 6 November 1956: "While the General Assembly is
able to establish the force with the consent of those parties
which contribute units to the force, it could not request the
force to be stationed or operate on the territory of a given
country without the consent of the Government of that
country."(47)

Two years later, the secretary-general submitted the same
views in a report to the Assembly on the experience derived
from the establishment and operation of peacekeeping forces.
In that report, he was more assertive when expounding on the
necessity to respect the general principles of international law
as well as the provisions of the United Nations Charter.   He
wrote that:

> As the arrangements discussed in this report do not
> cover the type of force envisaged under Chapter VII
> of the Charter, it follows from international law and
> the Charter that the United Nations cannot under-
> take to implement them by stationing units on the
> territory of a Member State without the consent of
> the Government concerned.   It similarly follows from
> the Charter that the consent of a Member Nation is
> necessary for the United Nations to use its military
> personnel or material.   These basic rules have been
> observed in the recent United Nations operations in
> the Middle East.   They naturally hold valid for all
> similar operations in the future.(48)

The point to be examined now is to what extent this basic rule
was followed in 1973.   As a point of departure, it should be
noted that the relevant documents on the establishment of
UNEF II did not explicitly refer to the element of "consent."

The Security Council resolutions made reference in very
general terms to "all Member States to extend their full cooperation to the UN."(49)   The secretary-general,
furthermore, wrote in his report to the Council that the
effectiveness of the force depended on three essential
conditions: "Firstly, it must at all times have the full
confidence and backing of the Security Council.   Secondly, it
must operate with the full
cooperation of the parties concerned.   Thirdly, it must be able
to function as an integrated and efficient military unit."(50)
Even the letter addressed to the secretary-general to confirm
Egypt's acceptance of the presence of UNEF II on its territory
was carefully drafted and deliberately couched in a general
manner to avoid specific reference to the word "consent."   The
relevant part read:

> The Government of the Arab Republic of Egypt
> considers that the presence of the United Nations

> Emergency Force on its territory is of a temporary
> nature and is, moreover, governed by the Charter
> of the United Nations, its purposes and principles
> and the general principles of international law which
> safeguard Egypt's sovereignty and territorial in-
> tegrity."(51)

How should this deliberate absence of any reference to the
element of consent be interpreted? And does it entail any real
erosion of the previously enunciated rule regarding the necessity to secure the consent of the host country?

It is to be noted that the Egyptian letter clearly pointed
to the fundamental principles that are applicable with respect
to the presence of the United Nations peacekeeping force on
the sovereign territory of states. The letter emphasized, in
particular, the temporary nature of the force. It also referred
to the UN Charter and the general principles of international
law which "safeguard Egypt's sovereignty and territorial
integrity" (S/11055 para. 3 dated 27 October 1973). The
combined effect of the aforementioned ingredients should
demonstrate that Egypt was determined to assert that UNEF
II's presence on its territory would continue to be subject to
its consent in a manner similar to the UNEF I 1956 arrangements. The only logical explanation for avoiding the use of the
word "consent" seems to be its possible association with the
events of May 1967 which, to the general public, tarnished to
some degree the credibility of UN peacekeeping. Thus, the
absence of the word "consent" could in no way be interpreted
as affecting the sovereign rights of the host country.

One knowledgeable authority on UN practice wrote
recently that, under the UNEF II guidelines, only the Security
Council could decide on the withdrawal of a force once it had
been established.(52)   He believes, however, that this
limitation on the consent principle operated only during the
duration of the force as authorized by the Security Council.(53)   This view is shared by others who are inclined to
consider that an attempt was made in 1973 to limit the principle
of consent.

It should, however, be made clear that the Security
Council was not proceeding to establish the type of force
envisaged under Chapter VII of the Charter.(54)   All the
resolutions adopted as well as the secretary-general's reports
were cautiously drafted to avoid any such impression and to
indicate that the force's effectiveness depends on the
cooperation of the parties concerned. It should be pointed
out, moreover, that no determination by the Council of the
existence of a threat to international peace and security was
publicly made and incorporated in any official document. The
Security Council was clearly basing its actions on the established guidelines for peacekeeping operations as developed and

elaborated during the previous two decades. To conclude this point, it should be stated that the constitutional and legal requirements contained in the Charter necessitate that a peacekeeping force operate only with the consent of the parties concerned. This does not contest the vast powers vested in the Council to enforce its decisions on any member states. These powers, however, are to be executed within a defined framework which was not followed, or even seriously considered, in 1973.

Thus, it is possible to assume that the validity of arguments supporting the erosion or limitation on the consent principle should be questioned, particularly when based mainly on the absence of the word "consent."

As a related issue, a distinction should be drawn between "concerned parties" and the "host country." The former may include all the parties involved in the conflict as well as the states that contribute contingents and extend facilities to the force, while the latter is always the states, or state, on whose territory the mandate of the force is being carried out. It follows that the appropriate agreement on the "Status of the Force," similar to the agreement of February 1957 with Egypt, could only be concluded with the host country. The UN is, of course, free to enter into contractual arrangements with any or all the other concerned parties. The scope and the area of application should, however, be confined to each party's respective territory and not be extended to the territory of the host country without its approval. A "Status of the Force" agreement defines certain corresponding obligations considered necessary for the proper functioning of the force. These obligations involve, inter alia, freedom of movement, jurisdictional issues, right to entry, and overflights. It is inconceivable that such facilities be extended to the force by another state as a result of its physical occupation of a part of the host country's territory. Such an infringement of the sovereign rights of the host country could not be condoned by the United Nations. It seems, however, that the various dimensions and implications of this basic legal principle were not fully realized when the UN officials embarked on negotiations with both the Egyptian and the Israeli authorities to conclude "Status of the Force" agreements. When Egypt was informed of the possibility of concluding such an agreement with Israel with a view of regulating the presence and functioning of UNEF II on Egyptian territory, it lodged a strong protest with the UN secretariat.

The UN attempted to justify its position by pointing out that, as a practical matter, UNEF II would perform part of its functions on territories occupied by Israel. It was, moreover, revealed to Egypt that Israel would insist on concluding an agreement with the UN as soon as one was signed with Egypt. In order to ensure that the UN would never reach any contractual agreement with Israel affecting its sovereign territory, in mid-1976, Egypt terminated all negotiations to finalize an agreement with the UN. Furthermore, Egypt made very clear to the concerned UN officials, in both the legal and political fields, that any agreement with Israel would be viewed with extreme gravity and that Egypt would not hesitate to raise the whole issue in the Security Council. There was no doubt that the Council would fully endorse the Egyptian position. This firm reaction brought the matter to an early conclusion and no further attempts were undertaken. Recognizing, however, the necessity to regulate UNEF's presence and functioning on Egyption territory, agreement was quietly and orally reached between Egypt and the UN to apply, mutatis mutandis, the provisions of the 1957 Agreement.(55) This arrangement proved to be adequate and was in force until the mandate of UNEF II was finally not renewed by the Security Council in July 1979.

The Functioning of UNEF II

The original mandate of UNEF II, as proposed by the secretary-general and endorsed by the Security Council in October 1973, underwent many changes as additional tasks were assigned according to the requirements of the agreements reached between the parties. The terms of reference and the general guidelines, as originally defined in the secretary-general's report (S/11052/Rev. 1), have not, however, been altered. Before examining the various phases of UNEF II, it might be appropriate to point out briefly that from the outset it became evident that UNEF II would be called upon to undertake a host of new and unprecedented functions. Even the general orientation of the functions underwent considerable changes. The salient points could be summarized as follows.

The commander of the force was designated as chairman of the military talks in November 1973. He exercised this capacity on many occasions throughout the following two years. He performed very valuable services and took an active part in bridging the gaps between the Egyptian and Israeli representatives. A United Nations official who participated in all these talks described this new role very accurately by writing:

> In the stress of the October war, Egypt was prepared to meet with Israeli military officers but only under a United Nations flag, symbolized by the commander of UNEF. The availability of this United Nations umbrella contributed to the attainment of other arrangements between the parties. Significantly, in contrast to the mixed armistice agreements of 1949, UNEF's commander signed as witness the

two separation of forces agreements and the interim agreement between Egypt and Israel (1975) that have been concluded since the October 1973 war.(56)

Another novel function emanated from what was only alluded to in the first secretary-general's report. In that report, he laid down the terms of reference for the force which included ". . . and cooperate with the International Committee of the Red Cross in its humanitarian endeavours in the area."(57) This cooperation was soon to expand and evolve considerably. At one point, it entailed the supervision of the nonmilitary nature of supplies as well as the actual transportation of the supplies through Israeli lines.(58)

A third completely new task was a result of the disengagement and separation of forces agreements which created buffer zones.(59) UN supervision was required to ensure the continuing nonmilitary character of these zones. It will be recalled that both UNTSO and UNEF I did help, under the provision of the 1949 General Armistice Agreement in patrolling demarcation lines and assuring that no party violated the Armistice Agreement. UNEF II was assigned a more complicated and sensitive task. In practice, it amounted to being in control of vast portions of Sinai. If undefined and put in the proper perspective, it could have been mistaken for full administration of Egyptian sovereign territory.(60) UNEF II activities underwent three phases.

First phase

The initial activities of UNEF II took place in the areas of actual confrontation between the armed forces of Egypt and Israel. They involved supervision of the cease-fire in cooperation with UNTSO observers, patrolling and interpositioning, where possible, between forward elements on each side. The force also cooperated with the international committee of the Red Cross on matters of humanitarian concern. It participated in the arrangements for the transfer of supplies through Israeli-held territory to Egyptian troops on the east bank of the Suez Canal.

Second phase

On 18 January 1974, at a meeting held at kilometer 101, an agreement on the disengagement of forces in pursuance of the Geneva Peace Conference on the Middle East was signed by the military representatives of Egypt and Israel and by the commander of UNEF II as witness (S/11198). After the completion of the disengagement operation, the main task of UNEF II was the manning and control of the zone of disengagement; and, in this connection, it established static checkpoints and

observation posts and conducted mobile patrols. The force
commander continued the practice of separate meetings with the
military authorities of Egypt and Israel concerning the implementation of the terms of reference of the force and the
inspections carried out by UNEF II, and he continued to lend
his assistance and good offices in cases where one of the
parties raised questions concerning the observance of the
agreed limitations of forces and armaments.

Third phase

On 4 September 1975 another interim agreement was
concluded between Egypt and Israel. Article V stipulated that
"The United Nations Emergency Force is essential and shall
continue its functions and its mandate shall be extended
annually."(61) A protocol to the agreement was later worked
out in the Military Working Group of the Geneva Peace Conference under the chairmanship of General Siilasvuo, the chief
coordinator of the UN peacekeeping missions in the Middle
East.(62) The negotiations to draft the protocol were arduous
and painstaking. When the two weeks specified in the annex
to complete a detailed protocol elapsed without reaching
agreement, the parties resorted to a technical device by
stopping the clock before midnight and continued to negotiate.
The agreement provided, inter alia, for the establishment
of buffer zones controlled by UNEF (buffer zone I in the north
and buffer zones 2A and 2B in the southern area). It also
provided that there would be no military forces in the
southern area south of line E and west of line M (Ras Suday
and Abu Rodeis areas). Finally, the agreement set up a joint
commission under the auspices of the chief coordinator to
consider any problems arising from the agreement and to assist
UNEF II in the execution of its mandate. In his report to the
Security Council of 17 October 1975 (S/11849), the secretary-
general noted that the responsibilities entrusted to UNEF II
under the agreement of 4 September and spelled out in detail
in the protocol of 22 September were more varied or extensive
than those it had so far and the new operational area was
much larger.
After the completion of the redeployment, UNEF II carried
out the long-range functions defined in the protocol. In the
southern area, its task was to assure that no military or
paramilitary forces, fortifications, or installations of any kind
were in the area. To perform that task, it established
checkpoints and observation posts in accordance with the
protocol and conducted patrols throughout the area, including
air patrols.
In buffer zones 2A and 2B in the southern area, it
maintained permanent checkpoints along the buffer zone lines.
It further supervised the use of the common road sections by

the parties in accordance with the arrangements agreed to by them and it provided escorts in those sections when necessary.

The functions of UNEF II in buffer zone 1 in the northern area were carried out by means of a system of checkpoints, observation posts, and land patrols. In the Early Warning Systems area, which was located in the buffer zone, UNEF II provided escorts, as required, to and from the United States watch stations and the Egyptian and Israeli surveillance stations. UNEF II was also entrusted with the task of ensuring the maintenance of the agreed limitation of forces and armaments within the areas specified in the protocol and, to this effect, it conducted bi-weekly inspections.

The Status of the Buffer Zones

As outlined earlier, the September 1975 agreement established three areas designed as buffer zones. The agreement and its annexes, however, did not define or elaborate upon the legal status of the zones. Two issues of a practical nature arose with respect to this status. One broke during the negotiations regarding the Egyptian civilian population returning to their homes in the northern area following the withdrawal of the Israeli forces. The issue of the civilian population proved to be the thorniest and most insoluble. In effect, resolving it could not be achieved during the two weeks allocated for the drafting of the protocol. Several hours after the specified deadline were needed to work out an acceptable formula. What is of relevance to this study is that the final outcome, contained in an unpublished letter addressed from the head of the Egyptian military delegation to General Siilasvuo, reconfirmed Egypt's sovereign right to issue identity cards to its civilian citizens who wished to return to the northern buffer zone. The letter also confirmed Egypt's responsibility to accord the residents of the area the medical, educational, and other services necessary for their livelihood. It should be clarified that the letter was drafted in such a manner as to ensure that it could not be used by Israel as a basis for claiming any rights regarding the Egyptian residents in the buffer zones. It was made clear that it was being communicated to General Siilasvuo for informational purposes and that it was not part of the contractual arrangement with Israel.

The second issue occurred some months later and related to the right of Egypt to exploit the natural resources in the buffer zones. Egypt and Israel advanced strong and contradictory views. Their arguments centered on whether Egypt could or could not exercise fully its sovereign rights in the buffer zones. To put it more accurately, they were in conflict over the nature of the limitations stemming from the provisions of the agreement and the annexes. Egypt's position was that the only limitations imposed on its sovereignty were to ensure the nonmilitary nature of the zones for the duration of the agreement. It followed that all civilian activities, including the exploitation of natural resources, particularly when carried out through third parties, were permissible. Egypt insisted that the buffer zones were integral parts of its sovereign territory and that it could exercise all its sovereign rights once the Israeli military occupation was terminated.

Israel, on the other hand, was of the view that the terms of the agreement implied that only the activities specified therein were permissible. Israel, moreover, interpreted the agreement as providing it with a right to be informed of all activities conducted in the zones. It also considered that it possessed a right to veto any activities which in its judgment would prejudice its national security.

This issue could have remained of an abstract legal value if the area under consideration were of no economic importance. However, the discovery of oil in Sinai, some by Israel itself, transformed the outlook and approach to the once neglected peninsula. Oil companies were attracted to its potential riches and competed actively to be granted concessions by the Egyptian government.

Egypt's oil minister inquired of the Egyptian foreign ministry in April 1976 about the possibility of granting concessions to foreign firms in the buffer zones and certain off-shore areas. After thorough study, the foreign ministry's reply was in the affirmative on both issues. It was made clear that the only limitations on Egypt's exercise of its sovereign rights pertained to:

- The obligation to maintain the nonmilitary character of the area for the duration of the Agreement.
- The obligation to inform UNEF II and coordinate the entry to and exit from the buffer zone through UNEF's checkpoints.

Upon receiving this reply, Egypt's oil ministry granted concessions to three American oil companies. Israel learned of the granting of concessions, protested to and even threatened the UNEF II authorities, and demanded that no oil drilling take place. Several contacts were made between Egyptian and UN officials on the subject. It became clear to Egypt that the UN was in a dilemma and, though its officials were inclined to agree with Egypt, they were anxious not to blow up the issue into a crisis.

The Egyptian military authorities refused to allow foreign oil companies access to Sinai during a state of belligerency with Israel. In short, they vetoed the whole project and the matter was quietly and permanently shelved.

Notwithstanding the final outcome, it still seems appropriate to offer an analysis of the status of the buffer zones. To examine the rights and duties of the United Nations, of the territorial sovereign, and of the former military occupying power proved to be a formidable task, particularly since references to the nature and status of the buffer zones in the agreement and annexes proved to be inadequate. Guidance had to be sought elsewhere. A wider framework encompassing the Charter provisions and the general principles of international law and based on the factual circumstances would be more appropriate.

The agreement and its annexes specified the following three points:

1.   UNEF II would be stationed in the buffer zones to ensure that no military forces of any kind, military fortifications, or military installations were in existence.
2.   UNEF would allow entry to and exit from the area by land, by air, or by sea through UNEF II checkpoints to authorized persons and cargoes only.
3.   The joint commission established by the provisions of article V of the protocol would hold its meetings in the buffer zone.(63)

It would thus seem clear that:

•   No obligation existed to prohibit Egypt from conducting nonmilitary activities.
•   Israel was not provided with any right to become a partner with Egypt in administering the buffer zone.
•   The United Nations' role was confined to ensuring the maintenance of the nonmilitary character of the area.

It is submitted that the UN Charter, Security Council resolutions, and the principles of international law in general would confirm these conclusions.

The United Nations Charter reaffirms the sovereignty, territorial integrity, and political independence of all member states. The Charter, moreover, commits the UN to remove threats to the peace and suppress acts of aggression. The UN cannot, therefore, acquiesce when the territory of a state is occupied by force. These principles were faithfully reflected when the Security Council adopted resolution 242 on 22 November 1967. The preamble to that resolution emphasized the well-established legal principle on the inadmissibility of the acquisition of territory by war. The operative part of the resolution affirms, inter alia, that the fulfillment of the Charter principles requires the respect for and acknowledgment of the sovereignty, territorial integrity, and political independence of every state in the area. The Charter principles would, therefore, preclude the UN from recognizing the existence of any rights to Israel as a result of its military occupation.

The general principles of international law which regulate the various consequences of armed conflict are generally based on the 1907 Hague Regulations and the 1949 Geneva Conventions. From the above, the following would be a fair summary of the provisions of the two legally binding international instruments as well as the customary norms developed since World War II:

1. Egypt is the sovereign with regard to the Sinai peninsula and its territorial waters.
2. Israel was a belligerent occupant of certain portions of the Sinai it invaded by force in 1967.
3. Once Israel's military occupation is terminated, no special rights accrue to Israel as a result of its physical occupation.

The Termination of the Mandate

As pointed out earlier, since the conclusion of the 1975 interim agreement, the mandate of UNEF was renewed annually. When the October 1978 renewal date approached, the Soviet Union, under pressure from some hardline Arab countries, objected to a further one year renewal. After some negotiations the Council adopted resolution 438 (1978), which renewed the mandate for a period of nine months, that is, until 24 July 1979. Both the Soviet Union and Czechoslovakia abstained.

Developments in the Middle East were bound to reflect on the consideration of the Council of all relevant issues. Some extremists in the Arab world were demanding that the UN should not be involved in any matter pertaining to the implementation of the Egyptian-Israeli peace Treaty.

The USSR was undecided on the position it should adopt. It was reported that during a trip to Moscow in the Spring of 1979, the Soviet leadership informed the Secretary-General that the matter is still under consideration and that their position will be influenced by the views of other concerned parties in the Arab world. Soon thereafter the Soviet Union was on record that they would oppose the renewal regardless of the degree of support of other Security Council members.

Egypt, motivated by a keen interest in maintaining a UN peacekeeping presence in the Sinai, was of the view that UNEF's mandate should be renewed. Israel, on the other hand, persisted with its deep rooted suspicion in the UN and demanded that the United States create a multinational force outside the UN system. As a second best alternative, Israel would prefer joint patrolling by the parties with U.S. assistance.

It is evident that notwithstanding the threat of the Soviet veto, Egypt did have the required majority to renew the mandate. However, following informal consultations between Council Members, a compromise was reached. It was composed of two elements:

A.   A general agreement to allow UNEF's mandate to elapse quietly. The Secretary-General reflected the views of the Council when he stated in a press release dated 24 July 1979 that "it is my understanding that members of the Council are agreed that there should be no extension of the UNEF mandate, which will accordingly lapse at midnight tonight, 24 July. It is my intention therefore to make all the necessary arrangements for an orderly withdrawal of UNEF." A matter which gave satisfaction to the Soviet Union who were obviously not keen on exercising their veto power.

B.   An agreement to allow the observers from UNTSO to continue their presence in the area in accordance with the mandate conferred on the Secretary-General in 1949. It will be recalled that on 11 August 1959, the Security Council adopted resolution 73 which requested the Secretary-General "to arrange for the continued service of such of the personnel of the present Truce Supervision Organization as may be required in observing and maintaining the cease-fire, and as may be necessary in assisting the parties to the Armistice Agreements in the supervision of the application and observance of the terms of those Agreements, with particular regard to the desires of the parties."

In the aforementioned press release, the Secretary-General stated that "it is my intention to make, in accordance with existing decisions of the Security Council, the necessary arrangements to ensure the further functioning of UNTSO."
A full analysis of the roles performed by the Secretary-General, the parties and the Members of the Council in general may be, at present, premature. Suffice it to say that a valuable and successful peacekeeping operation was terminated while its tasks were still incomplete. It was a classical situation when power politics prevailed over vision, when expediency overwhelmed the avowed commitment to the lofty purposes and principles of the United Nations Charter.

NOTES

1.   For detailed examination of the establishment, functioning, and withdrawal of UNEF I, see Elaraby, Nabil, "United Nations Peacekeeping by Consent: A Case Study of the Withdrawal of

the United Nations Emergency Force," New York University Journal of International Law and Politics, vol. I, 1968.

2. The Egyptian delegation consulted the secretary-general before the ballot.

3. UN Document A/3295 (1956).

4. UN Document A/3943 (1958) p. 53, para. 132.

5. Ibid. (emphasis added).

6. E. Gross, The United Nations: Structure for Peace, p. 31.

7. W.   Frye,   A United Nations Police Force, New York: Oceana Publications (1957) p. 17.

8. E. Gross, The United Nations, p. 31.

9. Ibid.

10. Ibid.

11. Ibid., p. 32

12. Ibid.

13. UN document A/3943 (1958), p. 53, para. 132.

14. E. Gross, The United Nations, p. 32.

15. UN document A/3375/Annex (1956).

16. G.A. Res. 1121, 11 U.N. GAOR Supp. 16 p. 61, UN document A/3572 (1956).

17. UN document A/3375/Annex (1956).

18. UN document A/3375 (1956).

19. UN document A/3526 (1957).

20. UN document A/3375 (1956).

21. 11 UN GAOR Agenda, item 66 at 348 (1956).

22. UN document A/3512.

23. G.A. Res. 1125 (XI).

24. Ibid.

25. Article 98, UN Charter.

26. UN document A/3943 (1958) at para. 158.

27. UN document S/7906 (1967) p. 2, para. 4.

28. UN document A/6730/Add. 3, 19-22.

29. Ibid. p. 12, para. 34.

30. UN document S/7906 (1967) p. 18, para. 50.

31. Ibid., pp. 23-26, para. 75-82.

32. The aide-memoire was reprinted in International Legal Materials 6, Current Documents 593. See also comments by Gross, pp. 581, 603. Basically, Hammarskjold's aide-memoire stated his understanding that the withdrawal by Egypt of consent, prior to completion of the task of the force, would run counter to acceptance by Egypt of the General Assembly's resolutions and actions.

33. UN document S/7906 (1967) p. 22, para. 73.

34. Ibid.

35. Maxwell Cohen, "The Demise of UNEF," in International Journal XXIII, Toronto: Canadian Institute of International Affairs, Winter 1967-68, p. 42.

36. UN document A/3573/Annex I (1957) p. 1, para. A-2.

37. Ibid., para. B-2.

38. S.C. Res. 339 (1973).

39. S.C. Res. 340 (1973).

40. S/11052/Rev. 1, para. 4(a).

41. G.A. Res. 1001 (ES-1) para. 8.

42. G.A. Res. 1001 (ES-1) para. 9.

43. A/3943, para. 132.

44. S.C. Res. 341 (1973), para. 2.

45. S.C. Res. 338 (1973), para. 2.

46. Ibid., para. 3.

47. A/3302 at 4, para. 9.

48. A/3943, para. 155 (emphasis added).

49. S.C. Res. 340 (1973), para. 5.

50. S/11052/Rev. 1, para. 3.

51. S/11055, para. 3 dated 27 Oct. 1973.

52. James Jonah, "Peacekeeping in the Middle East," International Journal, 1975, p. 115.

53. Ibid.

54. Art. 42 states "Should the Security Council consider that measures provided for in Article 41 would be inadequate or have proved to be inadequate, it may take such action by air, sea, or land forces as may be necessary to maintain or restore international peace and security. Such action may include demonstrations, blockade, and other operations by air, sea, or land forces of Members of the United Nations."

55.   In his capacity as Legal Advisor to the Egyptian Foreign Ministry, the author carried out the relevant negotiations with the United Nations in 1976.

56.   Jonah, "Peacekeeping in the Middle East," p. 106.

57.   S/11052/Rev. 1, para. 2(B).

58.   Nonmilitary supplies included food, water, clothes, and medicine.

59.   Three interim arrangements were reached in the period from November 1973 to September 1975.

60.   The structure and the various implications of the buffer zones will be discussed separately.

61.   S/11818 and Add. 1-4.

62.   The parties decided to consider the Agreement and all its annexes as an integral part.

63.   Article II, UN Charter, para. 2(B) of the Protocol.

4
UN Peacekeeping:
The Israeli Experience
Michael Comay*

Israel has a longer and more intimate experience of United Nations peacekeeping than has any other of the 151 UN member states.

On 29 November 1947, the UN General Assembly adopted Resolution A/181 (II), providing for the establishment of sovereign Jewish and Arab states in Palestine. The Arab side rejected the decision. Disturbances broke out in Palestine; irregular Arab forces entered it from neighboring territory; and the adjacent Arab states openly prepared for invasion. The UN Palestine Commission, set up to supervise the transition to independence, turned to the Security Council for armed forces to help preserve law and order. The permanent members of the Council were unable to reach agreement on this request. Instead, the Council asked the secretary-general to convene the General Assembly so that the question of the future of Palestine could be reopened. When the Palestine mandate ended, on 14 May 1948, Israel unilaterally proclaimed its independence, and had to stand its ground against the Arab armies that advanced upon it.

Israel never forgot this prenatal lesson. It had learned that the United Nations did not have the capacity to carry out its primary peacekeeping function, as contemplated by the collective measures provided for in the Charter. In the years to come, Israel would cooperate with UN "peacekeeping by consent," but never as a substitute for its own self-defense.

---

*The author no longer holds an official position and this chapter expresses his personal views. This essay reflects developments up to 31 August 1979.

THE PHASES OF PEACEKEEPING

Since its birth, Israel has been through five wars with its neighbors: the War of Independence (1948-49), the Sinai Campaign (1956), the Six-Day War (1967), the War of Attrition (1969-70), and the Yom Kippur War (1973). The periods between and after hostilities have seen a series of truces, armistice agreements, cease-fires, and disengagement pacts. In one form or another, a UN peacekeeping presence has been woven through all these interim arrangements. The history of the peacekeeping machinery may conveniently be divided into chronological phases.

Phase One: 1948-49

On 14 May 1948, Count Bernadotte of Sweden was appointed as a UN Palestine mediator. During a four-week truce that began on 29 May, he improvised a group of about 160 foreign military observers under a Swedish staff. In the second truce, from 15 July onward, the personnel in the observation group expanded to about 700, with a Central Truce Board to coordinate its activities. That was the genesis of UNTSO (the UN Truce Supervision Organization) that came into existence in 1948.

Phase Two: 1949-56

In the first part of 1949, armistice agreements were separately concluded with Egypt, Lebanon, Jordan, and Syria, and endorsed by the Security Council. Each agreement set up a Mixed Armistice Commission (MAC), consisting of two representatives from each side (three each in the Israeli-Egyptian MAC) with the chief-of-staff of UNTSO, or a senior observer nominated by him, as chairman. To service the armistice agreements, UNTSO started with some 70 military observers (UNMOs). The number was increased, and in the two years before 1967, ranged between 130 and 140, drawn from 17 countries.

The MAC procedure proved ineffective. When one party submitted a complaint of a violation of the agreement by the other party, a team of UNMOs would investigate and submit their report. At a formal meeting of the MAC, the representatives of the two parties would make their conflicting submissions, leaving the UN chairman to decide the issue by his vote. This litigious proceeding resulted in hundreds of decisions accumulating in the files, with little impact on the situation, together with hundreds of complaints that failed for lack of conclusive evidence. The MACs were of value to the extent that they served as a framework for informal contact and discussion between the parties. Where the two sides had a common interest in avoiding trouble, understandings were reached and working arrangements made without a vote.

The real problem with the armistice regime was not inadequate machinery, but the broad political and military context in which it had to operate. The text of each armistice agreement explicitly stated that it was a temporary measure pending the conclusion of an early peace. The peace negotiations initiated in 1949 under the auspices of the UN Palestine Conciliation Commission (PCC) proved abortive and petered out by 1951. Arab belligerency against Israel grew and expressed itself in propaganda attacks, increased border raids, and the maintenance by Egypt of shipping blockades through the Suez Canal and the Straits of Tiran. As a result, the armistice regime was eroded to the point of collapse.

Even before the 1956 Sinai campaign, the Israeli government repudiated the agreement with Egypt. The agreements with Syria and Jordan also came under intolerable strains, and the MAC machinery ground to a halt in these two cases. Regular meetings of the Israel-Syrian MAC came to an end in 1951, over the unresolved disputes and recurrent incidents concerning the demilitarized zone. On the Jordanian border, raiding and infiltration by armed terrorist groups reached a climax in 1954, and Israel withdrew from participation in the MAC. Only the Israel-Lebanese agreement continued to function normally, due to the relative tranquillity on that border at that time.

In the spring of 1956, the Security Council authorized the secretary-general to carry out a special mission to the Middle East, in an effort to salvage the armistice regime, and, in particular, to defuse the growing tension between Israel and Egypt. The mission was unsuccessful. In October of that year, the United Nations was suddenly plunged into the Suez crisis, precipitated by the Anglo-French landings at Port Said and the Israeli military occupation of the Sinai Desert.

Phase Three: 1956-67

In November 1956, the General Assembly, acting under the Uniting for Peace Resolution of 1951, gave birth to UNEF I. The force was proposed by the Canadian foreign minister, Lester Pearson, and improvised with remarkable speed by the secretary-general, Dag Hammarskjöld. It marked a great leap forward in UN peacekeeping. Instead of groups of individual military observers, UNEF was a paramilitary force of more than 6,000 men, made up of national contingents, and interposed between regular armies. In an article in Foreign Affairs,

Mr. Pearson described it as "an intermediate technique between merely passing resolutions and actual fighting."

UNEF's initial task was to act as a face-saving device for the withdrawal of forces from Egyptian soil, first those of Britain and France, and then, over several months, those of Israel. In February 1957, UNEF I was given a further long-range mandate to remain on the armistice demarcation line in the Gaza Strip and the international frontier in Sinai "with a view to assist in achieving solutions conducive to the main-tenance of peaceful conditions in the area." The Israeli government refused to agree that the force should operate on the Israeli side of the line as well.

For the next decade, UNEF I uneventfully carried out its functions, which were to act as an informal buffer between the armed forces, to observe and report on violations of the demarcation line, and to prevent illegal crossings of these lines by civilians.

On the face of it, UNEF I was successful in keeping the peace. But the spectacle of stability was misleading. The intervening years were spent by President Nasser in building up and equipping the Egyptian armed forces with Soviet help. In any case, the thrust of Egyptian policy during that period was to establish hegemony over the Arab world. That aspi-ration produced the short-lived union with Syria from 1958 to 1961, the 1958 crisis in Lebanon and Jordan, and the large-scale Egyptian involvement in the Yemen war from 1962 to 1964. By May 1967, Nasser was ready to move against Israel. He massed troops and equipment in the Sinai Desert near the Israeli border, concluded military alliances with Syria and Jordan, ordered UNEF to get out, and reimposed the blockade at the Straits of Tiran. These actions precipitated the Six-Day War of June 1967.

The abrupt demise of UNEF I came as a severe shock to peace-loving member-states such as Canada that had seen in the force a model for a more extended United Nations peace-keeping role in the future.

Phase Four: 1967-73

The Six-Day War replaced the old 1949 armistice demarcation lines with new cease-fire lines, except on the Lebanese border. Israel now regarded the whole of the 1949 armistice regime as having been swept away by the war. In practice, the armistice agreements with Jordan and Syria remained defunct after 1967, as the agreement with Egypt had done since 1956. Only Lebanon, with its border unchanged, continued to assert that its armistice agreement with Israel was still operative. It submitted complaints to the UN chairman of the MAC, which were noted in the periodic reports of the

UNTSO chief-of-staff. A few UNTSO observation posts have been maintained on the Lebanese side of the border, but they have had little more than a symbolic value.

To implement the 1967 cease-fire, the parties agreed to the stationing of UNTSO observation posts on both sides of the Golan Heights line and on both sides of the Suez Canal. Jordan, however, was unwilling to accept UN supervision of its cease-fire with Israel. Ironically, recent years have seen a marked relaxation of tension between Israel and Jordan, with hundreds of thousands of Arabs passing back and forth across the "open bridges" on the Jordan River.

In the Suez Canal sector, the cease-fire remained intact till the spring of 1969. Under an umbrella of Russian SAM missiles, Nasser then launched a "war of attrition," pounding the Israeli positions with massed artillery and infiltrating them with commando raids. In reply, Israel not only demolished parts of Suez and other targets within artillery range, but managed to penetrate deep into Egyptian air space and gain virtual air supremacy over the Nile Valley.

In these battles, the UN observers along the canal ceased to serve any useful purpose and became what the secretary-general described as "defenseless targets in a shooting gallery." A number of the observation posts were closed down and the observers withdrawn. In the summer of 1970, the "war of attrition" ended with a renewed cease-fire and military standstill, on the diplomatic initiative of the United States. A formula was at the same time accepted for reviving the stalled Jarring Mission. UNTSO then reoccupied the abandoned observation posts along the canal.

Phase Five: 1973-78

The Yom Kippur War of October 1973 once more changed the situation on the ground in the Suez Canal and Golan Heights sectors. It also brought two new UN peace forces into existence.

By the Disengagement of Forces Agreement signed on 18 January 1974 by Egypt and Israel, the Israeli forces were withdrawn east of the Suez Canal and a buffer zone was occupied by the United Nations Emergency Force (here called UNEF II for convenience). On either side of this disengagement zone there was a restricted zone, with the agreed level of troops and weapons to be checked by UNEF II. The force was established by the Security Council for an initial six-month period, and its mandate was renewed each six months after that until its withdrawal in July 1979.

A similar disengagement agreement was signed between Israel and Syria on 5 June 1974. To supervise it, UNDOF (UN Disengagement Observer Force) was established, largely by transferring units from UNEF II. Its mandate was also renewed at six-month intervals.

On 1 September 1975, further "shuttle diplomacy" by Henry Kissinger, the U.S. Secretary of State, produced another interim Egypt-Israel agreement. It created an enlarged buffer zone further to the east, with redefined restricted areas. A strip along the eastern shore of the Gulf of Suez, including the oilfields in the area, was restored to Egyptian administration, but was demilitarized. A novel feature of the agreement was an electronic early warning system within the buffer zone, with Israeli and Egyptian surveillance stations and a series of watch-stations and sensor fields operated by United States civilian personnel. The United States also undertook to make available to the parties the results of its regular aerial reconnaissance missions over the area. A joint Israeli-Egyptian Commission was set up as a forum for discussing problems of implementation, under the aegis of the UNTSO chief-of-staff, Major-General Siilasvuo, who had taken up the newly-created position of chief coordinator of the UN peacekeeping mission in the Middle East. The combined strength of the two forces was initially nearly 6,000, of which about 1,250 were in UNDOF. The estimated combined cost for 1976 was $112 million.

Apart from its token presence on the Lebanese side of the Israeli-Lebanese border, UNTSO had been left with no independent role since 1973. It acted as an auxiliary organ to the two peace forces. About ninety UNTSO observers were seconded to UNDOF, and more than a hundred were "lent" to UNEF II for periodic inspection duties.

Phase Six: 1978-79

The final period to be discussed in this chapter saw two developments: the end of UNEF II, and the establishment of the United Nations Interim Force in Lebanon (UNIFIL).

By a twist of irony, the UN peacekeeping role in the Sinai may have fallen victim to the peace treaty signed by Egypt and Israel in Washington on 26 March 1979. The treaty provided that "the Parties will request the United Nations to provide forces and observers to supervise the implementation of this Annex and employ their best efforts to prevent any violation of its terms" (Annex I, Article VI(1)). The role contemplated for the UN would cover the three-year phased withdrawal of the Israeli army from the Sinai Desert and would then extend into a postwithdrawal period of indefinite duration. The UN peacekeeping mission would supervise the transfer of territory and the redeployment of the parties' armed forces, occupy a buffer zone between them, check the limited forces zones on either side of the buffer zone, and ensure freedom of navigation through the Straits of Tiran at the entrance to the Gulf of Aqaba. For these purposes, it would operate check points, reconnaissance patrols, and observation posts. By the Agreed Minutes signed in Washington with the treaty, the parties would agree on the nations from which the UN forces and observers would be drawn, and the permanent members of the Security Council would be excluded. The United States undertook to continue its aerial monitoring.

By that time, UNEF II had successfully functioned in the Sinai for six years under the disengagement and interim agreements. It was natural to expect that it would assume the United Nations role provided in the peace treaty, with suitable adjustments in its size and composition. Its mandate was due for renewal by the Security Council on 24 July 1979. But the peace treaty was vehemently opposed by the Arab Rejection Front, with the political backing of the Soviet Union. The latter let it be known that it would veto the renewal of the force in the Security Council. After behind-the-scenes consultations, the secretary-general announced that the mandate would be allowed to lapse.

That contingency was not unforeseen. Simultaneously with the signing of the peace treaty, President Carter addressed similar letters to President Sadat and Premier Begin, undertaking that if the Security Council failed to carry out the peacekeeping arrangements of the treaty, he (President Carter) would take steps to establish an "acceptable alternative multinational force." When put to the test, however, this undertaking was not put into effect. Instead, the United States reached an understanding with the Soviet Union that UNTSO would take over from UNEF II. The Russian position apparently was that UNTSO, as the permanent UN peacekeeping mission in the area, could supervise the Israeli withdrawal in fulfillment of Security Council resolution 242, without involving the United Nations in the implementation of the peace treaty itself.

This proposal was rejected by Israel. It pointed out that, as a party directly concerned, it had not agreed to or even been consulted about such an arrangement. In any case, Israel maintained, UNTSO was inherently incapable of performing the functions allotted to the "forces and observers" under the treaty. The Israeli government called upon the United States to carry out the undertaking in President Carter's letter. Meanwhile, Israel and Egypt agreed to establish joint observation posts and patrols, pending a long-range solution to be worked out between them and the United States.

The fate of UNEF II, denoting an extremely reserved United Nations' attitude towards the Egyptian-Israeli peace treaty, increased skepticism in Israel as to whether the United Nations was capable of playing a constructive part in the Middle East peace process.

UNIFIL was born in the aftermath of the civil war in Lebanon. The situation in that unhappy country had remained brittle and confused. A Lebanese government had taken office in Beirut but had been able to exercise little real authority. The dominant power lay in the hands of a Syrian army, some thirty thousand strong. It had been involved in the civil war and remained as a "peacekeeping force" under the auspices of the Arab League. By an implicit understanding with Israel, the Syrian forces kept out of South Lebanon below the Litani River, as Israel had made it clear through American channels it would not acquiesce to Syrian military deployment in the vicinity of the border. Palestinian Arab terrorist groups affiliated to the Palestine Liberation Organization (PLO) had resumed raids from South Lebanon against the Israeli civilian population. An enclave along the border remained under the control of Christian and Shia Moslem militias commanded by a Lebanese army officer, Major Haddad. These militias and the local population from which they were drawn regarded themselves as fighting a battle for survival against the PLO and its leftist allies. They appealed for help to Israel, which provided them through the "good fence" on the border with humanitarian assistance (food, water, medical aid, and employment) and logistical support. In March 1978, after a particularly gruesome terrorist exploit of the PLO inside Israel, the Israeli army occupied the Lebanese area between the border and the Litani River, drove out the terrorist groups, and demolished their bases.

It was against this complex background that Security Council resolution 425 of March 1978 was adopted. It called for the withdrawal of the Israeli forces (to which Israel agreed) and the establishment of UNIFIL. Its terms of reference were threefold: to confirm the Israeli withdrawal (phased over two months); to maintain international peace and security in the area; and to assist the Lebanese government to regain effective authority in South Lebanon. The first of these tasks presented no problem. The second met with indifferent success (see below). As for the third, it was unrealistic to expect the government in Beirut to reassert its authority in South Lebanon as long as it was unable to do so in the rest of the country, and remained propped up by the Syrian army.

Disengagement and Withdrawal

After each bout of Israeli-Arab hostilities, United Nations
peacekeeping machinery has performed the short-range function of supervising the withdrawal of forces and their
redeployment behind agreed lines, including the demarcation of
these lines where they have differed from the previous ones.

Observation

In spite of its name, UNTSO was not designed for a general
observation function. A small number of military observers
could not be expected to be stationed along or patrol the 600
miles of open border, most of it running through desert or
rough hill terrain. The duties of UNTSO were confined to
investigating specific complaints by one or the other party,
together with supervision of certain specific demilitarized
zones.
          UNEF was a different matter. It was a genuine observer
force, deploying thousands of men along a single border that
lay between Israel and Egypt. The methods used by UNEF
varied according to the sector. Around the perimeter of the
Gaza Strip it maintained fixed observation posts by day and
mobile patrols at night. The international frontier in Sinai
was patrolled by jeep, supplemented by air reconnaissance in
the mountainous southern area. At Sharm-el-Sheikh, adjacent
to the Straits of Tiran, a company post was kept to observe
and report on passing vessels.
          Between the Six-Day War of 1967 and the Yom Kippur War
of 1973, UNTSO assumed a real observation task on two limited
cease-fire lines: the Suez Canal and the Golan Heights. For
this purpose, it relied on static observation posts spaced out
on both sides of the lines.
          From 1973, the two peace forces, UNEF II and UNDOF,
had extensive observation duties. They included supervision
of the buffer zones, regular inspection of the restricted areas
on each side, and investigation of complaints that the agreements had been infringed upon. These remain the duties of
UNDOF.
          It has always been the Israeli view that, where regular
armies are involved, the most effective and desirable means of
inspection and patrol should be through mixed teams of the
parties themselves. That possibility was revived by Israel in
the summer of 1979 in connection with the arrangements in the
Sinai for implementing the peace treaty with Egypt, after the
mandate of UNEF II had been allowed to lapse.

UNIFIL has divided its "area of operation" into eight subareas, with one of its national contingents allotted to each. The techniques used include checkpoints and road blocks along the roads, observation posts along key infiltration routes, foot and mobile patrols, random nighttime listening posts, and small detachments stationed in selected villages for brief periods of one to three days. Uniformed or armed personnel and military supplies are turned back when intercepted.

Local Agreements

In the past, one of UNTSO's important functions has been to act as a go-between in halting armed clashes and outbreaks of firing and restoring the cease-fire. In addition, UNTSO was instrumental in promoting several local agreements to reduce tension and friction at particular trouble spots. Examples of such agreements include the arrangements for supply convoys through the Jordanian line to the Israeli enclave on Mount Scopus in Jerusalem; the establishment of a line separating Israel and Arab cultivation in the Latrun no-man's-land; and the "no sailing agreement" on the Suez Canal.

Buffer Zones

In the course of the Israeli-Arab conflict, a variety of demilitarized zones, no-man's-lands, and special enclaves came into existence and were placed under United Nations control or supervision. Such buffer zones themselves became sources of tension and conflict where the national jurisdiction over them remained in dispute, and where the United Nations was given responsibilities concerning civilian life in the zones.

Under the armistice regime, that was the case with the el-Auja demilitarized zone on the Israeli-Egyptian border; the Mount Scopus area, the Government House area, and the no-man's-land in Jerusalem; the Latrun no-man's-land; and the demilitarized zone on the Israeli-Syrian border. The status of these areas and the administrative responsibility for them were left somewhat vague in order to get the armistice agreements signed. It was hoped at the time that the agreements would soon be superseded by a peace settlement, when all the loose territorial ends could be tied up. This expectation proved overoptimistic. In the years to come, each of these enclaves had a tangled history, often punctuated by gunfire.

The most complex and troublesome of them was the Israeli-Syrian demilitarized zone. The controversy had a much wider dimension because the zone was caught up in major Israeli development projects concerning drainage, irrigation, and hydroelectric power. The UN peacekeeping machinery, and

behind it the Security Council, became deeply embroiled in
questions of sovereignty, jurisdiction, and civil administration,
which were beyond their capacity to settle. The problem was
resolved only when the demilitarized zone was engulfed by the
Israeli advance in the Six-Day War of 1967, and the whole
armistice agreement with Syria ceased to operate.

The 1967 War also disposed of the other buffer zones and
enclaves created by the armistice agreements. In particular,
the Mount Scopus enclave and the no-man's-land running
through the center of the city vanished with the reunification
of Jerusalem. A shrunken Government House area continues to
serve as UNTSO headquarters, but without any longer trying
to regulate civilian activities since it has ceased to be an "area
between the lines."

In the demilitarized buffer zones established after the
Yom Kippur War, questions of sovereignty did not arise. The
disengagement agreements carefully avoided giving the UN
peace forces any responsibility regarding civilian administration. For the "area of separation" occupied by UNDOF on
the Golan Heights, it was expressly provided that the force
would comply with Syrian laws and regulations and that the
civilian administration in the zone would be in Syrian hands.

Similarly, by the Egypt-Israel interim agreement of 1975,
the strip of territory along the Gulf of Suez (including the
oilfields) evacuated by Israel, was restored to Egyptian civilian
administration, while UNEF II was made responsible only for
supervising its demilitarization and controlling a joint road.
No special provision of this kind was thought necessary for
the buffer zone in the Sinai Desert occupied by UNEF II, since
it was regarded as uninhabited desert. The force was obliged
by the agreement to keep out of the zone any personnel not
expressly authorized to enter. About 170 American civilians
were engaged in the early warning system inside the zone.
These arrangements worked satisfactorily for six years until
1979.

The above summary suggests certain broad conclusions.
The peacekeeping machinery is on a sound footing when supervising a buffer zone for the sole purpose of separating the
regular armed forces of the two sides. On the other hand,
the United Nations finds itself in difficulties where
responsibility for a demilitarized zone involves it in questions
of territorial status, national jurisdiction, or civilian
administration.

The "area of operations" of UNIFIL did not resemble any
of the demilitarized areas with which UN peacekeeping missions
had been concerned elsewhere in the region. No question
arose in principle regarding the territorial status of the area
or Lebanese sovereignty over it. Moreover, UNIFIL had no
responsibility for civilian administration of the local population.
But, in practice, UNIFIL operated in a vacuum. There was no

functioning government authority in the area, either military or civilian. Under these abnormal conditions, to what extent could UNIFIL have been able to make of its area of operations an effective demilitarized buffer zone? The answer must be a heavily qualified one.

As seen from Israel, the source of the continued trouble and tension in South Lebanon was that the PLO continued to use the area as the main base for its proclaimed "armed struggle" against Israel. According to Israeli intelligence estimates, in the summer of 1979, there were 15,000 armed Palestinian Arab terrorists in Lebanon, well endowed with military equipment. Of these, some 4,000 were established in fortified bases in a zone just north of the Litani River, adjoining UNIFIL's area of operation; and 1,500 more were concentrated in the southern Lebanese port city of Tyre, which UNIFIL had excluded from its area. About 500 had infiltrated into the UNIFIL area, some of them by the simple device of coming in unarmed and then picking up their weapons from supporters living on the inside.

From time to time, Israel had carried out pre-emptive strikes against territorist concentrations and bases, in exercise of its legitimate right of self-defense. It maintained that these actions forestalled a number of planned terrorist raids into Israeli territory. Israeli detachments also crossed the border in "hot pursuit" of small groups of terrorists operating from within the UNIFIL area. There have been periodic artillery barrages from the PLO bases directed at the towns and villages in the Christian enclave, with fire returned from the enclave. UNIFIL has suffered some casualties in clashes with either the PLO or Major Haddad's militiamen.

On paper, the Christian enclave, about 10 kilometers wide along the Israeli border, is included in the UNIFIL area of operation; but, in practice, UNIFIL has no control over it. UNIFIL puts part of the blame on Israel for this frustration. It has complained that Israel failed to hand over the enclave to UNIFIL, and that anyway Israel should keep a tighter check on the militias. To this, Israel has replied that the Security Council only called on it to withdraw its troops, not to hand over Lebanese territory to UNIFIL against the will of the local inhabitants; that it does urge self-restraint on the Lebanese militias, but cannot give them orders; that it has assumed a moral obligation to help the population of the enclave survive and protect itself; and that it has a common interest with the militias in keeping the PLO terrorists away from the border.

The "peace and security" aspect of UNIFIL's mandate is, therefore, a somewhat relative term. It was wishful thinking from the beginning to contemplate that UNIFIL would move in, soon restore order, hand over responsibility to a resurrected Lebanese government, and retire after a short-term mission. Yet, any fair assessment of UNIFIL during this period would hold that UNIFIL was a factor of stability in a very unstable situation, that it had damped down the quantum of violence, and that the position in South Lebanon would likely have deteriorated if UNIFIL had been withdrawn.

Under the Egyptian-Israeli peace treaty, the UN "forces and observers" would maintain temporary and interim buffer zones until the final Israeli withdrawal from the Sinai, three years after ratification of the treaty by the parties. The permanent treaty arrangements, to take effect after the three years, divide the Sinai Peninsula into three parallel zones running north-south from the Mediterranean coast to a point near the southern tip of the Sinai Peninsula, with a fourth narrow zone on the Israeli side of the international boundary.

In the western and central zones, Egypt will be entitled to station only certain limited and specified forces. The eastern Sinai zone, running west of the international boundary and the Gulf of Aqaba, will be demilitarized and controlled by Egyptian civilian police and UN personnel. The UN force will maintain two camps, one at the northern end and one at Sharm-el-Sheikh at the southern end. It will be responsible for verifying compliance with the restrictions regarding the three limited forces zones, two in the Sinai and one inside Israel.

The peace treaty thus accepts the concept that the arid and almost unpopulated Sinai Desert should be maintained as a natural security buffer between Egypt and Israel, either demilitarized or with limited forces, and under the supervision of a UN peace force. With the demise of UNEF II, it remains an open question how a UN presence can be retained in this framework, if at all.

A demilitarized zone on the Golan Heights would be more problematical, as there is insufficient room for a zone wide enough to keep the armed forces out of range of each other.

In any future peace treaty, Israel would insist that any part of the West Bank evacuated by it should be demilitarized except for forces needed for internal security. A glance at the map shows that if this was not done every inch of Israeli territory and the whole of its air space would be exposed to missiles, rockets, and heavy artillery located on the West Bank. Under the Camp David autonomy proposal negotiated by Israel, Egypt, and the United States, Israeli troops are redeployed in specified security locations during the interim five-year period.

Terrorist Infiltration

In the history of United Nations peacekeeping in the Israeli-Arab conflict, a most corrosive factor has been terrorist infiltration into Israel from neighboring Arab states.

The 1949 armistice agreements expressly prohibited attacks or incursions across the demarcation lines by military,
paramilitary, or nonregular forces. Yet, in the next few
years, there was constant marauding by armed gangs from
Jordan-held territory and from the Gaza Strip under Egyptian
occupation. Transport was attacked; roads mined; houses and
installations blown up; and civilians killed traveling in buses,
working in the fields, or sleeping in their homes at night.

Israel lodged hundreds of complaints with the MACs
concerning these incidents, but the armistice machinery proved
wholly ineffectual in dealing with the problem. In each case,
a team of UN military observers would investigate the complaint
and note the injuries and damage. But unless the tracks of
the perpetrators could be followed on the ground between the
scene of the outrage and the border (which was hardly ever
possible), the complaint was rejected for want of conclusive
evidence, and the government of the Arab state concerned was
absolved from responsibility, though the facts were common
knowledge. The peacekeeping operation, therefore, became
irrelevant to the pattern of terrorist infiltration.

Under these circumstances, Israel took its own measures
to defend its territory and its citizens against armed attack.
From the early 1950s, there were from time to time local
military actions by Israeli forces across the border. The
objectives were to harass and disperse terrorist groups, to
discourage villagers across the line from harboring and
cooperating with such groups, and to put pressure on the
governments concerned. On a number of occasions, the
Security Council censured the Israeli counterattacks, without
even referring to the terrorist activities that had led up to
them. Israel continued to invoke its inherent right of self-
defense, and to insist that the primary responsibility for
curbing infiltration lay with the Arab state from which it
emanated.

From 1953 to 1956, the main base for incursions was the
Gaza Strip. The fedayeen (terrorist) groups that carried them
out were recruited, trained, equipped, and dispatched by the
Egyptian army. One of Israel's major objectives in the Sinai
campaign was to put an end to the fedayeen raids by occupying the Strip. For the decade after the Suez crisis, it was a
matter of major Egyptian policy to avoid stirring up trouble on
the border with Israel. The fedayeen raids were not resumed,
and at not stage in its existence was UNEF I required to cope
with a serious infiltration problem.

From about 1965, terrorist attacks flared up again on
Israel's borders with Syria and Jordan, with the emergence of
the El-Fatah terrorist organization. The systematic Fatah
attacks were one of the causes of tension that led up to the
Six-Day War of 1967. In the civil war in Jordan in 1970-71,
the terrorist organizations were ousted and their main base

became Lebanon. Their role as one of the combatants in the
Lebanese civil war of 1975-76 has raised serious problems for
the Arab governments themselves about the uncontrolled armed
activities of the Palestinian Arab groups. Israel made it plain
that it would not tolerate the resumption of terrorist raids
from Lebanon. That policy led to the Israeli occupation of
southern Lebanon in March 1978, and the birth of UNIFIL.
    In negotiating the disengagement agreement of 1976
between Israel and Syria, the United States obtained an
unpublished undertaking from the Syrian government that
terrorist activities would be prevented across the cease-fire
line. In presenting the agreement for parliamentary approval,
the Israeli Prime Minister, Mrs. Golda Meir, declared that she
was authorized to state the United States' position as follows:

> Raids by armed groups or individuals across the
> demarcation line are contrary to the cease-fire.
> Israel, in the exercise of its right to self-defense,
> may act to prevent such actions by all available
> means. The United States will not consider such
> actions by Israel as violations of the cease-fire, and
> will support them politically.

This important endorsement of the Israeli position marked a
growing international recognition that: (1) the country that
plays host to terrorist organizations is responsible for what
they do; (2) that the target country is entitled to act in its
own defense; and (3) that the United Nations has no answer to
this problem.
    It is noteworthy that the Egyptian-Israeli Peace Treaty
expressly provides that "Each Party undertakes to ensure that
acts or threats of belligerency, hostility, or violence do not
originate from and are not committed from within its territory,
or by forces subject to its control or by any other forces
stationed on its territory, against the population, citizens or
property of the other Party" (Art.III(2)).

ATTRIBUTES OF PEACE FORCES

Composition of the Force

In setting up UNEF I, Hammarskjöld laid down several principles that were endorsed by the General Assembly. The
permanent members of the Security Council were ruled out as
participants, also member states having a "special interest" in
the conflict - presumably an implied reference to the Arab
states and Israel. The exclusion of the permanent members
has been a precedent followed in other peace forces since

UNEF I, including UNEF II and UNDOF. (The only exception
to the rule has been the British participation in UNFICYP, the
peace force in Cyprus).

Since the Yom Kippur War of 1973, the proposal has been
mooted in different quarters that the United States and the
Soviet Union should be directly involved in peacekeeping in
the Israeli-Arab conflict. It is argued that the two superpowers acted jointly to halt the October War and to set up new
negotiation machinery under their joint chairmanship; that they
are the only external factors that have serious leverage on the
parties to the conflict; that a peace force based on their
participation would provide a stronger deterrent to renewed
fighting; and that such a peacekeeping role by the superpowers could develop into a joint guarantee of a future
political settlement.

These arguments are persuasive in theory, but it is not
surprising that Israel's attitude is negative, as is that of
Washington. The interests and policies of the two great
powers in the Middle East remain incompatible, and there is
little pretense that they are governed in this region by
whatever detente may exist elsewhere. A Soviet military
presence in the area under United Nations auspices would, it
is feared, be exploited for Soviet purposes. With its
one-sided support for the Arab cause, its lavish military
assistance to Arab client-states, and its refusal to renew
diplomatic relations with Israel, the Soviet Union does not
commend itself to Israel for the role of a "disinterested"
peacekeeper. For different reasons, reservations would be felt
by Arab states, such as Egypt that is trying to disengage
itself from dependence on the Soviet Union, and by other Arab
states, such as Saudi Arabia and Jordan, that are still within
the Western orbit. In any case, there would be resistance in
Washington to committing U.S. troops to any fresh tasks
abroad. It was difficult to get congressional approval even for
sending less than 200 American civilian technicians to the
buffer zone in the Sinai Desert. In these circumstances, the
peacekeeping forces in the area are likely to remain composed
of contingents from smaller powers that are physically removed
from the region, and not involved in the conflict. That rule
was followed for UNEF II, UNDOF, and UNIFIL.

The requirement that a geographical balance be maintained
in the peace forces creates certain problems of its own. The
wide diversity of units also creates marked inequality in
conditions of service within the same force. Differences of
language, training, and working methods are especially felt in
a multinational force headquarters. It would be desirable if a
peace force could be provided with a homogeneous headquarters staff from a single developed national army, with liaison
officers attached to it from each contingent in the force.
Moreover, staff officers should be rotated at longer intervals
than other personnel.

Should the composition of peace forces be subject to the approval of the parties to the conflict? When UNEF I was established in 1956, Hammarskjöld proposed that its composition should be determined by the secretary-general "in consultation with" the host country. That formula ran into trouble when the Egyptian government vetoed three member states on the secretary-general's balanced list - Canada, New Zealand, and Pakistan - as they were in the British Commonwealth. Hammarskjöld deleted two of these countries, but persuaded Nasser to accept the participation of Canada, though only in a logistics role. The practical effect, therefore, was that no participating country was imposed on Egypt against its will.

When UNEF II and UNDOF were set up, there was no consultation with the governments concerned regarding the composition of the forces. Israel objected to the inclusion of four countries that did not have diplomatic ties with it - Ghana, Indonesia, Senegal, and Poland - but the objection was not accepted. Israel thereupon made known that personnel from these national contingents would not be permitted to pass through its lines and enter the territory under its control, unless special permission was obtained in each case. As against that, the secretary-general maintained that each peace force must be regarded as an integrated whole without any distinction being drawn between its component units. It is submitted that the Israeli position embodies a valid principle, namely, that the peacekeeping units should be drawn from countries having normal relations with both sides to the conflict, and accepted by both sides as impartial. UNIFIL has also included units from states that do not have diplomatic relations with Israel, such as Iran, Senegal, and Nigeria, although it was laid down that there should be consultation regarding these matters with the parties concerned.

Status of the Force

UNEF I had the status under the Charter of a subsidiary organ of the General Assembly. UNEF II, UNDOF, and UNIFIL have an equivalent status as subsidiary organs of the Security Council. These peace forces are, therefore, covered by article 105(I) of the Charter, elaborated in the General Convention on the Privileges and Immunities of the United Nations. The detailed application of the Convention to the functioning of UNEF I on Egyptian territory was worked out in a Status of Forces Agreement between the United Nations and the Egyptian government.

After 1973, the UN secretariat initiated talks for similar agreements with Israel and Egypt concerning UNEF II, and with Israel and Syria concerning UNDOF. In the talks with Israel, it proved difficult to find agreed formulations on such questions as the application of Israeli laws, the extent of UN immunities, and freedom of movement for UN personnel. For their part, the two Arab governments showed little interest in concluding such agreements, since they were anxious to make clear that the peace forces were transient in nature. The negotiations with the parties were inconclusive, and have remained in abeyance. Meanwhile, practical problems, including criminal offenses, have been dealt with on an ad hoc basis. UNIFIL was set up and deployed at the request of the Lebanese government, but no Status of Force Agreement was negotiated.

What is the "host country"? In the original case of UNEF I, the force operated only on Egyptian territory or territory under Egyptian military control (the Gaza Strip). The arrangements concerning its status were, therefore, negotiated only with Egypt. UNEF II and UNDOF, however, operated on both sides of the cease-fire lines; and, by agreement between the opposing states, served as a buffer between their armed forces. In their case, national sovereignty became irrelevant, and the UN peacekeepers dealt with the authorities that physically occupied and controlled the territory on the two sides of the line.

Apart from its relations with the parties to the conflict, the United Nations also entered into separate agreements with the countries contributing units to the peace forces. By these agreements, the participating state retained exclusive criminal jurisdiction over its own nationals in the force; while the discipline, ranks, and other normal service matters within a unit remained the independent responsibility of that unit, under the regulations of its own national army.

The peace force was thus governed by a combination of factors: agreements between the parties; agreements or understandings between the United Nations and the parties; agreements between the United Nations and the troop-providing states; the internal regulations applying to UN missions in the field; and directives from the UN secretariat to the force commander. It should be noted that the states providing contingents to a peace force had no direct dealings with the parties to the conflict concerning those contingents.

The principle of freedom of movement for UN peacekeeping personnel has produced differences of opinion between the United Nations and the parties. Israel is very much concerned about military security in sensitive border areas, and is reluctant to allow the personnel of foreign armies to move freely in these areas, even if they temporarily wear a blue UN arm band. From time to time, the Israeli army has for operational reasons imposed certain restrictions. Particular areas or roads may be temporarily closed to UN personnel; the radius of movement around UN observation posts limited; and overflights by UN planes confined to prescribed corridors.

Political Control of the Force

On the whole, UNTSO and the four peace forces have functioned on the day-to-day operational level with remarkably little political bias or interference. Officers and men from different regions and backgrounds have worked well together, and have carried out their task with diligence and patience. The chiefs-of-staff of UNTSO and the commanders of the peace forces have been appointed from neutral countries, after sounding out the parties whether the appointments would be acceptable to them. The secretary-general and his senior officials have exercised broad and flexible powers in the administration and executive control of the peace missions. The participating states have not tried to influence their national units in the carrying out of their UN duties.

However, the question of control becomes more complex and controversial at a higher political level. The secretary-general has acted on the authority and according to the directives of the Security Council - or, in the case of UNEF I, the General Assembly. Both these principal UN organs suffer from a chronic and built-in bias where the Israeli-Arab conflict is concerned.

When an Israeli-Arab dispute comes before the Security Council, the Arab party to the dispute can usually command a Council majority and avail itself of the Russian veto where needed, or, in the case of UNEF II, the threat of a veto. The decisions of the Council have been of positive value only when they have been based on a consensus that includes the states directly concerned. That has been the case with resolutions 242 and 338, setting out the guidelines for a peace settlement, and with the establishment of the peace forces. In the last resort, Israel would withhold its cooperation from a peacekeeping venture where the conditions were unacceptable.

In the General Assembly, the 20 Arab member states, together with the non-Arab Moslem states, the Communist bloc, and a number of Third World countries, command an overwhelming and automatic parliamentary majority. Whatever implications this may have for the Israeli-Arab conflict on the political and propaganda fronts, it is improbable that the General Assembly will again launch a peacekeeping operation, as it did with UNEF I in 1956. Today, neither the Western powers nor the Soviet Union look for crisis control in an Assembly with a runaway preponderance of Third World countries. The Uniting for Peace Resolution has been pigeonholed.

Where the two superpowers become dangerously involved on opposite sides of the crisis, and have a common interest in defusing it, they are liable to act jointly, through the Security Council. The way the Yom Kippur War of 1973 was halted provides a striking illustration.

To sum up, the UN peacekeeping operations in the Israeli-Arab conflict have been under impartial and apolitical control up to the level of the secretary-general. Beyond that, the peacekeeping can function only to the extent that it can be insulated from the voting balances in UN organs, and from rivalry between the major powers. The two primary conditions for peacekeeping are the consent of the parties to the conflict, and a consensus in the Security Council.

The Financial Aspect

The United Nations crisis over peacekeeping costs made the original UNEF principle of obligatory assessments unworkable, and it was abandoned in practice after the Congo involvement. Later peacekeeping operations were paid for by voluntary contributions, with the main burden being assumed by those states that had a special interest in the specific situation concerned.

With the establishment of UNEF II and UNDOF by the Security Council in 1973-74, the General Assembly reverted to financing them on the basis of assessments on the whole membership, as expenses of the organization in terms of article 17(2) of the Charter. This was done by general consensus because of the importance attached to the peacekeeping operation after the Yom Kippur War, and because of the joint sponsorship of the cease-fire by the two superpowers. To bypass the unresolved legal and political issues that had paralyzed the Nineteenth Session of the General Assembly, the assessments were described in the relevant resolution as "an ad hoc arrangement, without prejudice to the positions of principle that may be taken by member-states. . . ." The costs were apportioned among groups of member states according to a novel formula. The five permanent members of the Security Council contributed nearly two-thirds. A list of 23 developed countries accounted for another third of the total. About 2 percent was paid by the remaining 110 member-states, classified as "less developed." A few member-states still refused to participate in the costs and their assessments were written off as "noncollectable."

The costs referred to above do not include the regular expenses for their own units borne by the participating countries. The United Nations reimburses them only for "extra and extraordinary costs." These reimbursements include a flat monthly rate per man, and depreciation for equipment.

For the expenses of UNIFIL, the precedents of UNEF II and UNDOF have been followed.

Duration of the Mission

When UNEF I was proposed in 1956, the Egyptian government stipulated that "consent of Egypt is indispensable for entry and presence of United Nations forces in any part of its territory. If such consent no longer persists, these forces shall withdraw." Hammarskjold sought a voluntary commitment from Egypt that the force would remain in being until its task had been completed, a matter to be decided by the General Assembly. On a visit to Cairo, Hammarskjöld obtained the agreement of Nasser to an ambiguous "good faith" formula in this spirit. It was embodied in an aide memoire annexed to a report by the Secretary-General and endorsed by the Assembly.

When put to the test in May 1967, however, the undertaking proved worthless. Nasser ordered the expulsion of UNEF and secretary-general U Thant withdrew it at once. In a lengthy report explaining and defending his action, U Thant maintained that Egypt was entitled to withdraw its consent; once this was done, the continued existence of UNEF in Egypt became impossible. U Thant complained that the criticism directed against him did not take account of "the essentially fragile nature of the basis for UNEF's operation throughout its existence."

The duration of UNEF II and UNDOF is a different problem. After the Yom Kippur War, neither of the two Arab states were willing to consider a peace force with a mandate for a long or indefinite period. Each time the six-month mandate of UNDOF was about to expire, Syria would withhold its consent until the last moment, and demand political concessions as the price for renewal. In a less blatant way, Egypt also created uncertainty about an extension of the mandate of UNEF II and used international anxiety on the matter as a means of political pressure. It is a paradox that UN peacekeeping agencies, intended to relax tensions, should themselves become a focus of tension.

In the negotiations for the 1975 Israeli-Egyptian interim agreement, the mandate for UNEF II was made renewable annually for a minimum period of three years. If Egypt were to withdraw its consent during that period, it could be accused of a breach of faith, but the position of the peace force would become untenable.

The life span of a peace force is germane to the concept of international guarantees, which Israel is frequently urged to accept as a substitute for defensible frontiers. The nature of such international guarantees has never been clarified. The United Nations has no army - and even if it had, armed intervention against Arab states, or even economic sanctions against them, would be inconceivable in the light of present-day realities. Nor is there any prospect of an American or

Western security pact that would commit the armed forces of those countries to Israel's defense, as they are committed in NATO. To the extent that the "guarantees" would rest on UN peacekeeping arrangements, they would be brittle, for there is no effective way to make the parties cooperate any longer than they wish to.

THE POLITICAL CONTEXT

Peacekeeping does not function in a vacuum. Its viability is affected by the political and juridical situation between the parties to the conflict.

In the Israeli-Arab conflict (which in this context does not include the current situation in southern Lebanon involving UNIFIL), the term "peacekeeping" is a misnomer. The peace-keepers have operated in interim situations that have been neither war nor peace. Two questions, therefore, become relevant:

- What has been the relationship between the peacekeeping efforts and the peacemaking efforts?
- Does the peacekeeping rest on nonbelligerence, or a formal termination of the state of war – that is to say, does it rule out a resort to force?

Peacekeeping and Peacemaking

In theory, peacekeeping and peacemaking are interdependent. Peacekeeping is not an end in itself, but a means to relax tension and provide a measure of stability while peace talks proceed; conversely, the fact of simultaneous peace talks justifies and maintains the interim peacekeeping.

This concept underlay the 1949 armistice agreements, which were concluded for the express purpose of promoting the return to permanent peace. The United Nations then set up parallel peacemaking machinery in the Palestine Conciliation Commission (PCC). The cease-fire arrangements set up after the Six-Day War in 1967 were followed by Security Council resolution 242 and the Jarring Mission. In 1973, after the Yom Kippur War, UNEF II and UNDOF were established against the background of Security Council resolution 338 and the Geneva Conference. Only in 1956 did the United Nations refuse to launch another peacemaking effort at the same time as UNEF I was set up. The Israeli government pleaded that this should be done. Hammarskjöld rejected the Israeli position almost with moral fervor, and was supported by the General Assembly. In the atmosphere then prevailing, a fresh peace move was dismissed as an unmerited reward to Israel for its military action.

While peacemaking and peacekeeping in principle support each other, the theorem can be overstated. The correlation between the two processes has in practice been blurred and inconclusive. At times, peacekeeping may even have been the enemy of peacemaking. Where the interim situation has seemed to settle down, and the crisis atmosphere has subsided, the parties have been less inclined to consider painful concessions, while international concern has turned to more acute situations elsewhere. That seems to have been the case during the decade from 1956 when UNEF I sat quietly in the Gaza Strip and at Sharm-el-Sheikh, while no serious international attempt was made to come to grips with the underlying conflict.

As seen from Jerusalem, the recurrent hostilities and the lack of progress toward peace both derived from the same underlying cause. The main problem has been the unwilling-ness of the Arab world to accept the Jewish state as an irreversible fact of history, with the consequence that Arabs cling to a "military option." Even Egypt's 1975 interim agreement with Israel was denounced by an Arab Rejection Front that included Iraq, Syria, Libya, Nigeria, and the PLO.

A dramatic breakthrough came with Sadat's visit to Jeru-salem in November 1977. The peace process it initiated led to the Camp David Accords, the Egyptian-Israeli peace treaty, the autonomy talks regarding the West Bank and the Gaza Strip - and a wider and stiffer Arab Rejection Front. As regards UN peacekeeping, the result has been paradoxical. The parties to the peace treaty have lost their peacekeeping force (UNEF II) while UNDOF continues to function smoothly between Israel and Syria, a vociferous member of the Rejection Front.

A meaningful peace dialogue between the parties directly concerned is essential in its own right, for without that the conflict cannot be resolved. However, the viability of the peacekeeping operations has so far depended less on conduct-ing a parallel process of peacemaking than on the question of belligerency.

Peacekeeping and Belligerency

In the negotiations for the 1975 Israeli-Egyptian interim agreement, the term "elements of belligerency" was loosely used to include manifestations of political, economic, and propaganda warfare. Belligerency in the present context refers only to armed attack and the imposition of blockades on sea routes.

The armistice agreements of 1949 unequivocally put a permanent end to belligerency. The first two articles in the

agreements prohibited attacks or incursions across the demarcation lines by military, paramilitary, or nonregular forces,
and guaranteed the right of each party to its security and
freedom from fear of attack. Unlike the rest of the agreements, these articles could not be revoked or altered even by
subsequent agreement between the signatory governments. In
August 1949, when the agreements came before the Security
Council for endorsement, the acting mediator, Dr. Ralph
Bunche, stated that they were "not the final peace settlement,
but the only possible interpretation of their very specific
provisions is that they signal the end of the military phase of
the Palestine situation." In his report of 24 January 1957 to
the General Assembly, Secretary-General Dag Hammarskjöld
described the armistice regime as a "nonaggression pact,
providing for mutual and full abstention from belligerent acts."

In 1951, Israel complained to the Security Council about
the continued Egyptian blockade of the Suez Canal, and the
seizure of ships and cargoes bound for Israeli ports. Egypt
maintained that it was entitled to exercise belligerent rights
against Israel, since an armistice was by definition not a
termination of hostilities but only a temporary suspension of
them. This contention was rejected by the Council, which
held that "since the armistice regime . . . is of a permanent
character, neither party can reasonably assert that it actively
is a belligerent or requires to exercise the right of visit,
search and seizure for any legitimate purpose of self-defense."

Egypt ignored that decision, and continued to assert the
doctrine and practice of a "state of war." In the General
Assembly debates during the Suez crisis, the Israeli representative declared that "the rock on which the armistice agreement
foundered was that of belligerency. For eight years an effort
was made to keep this agreement alive in conditions quite
incompatible with its existence."

In securing Israeli withdrawal from Sinai and the Gaza
Strip and establishing UNEF I, the United Nations did not call
upon Egypt to renounce a state of war. In May 1967, when
UNEF I was ejected, Egyptian troops reoccupied Sharm-el-
Sheikh, reimposed the blockade of the Gulf of Aqaba, and
justified it on the same juridical grounds as before. That act
precipitated the Six-Day War. The Sharm-el-Sheikh story
illustrates the basic difference between peacekeeping based on
nonbelligerency and peacekeeping that has to coexist with
belligerency.

In the negotiations for the 1975 Egypt-Israel interim
agreement, Egypt again refused in principle to renounce a
state of war and to stop all belligerent practices, though the
agreement did contain important elements of nonaggression.
The 1979 peace treaty finally settled this question between
Egypt and Israel. Article I(1) reads: "The state of war
between the Parties will be terminated and peace will be

established between them upon the exchange of instruments of ratification of this Treaty." (The exchange took place soon after.)

As between Israel and the other neighboring Arab states, the question remains whether a juridical state of belligerency or a state of war continues to exist.

Peacekeeping and Peace

In laying down guidelines for a peace settlement, resolution 242 affirms "the necessity . . . for guaranteeing the territorial inviolability and political independence of every State in the area, through measures including the establishment of demilitarized zones." It was envisaged at the time that, for a number of years after a peace settlement, the United Nations would probably be called upon to keep peace forces on the ground for the supervision of buffer zones.

As has been noted, that was written into the Egyptian-Israeli Peace Treaty. It remains to be seen whether the United Nations will be allowed to project its peacekeeping role into the new and different political framework of peace – at present between Israel and Egypt, and potentially in a comprehensive Middle East settlement. Such a role would be derived from the wealth of experience already accumulated in the course of UN peacekeeping in the Middle East over more than thirty years.

Seen in perspective, that experience has brought into focus the built-in conditions for UN peacekeeping. They include:

- the consent of the states directly concerned;
- a Security Council consensus that includes the major powers;
- national contingents made available on a voluntary basis by countries from different geographical regions;
- agreement among the general membership of the United Nations concerning the costs; and
- recognition that each government in the peacekeeping area is responsible for preventing its territory from being used for attacks by irregular forces and terrorist groups.

National policymakers and international peacemakers should have a clear grasp of what UN peacekeeping can or cannot do. They should then seek to utilize its positive features while taking account of its frailties.

5
Canadian Attitudes to Peacekeeping
Geoffrey A.H. Pearson*

COLLECTIVE SECURITY

The idea of collective security haunted the imagination of
European statesmen after World War I and led to the creation
of the League of Nations. It is less well known that Canada
shared the skepticism of the United States about this idea until
1939, viewing it as, in some sense, a European device for
committing Canadian participation to European conflicts over
which Canada had little influence and which were marginal to
its own security. As a member of the League, Canada opposed
sanctions and the use of coercion to punish aggression. World
War II shattered the illusion that Canada could avoid the
consequences of European rivalries, but it also strengthened
its determination not to be committed to war again without
having a voice in the arrangements made to preserve the
peace. Moreover, this voice would be a strong one, for
Canada emerged from the war with armed forces of almost a
million men and the fourth or fifth largest GNP of the members
of the new world organization.

Canada's hopes and expectations were frustrated. It was
not elected to the Security Council in 1946, having to wait
until 1948; the armed forces which it was ready to earmark for
UN service under the provisions of Chapter VII of the Charter
were not summoned, the UN Security Council being unable to
agree on the nature of UN forces; the Council, in fact,
showed an alarming tendency toward paralysis. Canadian
leaders began to hint in these circumstances that the idea of

*The views expressed are those of the author and do not
necessarily represent the views or policy of the Canadian
Department of External Affairs.

collective security had perhaps best be implemented in some other way, and especially through article 51 of the Charter on regional defense arrangements. In 1947-48, both Britain and Canada sent signals to Washington that it was time to consider a North American guarantee of the defense of Western Europe. For Canada, this meant both reciprocity of commitments and an equal voice in the security policies of all concerned. The birth of NATO in 1949 coincided with increasing disillusion in Ottawa with the Security Council, on which Canada now served, although the UN response to war in Korea the next year revived the Canadian hope that collective security could be made to work in the wider context. The key to success now appeared to be the General Assembly where the majority could be counted on to support Western policies.

The Korean War provoked hesitation and confusion in Canada about the nature of Canada's collective security commitments. It was politically convenient to interpret the essentially American initiative to employ the UN for enforcement action in Korea as an exercise in collective security, but defense planning clearly gave the European theatre priority. Accordingly, the special force which was raised for duty in Korea was earmarked for NATO as well as for the UN. After the end of the Korean War, the NATO commitment to the UN remained on the books. Canada hoped in 1950 that the Korean War would lead a number of countries to earmark forces for the UN and was disappointed when this did not happen.(1) The purpose of such forces was still thought to be that of repelling aggression rather than the more neutral function of monitoring armistice agreements, in which the UN was then engaged in the Middle East (UNTSO) and Kashmir (UNMOGIP). NATO and the UN were still seen as complementary institutions in the search for collective security.

ALLIANCE DIPLOMACY

A second influence on Canada's approach to peacekeeping was its vital stake in North Atlantic defense and the delicate brokerage relationships it cultivated in dealing with transatlantic issues. On the one hand, Canada was concerned to muffle and restrain what it perceived as United States tendencies to convert the UN into an anticommunist organization, especially vis-a-vis China (although Canadians generally shared the view that the Soviet Union was chiefly responsible for the breakdown of the UN security system); while, on the other hand, Canada attempted to soften European perceptions of the UN as an increasingly anti-European organization determined to end European dominance in most of Africa and in parts of Asia. Canada's relations with India throughout the 1950s were of significant importance in both these respects. In 1954, Canada was asked to participate in the International Control Commission established to monitor the Indochina settlements, partly no doubt as a reflection of these multifaceted relationships which gave it the reputation of a relatively impartial (though clearly Western) observer acceptable to all sides. Starting with this Indochina assignment, and with the appointment of General E.L.M. Burns as commander of UNTSO the same year, Canada viewed her role in peacekeeping as one of disinterested objectivity (an assumption which was not, of course, always shared by others, especially in Indochina).

Canada's diplomatic role among her Western partners and in the new Commonwealth was also much in evidence at the start of UNEF I and UNFICYP, where the unity of the NATO alliance was threatened by decisions to use force without consultation. The split between the United States and Britain/France over Suez was a particularly shattering blow to Canadian officials, who feared the break-up of the Commonwealth as well as NATO. In desperation, it almost seems in retrospect, Canada picked up a British idea of using a UN label to make Franco/British intervention respectable and turned it into a device to expedite their withdrawal before more drastic actions might be taken. Again, in 1964, when the situation in Cyprus threatened to bring Greece and Turkey to the brink of war, to disrupt NATO, and to tempt intervention by the superpowers if nothing were done, Canada responded to the entreaties of her allies and especially her neighbor to participate in a new force, despite simultaneous service in UNEF I and, by now, the UN force in the Congo.

MIDDLE POWER

Canada's contribution to peacekeeping has also been based on its reputation as a "middle power." There are several meanings to this term. First, Canada possesses human and material resources which enable it to raise and equip substantial military forces if and when necessary. This is a relative concept: in 1950, Canada was stronger than now compared to other countries, but, in 1976, Canada was still thirteenth in terms of military expenditures even though the amount spent on defense was less than 2 percent of GNP. Middle powers have skills, equipment, and a capacity to incur debts (if they are Western middle powers) which qualify them for peacekeeping. Canada has participated in thirteen UN peacekeeping operations and the two independent operations in Indochina. In all, Canadian personnel served 33,174 man years in peacekeeping operations from 1949 to 1980 at a total cost of $266 million, representing the rather modest 0.4 percent of the total military budget for that period.(2)   This is a high cost for one state to bear when, at least in theory, peacekeeping is a collective UN responsibility.

Canada is also a middle power in the sense of being accustomed to searching for the middle way, both in its domestic affairs and as a long-term interpreter of Empire and Commonwealth to puzzled Americans and suspicious recruits from Asia, Africa, and the Caribbean.   General Burns, for example, wrote about his experiences in Between Arab and Israeli, although few Canadians would claim to be able to "fix" that particular quarrel, despite a good deal of experience.

The Commonwealth has not evolved a firm policy of its own for the practice of peacekeeping.   But Commonwealth members have been the backbone of most UN operations, and have taken a significant part in moving the resolution of the Rhodesian conflict through the creation of the Commonwealth Monitoring Force (largely composed of United Kingdom military personnel with additions from Fiji, Kenya, and New Zealand troops and directed by the United Kingdom), and the implementation of the Commonwealth Observer Group to witness the elections to determine whether or not they were "free and fair."   The Commonwealth role was substantial and could well become a precedent for the future.

Finally, there is a sense in which Canada is midway between the most industrialized and developing countries, sympathetic to the needs of the latter but enjoying the standard of living of the former.   The sympathy is partly based on the common experience of "colony to nation" experience which includes the political economy of resource development and foreign ownership.

MAKING THE UN WORK

Canada has found the world of the UN congenial diplomatic ground, challenging, and eliciting a disposition to conciliate and to harmonize.   Unlike the United States, France, and Britain, it has not been a party to disputes before the Security Council.   Though seriously committed to finding means of developing a "New Economic Order," Canada, unlike the developing countries, does not expect to convert the UN into an agency for the redistribution of power and wealth.   It is not primarily interested in the UN as upholder of international virtue and order, conscious of the fact that the Charter was negotiated principally among the great powers and that two-thirds of the current membership were not even present at San Francisco for the signing of the Charter. Instead, Canada has found in the UN "a place to stand," a means of maximizing opportunities for the enhancement of both interests and status. The Canadian interest in the capacity of the UN to settle disputes peacefully has already been suggested: collective security arrangements would provide a means to exert influence on major allies and powerful neighbors as well as help to maintain peace; and Canada's armed forces would give substance to diplomatic goals outside North America, where the role of junior partner was inevitable. NATO helped to satisfy these requirements but left out of account the Commonwealth connection, which was strongly reinforced by the new nations of Africa after 1960. The circumstances of Suez in 1956 were unique for all concerned. In Canada, they had the effect of galvanizing what had been a dormant impulse to clothe the UN with real authority and to give meaning to the commitment to earmark forces for UN service. The ten years of UNEF I were the crest of the peacekeeping wave – for a short time in 1964 Canada made substantial contributions to three major operations simultaneously (UNEF I, ONUC, and UNFICYP) and again in 1978 (UNEF II, UNDOF, and UNIFIL).

Canada has focused attention on three aspects of the potential UN contribution to the peaceful settlement of disputes – national preparations for peacekeeping, improvement of such international arrangements as existed, and the link between peacekeeping and peaceful settlement. As already stated, Canada earmarked forces for service with the UN as early as 1950, although it was not until 1956 when UNEF I came into being that a standby battalion was actually formed. Canada has occasionally suggested that such arrangements be made outside the UN, e.g., in 1964 the prime minister proposed that interested countries agree jointly to establish "an international peace force . . . specifically tied to carrying out UN decisions" and at the request of the UN. The Ottawa conference of military representatives from 23 countries held as a result of this initiative was not able to go that far and eventually nothing was done, although Canada and the Scandinavian governments have kept in touch on standby arrangements. Canada has urged that most if not all UN members make similar standby arrangements. To this end, it has provided detailed information to the UN on the organization and training of those elements of the Canadian armed forces on peacekeeping standby, as well as views on the proper procedures to follow in authorizing and pursuing operations, the facilities and services required, and the selection and training of personnel.

From the early 1960s, Canadian officials have concentrated as well on improving the financing and control of peacekeeping operations. Canada has maintained the view consistently that peacekeeping costs are expenses of the organization under article 17 of the Charter and therefore subject to apportionment among all members by the General Assembly. This view is based on the assumption mentioned above that the security functions of the UN arc a matter of the collective interest, and that a volunteer fire brigade is an anomaly as well as an injustice. This is not, of course, a unanimous view. Others believe that the "aggressor" should bear the costs of aggression, or that only those principally concerned should do so. Special scales of assessment have had to be devised so as to lessen the burden on developing countries. Canada has regretted in particular that two permanent members of the Security Council, charged with special responsibilities for the maintenance of peace, should have been significant defaulters on the peacekeeping account (the USSR has never contributed to the most recent UN operation to be authorized by the Security Council - the UN Interim Force in Lebanon - and China only began to contribute in 1982).

In regard to command and control, Canada's views have been shaped even more by its interests as a prominent contributor anxious that its troops should not be endangered nor their function made impotent by political disagreement in New York. Canada has, therefore, resisted attempts to weaken the prerogative of the secretary general and the force commanders to exercise efficient and timely control of all aspects of operations (see J.D. Murray, "Military Aspects of Peacekeeping," chap. 8 in this volume), while recognizing that the Security Council must retain ultimate authority and that the secretary general must keep its members informed of his plans to carry out the mandate given him. A key question is the nature of this consultation with the Council. Suggestions have been made that a subcommittee of the Council act as liaison between the Council and the secretary-general or that the military staff committee, composed of representatives of the permanent members, be revitalized for this purpose. (Canada proposed in 1972 that representatives of troop contributor states be invited to participate in the work of the military staff committee if it were to be given such functions.) In the Canadian view, however, there is no adequate substitute for the competence and efficiency of the secretariat, qualities which are not easy to establish and maintain in a body of such disparate loyalties and standards (see Brian Urquhart, "Peacekeeping: A View from the Operational Center," chap. 7 in this volume). Troop contributors can and do play some part in the process of management and control, but there arc limits to the influence which governments can exercise in any formal way outside the structure and procedures of the Security Council.

The work of the Special Committee on Peacekeeping Operations (the Committee of 33), established by the Assembly in 1964, illustrates these limits. Its efforts to reach agreement on guidelines for the establishment, control, and financing of operations, and on practical measures which governments might take to prepare for such operations have yielded only modest results.(3) Canada has advocated that the committee approve measures of advance planning and training, even though the political differences over guidelines for the control of operations remain deep. (The formulas for command, control, and financing actually agreed upon for UNEF II and UNIFIL are likely to be the model for any eventual guidelines.) The need to exchange information and to organize cooperation between states about the practical techniques of peacekeeping will grow as more countries are invited to participate and accept such invitations. Some or all of the following steps could be taken: preparation of a manual of standard operating procedures for forces in the field, of a standard guidance letter from the secretary general to potential troop contributors on what is expected of them, training courses for officers designated by governments as UN observers or staff officers, and the creation of a single secretariat headquarters bureau for peacekeeping affairs. With some 13,500 men from 26 countries participating in UN operations in mid-1979, it is difficult for Canada to accept that planning must remain uncoordinated and that crisis management is the only technique of control.

The third major concern of Canada was that a link be forged between peacekeeping operations and the settlement of the disputes they were called upon to monitor. The United Nations is not empowered to enforce settlements of disputes unless it acts under Chapter VII of the Charter with the agreement of its permanent members. Lacking such agreement, member states must give their consent to procedures and terms tor the settlement of disputes between them. Yet, peacekeeping questions may appear to rob the parties of any incentive to negotiate seriously, inasmuch as the consequence of not doing so - the threat or use of force by either party - is discouraged by the UN presence between them. The operations themselves may then continue indefinitely and contributors find themselves apparently locked into quasi-permanent obligations.

Canada has, therefore, emphasized the responsibility of the Security Council to incorporate in the mandates of peacekeeping forces, or in associated resolutions, either the principles of a future settlement or at least the commitment to negotiate in good faith, with the assistance of the UN, such a settlement. Arrangements for mediation have, in fact, been approved by the Council in most instances; and, in the case of the Arab-Israeli dispute, Canada participated in 1967 in the drafting of resolution 242 which outlined the principles of a settlement. Nevertheless, the disputes with which Canadian forces are most familiar, in Cyprus and the Middle East, have been the most resistant to peaceful settlement. Canadian governments have been sensitive to the value of these operations in helping to keep what peace there has been and have not accepted the view that peacekeeping is a failure unless negotiated settlements follow.   But they have been equally sensitive to the demonstrated willingness of the parties to negotiate and to the attitudes of those outside powers which have a direct interest.   In the case of UNFICYP, the apparent unwillingness of the parties to compromise sufficiently to bring about agreement and the clear absence of sufficient financial support for the operation have led to repeated expressions of doubt by Canada that the force has enduring value and of concern that only a few countries should bear the burden of peacekeeping risks and costs.

DISILLUSION?

A number of events in 1967-68 combined to bring about a review of the peacekeeping commitment.   The somewhat inglorious withdrawal of UNEF I in 1967, closely followed by renewed fighting between Israel and Egypt, led the government to question the decision of the secretary general not to consult the UN formally before agreeing to withdraw, and the opposition to raise questions about peacekeeping mandates. Two other operations were not going well.   In Vietnam, Canada appeared to some Canadians to be taking the American side and to others to be part of a cover for subversion and indirect aggression.   In Cyprus, there was political stalemate and few volunteers to pay the costs, which were absorbed in part by the troop contributors.   Canadian and other initiatives at the UN to put peacekeeping on a sound military and financial footing had failed.   In these circumstances, it was inevitable that many would question the likelihood of further demands on the UN to keep the peace and the capacity of the organization to respond.   Moreover, the image of Canada as "helpful fixer" was wearing thin.

Foreign policy for Canadians in 1970 and the "Defence White Paper" of 1971 appeared to reflect a change of heart. Terrorism at home drew attention to a more basic priority for the armed forces, which was put first in the following listing of their roles in the White Paper:

- the protection of Canada;

- the defense of North America in cooperation with U.S. forces;

- the fulfillment of such NATO commitments as may be agreed upon; and

> •   the performance of such international peacekeep-
>   ing roles as we may from time to time assume.

The assumption of Canada might look with suspicion on invitations to participate in new peacekeeping operations seemed to
be confirmed in January 1973 when the Secretary of State for
External Affairs outlined conditions for accepting any new
assignment in Vietnam. These included the prospect for
effectiveness of the operation expressed through its mandate,
the commitment of the parties to the terms of any agreement
and to the negotiation of a settlement, the existence of a
political authority which would assume responsibility for the
settlement as a whole and to which the peacekeepers would
report, freedom of movement, acceptability of the force and of
Canada to all the parties, and the fair sharing of costs.
Canada, in fact, agreed to participate in a new Vietnam
operation for sixty days but later withdrew when it became
clear that some of the conditions it had specified were not
being observed. (See David Cox, "The International Commission of Control and Supervision in Vietnam, 1973," chap. 13 in
this volume.)
    Only six months after Canada left Vietnam, it agreed to
participate in UNEF II. In explaining the decision to the
House of Commons, the Secretary of State for External Affairs
elaborated the conditions which he had listed earlier in the
year apropos of Vietnam. He contrasted the establishment of
UNEF II with UNFICYP and with UNEF I. He pointed out that
the cost of UNEF II would be shared among the members,
unlike UNFICYP, and that UNEF II (unlike UNEF I) had the
backing of four permanent members of the Security Council.
Moreover, its mandate was more clearly set out and could not
be changed without the concurrence of the Council. He
repeated the view that a cease-fire was not enough; it must
lead to political negotiations for a settlement. He expressed
hope that such negotiations would be more likely to take place
than had been the case in the past. He ended on another
characteristic Canadian note: "We consider that we have a
responsibility to the world community and to all the peoples of
the Middle East to do what we can to give them another chance
to achieve a peaceful settlement."
    In 1978, Canada agreed to participate in the United
Nations Interim Force in Lebanon. The commitment was more
modest in comparison to Canada's contributions to other UN
forces, but significant in the supply of a vital logistics
component, about 100 men, and was limited to six months.
These restrictions reflected an increasing strain on Canada's
military capacity to serve United Nations peacekeeping. The
total commitment of some 1,700 men actually on station plus
several hundred more in a back-up role was perhaps less of a
burden than the depletion of strength in special areas, espe-

cially signals. On the other hand, Canada's decision to accept even a limited commitment was continued evidence of a basically positive attitude to UN peacekeeping, despite its vicissitudes. Canada was serving her fourth term on the Security Council in 1978 and had taken part in efforts to establish the new force, the fourth to be introduced into the Middle East and the fourth to include a Canadian component.

THE FUTURE

Cross-border violence in southern Africa and in southeast Asia has not led to requests from the states concerned for UN peacekeeping assistance, although other states have proposed the establishment of UN forces in southern Africa. It is unclear at the time of writing whether such forces will be sent. In the meantime, one UN force, UNEF II, has been disbanded, and a non-UN force is to be established in the Sinai under the terms of the Camp David Accords following the Israeli withdrawal from the Sinai in April 1982. It seems safe to predict, however, that interstate violence and war will continue, and perhaps grow. As in the past, UN intervention will depend on whether consensus exists among the permanent members of the Security Council that the situation calls for intervention and that UN intervention is preferable to their own or to that of some other body. Where regional organizations exist, they are likely to be favored over the UN unless one of the parties, e.g., South Africa, does not belong to them. The prospects for UN peacekeeping are, therefore, likely to remain more or less what they are now - fairly certain in the Middle East, not unlikely in Africa, and unpredictable in Asia. It is notable that, apart from the region of the eastern Mediterranean, there is only one UN military presence still extant (on the Kashmir border in Pakistan).

If requests are made to Canada to participate in future operations, Canada's response will be governed in part by its military capabilities. These are now stretched very tight, especially in respect of specialists such as communications personnel. One infantry battalion might still be made available if a political decision were made to contribute; but, even so, it would not be unreasonable for Canada to ask the UN to release it from a current obligation if it were to accept a new commitment. The question of costs might be important in this respect; the extra expenses are more easily borne if the major contributors to the UN budget pay their share. Otherwise, much would depend on the exact circumstances of the operation, the nature of the mandate, the attitudes of Canada's allies, and the nature of the threat to peace.

The attitudes of the permanent members of the Security Council will be a key factor. Continuing disagreement between them on command, control, and financing of operations will act as a disincentive to further contributions by Canada, for even though UN forces may remain more or less viable, lack of strong political support in New York is a source of anxiety, especially at times of tension. It is unlikely, however, that in the near future great power rivalries will dissipate to the point of allowing such support. Improvisation and crisis bargaining may have to suffice, perhaps with the tacit acceptance of standard operating procedures. Despite these prospects, Canada may prefer the UN as a controlling framework to ad hoc and temporary arrangements which derive their authority from the parties alone, as was the case in Indochina, or to the substitution of other organizations, such as the Commonwealth, where there is limited, though significant experience of this kind of international cooperation.

The Canadian government is now undergoing a review of its peacekeeping policy. There are many demands placed on the armed forces establishment, particularly the current emphasis on upgrading its NATO commitment. However, in light of Canada's valued record, its membership in the Western Five which are negotiating the UN transitional arrangements for Namibia, and the statement of the Secretary of State for External Affairs, Mark MacGuigan, at the meeting of the Association of South Asian Nations to the effect that Canada would entertain a request for peacekeeping forces for a Kampuchea/Thailand operation, it appears that there will be no basic change in Canada's policy based on a careful assessment of each situation and the availability of the requisite military personnel. Having worked so long to strengthen the UN as an organization, Canada is not likely to abandon it in favor of "real" or even "ideal" worlds.

Finally, it may be that international agreements involving third party verification will offer new opportunities to the UN to monitor disputes in situations short of conflict. A treaty on the law of the sea, for example, could well lead to new means of dispute settlement. Outer space is another subject which will call for new thinking about management and control. Keeping the peace is a flexible concept. Soldiers in uniform are not necessarily an essential part of it. But the skills of the soldier/diplomat are bound to continue to be in demand. Canada will have the personnel to help satisfy some reasonable share of the demand, and will probably be inclined to do so if the UN provides the conditions for effective operating procedures and adequate political support.

NOTES

1. Speaking to the Political Committee of the Assembly on October 11, 1950, the Canadian delegate expressed the hope that the General Assembly might "provide the germ of an international force by making it possible to earmark national contingents for United Nations purposes." He referred to Canada's action in recruiting a Special Force and hoped that the great majority of United Nations members would take similar action. "If so and if we are again confronted with an emergency such as that which faced us last June, we who accept our obligations under the Charter and desire to do what we can to carry them out will be in a better position to make a speedy and effective contribution to the defeat of aggression." The debate on this subject resulted in the General Assembly Uniting for Peace Resolution 377 (v) of November 3, 1950.

2. See Albert Legault, "La contribution du Canada aux operations du maintien de la paix," paper presented to a joint seminar of the International Peace Academy and the Norman Paterson School of International Affairs, Ottawa, October 22, 1981.

3. Though dated, the basic issues of command and control are discussed in H. Wiseman, "Peacekeeping: Debut or Denouement?" CIIA Behind the Headlines, Vol. XXXI, Nos. 1-2, 1972.

6
Peacekeeping and Canadian Defense Policy: Ambivalence and Uncertainty
Rod B. Byers

Since the 1950s, peacekeeping has been acknowledged as a cornerstone of Canadian foreign and defense policies. The role has been officially designated as a priority for the Canadian Armed Forces (CAF); and, over the years, politicians, especially the late Lester Pearson, have vigorously advocated strengthening the international peacekeeping aspects of the United Nations. Canada has participated in all UN peacekeeping operations and has been one of a small minority of countries which has officially designed troops for such purposes. On the military side, the CAF have incorporated peacekeeping into their ethos, planning, training, equipment, and resource allocations. All these factors suggest a long-standing and serious commitment on the part of successive Canadian governments. While the reasons underlying this commitment are complex and numerous, it has often been argued that peacekeeping is a role that a middle power such as Canada can undertake in order to make a meaningful contribution to international peace and security.

The foregoing summary, while oversimplified and abbreviated, typifies the stereotype of the Canadian peacekeeping record.(1) On the surface, the overall record appears exemplary and, in many respects, the Canadian case can serve as a model for other states in the international system who wish to undertake the peacekeeping role. Yet this conclusion should only be drawn if it is understood that the Canadian experience has been fraught with uncertainty, ambivalence, and difficulty.

At the governmental level, the priority and importance attached to peacekeeping vis-a-vis other defense activities has, not surprisingly, been cyclical. Peacekeeping has served to fulfill a number of foreign policy objectives. Yet Canada's relationship to NATO and the defense of North America, for example, has remained either obscured or ignored. In terms of officially declared policy, the fortunes of peacekeeping have hit both the top and the bottom of defense priorities. While this may reflect the reality of international politics and the international environment, it could also reflect uncertainty and ambivalence in the formulation of the country's foreign and defense policy objectives.

Needless to say, a relationship exists between declaratory policy and the implementation of such policy by the CAF and the Department of External Affairs. In the case of peacekeeping, the shifts in policy emphasis have complicated planning, training, equipment purchases, resource allocation, and personnel requirements. From the perspective of the CAF, it should be remembered that the composition of the Canadian contribution has varied with each operation and that the government's offer to supply integrated military units has not been taken up by the UN. One result has been the cannibalization of military units in order to supply the required number of communication and logistics specialists. A by-product of this type of arrangement has been a partial loss of expertise and operational capability within the CAF land forces. Furthermore, it is not clear that senior military personnel attach the same degree of importance to peacekeeping as do their political masters.

These aspects of Canada's peacekeeping involvement are apparent to the close observer, but are not sufficiently understood or appreciated. This being the case, it is important to assess the Canadian record, taking into account the uncertainties, ambiguities, and difficulties of both policy and practice. Such an assessment should offer insights into future Canadian participation and possibly assist other states in their formulation of peacekeeping policy and practice so that they may avoid some of the pitfalls of the Canadian experience. In order to pursue this argument more fully, the Canadian experience will be assessed first from the viewpoint of the policy dimension, second in terms of the perceived utility of peacekeeping, and third in terms of its military implications.

THE POLICY DIMENSION

It is well known that peacekeeping emerged as a central instrument of Canadian foreign and defense policy after World War II. However, prior to the mid-1950s, the Canadian government had not clearly articulated which foreign policy objectives and interests were being served by peacekeeping; and no official government statement explicitly linked peacekeeping to other foreign and defense policy instruments.

Yet, in fairness to the Canadian government, it should be remembered that, in the immediate postwar era, peacekeeping was not a major concern as attention was first focused on collective security and subsequently on collective self-defense via NATO, once it became clear that the UN was unable to fulfill its collective security mandate. The contemporary regime of peacekeeping began to emerge only in early 1949 with the formation of the UN military observer group in India-Pakistan (UNMOGIP). Canada acceded to the UN request in the case of UNMOGIP but did so with minimum publicity and without declaring how participation related to Canadian foreign policy objectives. In fact, from 1949 through 1955, peace-keeping rated no mention in the annual reports of the defense department; and government policy remained unclear. During this period, the thrust of Canadian military activity focused primarily on NATO and participation in the Korean war. To some extent, the genesis of Canada's willingness to earmark and allocate military personnel for UN duty on a continuing basis can be traced to the Korean war, but this was within the context of the 1950 "Uniting for Peace" resolution of the UN General Assembly which was deemed to fall within the frame-work of collective security. Initially, therefore, peacekeeping was a limited and relatively unimportant aspect of postwar Canadian foreign policy, and it is probably correct to argue that "the policy of the Canadian government toward the peacekeeping initiatives of the United Nations can only be described as uninspired in the early 1950s."(2)

Despite the undifferentiated approach to early peace-keeping activities, successive Liberal governments, over time, attached increasing importance to the role as an instrument of Canadian foreign policy. Here, the preferences and impact of Lester Pearson, as Secretary of State for External Affairs, influenced the actions of the Liberal government; and, as early as 1954, a pattern of continued participation emerged as the norm. For example, despite reservations over possible participation in the International Commission for Supervision and Control (ICSC) in Indochina, it has been argued that "there never had been a moment's doubt that this was an obligation that Canada had to accept."(3) During this early period, however, it should be remembered that participation required few personnel and only limited resources. In other words, a capability factor to perform the role was never a serious consideration. Nevertheless, with active Canadian involvement in early UN operations and the ICSC, the Liberal government of the day should have formulated a policy per-spective which related peacekeeping to other defense roles and priorities. The lack of explicit objectives meant that Canadian participation in UNEF I in 1956 was undertaken without the benefit of a clear policy framework and with inadequate understanding of how large-scale participation would affect the future requirements and needs of the CAF. Unfortunately, UNEF I tended to become the "model" for Canadian peacekeeping activities and, for some time, constituted the norm for future operations. Yet, in actuality, Suez turned out to be the exception rather than the rule.(4)

After the 1957 general election, the Conservative government of John Diefenbaker made no immediate attempt to clarify the policy dimension. Observers generally argued that the Conservatives would be less receptive to peacekeeping than the Liberals, even though in principle all-party agreement had emerged with respect to Canadian participation in UNEF I. Yet, the Diefenbaker government responded positively when asked to participate in the 1958-59 Observation Force in Lebanon (UNOGIL); and it was during this period that Canada officially earmarked a military unit as a standby force for possible UN operations. Such actions were entirely consistent with past Liberal practice.

In 1959, the Conservatives made a limited attempt to specifically link military activities to broader foreign and defense policy objectives. Defence, 1959 stated that Canada would provide military forces for the defense of North America, for NATO in Europe and the North Atlantic, and for "the United Nations to assist that organization in attaining its peaceful aims." The annual report went on to outline the existing level of Canadian participation, but made no reference to future operations. Neither did the report explicitly address itself to the relationship between peacekeeping and the other major defense roles. Nevertheless, the Conservative government implied that NATO constituted the preeminent defense activity. This view remained consistent throughout the Diefenbaker era, despite a sizeable commitment to the Congo operation (ONUC) in 1960. On balance, the Conservatives agreed to participate in peacekeeping operations when the opportunity arose, but did not place particular emphasis on the role. It should be remembered, however, that the issue of nuclear weapons split the government and tended to push other foreign and defense issues into the background during the early 1960s.(5)

Prior to 1964, therefore, the lack of a clearly defined policy dimension for peacekeeping allowed Canadian participation to be interpreted from two rather different perspectives. One view held that peacekeeping could be perceived as a separate role in its own right to be pursued when the opportunity arose. Within this context, peacekeeping was accorded an unduly elevated status, almost a foreign policy objective, which enhanced Canada's stature within the international system. Alternatively, peacekeeping could be considered as one of a range of foreign policy instruments to be exercised as appropriate. In this case, it was considered less significant than the main defense commitments undertaken within the NATO and NORAD context. As a generalization, it could be argued that federal politicians tended to be motivated by the peacekeeping as "objective" perspective, while senior members of the armed forces were more concerned with matters of function and priority. Under these circumstances, it was not surprising that uncertainty from the policy perspective seemed the order of the day.

The Liberals formed the government after the 1963 general election, and it was widely assumed that Canada's foreign and defense houses would be put in order. On the defense side, the 1964 Defense White Paper(6) constituted an ambitious, and to that date most complete, attempt to articulate Canadian defense policy within the domestic and international environments, and then relate military roles to broader policy objectives. The white paper properly started with the premise that defense policy could not be divorced from foreign policy and listed three major objectives: "To preserve the peace by supporting collective defence measures to deter military aggression; to support Canadian foreign policy including that arising out of our participation in international organizations; and to provide for the protection and surveillance of our territory, our airspace and our coastal waters." In order to fulfill these objectives, the government agreed on the following set of priorities:

1. Forces for the direct protection of Canada which can be deployed as required.

2. Forces in-being as part of the deterrent in the European theatre.

3. Maritime forces in-being as a contribution to the deterrent.

4. Forces in-being for UN peacekeeping operations which would also be included in 1 above.

5. Reserve forces and mobilization potential.

Here, UN peacekeeping was ranked fourth, but then multi-tasked with forces allocated for the defense of Canada. The overall effect and impression was to upgrade peacekeeping in comparison to the priority allocated the role by the Conservatives.

The upgrading of peacekeeping was based, in good part, on the assumption that Third World "instability will probably continue in the decade ahead and called for containment measures which do not lend themselves to Great Power or Alliance action. The peacekeeping responsibilities devolving upon the United Nations can be expected to grow correspondingly."(7)   In general, the Pearson government adopted the view that instability existed in the international system, that deterrence should be maintained across the entire range of the force spectrum, and that Canada could make a meaningful contribution at the lower end of the spectrum.   Thus, the white paper claimed "it is essential that a nation's diplomacy be backed up by adequate and flexible military forces to permit participation in collective security and peacekeeping, and to be ready for crises should they arise."   Based on this set of factors, the white paper stated that "It is the policy of the government, in determining Canada's force structure for the balance of the decade, to build in maximum flexibility.   This will permit the disposition of the majority of our forces in Canada where they will be available for deployment in a variety of peacekeeping activities."   At the same time, however, the white paper clearly indicated that Canada's main defense contribution would continue to be collective self-defense via NATO.

On balance, the Pearson government adopted the view that the peacekeeping role complemented other military activities, including NATO.   Thus, the stated objective of reequipping the CAF in order to increase mobility and flex-ibility was considered compatible across the entire range of Canadian defense activities.   Major reequipment expenditures for the army were to produce a mobile force with an air-sea lift capability for immediate deployment outside Canada.   This objective dovetailed with the increased emphasis placed on peacekeeping and assumed a high degree of compatibility between existing NATO commitments and future peacekeeping operations.   Both government and senior military personnel seemed to share the view that compatibility between the two types of commitments could and should be maintained.(8) This, of course, was based on the premise that the CAF had sufficient manpower to fulfill NATO commitments and con-currently participate in peacekeeping operations.

For peacekeeping, the 1964 Defence White Paper repre-sented the high water mark in terms of declared government policy.   According to one observer: "The white paper is a milestone in the development of Canada's peacekeeping policies, not becuase it marks the beginning of a radically new policy, but because it indicates the importance that the government attaches to peacekeeping responsibilities and to the necessity to integrate defence and foreign policies."(9)   In more practical terms, the government set out a framework within which the defense department could undertake planning, training, and, to a lesser extent, equipment acquisition as well as budgetary allocations.   This clearly indicated that, in policy terms, peacekeeping was deemed as one instrument, albeit one of the more important instruments, to support the country's foreign and defense policy objectives.   Needless to say, in

principle, the articulation of the relationship between objectives and goals constituted a major step in the right
direction.

If 1964 represented a peak, then 1971 represented official
disillusionment over the utility and future prospects for
peacekeeping. By this time, Mr. Trudeau had been prime
minister for three years and, to some extent, his personal
stamp had been placed on the country's foreign and defense
policies. At the same time, Defence in the 70s(10) could, with
justification, give examples which pointed to the demise of
peacekeeping. The rather ignominious withdrawal of UNEF I
from the Middle East in 1967, the inability of the UN to reach
an agreement on a general peacekeeping formula as well as the
problems of financing peacekeeping operations, the ineffectiveness of the ICSC in Indochina, and the presumed reduced
future demand for peacekeeping represented factors which
caused the government to reevaluate the country's commitment
to the role. In addition, the inability to move from peacekeeping to peacemaking contributed to a sense of frustration in
government circles. The 1971 white paper argued that "the
scope for useful and effective peacekeeping activities now
appears more modest than it did earlier, despite the persistence of widespread violence in many parts of the world."
Based on this set of premises, peacekeeping was deemed the
least important defense priority as the Trudeau administration
allocated greater priority to the protection of Canadian
sovereignty, to the defense of North America, and to NATO in
that order. In effect, this set of declared priorities
reallocated the peacekeeping role to its pre-1964 position
vis-a-vis other defense activities. Yet, the underlying basis
of mobility and flexibility which had been outlined in the 1964
white paper was retained as the government stated its intention "to maintain within feasible limits a general purpose
combat capability of high professional standard within the
Armed Forces, and to keep available the widest possible choice
of options for responding to unforeseen international developments." More specifically, the commitment for a standby
peacekeeping battalion was retained and personnel continued to
receive training for such operations. In addition, the
necessary linkages between peacekeeping and other defense
roles remained a key element in the 1971 white paper. That
is, the practice of relating defense activities to broader
foreign and defense policy objectives remained central.

Events since the publication of Defence in the 70s have
tended to contradict the premises of the white paper as the
scope for peacekeeping operations expanded during the
mid-1970s. Canadian military personnel became involved with
the abortive and short-lived ICSC in Vietnam, with UNEF II,
UN Disengagement Observer Force (UNDOF) and UN Interim
Force in Lebanon (UNIFIL) on the Syrian-Israeli border. This

rather abrupt turn of events had to be taken into account when the defense department undertook its force structure review in late 1974. Upon completion of the first phase of the review in November 1975, the defense minister reaffirmed in the House of Commons the priorities of the 1971 White Paper and stated that "the structure of the Canadian Armed Forces will provide up to 2,000 personnel to be available for United Nations peacekeeping purposes at any one time."(11)

In effect, the demand for peacekeeping during the mid-1970s meant that the Trudeau administration remained as, or even more, committed than had the Pearson government during the 1960s. From the policy perspective, the major difference was one of emphasis as the Trudeau government consistently maintained a more skeptical attitude toward peacekeeping. This clearly affected perceptions of the utility of peace-keeping. Here it could be argued that the policy was clear, the practice was clear, but the outcome was one of official ambivalence. Increasingly, therefore, during the late 1970s, members of the Trudeau administration adopted the position of reluctant participation - particularly in the case of Cyprus. Statements by spokesmen for the government of Joe Clark indicated that the Conservatives would retain the general policy posture of the Trudeau government on the question of peacekeeping even though no definitive position had been adopted by the end of 1979. To some extent, the current peacekeeping policy of the Canadian government seems to have come full circle to that of the early 1950s. Consequently, it became incumbent upon the newly elected Conservative govern-ment to clearly formulate its policy posture regarding the peacekeeping role.

But before that could happen, the Clark government was defeated and Trudeau returned to power. It was this government, which, somewhat reluctantly, acceded to the secretary-general's "insistence" that Canada contribute to UNIFIL - despite misgivings about the viability of the oper-ation and the strain on logistical manpower in the CAF.

On an informal basis in the summer of 1981, the United States "sounded out" Canadian attitude toward participation in the non-UN multilateral peacekeeping force in the Sinai following the final and complete Israeli withdrawal from Egyptian territory according to the Camp David Accords. Middle East foreign policy concerns and the non-UN character of the operation strongly inclined Canada not to participate; however, because of the "informality" of the request, no formal refusal was made.

THE UTILITY OF PEACEKEEPING

The degree of uncertainty and ambivalence toward peacekeeping from the policy perspective can, in part, be explained by
the difficulties which face any nation-state in terms of the
interface between the formulation of declared policy and its
actual implementation.   Obviously, the policy process and
conflicting priorities - both domestic and external - have had
an impact on the ability of successive governments to
implement declared policy.   In the sphere of international
relations, however, the major variables which affect policy
implementation are often outside the control of individual
governmental decision makers. Peacekeeping is a good example
of this situation.   Obviously, Canada and other peacekeepers
have a considerable degree of latitude concerning the first
order decision - that is, whether or not to agree in principle
with the peacekeeping role as a foreign policy instrument.   In
terms of first order decisions, the policy discussion can be
explicitly (and possibly rationally) articulated vis-a-vis other
foreign and defense activities.   Both the Pearson and Trudeau
administrations attempted this process.   Yet, the second order
decisions, including the terms of commitment to a specific
operation, tend to be outside the control of the peacekeeper.
Not surprisingly, therefore, the policy dimension becomes
difficult, at times impossible, to implement as originally
anticipated.   Under these circumstances, skepticism toward the
utility of peacekeeping increases.   Within this context,
Canadian views could express common themes and concerns
perceived by other states that undertake a peacekeeping role.
       One set of factors which have adversely affected per-
ceptions of utility stems from the inability of members of the
UN to reach agreement on the establishment, administration,
command and control, and financing of peacekeeping operations. The ad hoc approach forced upon the secretary-general
and the ambiguous nature of his powers in this area along with
disagreement among members of the Security Council have
complicated most peacekeeping operations.   The inability of the
Special Committee on Peacekeeping Operations (the Committee
of 33), set up in 1965, to establish principles and guidelines
for peacekeeping reflects the inherent difficulties which exist
within the UN.   These factors have been discussed at length
from a Canadian perspective by academics, by the House of
Commons Standing Committee on External Affairs and Defense
(SCEAND), and in Canadian submissions to the Committee of
33, which all indicate, in varying degrees, dissatisfaction and
disillusionment with the UN situation.(12) However, it should
be remembered that UN difficulties have been a continuing
feature of the organization when security issues have arisen.
This has been the case for collective security in Korea, peace

observation missions, or larger peacekeeping operations in the Congo and Middle East. Obviously, the utility of peacekeeping would be enhanced if the UN resolved some of the problems which continually arise. Yet, peacekeeping operations have been mounted despite opposition from certain members of the UN. Thus, while each operation has been undertaken within a context of uncertainty at the UN level, this, by itself, has not been crucial in terms of Canadian support or disillusionment.

States that have expressed a willingness to undertake the peacekeeping role have come to realize that they do so with very little control over when, where, or how they will be called upon.(13) The fulfillment of the role is dictated by events and actors which leave the peacekeeper in a reactive rather than an initiatory position. The terms and conditions of involvement depend in part upon the superpowers and in part upon the participants to the conflict. This is to point to the obvious. Yet, the implications for Canada of Nasser's rejection of the Queen's Own Rifles for UNEF I were not sufficiently appreciated by either the Diefenbaker or the Pearson governments. It was only after the sudden rejection of the UN force in 1967 that the Pearson government realistically appreciated the inability of the peacekeeper to influence the outcome of such operations. In many respects, this constituted a rude and sudden shock to Canadian officials and members of the attentive public.

In addition, as a result of superpower politics, other operational conditions circumscribe the role of the peacekeeper. In 1954, Canada joined the three-member Indochina commission of the ICSC as a surrogate of the West, and while government spokesmen played down this criterion, it remained a central consideration (see chap. 13 by David Cox in this volume). This emerged even more clearly with the formation of the short-lived ICCS in Vietnam. With the formation of UNEF II in 1973, the concept of "balance" between NATO and Warsaw Pact members established a new precedent within the UN context. Here, Canada clearly represented NATO while Poland represented the Warsaw Pact. In this particular instance, cooperation between the Canadian and Polish contingents were relatively effective. Yet, the precedent adds a further complicating factor for future UN operations. These examples indicate the extent to which the superpowers have affected the utility of peacekeeping irrespective of the views and wishes of those states that explicitly relate their foreign and defense policies to the peacekeeping role.

These factors accounted, at least in part, for the increased circumspection adopted by the Trudeau government on the peacekeeping front. Defence in the 70s referred to operations which have "been severely hampered by inadequate terms of reference and by a lack of co-operation on the part of those involved. Other detrimental factors have been the absence of political support by some of the great powers, and insufficient logistic and financial resources." Consequently, in the future, "the major factor affecting Government's decision [to participate] would be the existence of realistic terms of reference. They would have to reflect a consensus by all parties on the purposes which the operation was intended to serve and the manner in which to discharge its responsibilities." The Trudeau government attempted to implement these principles in the case of ICCS participation. Despite the best of intentions, only one of four conditions was observed.(14) This experience served to increase Canadian disillusionment, even though useful functions were performed by participation. In part, Canada's role should have improved relations with the United States, but one suspects that the memory of Washington officials is rather short-lived.

Based on these considerations, the reader could be forgiven if the conclusion were drawn that Canadian decision makers were ready to forego the peacekeeping role. Yet this is not the case. Data collected in 1975-76 via the Canadian International Image Study (CIIS) indicated that the Canadian Foreign Policy Elite (CFPE), composed of some 251 federal politicians, officials, and academics, almost unanimously (97.5 percent) supported continued participation in peacekeeping operations.(15) In fact, the degree of support for peacekeeping was more extensive than support for NATO (92.5 percent) or for NORAD (85.9 percent). Furthermore, when asked to rank order ten possible defense roles for Canada, the CFPE allocated the top position to peacekeeping ahead of sovereignty, surveillance, NATO, and NORAD to name the most obvious. In other words, on the surface, the Canadian commitment appeared deep-rooted. This did not mean, however, that Canada should become involved in all peacekeeping operations as only 13.2 percent of the CFPE supported the proposition that Canada should automatically volunteer troops whenever the UN establishes a peacekeeping operation. Thus, while support in principle exists, this latter finding indicated that a certain sense of caution pervaded the Canadian foreign policy community.

Nevertheless, there would appear to be a real dichotomy or almost schizophrenia in Canada concerning the utility of peacekeeping. On the one hand, the Trudeau government officially downgraded the role as an instrument of Canadian foreign and defense policies, and repeatedly questioned its utility. The Conservative government of Joe Clark adopted a similar posture. On the other hand, members of the foreign policy community almost unanimously supported continuation of the role. Clearly, then, it becomes essential to try to explain this seemingly anomalous situation.

Perceptions of utility have, in part, been a function of the extent to which operations contributed to system and subsystem stability, to conflict avoidance between the major world powers (especially the superpowers) and, to conflict management at the regional subsystem level. The linkages among these factors are obvious in the sense that the second and third clearly enhance stability at the system and subsystem levels. Not surprisingly, therefore, the CFPE, when asked to explain their support for Canadian participation, attached greater importance to the stability rationale (nearly one-third of the respondents) than to any other single factor. Going beyond this general response category, however, only a small number (2.6 percent) specifically referred to conflict avoidance, and conflict management did not emerge as a distinct category for the decision makers. This finding was rather surprising as the conventional wisdom contained in the literature cites numerous references to the linkage between peacekeeping and conflict avoidance.(16) Furthermore, Canadian politicians have referred to this rationale on any number of occasions. For example, Lester Pearson argued that Canada's vital interest in the 1956 Suez crisis was to reduce tension among traditional allies. Without UNEF I, it was feared that the conflict would escalate into a broader military confrontation. Similarly, the deployment of UN forces in the Congo helped to limit the extent of superpower involvement. Pearson claimed that countries such as Canada "are and will remain the backbone of a collective effort to keep the peace as long as there is fear and suspicion between the great power blocs."(17) The lack of response on behalf of the Canadian foreign policy community to this aspect of peacekeeping (conflict avoidance) suggests that it is no longer (if it ever was) deemed sufficient cause for Canadian participation.

Since peacekeeping forces are normally deployed after the outbreak of hostilities, the contribution to conflict avoidance at the subsystem level is severely limited; but the conflict management aspect has been a continuing justification for the peacekeeping role. For Canada, the 1964 Defence White Paper referred to problems in the Third World and argued that "instability will probably continue in the decade ahead and call for containment measures which do not lend themselves to Great Power Alliance. The peacekeeping responsibilities devolving upon the United Nations can be expected to grow correspondingly." The 1970 peacekeeping report of SCEAND to the House of Commons agreed: "Properly effective peacekeeping activity will be of enormous value in defusing difficult security crises, in providing time for mediation and settlement efforts, in establishing the facts in confused situations and - above all - in reducing the chances of superpower confrontation and the dangers of escalation."(18) While the Trudeau government tended to be less enthusiastic, the 1971 White Paper employed much the same rationale as it argued that peacekeeping "helps to prevent the outbreak or spread of

hostilities in other areas of tension, so that underlying
political problems can be settled through negotiation or a
process of accommodation, and so that the probability of Great
Power conflict is minimized."

The arguments supporting the conflict avoidance function
are fairly persuasive, but critics have rightfully pointed out
that the conflict management function, while introducing an
element of greater stability into a crisis situation, all too often
reinforces the status quo - political and/or territorial - and
thus draws out the peacekeeping role: "All too often the
negotiations never took place or got nowhere. Peacemaking
almost never followed peacekeeping. The result was a decay
of world morale, a lessening of faith in the UN. The disillusionment was felt in Canada, too. Suez 1956 had stirred
hope, but Suez 1967 destroyed it. Suddenly Canadians began
to question why peace had not followed peacekeeping. . . . A
sense of futility was very sharp."(19) The mid-1974 outbreak
of hostilities in Cyprus contributed to a hardening Canadian
position on the question of utility. In his September 1974
address to the General Assembly,(20) the Minister for External
Affairs claimed that "fighting has taken place on an unprecedented scale because the long-smouldering political problem
remained unresolved. Moreover, it has been demonstrated
once again in Cyprus that without the agreement and cooperation of the disputants, the constructive role of a
peacekeeping force is severely circumscribed." On the more
general issue of participation in future operations the Minister
pointed out that "Canadians are today becoming less inclined to
accept in an unquestioning way the burden of participation.
Their concern springs mainly from the fact that peacekeeping
endeavours often seem to do no more than perpetuate an
uneasy status quo. . . . It must be accompanied by a parallel
effort on the political level, especially by the parties most
directly concerned, to convert the temporary peace . . . into
something more durable. If this is not done . . . governments will be less willing to respond to future requests for
troops." This view has been increasingly shared within
Ottawa circles and only a small minority (3.9 percent) of the
CFPE mentioned the peacemaking function. While in opposition
spokesman for the Conservatives urged the Liberals to withdraw from Cyprus unless there was some progress towards a
peaceful resolution of the conflict. This view has also been
expressed by the newly appointed Conservative Minister of
Defence and the Clark government could be laying the ground-
work for withdrawal. Should a UN peacekeeping operation be
established with a Canadian contingent in Namibia then the
pressure to opt out of Cyprus would be substantially increased. There are reasonable grounds to argue that fifteen
years in one operation is long enough. If this should occur,
however, it should not be interpreted as an end to the
Canadian peacekeeping role.(21)

Yet unilateral withdrawal from an operation such as Cyprus would raise the question of how the action would be perceived by other actors in the international system. After all, if Canada acquired an "opting-out" reputation there would be greater hesitancy to make an initial request in the case of future operations. But, within this context, withdrawal from the ICCS may have raised some doubts in the international community. Withdrawal from Cyprus would certainly add to this particular problem. If the Trudeau government decided to cut back on Canada's commitment to peacekeeping, then the Cyprus route makes some sense from the narrow perspective of national self-interest. Yet, there could be repercussions in terms of Canadian reliability and credibility in the eyes of some UN members; and, if withdrawal were later linked to further serious problems on the southern flank of NATO, Canada's position within the Western alliance could be undermined.

The reliability factor should not be dismissed out of hand, as nearly one-quarter of the CFPE supported participation on the grounds that Canada is perceived by other actors as possessing the necessary foreign policy attributes to perform this particular role. Thus, Canadian reliability, credibility, detachment, neutrality, and pragmatism emerged as attributes which enhanced the country's peacekeeping ability. Here, the argument becomes somewhat circular as these terms are perceived important because Canada has actively participated and done so in a reliable manner. Should the opting out and/or nonparticipatory routes be adopted, then this set of factors would clearly be less significant in the eyes of other states in the international community and thus no longer constitute cause for Canada to maintain the peacekeeping role. It might be pointed out, however, that in international politics linkages generally exist between various components of a state's foreign policy posture and positive aspects of that posture should not be jeopardized without due cause.(22)

Having made this observation, however, it should be pointed out that Canadian decision makers do not attach a great deal of importance to national self-interest factors when expressing support for peacekeeping. In the case of both NATO and NORAD, self-interest factors were considered far more significant than in the case of peacekeeping. Only a small minority referred to peacekeeping as augmenting Canada's prestige (7.8 percent), international role (7.8 percent), and benefits to the CAF (5.2 percent). Indirectly, of course, positive foreign policy attributes are beneficial to Canada, but self-perceptions of attributes supposedly held by others hardly constitute national self-interest criteria. Thus, from the perspective of most Canadian decision makers, participation in peacekeeping operations is not particularly relevant in terms of direct self-interest. That is, the tangible benefits to Canada and to Canada's role and position in the international system are not explicitly linked to continued support for peacekeeping. This suggests that the role, despite its first-order ranking in terms of preference for defense commitments, could be downgraded without adversely affecting Canadian self-interest.

In part, the utility of peacekeeping can be linked to the "voluntarist" component of Canadian foreign policy.(23) That is, Canada participates in peacekeeping out of a sense of responsibility to the international community, and actions in this policy sphere constitute an "ought" for the policymaker. Thus, over one in ten (13.0 percent) members of the CFPE argued that there is a "need" for peacekeeping in the international system, while an almost equal number (12.5 percent) stated that Canada has an obligation to participate. When coupled with those respondents who indicated that it is important to maintain the UN as an organization and support its objectives (7.8 percent) and that the moral factor should be taken into account (5.2 percent), the voluntarist rationale for peacekeeping emerged as quite significant. Unfortunately, the altruistic component of a state's foreign policy can often be circumscribed by events beyond its control. In other words, it is laudable to justify the utility of peacekeeping from such a perspective but, should the circumstances which caused altruism to become a factor alter, this particular rationale could dissipate rather quickly. Here, the continued decline of the perceived viability of the UN as an organization coupled with the increasing lack of sympathy toward various aspects of Third World politics could have a spill-over into the peacekeeping sphere.

On balance, therefore, Canadian rationales regarding the utility of peacekeeping indicate two rather different trends. On the one hand, declared government policy and statements have, particularly during the 1970s, called into question the role of peacekeeping as a central foreign policy instrument in spite of continued participation. On the other hand, support for peacekeeping would appear to be solidly entrenched among members of the foreign policy community. Yet, reasons for support tend to be in the sphere of intangibles (voluntarism, perceived attributes) rather than more tangible factors (self-interest). There are two exceptions. The first is that of system and subsystem stability. As long as peacekeeping is perceived as making a contribution to international stability, its utility will be enhanced - provided there is also progress in terms of peacemaking. For the most part, this has not occurred - particularly in Cyprus. The second exception involves the military dimension and the extent to which the CAF has the capability to undertake the role. It is to this last set of considerations that we now turn.

THE MILITARY DIMENSION

The military dimension is directly and indirectly affected by both the policy dimension and perceptions of the utility of peacekeeping. Policy objectives, statements, and priorities require translation into specific commitments, force levels, equipment, and training. Indirectly, the policy dimension affects the Canadian armed forces in terms of military professionalism, the relationship between defense roles, and multi-tasking. If the policy dimension is unclear or a low priority is attached to peacekeeping, coupled with a sense that the utility is questionable, then the emphasis placed on the military dimension by the armed forces is bound to be circumscribed. If the opposite conditions exist, then the degree of emphasis from the military perspective is bound to be considerably higher. The latter circumstances existed during the middle and late 1960s when peacekeeping was given a high profile and considerable attention. During this period, a number of military uncertainties remained beyond Canada's control, but these did not affect Canadian support for the role. However, during the 1970s and into the 1980s, a combination of the change in defense priorities and increased doubts regarding the utility of peacekeeping led to greater uncertainty within the CAF.

One of the more important military concerns is the question of professionalism(24) – that is, the extent to which peacekeeping is considered to be, or can be equated with, the raison d'etre of the military establishment. As in most Western industrialized countries, a study by the CAF on professionalism(25) argued that "the raison d'etre of a professional military force is to apply, or to threaten to apply force on behalf of the state and at the lawful direction of the duly constituted government of the nation." The report went on to state that this function "quite rightly dominates the thinking and outlook of the military profession" and "is reflected in its development processes . . . and leadership style." Defence in the 70s had adopted the same philosophy with its objective to retain a high general purpose combat capability.

Yet, the relationship between roles and commitments on the one hand, and the application of force on the other must be appreciated by both politicians and military personnel. The existing ethos of the CAF raises a problem as the roles assigned by the government are of three types: military, quasimilitary, and nonmilitary. For military roles, the potential application of force constitutes the primary purpose of the task via NATO and NORAD commitments. Quasimilitary roles may require the application of force, but the potential application is normally not central to the task. Here, surveillance and control of territory, air space, and coastal waters, as well as internal security constitute the most appropriate examples. Nonmilitary roles do not require the application of force and can be undertaken by civilian agencies and departments, e.g., disaster relief, pollution control and cleanup, and national development projects. In terms of these three role types, only the first clearly corresponds with the core of the prevailing professional military ethos.

Even though the CAF has undertaken quasimilitary and nonmilitary tasks, they have not been allocated the same degree of precedence as military tasks, i.e., they are undertaken with a certain degree of ambivalence. While the CFPE as a whole ranked quasimilitary roles as being the most significant (peacekeeping, sovereignty, and surveillance), respondents from the Department of National Defence (DND) ranked traditional military roles (NATO and NORAD) as being most important. The quasimilitary role of sovereignty was ranked third by DND respondents followed by the need to counter the Soviet military threat. The implications of this pattern are several. First of all, it contrasts rather sharply with the order of priorities laid down in the 1971 white paper. Second, preferences for resource allocation - equipment, personnel, training, etc. - within the CAF would emphasize NATO and NORAD and downplay requirements for quasimilitary roles. Third, there could be disagreement between DND and other departments in Ottawa when foreign policy issues arise which involve military considerations.

Obviously, attitudes toward peacekeeping are affected by the value system of the military. Nevertheless, it was surprising that DND respondents in the CIIS of 1975-1976 ranked peacekeeping as the fourth least important defense commitment, i.e., seventh out of ten. In part, the deviation from the overall CFPE pattern could be explained by the fact that peacekeeping normally does not require the application of force. The operations in Cyprus, the Middle East, the Congo, and Vietnam could all be classified as quasimilitary, while the peace observation missions could probably be more correctly labeled as nonmilitary. The fact that peacekeeping units make no concerted attempt to match the armament and force levels of the disputants in an interposition situation only further emphasizes the quasimilitary nature of the role. While various Canadian peacekeeping units have had to resort to the use of force on occasion, the primary emphasis has been, and is, on interposition between opposing sides in a conflict.

It could be argued that the Congo operation deviated from the norm in that UN forces became involved during various parts of the operation in war-fighting situations. This could have accounted for the brief employment of the term "peace-restoring" during the late 1960s. At that time, the Chief of Defence Staff explained to SCEAND that the philosophy behind Mobile Command was to provide a force which could operate independently within a peace-restoring context.(26) If implemented, this would have fundamentally altered the philosophy behind peacekeeping as the application of force would have become more central to any operation. In reality, of course, this concept was never feasible and, for the most part, constituted wishful thinking on the part of some senior defense planners. Yet, this example was important as the desire to move in the direction of peace restoration indicated ambivalence within certain sectors of the CAF.

There must be a wider range of factors, however, which can explain the low rank allocated to the peacekeeping role by some members of the CAF. A related issue is the extent to which peacekeeping can be considered as complementary to other defense roles. In the main, senior military personnel have adopted the view that peacekeeping can be successfully undertaken by units and personnel expected to fulfill more traditional military roles. For example, a positive spin-off is deemed to result from the training and experience gained within the NATO context which then allows Canadian personnel to be peacekeepers par excellence. The SCEAND report on peacekeeping accepted this view and noted that "the normal professional training and discipline of Canada's regular forces accounts for the effectiveness they have shown in past operations."(27) To some extent, this claim has been substantiated by the Canadian experience. Yet constraints on the use of force, the type of equipment and arms, the operational environment of the small squad, the need to exercise personal diplomacy, and the need for noncommissioned personnel to make rapid, on-the-spot decisions tends to be at variance with some aspects of "normal" professional training for military type roles. The operational environment of NATO's central front is rather different than that of the Green Line in Cyprus - with the exception of the Canadian defense of the airport at Nicosia during the attack by Turkey in 1974.

In other words, the peacekeeper has to be aware of the nature of the operational environment and realize that the skills and training can differ from the traditional norm of military professionalism. In some instances, military units and personnel who are tasked with an internal security role by their government may, in the first instance, more effectively perform the peacekeeping role. This being the case, the Canadian example may not necessarily be applicable to other military establishments.

Other aspects of the complementary issue involve the organizational and structural implications of the relationship between peacekeeping and other defense roles. The prevailing view within the CAF has generally supported the argument that armed forces should be structured to perform military tasks and then adapted as necessary to meet the contingencies of peacekeeping. This position was most clearly articulated in

1967 by the then retired Chief of Defence Staff: "I do not believe we should ever design forces for peacekeeping only. . . . We should design forces for war as we know it and then adapt them to the peacekeeping role or any other role that happens to fall to them in line with Canada's National Policy."(28) During the debate over unification of the CAF in the late 1960s, some senior retired military personnel expressed the fear that the Liberal government's emphasis on peacekeeping would adversely affect the CAF's capability to adequately fulfill the NATO and NORAD commitments.(29) While this view was rejected by government spokesmen, the discussion served to emphasize that peacekeeping can be perceived as a competitor to traditional military roles and that any serious attempt to upgrade peacekeeping at the expense of NATO and NORAD would be opposed by segments within the CAF.

To some extent, wariness regarding peacekeeping can be linked to the more practical aspects of the military dimension. In light of concurrent commitments, especially NATO, and multitasking, it must be asked whether the CAF have the necessary force levels and capability to adequately undertake peacekeeping operations. On the surface, in light of past and current contributions, this might appear as a nonissue, yet it should not be dismissed out of hand. On the positive side, nearly one quarter (22.6 percent) of the CFPE supported continuing Canadian participation on the grounds that the CAF had the capability to successfully fulfill the role. For this segment of the foreign policy community, the capability factor emerged as most significant. But were they being overly optimistic?

As a generalization, the larger the size of a country's armed forces the more likely it is that peacekeeping can be undertaken without adversely affecting the capability to carry out other commitments and, at the same time, retain a reserve capability. In the Canadian case, force levels have steadily declined from 126,000 in 1962 to 80,000 in 1981. Over this period, the decline of some 37 percent has been quite drastic and, while all elements of the CAF have been affected, the reduction for the land environment (army) has been of a greater magnitude than on the air and sea side. For example, in 1962, with a force level of 52,000, the army constituted 41 percent of the total military manpower. By 1978, with 29,300 personnel, the land environment had dropped to 36.6 percent of the CAF. In 1977, the Liberal government announced that the CAF would be increased by some 4,700 personnel to bring them to the 1974 level of 83,000. Yet, most of the increase was to be allocated to the support arms, and the infantry component would be limited to an increase of some 600 personnel. Because of budgetary restrictions, the Trudeau administration subsequently slowed down the announced aug-

mentation program, and it remains unclear when, if at all, the
83,000 figure will be reached.

The major question for the Canadian government is
whether the existing force ceilings are sufficient to allow the
armed forces to effectively undertake and fulfill commitments
negotiated by the government. For example, in 1964, during
the debate over further reductions, the Chief of Defence Staff
argued that "we can meet our commitments within our present
ceiling of 83,970. I am equally sure that we cannot do it with
less. . . . My position is that unless we eliminate a major
commitment, we cannot do our job with fewer people."(30)

The overall situation for the land environment has been
complicated by peacekeeping commitments as deployment levels
have varied considerably over time. In 1962, approximately
1,140 personnel were assigned to such duties. By 1966,
deployment had increased to some 1,800 personnel and then
declined to 460 by 1970. By 1974, the level had risen to some
1,700 and this figure remained constant into 1979. Thus, as
overall army force levels declined during the 1970s, the
commitment to peacekeeping increased. With the disbandment
of UNEF II, some 880 Canadian personnel became available for
reassignment to other duties which has eased some of the
personnel problems. As of 1982 some 756 personnel were
assigned to peacekeeping duties. On balance, however, the
extensive involvement coupled with uncertainty in the policy
dimension has contributed to military ambivalence - particularly
as fewer personnel have been available for military type tasks.
To help overcome this situation, reserve personnel have been
employed on peacekeeping operations, but this only constitutes
a stop-gap solution.(31)

In order to cope with the variety of requirements and
commitments, multitasking has become the norm, and nearly all
segments of the CAF are now multitasked.(32) In principle,
the concept constitutes a rational approach to defense planning
and resource utilization. Furthermore, most military establishments rely upon multitasking in order to meet the range of
commitments which support a country's domestic and foreign
policies. However, should multitasking become excessive or be
based on insufficient force levels, then the capability to carry
out primary tasks will be adversely affected.

The CAF is currently at a force level and posture which
cannot realistically meet the extent of multitasking deemed
necessary by government requirements should a crisis occur.
This issue was extensively reviewed in the mid-1970s within
the context of the force structure review which utilized the
roles of the 1971 defense white paper. Some 55 tasks were
identified, and apparently all of these were retained for
planning purposes. A sense of the extent of multitasking was
ascertained from the annual reports of the defense department.
For example, the 1974 annual report outlined approximately 24

separate tasks which were assigned to the six commands in
Canada with a high of eight being assigned to maritime
command. Even though some tasks are more important than
others, conflicting demands on manpower and equipment can
hardly be avoided. In the case of mobile command, in 1976,
some 5,000 of 17,600 personnel were attached to secondary
units, including headquarters and training centers, while the
three major combat groups accounted for only 12,600 personnel. Even though mobile command was restructured during
1977, the situation, as of 1982, has not been appreciably
altered.

Most of the multitasking for the land element is the
responsibility of the two combat groups and the Special Service
Force. At present, the land element is multitasked in five
areas: NATO, Canada/U.S. Defense (CANUS), peacekeeping,
internal security, and national development. Within these five
areas, multitasking can be either explicitly specific commitments, as in the case of NATO and peacekeeping, or
unspecified commitments, as in the other three areas. In the
former category, approximately 4,500 personnel are currently
serving overseas in Europe or on peacekeeping assignments,
that is, nearly one-sixth of the total land force. Furthermore,
the government has explicitly committed a Canadian air-sea
transportable combat group to the NATO flanks. The
remaining explicit commitment is to provide up to 2,000
personnel for peacekeeping. Taken together, these commitments represent a further 12 percent of the total land force;
and, if drawn primarily from mobile command, the manpower
problem would become even more acute. In other words,
multitasking has serious implications for the land environment.
If the overseas commitments are called upon at the same time
as a major unspecified commitment turns into a specific
commitment, only two-thirds of the total land element remains
available as a manpower pool.(33) Since the major combat arms
constitute only one-third of the land environment, the
difficulties of coping with multitasking become obvious. While
peacekeeping is not a direct cause of this problem, it is part
of the overall context, and the uncertainty of the demand for
peacekeeping forces contributes to ambivalence regarding its
role.

The ad hoc approach to the formation, composition,
financing, and operationalization of peacekeeping operations
has complicated defense planning. Some of these problems
have been discussed at length elsewhere in this volume and
partially explain the disenchantment in both the policy dimension and the practical area of peacekeeping. However, the
Canadian case deserves greater elaboration as a serious gap
has existed between the type of prior commitment recommended
by Canadian governments and the final composition of Canadian
peacekeeping contributions. Dating back to UNEF I, the

Pearson government had offered a major operational combat unit to the UN as the preferred contribution. In every case except Cyprus, such offers have been rejected with the result that the Canadian land forces for UN operations have been drawn from administrative and support personnel. The 1964 defense white paper noted this situation as "requests from the Secretary-General for assistance have been for specialists of various kinds, mainly from the Canadian army and the RCAF." However, the white paper later stated that training for peace-keeping would still be undertaken at the unit level even though the possibility of this type of deployment remained remote.

The 1971 defense white paper adopted much the same position as the government continued to commit a battalion group for UN standby even though it seemed unlikely to be deployed. This was the situation in October 1973 with the offer to commit the Canadian airborne regiment, in the Middle East. This contribution was not deemed essential by the secretary-general who responded with the request for a logistics component - air support, transport, communications, and other administrative and support personnel. In order to comply with this request, the CAF had to draw personnel from a variety of units and commands. This resulted in a diminution of support elements within the combat groups, as well as a reduction of administrative personnel elsewhere in the system. This type of situation served as a double source of frustration for the CAF. First, most personnel realized that peacekeeping training at the unit level would not result in unit deployment even though it could serve as a useful function for contingency purposes. Second, the major support units tend to be cannibalized which, in turn, would adversely affect the overall combat effectiveness of the major units should they be involved in other multitasking situations. Even without active deployment, the normal training and operational effectiveness of combat groups tends to be impaired as key support and administrative personnel are serving elsewhere. On balance, therefore, there are solid grounds for being concerned with the military dimension.

THE CANADIAN EXPERIENCE: SOME CONCLUDING OBSERVATIONS

This chapter has focused exclusively on the Canadian example and thus has been primarily directed at the Canadian policy-maker with the view of clarifying certain aspects of current policy and practice. Nevertheless, the Canadian case can be considered illustrative of the types of problems faced by most nation-states that have undertaken the role of peacekeeper.

Policymakers in other states may consider it of some value to assess their situation and aspirations in light of the Canadian experience.

In terms of the policy dimension, at least four observations come to mind: (1) The articulation of policy and policy objectives lagged behind the practice of peacekeeping, i.e., while Canada participated in its first peacekeeping operation in 1949, the policy implications were not clearly and officially spelled out until the 1964 defense white paper. (2) The priority and relationship between peacekeeping as an instrument of foreign policy and other instrumentalities has often been difficult to ascertain. Despite serious attempts to explicitly develop a coherent framework covering the range of Canadian roles and instruments, it has been difficult to implement policy as anticipated. (3) Despite the long-standing commitment on the part of successive Canadian governments to the principle of peacekeeping, the degree of support has varied considerably. (4) It could be pointed out that, upon the outset of the 1980s, the Canadian position on peacekeeping exhibited some of the characteristics of the mid-1950s. That is, the role and position of peacekeeping vis-a-vis other defense activities and foreign policy instruments required clarification, but there are no signs that the current Trudeau administration intends to undertake a policy review.

In part, problems in the policy dimension are a function of the perceived utility of peacekeeping. Not surprisingly, perceptions of utility have varied over time, and declared government policy has reflected these changing perceptions. According to policymakers and observers, three types of factors have shaped perceptions: (1) those that are rooted in the international system, such as the impact of superpower politics, as well as the preferences of disputants to a conflict on the selection and implementation of peacekeeping operations; (2) the internal difficulties within the UN system on the financing, establishment, support, etc. of peacekeeping; (3) the impact of the domestic environment including the commitments and capabilities of the Canadian armed forces. Thus, on the surface, the Canadian foreign policy community strongly advocated support for peacekeeping as an instrument of foreign policy but stressed the less tangible benefits of peacekeeping. Even though considerable emphasis was placed on the need for international stability, Canadian support for peacekeeping could dissipate rather quickly.

Linkages between the policy dimension and perceptions of utility must be taken into account when the military dimension is assessed. Obviously, the applicability of the Canadian experience will vary from country to country depending upon the structure, capability, and professionalism of individual military establishments. However, from the perspective of the CAF, peacekeeping has been undertaken with a certain sense of ambivalence. First, the professional ethic of the CAF is not entirely compatible with the peacekeeping environment. Furthermore, in terms of capabilities, the CAF is at a force level which calls into question its ability to successfully participate in major peacekeeping operations and also fulfill commitments in other areas. Third, there have been problems in relating the military dimension to the policy priorities and activities laid down by the government. This is particularly true when priorities appeared to deviate from declared policy.

In conclusion, it might be noted that the difficulties and problems which have arisen for Canada should be seen as illustrative of a nation-state that has made peacekeeping one of its major instruments of foreign policy and, in the process, has attempted to link policy and practice in as rational a manner as possible. This being the case, imagine the difficulties and problems faced by states in the international system that have not undertaken the peacekeeping role with the same sense of dedication and commitment.

NOTES

1. Alastair Taylor, David Cox, and J. L. Granatstein, Peacekeeping: International Challenge and Canadian Response. Toronto, Canadian Institute of International Affairs (CIIA), 1968.

2. Granatstein in Taylor et al., p. 107.

3. Ibid., p. 109.

4. James Eayrs, Canada and World Affairs, October 1955 to June 1957, v.IX. Toronto, CIIA, 1959.

5. P.V. Lyon, Canada and World Affairs, 1961-63, v.XII. Toronto, Oxford, 1968. For an American interpretation see Jon McLin, Canada's Changing Defence Policy, 1957-63, Baltimore: John Hopkins, 1967.

6. For references to the 1964 white paper see Canada, White Paper on Defence, Ottawa, Queen's Printer, 1964.

7. Ibid., pp. 11, 12, and 21 for quotes in this paragraph.

8. See David Cox, "Canadian Defence Policy: The Dilemmas of a Middle Power," Behind the Headlines, #5-6, v.XXVII, Toronto, CIIA, 1968.

9. See Cox in Taylor et al., p.49.

10. For references to the 1971 white paper see Canada, Defence in the 70s, Ottawa, Information Canada, 1971.

11. Canada, House of Commons, Debates, 1975, p. 9503.

12. See Henry Wiseman, "Peacekeeping: Debut or Denouement?", Behind the Headlines, v.XXXI, #1-2, 1972 and Canada, House of Commons, Standing Committee on External Affairs and National Defense (SCEAND), Subcommittee on Peacekeeping, May 21, 1970, #31.

13. One of the best studies on peacekeeping remains Alan James, The Politics of Peace-Keeping. New York: Praeger, 1969.

14. Despite some confusion the government considered four stipulations as essential: i. That the four major protagonists (the US, North Vietnam, South Vietnam and the Viet Cong) be bound by agreement to end the war. ii. That all four invite Canada to participate. iii. That a continuing political authority receive reports. Or iv. That the ICSC be given freedom of movement throughout Vietnam. Only the second of these conditions was observed.

15. For the background and explanation of the project see R. B. Byers, David Leyton-Brown, and Peyton V. Lyon, "The Canadian International Image Study," International Journal, v.XXXII, #3, Summer 1977.

16. For example see C. S. Gray, Canadian Defence Priorities: The Question of Relevance, Toronto, Clarke Irwin, 1972, p.109 and Alastair Buchan, "Concepts of Peacekeeping" in Michael Fry, ed., Freedom and Change, Toronto, McClelland and Stewart, 1975, p.17.

17. Quoted in David Cox, "Peace-Keeping in Canadian Foreign Policy," Stephen Clarkson, ed., An Independent Foreign Policy for Canada?, Toronto, McClelland and Stewart, 1968, p. 191.

18. SCEAND, Peacekeeping Report, p. 16.

19. Jack Granatstein in Canadian Forum, August 1974, p. 18.

20. Canada, Department of External Affairs, Statements and Speeches, September 25, 1974.

21. For pessimistic views on peacekeeping see F.S. Manor, "Case Against Peacekeeping," International Perspectives, July/August, 1977 and John Gellner, "Future of International Peacekeeping," ibid., Sept./Oct. 1973.

22. The case can be made that the Trudeau administration made this mistake with NATO in 1969. For example see R. B. Byers "Defence and Foreign Policy in the 70s: The Demise of the Trudeau Doctrine," International Journal, v. XXXIII, #2, Spring 1978, pp.312-38.

23. For a discussion of voluntarism see Thomas A. Hockin in Lewis Hertzman, John Warnock and Thomas Hockin in Alliances and Illusions, Edmonton, Hurtig, 1969, pp. 95-136.

24. For an overview of this issue see R.B. Byers and Colin S. Gray, Canadian Military Professionalism: A Search for Identity, Wellesley Paper 2, Toronto, CIIA, 1973 and Adrian Preston, "The Profession of Arms in Post-War Canada, 1945–1970," World Politics, XIII (1971), pp. 189–214.

25. Canada, Department of National Defence, Report of Study on Professionalism in the Canadian Forces, 1972.

26. House of Commons, Standing Committee on National Defence, 1967, p.275.   Also see Canada, House of Commons, Debates, 1966–67, pp. 14559–60.

27. SCEAND, Peacekeeping Report, p.28.

28. Standing Committee on National Defence, 1967, p. 2327. Also see p. 2315.

29. Ibid., p. 275.   For example, Lieutenant-General F. Fleury argued that "If you are going to have a Canadian defence force . . . for peacekeeping duties, and peacekeeping duties only, then I think perhaps you ought to have another favourable look at unification, because this might be the one circumstance that I can see where unification might be a real boon." (p.1305).

30. See John T. Saywell, ed., Canadian Annual Review, 1974, Toronto, University of Toronto Press, 1975, pp. 332–34.

31. For example at the end of 1978 some 130 reserve personnel served with UNEF II.

32. It should be pointed out that there had been reductions in other commitment areas.   In the mid-1960s Canada's NATO land commitment consisted of a 6500 man mechanized brigade group allocated to the European central front with a standby commitment of two brigade groups.   This was renegotiated by the Trudeau government and now the European land commitment consists of a 2800 man mechanized battle group to be deployed on the flanks of NATO with a standby commitment of one combat group stationed in Canada for flank deployment. Unfortunately the Canadian land forces have not been equipped with sufficiently modern equipment to effectively offset deployments within the Warsaw Pact armies.   The acquisition of 128 Leopard I tanks constitutes a partial attempt to rectify this situation, but the effectiveness of the Leopard I will soon decline with the new generation of main battle tanks being deployed by the USSR.   Furthermore, the CAF must acquire more rapidly the next generation of precision guided munitions or the decline in combat capability will continue.

33. An example of the problems posed by multi-tasking occurred during the FLQ crisis of 1970 when twelve of the fourteen major combat units stationed in Canada had to be deployed for internal security purposes.   Only two units

stationed with 1 Combat Group in Western Canada remained
uncommitted. If the crisis had coincided either with the
request for a peacekeeping contribution of the size deployed in
Vietnam or later with UNEF II the Canadian government would
have been unable to comply. This scenario indicates the
difficulties which could arise from unrealistic multi-tasking.

III

Operational Considerations: Political and Military

Introduction to Part III

Too little attention has been devoted to the complex and difficult conduct of the political and military management of peacekeeping operations in the fulfillment of their mandated objectives. Mandates (usually no more than a phrase, a sentence, or a paragraph) need to be transformed into the organizational structures, careful definition of functions, political control, efficient military command and deployment, and the sustainment of the forces in the field in difficult, at times dangerous, and almost always under sensitive and changing political conditions. The long chain of linkage between the resolutions of the Security Council and the performance of the soldiers in the field is axis upon which a mandate is effectively performed. Yet, that axis is constantly subject to political, administrative, and logistical pressures and controversy. Part III presents a full exposition of these matters from the varied points of view of the political control in New York to the military command in the field.

In the first of the chapters, "Peacekeeping: A View from the Operational Center," Urquhart puts forth the basic conditions required for the effective performance of peacekeeping operations, with special emphasis on the design of forces appropriate to the situation, swift implementation, disciplined denial of the use of force unless specifically defined and authorized, and the qualities which should guide the conduct of the under-secretaries-general for special political affairs, namely, "flexibility, capacity to act quickly, political sensitivity, a low profile, and general availability." Withall, the limitations of peacekeeping are clearly prescribed, noting that the UN has no defense ministry and is not capable of managing these operations in a manner consistant with national military policies and procedures. The political relations and functions of the Security Council and the secretary-general are

159

discussed. A look to the future suggests further UN operations, but cautions that "we shall have to continue for some
time with the present admittedly haphazard and improvised
system of peacekeeping, although we can certainly make a
number of improvements in its functioning and in its readiness
and capacity to act." The views expressed in this chapter
carry the weight of many years of experience at the fulcrum of
UN peacekeeping and an acute sense of the constraints and
bounds of discretion of the UN system.

In the next chapter, "Military Aspects of Peacekeeping:
Problems and Recommendations," Murray, who has served in
the field of operations, shows how different, and at times
contradictory, the military features of an operation contrast
with the political and administrative aspects of the New York
headquarters. This chapter, divided into the military
categories of strategy, tactics, and logistics, examines the
problems within the chain of command between the secretary-
general and the commander in the field, the difficulties which
can arise between a commander and a special political
representative of the secretary-general assigned to the field,
and the problems that frequently arise between command
headquarters and the battalion level. Other specific problem
areas are also noted, such as the differences in view on the
level of military capability required to functionally implement a
"political mandate," differing assessments of logistical
requirements and of the appropriate tactics required to meet
emergency situations under the constraints of the nonuse of
force, and the frequent curtailments of the freedom of movement. In effect, sharp disagreement is evident between the
military and political perspectives which require special
measures to be overcome.

Similar themes are dealt with by Beattie in "The International Peace Academy and the Development of Training for
Peacekeeping." Here, however, also based on direct military
peacekeeping service, the focus is on the need to train diverse
national military personnel in the special characteristics of
peacekeeping where, in contrast to national experience, there
is no enemy, and where a common and distinct doctrine is
required for international service. Unique communication and
negotiation skills are important requirements to manage the
predominantly political nature of peacekeeping, as are the
military and personal skills required to meet the particular
political/military contingencies which occur in the field. But
because the UN has not agreed to sponsor or guide national or
international training programs for peacekeeping and because
inexperienced personnel are frequently deployed in the field
with little advance notice, the lack of training creates many
problems and diminishes the efficiency of the force, factors
compounded by the general ad hoc nature of UN peacekeeping.

Apart from national training conducted by some contri-
butory countries, the only international nongovernmental
organization to provide this training is the International Peace
Academy. Its qualifications and extensive experience are
discussed, with recommendations for future development. In
recommending measures for improvement, Beattie draws on the
apt quote from Lester B. Pearson. "Are we to go from crisis
to crisis improvising in haste? or can we pool our experience
and our resources, so that the next time we, the governments
and peoples whom the United Nations represents, will be ready
and prepared to act?"

The essential and initial functions of all peacekeeping
operations are observing and reporting violations of cease-fires
and similar military arrangements. Yet, as Stokes points out
in "Technology and the Future of Peacekeeping," national
military forces employ the most sophisticated electronic
observation devices, whereas peacekeepers rely predominantly
on the human senses and only relatively primitive technology,
such as binoculars. The civilian Sinai Field Mission for the
first time introduced advanced surveillance and communications
equipment. There are many systems available - photography;
television; thermal imaging; light amplification with additional
magnetic, electro-optical, seismic, acoustic, and pressure-
sensitive or infra-red capabilities. Appropriately deployed,
they can contribute greatly to the effectiveness of observation
and early warning, perhaps reduce the number of peacekeeping personnel required to patrol and survey cease-fire lines
and related functions, balance differentials in the observation
capabilities of opposing sides, and provide notification of
violations to all parties, thereby fostering confidence between
the parties. Possible problems are political authorization,
initial costs, stock-piling, training, and above all, the
avoidance of surveillance intrusion into the sovereign
territories of the parties. But the potential advantages of the
use of sophisticated technology are considerable. Further
political and military feasibility studies are recommended.

7
Peacekeeping: A View from the Operational Center
Brian E. Urquhart

Peacekeeping operations are a novel addition to international machinery for the maintenance of international peace and security, and a serious assessment of peacekeeping must start from the general context in which these operations are mounted. Peacekeeping operations normally deal with regional conflicts which have a wider potential for threatening international peace and security. The initial call for peacekeeping was for two main reasons. Peacekeeping is not mentioned in the Charter and was evolved as a technique when it became clear that the Security Council was not going to be able to operate under the sequence of moves outlined in Chapters VI and VII of the Charter, resulting, if necessary, in enforcement action under the Charter. Peacekeeping represents a new approach to peace and security based on consensus, voluntary agreements, and cooperation, because it became clear that attempts to enforce peace were not politically or militarily realistic in the context of contemporary political and military circumstances. Another incentive for peacekeeping arose from the power vacuums which resulted from the decolonization process, as for example, in the Middle East, Cyprus, the Congo, and West Irian. Peacekeeping has now developed beyond this phase to become a useful device for maintaining the delicate balance of international peace when it is threatened by a regional conflict in which the great powers are likely to become involved. The role of an impartial and objective third party to pin down cease-fires and to form a buffer between conflicting states is particularly important when those conflicting states may, if they remain in conflict, steadily draw the nuclear powers closer to the heat of conflict. Apart from its value in pacifying a particular conflict situation, therefore, peacekeeping is an important instrument of the Security Council in preventing local or regional conflicts from becoming the detonators of a far wider conflict.

It is important to remember that peacekeeping is only one part of a large machinery for attempting, if not to keep the peace, at least to maintain some reasonable balance in international security. This effort includes the Security Council, the quiet diplomacy of the secretary-general, and the bilateral efforts of a number of governments, all of which are aimed at defusing conflict situations and preventing them from having wider repercussions as regards international peace and security. Peacekeeping also serves to keep the temperature down and to create an atmosphere conducive to peacemaking and the pursuit of basic solutions to international problems.

Peacekeeping can only function under certain conditions. If these are not present, it will either function ineffectively or will cease to function at all. The most important of these conditions is acceptance, first of all by the Security Council whose continuing support is essential, second by the countries or parties principally concerned in the conflict, and third by the states contributing troops to the peacekeeping forces. If any one of these acceptances is lacking, it is extremely difficult to maintain an effective peacekeeping operation.

The second condition is cooperation. As stated above, the cooperation of the Security Council at all points is essential to the effective maintenance of a peacekeeping operation. Even more important, the cooperation of all the parties concerned in the conflict situation is necessary if the peacekeeping operation is to function as intended. Peace-keeping operations have very little capacity for enforcement and are limited in their use of force to self-defense in the last resort. This means that any determined party, reasonably well-armed, can defy a peacekeeping force effectively. We have seen good examples of this in south Lebanon.

A third condition for successful peacekeeping is the nature of the mandate. When the mandate is clear and is based on terms which are specifically agreed by the parties to the conflict, peacekeeping does not present great problems as long as the parties are prepared to stick to their agreement. This has been true, for example, with UNEF II and UNDOF. When, however, the mandate is ambiguous or unrealistic and has not been agreed by the parties in advance, an operation is bound to be in for trouble. Sometimes there are overriding reasons for putting in a peacekeeping operation anyway; but, in such cases and when there is an inadequate or unrealistic mandate, the operation will face continual, and sometimes highly controversial, problems. This is now the case in south Lebanon with UNIFIL.

Another usual condition of peacekeeping operations is international political necessity. By this I mean that the Security Council should weigh the value of a peacekeeping operation in terms of conflict control and the maintenance of international peace as against the probable difficulties, and even casualties, it may face. The Council may decide that the primary requirements of international peace and security require that an operation be set up even if it is obvious from the beginning that it will not easily achieve the objectives set for it by the Council. It should also be clearly understood that the Council, in reaching decisions on such important matters, is unlikely to produce a mandate that is crystal clear, in view of the differing views of its members on certain key points. The decisions of the Council on peacekeeping operations have in the past sometimes resembled more the pronouncements of the Delphic Oracle than the clear executive instructions which would be most helpful in conducting peace-keeping operations. This is a political hazard which has to be accepted, although it can create very great difficulties for the secretary-general as well as for the commander and the forces in the field.

A peacekeeping force should never be expected to rely on force to achieve its ends. If it finds itself forced into such a position, it will already have lost its status as a peacekeeping operation and, in all probability, any reasonable hope of remedying the situation as well. It will cease to be above the conflict and will have become part of it.

In the heat of the moment, it is often suggested that peacekeeping forces should adopt forceful tactics. Such suggestions usually come from people who do not have to face the situation on the ground and who are also unaware of the consequences of an attempt to use force by a group which is not entitled to do so and can at best use force under such restrictions as to make it militarily unrealistic. If enforcement operations are required, the Council would have to agree on them, and so would the host country or countries. It is precisely because the Council cannot agree on enforcement operations that the peacekeeping technique has been devised, and it is precisely because an operation is a peacekeeping operation that governments are prepared to make troops available to serve in it. And, above all, it is because a peacekeeping operation is not an enforcement operation, with all of the implications for national sovereignty, that the parties to a conflict and especially the governments concerned are prepared to accept UN forces on their territories.

On the other hand, a firm military posture and a deter-mination not to be pushed around is absolutely essential in peacekeeping. This firmness usually takes the form of clear reactions to threats and the maintenance of positions and agreements with such consistency that any force wishing to change the status quo would have to engage in acts overtly hostile to the UN force. The parties to a conflict are usually reluctant to attack a UN peacekeeping force directly.

There are, in fact, considerable advantages in the non-use of force. One of them is that peacekeeping operations, since their presence and not their offensive military capacity is important, can be launched extremely quickly. In the Congo, the first troops arrived within 36 hours of the Security Council decision. In 1973, the first troops arrived in the Suez area within 24 hours. This would not have been possible if the troops had been required to fight on arrival. It was possible because the presence of the troops and their very noncombatant status was what was important.

A small and lightly armed body of troops can make its presence felt only if it does not attempt to engage in military contests. National forces are extremely reluctant to fire on United Nations troops with their noncombatant status and representing the collective decision of the United Nations. If, however, United Nations troops were to fire first and cause casualties, this compunction would quickly vanish. In fact, nonuse of force is one of the main strengths of peacekeeping forces. In this connection, it is worth remembering that, in the kind of situation the UN deals with, forceful methods do not usually work as well as the peacekeeping method. The British had nearly 50,000 fully armed combat troops in Cyprus before the UN peacekeeping force arrived. Although engaging daily in military operations, they were unable to maintain the peace between the two communities, which is why the United Nations was called in. The United Nations has never had more than 7,000 troops in Cyprus, but precisely because those troops have been noncombatant and represented the will of the international community, their status right from the beginning has been quite different and far more effective.

In considering the question of the changing character of peacekeeping mandates, it is worth briefly considering the evolution of peacekeeping. The phrase itself came into general currency in the early 1960s and is not mentioned in the Charter. The concept evolved in an equally haphazard manner, starting with military observers in northern Greece, the Middle East, and Kashmir and progressing to the first emergency force in 1956, after the Suez crisis when Lester Pearson observed, quite rightly, that military observers would not be adequate to meet the problem then existing in Sinai. These operations have been developed through improvisation and experience. All of the operations are different and require different treatment, different composition, and very often a different basic approach.

Operations which take place on accepted demarcation lines or frontiers between the conventional forces of conflicting parties are much easier to run than those involved in the internal life and difficulties of one or another country which deal with a variety of unauthorized armed groups. Thus, the Congo operation and the south Lebanon operation have proved to be unusually difficult. The operation in Cyprus was a mixed military and civilian operation, again dealing with internal matters within a country, and the same will be true of the Namibian operation, if it ever takes off.   Classical peacekeeping operations such as UNEF I and II or UNDOF are much easier to handle.

In the beginning, very little thought was given to the possible duration of peacekeeping operations. Usually there was an optimistic three or six-month initial target and, when the operation showed signs of lasting almost indefinitely, nobody was bothered unduly. UNTSO in the Middle East, for example, was set up originally to observe the truce ordered by the Security Council in July 1948 but it has lasted until the present time. UNEF I, originally set up to oversee the withdrawal of the three armies from Egypt, was then left to supervise the Egypt-Israel border and armistice demarcation line with no fixed termination date. However, at the request of the Egyptian government it was withdrawn in June 1967.

It was only in the light of these experiences that the member states began to wonder whether open-ended peacekeeping arrangements, apart from being expensive, were not also ineffective and, in some circumstances, even counterproductive in terms of the overall peacemaking process. There was also a feeling, especially in the Middle East, that the peacekeeping operations tended to sanctify the status quo and to give the impression after a number of years that it would remain forever. This was the main reason for the insistence on the short mandates of UNEF II and UNDOF and the show of reluctance which characterized their periodic renewal by the Security Council. UNIFIL has had a uniquely complicated history of mandate extension, the mandate being extended for different periods each time since its inception, with the general, if somewhat unrealistic, aim of encouraging political progress. As a purely practical matter, short mandates or constant changes in their length pose difficult military, logistical, and administrative problems. This practice detracts from efficiency and adds to expense. The political justification for it, therefore, should be of clear importance before it is embarked on.

As stated above, it is impossible to have a general blueprint for all peacekeeping operations since all are different. The mandates for each are worked out at the time by the secretary-general and the Security Council, and the method of operation has to be worked out in the light of the prevailing circumstances by the secretary-general and his staff - in this case the office of the under-secretaries-general for special political affairs. This office has to maintain as great a flexibility and simplicity of operation as possible if it is to cope with the changing circumstances and contexts of the various peacekeeping operations it has to set up and run.

The most important qualities which the office should have are flexibility, capacity to act quickly, political sensitivity, a low profile, and general availability.

The office of Special Political Affairs is often chided for not having a larger headquarters set-up and particularly for not having a large military staff. This criticism, though well-intentioned, is based on a false assumption, that this office is vaguely the equivalent of the defense ministry of a national government. It is no such thing. The United Nations has no sovereignty of its own and can run operations of a peacekeeping nature only on a specific mandate from the Security Council. It cannot engage in the kind of military contingency planning in which a ministry of defense engages, since such planning is an act of sovereignty and is based on existing establishments which, in the United Nations, are nonexistent. The fact is that, under the present political, constitutional, administrative, and budgetary arrangements of the United Nations, it is impossible for the organization to maintain permanent establishments. The maintenance of a permanent international force, which was advocated so enthusiastically long ago, has now ceased to be a practical possibility if it ever was one, simply because of the political implications of the existence of such a force in terms of United Nations authority and national sovereignty. We have, therefore, to live with the fact that we have to improvise, and that each peacekeeping operation has to be hand-tailored to the job at hand.

It will probably not be possible in the foreseeable future to put together a permanent force which will be ready to tackle any peacekeeping undertaking. Quite apart from any other considerations, matters of geographical composition would make this impossible. We have not yet arrived, unfortunately, at the stage where all governments accept that any United Nations operation, staffed by people of any nationality, is completely impartial and objective. This is particularly true in the military field. For these reasons, a large permanent staff, and especially a large permanent military staff, would have very little to do, and its activities would be likely to become controversial and unproductive. What is necessary is a small, highly-qualified staff, civilian and military, which is capable of initiating the necessary operations, usually under great pressure and urgency, and which is capable of expanding itself quickly through the recruitment of additional military and civilian personnel if a particular operation requires it. This approach is, in my opinion, best suited to the present stage of development of peacekeeping. A more grandiose set-up, bearing more resemblance to a national defense ministry, will only be possible and useful when certain fundamental conditions of United Nations peacekeeping have changed.

When an operation is set up, certain basic problems usually arise. There is the initial problem of command and staff which can often be solved, temporarily at least, with existing resources from observer operations or from neighboring peacekeeping operations. There are, almost invariably serious logistical problems since the United Nations has no permanent establishments and, therefore, does not have a worldwide logistical pipeline. These have to be solved by improvisation and by assistance from states which have logistical arrangements in various parts of the world. Usually the initial arrangements are far from perfect. We also have to face the fact that the United Nations dislikes the expenditures involved in operations and that, very often, the victims of the economy-mindedness of the administrative intergovernmental organs of the United Nations are the soldiers in the field. The secretariat does its best to mitigate such consequences as far as possible.

Once an operation is established, the degree of complication depends on the local conditions. In a well-based operation with firm and agreed guidelines, there is no particular problem about the operational aspects of the task. In a confused situation, with no local governmental authority, no clear mandate, and a wide selection of heavily armed, conflicting parties (such as exists in south Lebanon), the situation is more difficult. The commander has to come to terms with the simultaneous necessity for firmness and flexibility, and the natural desire of well-trained units to show their military prowess on the ground with the probable results of their doing this in terms of an escalation of hostilities involving the peacekeeping force itself. He also has to face the situation that the force is in the middle and must not become an extension of the military forces of any of the parties. This impartial position is likely to be unpopular with all of the parties concerned, who all believe that righteousness is exclusively on their side and that the United Nations should be fighting their battles for them. All of this requires good leadership and a constant effort to maintain the morale of the troops through their understanding of the task they are performing. Above all, the troops have to be made to understand that their usefulness is not simply in controlling the small and sometimes petty struggles that they are witnessing on the ground. Their basic task is the maintenance of international peace and security through the containment of conflict.

The role of the Security Council is of paramount importance in peacekeeping operations, and the relationship between the Council and its members on the one hand and the secretary-general and his staff on the other is an essential element in the maintenance of these operations. The history of peacekeeping has shown a steady and, on the whole, positive development of this relationship. The Security Council was very little concerned with the original observer operations except as a source for accurate, objective reports on incidents in the Middle East or Kashmir. Things became more complicated with the first peacekeeping force - UNEF I - which was established by the General Assembly, due to the paralysis of the Security Council by the British and French vetoes. This arrangement was challenged at the time as unconstitutional by some member states, and its basic weakness was displayed with dramatic results in 1967 when UNEF I was withdrawn. The Congo operation, with its enormous complexities of every kind, soon made it impossible for the secretary-general to run the operation effectively with the support of all members of the Security Council. The disagreements of the different political parties in the Congo were projected onto the world scene in the form of partisanship for one or another Congolese faction among the members of the Security Council and among the members of the United Nations at large. This led, in the end, to a formal challenge to the constitutional right of the secretary-general to conduct the operation at all, and to a withdrawal of recognition of his authority by some member states.

The fundamental controversy over peacekeeping which thus arose has resulted in a prolonged discussion of the basic principles of peacekeeping in the United Nations Special Committee on Peacekeeping Operations (Committee of 33), which has so far not managed to reach agreement on the fundamental principles involved, particularly those relating to the respective authority of the Security Council and the secretary-general and the description of that authority in practical terms.

Meanwhile, with the Cyprus operation, and particularly with the peacekeeping operations in the Middle East established in 1973 and 1974, there has been a practical and positive evolution of the relationship between the Security Council and the secretary-general as regards the conduct of peacekeeping operations. The guidelines for UNEF II, approved by the Security Council in 1973, were the fruit of the experience of the previous years and of the discussions which had taken place in the Committee of 33, and represented a practical solution to problems which had proved insoluble in principle. The fact that these guidelines were agreed to unanimously by the Security Council and have functioned well ever since says a good deal for this pragmatic approach.

While it is clear that the Security Council has primary responsibility for peacekeeping operations as an important instrument for the maintenance of international peace and security, it is also clear that there are some things which an intergovernmental body cannot in practice do and which can only be done by an executive body. These include the kinds of decisions that have to be taken when a peacekeeping operation runs into trouble, usually in the early hours of the morning, given the different time zones involved. Such decisions have to be taken urgently and, in any case, probably could not be taken in time by an intergovernmental political body, even supposing it were possible to call it into urgent session at three o'clock in the morning. It is generally accepted, therefore, that the secretary-general and his staff should do the job, reporting as and when necessary to the Security Council, which, of course, is free to disown those decisions.

In fact, it is greatly in the secretary-general's interest to keep the Security Council closely informed of developments in peacekeeping operations, and this is also welcomed by Security Council members. Where necessary, formal reports are made, or the secretary-general may inform the Council of a particular development in informal consultations with the members. As a matter of course, the secretary-general and his staff keep members of the Council and interested delegations informed of day-to-day developments. The Council and its individual members have tended to become more active in supporting the secretary-general in the conduct of peacekeeping operations in recent years. This has been particularly true of successive presidents of the Security Council in the difficulties which have been encountered in south Lebanon. The level of cooperation and understanding between the Security Council and the secretary-general and his staff is probably more comprehensive and satisfactory now than at any time in the past.

The cooperation of the host country or countries is of paramount importance in the conduct of peacekeeping operations since, without their consent and cooperation, very little can be done. When there is full agreement on the mandate of a force and its method of operation, relations with host countries present very little difficulty. When there is no such agreement, these relations can be very difficult. Normally, after the initial guidelines have been laid down, the day-to-day relations with host countries are conducted by the head of the peacekeeping mission in the area. In the Middle East, this arrangement is supplemented by the existence in Jerusalem of the chief coordinator for peacekeeping missions in the Middle East, General Siilasvuo, one of whose functions is high-level political contacts with all the governments concerned. On serious problems, it may be necessary for the secretary-general to deal directly with either the permanent representative of the government concerned in the United Nations or the prime minister or foreign minister in the capital. In any case, the secretary-general and his chief colleagues maintain close relations with all of the governments in whose territories peacekeeping forces are operating. It is often necessary for the secretary-general or his representatives from headquarters

to travel to the area and consult on outstanding problems with
the governments concerned and with the commanders of UN
operations. This has been particularly true of the situation in
south Lebanon. In any case, it is wise for all concerned to
keep close and continuous contact to avoid unnecessary misunderstandings.

Constant contact is also maintained with representatives of
the states contributing contingents to peacekeeping operations.
This is done formally by the secretary-general before the
renewal of each mandate by the Security Council. Meetings of
the representatives of troop-contributing states are held as
necessary at United Nations headquarters to keep them
informed of the situation in the field and on administrative and
logistical matters, as well as on particular developments as
they affect one or another contingent of a force. Representatives from most contributing states also visit the areas of
operation from time to time.

Regular communication with troop-contributing governments is of great importance. The provision of a contingent
for a peacekeeping operation is often a difficult decision for a
government, and this is particularly true when the operation
itself is difficult or controversial. If a contingent is in
difficulty or danger, and especially if it suffers casualties,
there are inevitably repercussions on the national political
scene which are of great concern to the government. Inac-
curate or sensational press reports often compound such
difficulties. It is essential, therefore, at all times, that the
best possible information as to what is really going on be
available to a troop-contributing government so that it can deal
with these repercussions and also, if necessary, correct
distorted information.

The provision of a peacekeeping contingent may also have
effects on the relations of a troop-contributing government
with other governments, especially those who are parties to
the conflict. Here also, it is very important for the
secretary-general and his staff to keep the governments as
well informed as possible so that political and diplomatic
repercussions can be dealt with and so that support can be
given to the governments concerned in difficult situations.

In view of the considerable complications which providing
peacekeeping contingents can cause for governments, it is
reassuring that, so far at any rate, there has been little
difficulty in getting the necessary contingents for United
Nations peacekeeping operations. In fact, a greater difficulty
is to ensure their acceptability to the governments and parties
concerned. From time to time, a government is compelled to
withdraw its contingent for domestic political, financial, or
other reasons. In such cases, it is usually possible, without
undue difficulty, to find replacements. In fact, there are
occasions when there are far more volunteers than there are
places to fill.

The fact that many governments have instituted training programs relating to United Nations peacekeeping as part of their normal military curriculum has certainly helped in ensuring that troops arriving for peacekeeping operations are reasonably aware of what it is they are expected to do. In cases where such training programs do not exist, the adjustment to peacekeeping duties can be painful and there have been noticeable difficulties in acclimatizing the troops to the unusual and unconventional nature of United Nations tasks. The idea that peacekeeping troops do not have "enemies" in the conventional military sense but are there to help all parties to keep the peace is of fundamental importance to a proper attitude.

The provision of qualified staff officers to run peacekeeping operations can present problems. Certainly, the more thought and training that can be given in advance to the nature and requirements of peacekeeping, the less mistakes are likely to be made in the operation itself. Officers and contingents who do not understand the wider political context of peacekeeping tend to develop negative attitudes toward the very difficult tasks they are asked to fulfill. Those who persist in comparing peacekeeping to normal military service and who hanker for the use of conventional force are likely to end up frustrated and defeatist. For this reason, training and indoctrination in advance of operations are absolutely essential.

I am constantly and agreeably surprised at the capacity shown by officers and men of almost all peacekeeping contingents for understanding their difficult tasks, for acclimatizing themselves not only to foreign and unusual circumstances but also to the psychological difficulties of being soldiers, and yet always being in the middle and having no enemies. Peacekeeping operations, at their best, are a microcosm of the truly international world we strive to achieve in the United Nations. A visit to one of these operations is an encouraging antidote to the frustration one sometimes feels at the diplomatic level. The fact that peacekeeping is one of the United Nations' more successful activities is in large part a tribute to the dedication and intelligence of the officers and men in the field.

It seems obvious to me that peacekeeping has a promising future, even if it remains within the present range of operations. These operations can be lifesavers in times of international crisis, and it is likely that they will be called for again and again in times of need. The question is whether we can develop this new and original creation from its present improvised state - where it is in the nature of the sheriff's posse set up in an emergency to deal with a particular situation - into something more consistent and permanent, and whether this would be a good idea. A more institutionalized and permanent system than our present ad hoc peacekeeping operations would clearly require basic changes in the international set-up. For a permanent international peacekeeping force to exist as a regular factor of the international situation would require a far greater degree of general disarmament. It would require a far greater and more consistent acceptance of the resolutions of the Security Council and of international law. It would require a much more reliable, comprehensive, and independent budgetary system. It would also require that those who work with the United Nations, whatever their nationality, be accepted without qualification by all member governments as impartial, objective, international servants. It would require a less adventurous attitude toward conflict on the part of many governments, and a general and firmly held belief that international peace and respect for the sovereignty of others is as desirable in the international community as law and order are in a national community.

We are not at present anywhere near to any of these developments, although we can see perhaps the beginnings of some of them. I am inclined to believe that we shall have to continue for some time with the present admittedly haphazard and improvised system of peacekeeping, although we can certainly make a number of improvements in its functioning and in its readiness and capacity to act. Much has already been done in this field and much more can certainly be done. But this will probably be the limit of our efforts until some of the fundamental conditions mentioned above have perceptibly changed.

8
Military Aspects of Peacekeeping: Problems and Recommendations

J.D. Murray *

With the exception of hostile action by one of the former combatants, the greatest military consideration in peacekeeping is the nonmilitary. This might appear to place the military commander in a novel situation. However, military history indicates that field commanders, in addition to fighting the war, have had to consider the nonmilitary objectives set by governments and to operate within the constraints which these governments imposed. It may be expected, then, that in peacekeeping, as in war, the military commander will be guided by the overall objectives of his political masters, constrained in the means through which he can meet these objectives, and restricted by the limited resources provided to him. In moderation, these nonmilitary aspects of peacekeeping have been accepted, but instances have arisen where they became excessive and an unnecessary burden on the commander and his military peacekeeping force.

This chapter will describe and analyze those aspects of international peacekeeping which impose burdens upon the military force and make some recommendations for their relief.

The writer has taken certain liberties with Liddell-Hart's main aspects of warfare(1) in discussing peacekeeping under the headings "Strategy," "Tactics," and "Logistics." An explanation is required. Liddell-Hart saw "grand strategy" as being superior to strategy, and he emphasized that it was the purview of the civilian government, not the military. Thus, it has not been used as a topic here. As far as peacekeeping is concerned, grand strategy has been the purview of the UN

*The observations and opinions expressed in this paper are those of the author and do not necessarily represent the views or policy of the Canadian Department of National Defence.

Security Council or General Assembly. The only grand strategy in evidence has been to place peacekeeping units from as
many member states as possible in the troubled areas in the
hope that world pressure would deter hostilities. "Strategy"
is used here to refer to the general modus operandi which the
commander selects for a peacekeeping force. "Tactics" will
refer to military tactics which have been adapted to peacekeeping line operations. The units which perform these
functions will be referred to as operational units. "Logistics"
include all the administrative and logistics functions required
to support peacekeeping operations. The units which perform
these functions will be referred to, individually, as administrative or logistics units and, collectively, as support units.
    It must be emphasized that the subject matter here is
peacekeeping, not peacemaking, and relates only to peacekeeping forces, not to observer missions and truce supervisory
organizations. The descriptive and analytical portion of this
chapter will draw upon examples from six of the peacekeeping
forces employed to date: UNEF I, ONUC, UNFICYP, UNEF II,
UNDOF, and UNIFIL. Statistical data on these forces can be
found in the Appendix.

STRATEGY

In 1956, as commander-designate of the first international
peacekeeping force, General E.L.M. Burns contemplated his
strategy for a divisional size force, with a brigade of tanks
and fighter aircraft.(2) Obviously, whatever strategy General
Burns contrived initially was quite different from that which
he developed as the force evolved. There were four main
reasons. First, the mandate decreed that UNEF would not
fight its way between the opposing armies but would deploy
with the consent of the host Egyptian government, after a
cease-fire was in effect. Second, General Burns was to find
that, in peacekeeping, he did not have the flexibility in
strategy selection that a commander would have in war.
Third, strategy application is dependent upon timely information. And fourth, the force capabilities were different from
what General Burns had envisioned. The development of
peacekeeping strategy will now be discussed under headings
which parallel the four reasons for General Burns' revised
strategy.

The Mandate

The mandate for UNEF I was instrumental in establishing the
main strategy used by subsequent forces - peacekeeping by
interposition. If the force was not to fight its way between
the opponents, but was "to secure and supervise the cessation

of hostilities,"(3) the only strategy available was for it, with the consent of the parties, to physically impose a presence between them to ensure that hostilities did not recommence. The strategy of interposition met the requirement, except in the final days when the host nation called for UNEF's withdrawal. With hostilities threatening, the force commander did not have the option of altering his strategy, as the UN did not strengthen his mandate but cancelled it.

The Security Council resolutions which amended the mandate for ONUC make it the classic example of how the mandate affects the commander's strategy. Initial resolutions called for the force to oversee the Belgian withdrawal and to provide the Congolese government with military assistance aimed at restoring law and order. Also, ONUC was forbidden from intervening in any internal conflict.(4) Thus, little more than military training assistance and police activities were sanctioned. A deteriorating situation caused the Security Council to add "measures to prevent the occurrence of civil war in the Congo, including arrangements for cease-fires, the halting of all military operations, the prevention of clashes, and the use of force, if necessary, in the last resort."(5) This required the commander to invoke the strategy of interposition. When the Katanga crisis erupted, the Security Council again strengthened the mandate by authorizing "vigorous action, including the use of a requisite measure of force"(6) for the removal of mercenaries from Katanga, which allowed the commander to undertake a military offensive to achieve the stated aim. This is the only instance in which a peacekeeping force commander has been given a mandate to select an offensive strategy.

The resolution establishing UNFICYP called for the force "to prevent a recurrence of fighting and, as necessary, to contribute to the maintenance and restoration of law and order and a return to normal conditions."(7) The main requirement, "to prevent a recurrence of fighting," led the force commander to adopt interposition as his principal strategy. The Turkish invasion of 1974, an action which UNFICYP was clearly not expected to subdue, brought with it a major change in the situation on the island. The Turkish armed forces had become a party to the dispute. Thus, even with a cease-fire in effect, UNFICYP had no mandate to pursue its duties in territory controlled by the Turkish forces. As the political climate in the UN was not conducive to seeking a new mandate, the secretary-general decided that the terms of the Geneva declaration of 30 July 1974, which included responsibilities for UNFICYP, plus three Security Council resolutions adopted during the crisis(8) would constitute recognition of the force under the circumstances existing in Cyprus. In reality, this interim solution left the force commander with a mandate which did not apply to all parties involved. While his strategy reverted to interposition, acceptance of his actions was contingent upon adherence by all parties to the 1974 declarations and resolutions. This interim situation persists, leaving the commander without an appropriate mandate to pursue that strategy which he may select.

The Security Council resolution, which established the peacekeeping forces of the 1970s, virtually predetermined that their principal strategy would be interposition.(9) In UNEF II and UNDOF, "Kissinger diplomacy" secured exclusive UN buffer zones which are a considerable advantage in the execution of a strategy of interposition.

Command

It has been general practice for the military commander of a UN peacekeeping force to report directly to the secretary-general. However, in ONUC this was not the case, and grave difficulties arose concerning the selection of an appropriate strategy. When the operation began, a civilian "Special Representative of the Secretary-General" was appointed the overall head of ONUC. Subordinate to him and of equal rank were the military "Commander of the United Nations Force" and the "Chief of Civilian Operations."(10) A controversy over strategy selection developed between the special representative, Dr. Ralph Bunche, and the force commander, Major-General Carl von Horn. General von Horn implemented a strategy of disarming the Congolese army as the method of fulfilling his "law and order" mission. But Dr. Bunche maintained that ONUC could not disarm these troops, except at the request of the Congolese government. Presumably, General von Horn could have accepted such direction as realistic in a UN context. Dr. Bunche, however, went one step further and ordered him to return those arms which had already been seized. General von Horn refused the direct order. Unperturbed, Dr. Bunche simply by-passed General von Horn and issued his order to the military units.(11) Had the force commander reported directly to the secretary-general, it is unlikely that this misunderstanding concerning strategy would have occurred.

Intelligence

Frequently, in a two-party dispute between sovereign states, political considerations impact at the international diplomatic level and have little influence on a force commander's strategy and its application. However, in peacekeeping situations which are multiparty, communal, or faction oriented, the local political climate can have a bearing on strategy. The 1978 UNIFIL situation gave rise to several incidents, including direct attacks on peacekeeping troops, which might have been prevented had the force had timely information on the intent of

the parties involved. An appropriate mandate and strategy
can be of little value if not translated into practice at the
required time and place. Thus, although military intelligence
has never been an acceptable facet of peacekeeping, the force
commander must have current and accurate knowledge of the
political and military aims of all disputing parties. The ONUC
operation and 1974 situation in Cyprus lead to the same
conclusion.

Force Capabilities

There must be a close correlation between the composition of
the peacekeeping force and its commander's strategy. Experiences from ONUC and UNFICYP illustrate the effect of national
foreign policy and UN nonmilitary considerations upon the
strategy selected.

The ONUC commander's strategy was affected by the
composition of his force from the aspect of loyalty rather than
effectiveness. Certain troop-contributing nations became
disenchanted with the UN's Congo policy and threatened to
order their troops to support anti-ONUC factions. Although
the threats were never carried out, the commander was forced
to adopt a strategy of assigning these less reliable units to
areas which were not likely to be sensitive.(12) Thus, the
capability of certain military units became a decisive factor at
a crucial time in ONUC's tenure.

In the early 1970s, UNFICYP was reduced in both personnel strength and equipment. This was done, not on the
advice of the force commander, but for UN political and
financial reasons. At the time of the 1974 hostilities, action
was underway for further reduction from peacekeeping force to
observer mission status.(13) Thus, when the force commander
decided, in accordance with his mandate, to defend certain
UNFICYP installations, most units were not capable of deter-
ring an attacker.

These events illustrate that foreign policy changes in
troop-contributing nations and UN nonmilitary considerations
can transform a force into one incapable of effecting its
commander's strategy in fulfillment of a mandate.

Strategy Summation

This review indicates that, while peacekeeping forces have
used military offensive and defensive strategies, the only
strategy developed by peacekeeping commanders, and the
principal one used by all forces, has been interposition.
Peacekeeping forces have had other tasks, such as law and
order, negotiation, observation, investigation, and reporting,
but none of these can be classed as a strategy. Force
commanders have encountered few problems with the strategy

of interposition under routine conditions, but have not always been as fortunate when an emergency prevailed.

A force commander may be called upon to adapt his strategy on short notice to meet an emergency. As most forces have been authorized in the haste of an existing crisis, little thought has been given to subsequent emergencies. Experience has shown that, if initial provision is not made for dealing with future emergencies, a situation may ensue whereby the appropriate authority will be unable to cope during such a crisis. If the force commander is to select and execute an effective strategy for both routine and emergency situations, he must be provided with:

1.   a mandate which establishes the authority of the force with respect to all parties to the dispute, gives broad guidelines for strategy selection, makes provision for subsequent emergencies, and can be revised to meet unforeseen circumstances;

2.   direct command under the secretary-general;

3.   a means to keep him aware of political and military developments which may affect his operation; and

4.   a force which is capable of giving full effect to the strategy which he has chosen within his mandate. (Conversely, if force capability is reduced, the mandate must be revised accordingly.)

TACTICS

After the force commander has selected his strategy, his subordinate commanders and staff must determine the tactics to be used by the peacekeeping units which are operating in contact with the disputing parties. They are crucial to effective operations.

The Mandate

The force mandate and the commander's strategy constitute the framework for the conduct of peacekeeping operations. The tactical and operational questions most frequently relate to the use of force and freedom of movement.

General Burns first broached the question of use of force with the secretary-general in 1957. The reply was that UNEF troops could fire in self-defense but were prohibited from taking the initiative in the use of weapons. This allowed them to fire in response to an armed attack against them, even though the attack might occur because of their refusal to accede to the attacker's demands.(14) General Burns' opposing view was that, if it were known that UNEF would not resist force, then troops of either party could infiltrate between UNEF posts without interference but, whereas if UNEF had the right to resist, neither side would run the political risk of attacking UN troops. The final decision - a virtual principle of peacekeeping - was "that UNEF should not become embroiled in hostilities with the armed forces of either side."(15) These rulings resulted in UNEF units developing tactics which deployed their soldiery in the best possible positions to intercept infiltrators.

When similar questions arose concerning UNFICYP, the secretary-general issued an aide-memoire stipulating that arms were to be used only in self-defense, and that UN troops were prohibited from taking the initiative in their use. However, a liberal interpretation of self-defense included the defense of UN personnel or property under armed attack, allowing UN troops to take action which might bring them into conflict with either Cypriot community in circumstances where fighting was likely to occur. Only the minimum force necessary was to be used and that only after peaceful measures had failed. Examples of the justified use of force were cited as resistance to force aimed at compelling UN troops to leave their positions or attempts to arrest UN troops.(16) UNFICYP adopted tactics similar to those of UNEF I and took special care in the marking of cease-fire lines. One unique UNFICYP tactic, in a major show of UN determination, was the use, in August 1964, of a multinational force in the Nicosia area to tear down fortifications and gun emplacements.(17) While some basis for this tactic could be found in the mandate, it was successful because it was used before either Cypriot community knew what was to be expected of a UN force. If attempted again, it is unlikely that either community would accept it.

An incident in UNEF II, prior to the "disengagement agreement," illustrates the need for early direction regarding the use of force. Israeli officers had agreed that their checkpoint near Suez be replaced by a UN checkpoint but, when troops of the Finnish battalion attempted to set up their post, they were interfered with by the Israelis. Faced with the dilemma of the requirement for a show of UN determination versus restraint in the use of force, the Finnish commander selected a novel course of action. He marched a body of men to the area, ordered them to ground their weapons and roll sleeves. He then ordered his troops to approach the Israelis. His appreciation of the situation was correct as the Israeli soldiers laid down their weapons and joined the fist-fight. The earnestness of the fighting remains open to question, but the Israeli withdrawal to a comfortable distance from the UN post testifies to its effectiveness.

Difficulty in implementing the principle of freedom of movement can be illustrated by the problems experienced in UNEF II. Although host country officials tended to interpret

freedom of movement in the manner which best suited their
own purpose, the principle was generally accepted at the
highest levels and ignored more and more at progressively
lower levels.   In 1973, Egyptian and Israeli officials took
different, but equally restrictive, approaches to UN movement.
As a general rule, Egyptian authorities either did or did not
permit movement into a given area.   Israeli authorities seldom
officially prohibited UN movement but, in their forward areas,
they provided an accompanying liaison officer.   This made it
easy to restrict or delay movement, as the liaison officer would
move only on the route which he had selected, or Israeli
authorities would state that all of their liaison officers were
occupied.   In the air, both sides prohibited UN flights in the
forward areas and restricted flying to a few international air
corridors and special narrow routes.   UN officials drew major
incidents of obstruction to the attention of the parties and
requested greater overall freedom.   However, during periods
when intensive political negotiations are taking place, it may
be inappropriate to raise questions which are obviously
sensitive to the disputing parties.   Further, in an age of
sophisticated military equipment, principally of superpower
manufacture, it may be reasonable to accept some restriction
on UN scrutiny as UN service does not prevent contingents
from retaining certain national interests.   In any case, the
requirement is for a clearly defined degree of freedom of
movement, equally applicable within the territory, airspace,
and national waters of all parties to the dispute, and that this
be agreed at the time the force is authorized.

Command

In peacekeeping as in war, there is a requirement for an
effective chain of command - the link from the commander to
his units.   In a peacekeeping command, language can be a
major problem.   Some units may have only two or three personnel who are fluent in the official language of the force.
Orders are less likely to be misconstrued if they are not
retranslated and retransmitted.   The ideal is to have no
intermediate headquarters between that of the force commander
and his units.
      In ONUC, this was not possible.   The Congo was subdi-
vided into territorial commands with a brigade headquarters in
each command.(18)   The military chain of command ran from
the force commander's headquarters to brigade headquarters to
the peacekeeping unit.   In a force of 20,000, this extra
command level was necessary and the system could have
worked except for an additional organizational quirk.   As seen
earlier, ONUC was headed by a civilian special representative
to whom the force commander was subordinate.   An extension
of this system placed a civilian UN representative, to whom the

brigade commander was subordinate, in each territorial command. Thus, the brigade commander was required to serve
two masters: his local civilian superior, and his military
commander in Leopoldville. A serious controversy occurred
when Dr. C.C. O'Brien, the UN representative in Katanga,
relayed an order for a major operation. The brigade commander complied but the operation failed. General McEoin, the
force commander, denied knowledge of the operation.(19)
Unity of command and a simple chain of command could have
avoided many such ONUC problems.

In early 1974, UNEF II deployed two brigade headquarters
and intended to place half its units under each. However,
when one of these headquarters was required to form the
nucleus of the new UNDOF headquarters, the overall plan had
to be dropped and the other brigade headquarters disbanded.

The 1978 UNIFIL deployment portrayed a proliferation of
headquarters from a different standpoint. On appointment,
the force commander, Major General Erskine, formed his
personal interim headquarters in Jerusalem. As troops
deployed, a forward headquarters was established at Naqoura,
and a main headquarters was ordered at Zahrani, both in
Lebanon. The result was a critical separation of the force
commander from his units (the chief of staff, an inexperienced
peacekeeper, headed forward headquarters), and of the operational staff and units from their logistics support. Notwithstanding the UNIFIL commander's direct responsibility to the
secretary-general, the existence in Jerusalem of the ranking
UN general, the chief coordinator, Lieutenant General
Siilasvuo, may have contributed to this complex command
arrangement. In any case, General Erskine recognized the
problems and consolidated his headquarters in Naqoura.

Most commanders would consider the command of ten
battalions to be too wide a span of control. However, as
peacekeeping operations are far less intensive than war, the
span of control principle does not outweigh the potential for
confusion in orders which intermediate or satellite headquarters
can cause. While span of control may be broadened, the
principle of unity of command remains as valid in peacekeeping
as in war.

Unit Capabilities

The requirement for a proper assessment of the capability of
peacekeeping units to perform their assigned tasks was
demonstrated in September 1961 when an ONUC formation failed
to remove mercenaries from Katanga. The operation failed
because the ONUC units were confronted by better equipped
troops, supported by the "Katanga Air Force," consisting of
one jet fighter aircraft.(20) Three months later, ONUC
achieved complete success by committing a larger force with a

full range of weapons and supported by newly acquired jet aircraft.(21) While the UN is unlikely to become involved in "offensive" peacekeeping actions again, this example illustrates that ground forces must have the numerical strength, training, and equipment to perform the tactical task. Further, as one "enemy" aircraft necessitated a tactical air element within the force, a similar scenario requiring a naval element can be envisaged.

The initial formation of UNEF II and of UNDOF was accomplished through the redeployment of units from existing peacekeeping forces. In UNEF II, four battalions were redeployed from UNFICYP; and, for UNDOF, UNEF II provided two battalions. This was possible because, in the first case, the national governments of the four battalions agreed to their transfer and to dispatch replacement units to UNFICYP and, when UNDOF was formed, UNEF II had sufficient reserve troops to release two battalions without replacement. In both cases, the proximity of the areas involved made these solutions ideal. This movement of units, in which every soldier has current peacekeeping experience, from an existing force to the area of current turmoil, contributes greatly to the prompt use of proven peacekeeping tactics.

When an international peacekeeping force is formed, one of the parameters is usually broad representation by political persuasion, race, or geographic area. This can result in the selection of a contributing nation which is not capable of providing an immediately effective peacekeeping unit. Worse still, this can detract from the capability of otherwise effective units. As an example, Nepal contributed an infantry battalion of excellent troops to UNEF II, but it arrived in the force area with no tentage, radios, or vehicles. The unit had to be placed in force reserve for several months until it could be supplied with sufficient UN equipment to enable it to undertake a full-time mission.(22) The equipment which the Nepalese unit required was in the shortest supply; therefore, other units already performing line missions had their effectiveness reduced by being unable to obtain new or replacement equipment. Lastly, as Nepal did not accept a continuing commitment to UNEF II, the battalion was not replaced at the end of its six-month tour. Thus, UNEF II and the UN received less than full value for their considerable effort regarding this unit. This illustrates that, because of overriding political factors, instances will occur where additional peacekeeping units are a liability rather than an asset.

Even if all units of a peacekeeping force are fully effective, the force cannot operate efficiently without a properly constituted headquarters. In all forces to date, the principle has been that the headquarters military staff be provided by the nations contributing contingents. After some initial delay, like that experienced during the formation of

UNIFIL, this practice has resulted in the headquarters being adequately manned. The problem, however, is that staff officers, schooled in a variety. of staff procedure methods, introduce facets of their national systems. Incompatibility of procedures can result in a lack of interface, or even conflict, between staff branches within a headquarters. Obviously, with the many nationalities, languages, and customs in an international headquarters, a simple and well-defined set of staff procedures would be an asset. This is not to deny that, over a period of time, the amalgam of procedures in a head-quarters becomes known and works reasonably well. The requirement is for a clear definition of the staff procedures to be used and for some degree of training to be provided to potential staff officers. This applies to administrative and logistics as well as to operations staffs.

The main operational unit in all peacekeeping forces has been the basic (even "stripped-down") infantry battalion. This is due to the flexibility of these units and their international availability. Given reasonable conditions of terrain and distance, infantry battalions could be the only operational units required for peacekeeping, but these conditions do not always exist. Thus, specialist units have been utilized in several forces. In UNEF I, reconnaissance units patrolled the long, wilderness-surrounded international frontier and regular, low-level, aircraft patrols were flown over it.(23) Reconnaissance units were also used for a time in UNFICYP to patrol in the sparsely populated areas. As UNEF II and UNDOF employed only infantry battalions, the commit-ment to station troops on Mt. Herman virtually escaped notice. When called upon to deploy troops to the Golan area, UNEF II was fortunate in having the Austrian battalion trained in mountain operations. It was assigned to UNDOF and, at each unit rotation, Austria has ensured that its new unit contains sufficient mountain trained troops to meet the Mt. Herman commitment. Thus, while future requirements for operational peacekeeping units will focus on infantry battalions, geo-graphic considerations could dictate a requirement for a variety of specialist land, air, or even sea units.

As any attempt to impose a solution by force or to remain in position in the face of open hostilities is generally accepted as being outside the routine peacekeeping scenario, the capabilities of units discussed above should suffice, except for emergency situations. Such an emergency occurred in Cyprus in 1974 and warrants examination. When hostilities broke out and UNFICYP units were tasked to defend themselves, UN installations, and Nicosia International Airport, most were understrength and lacked sophisticated defensive weaponry. During the July round of fighting, the British UNFICYP unit obtained armored vehicles - not through the UN but from the British sovereign bases in Cyprus - and supplemented the

lightly armed Canadian and Finnish troops defending installations in and around Nicosia. By the time the August fighting commenced, the Canadian contingent had been reinforced,
including armored personnel carriers and reconnaissance
vehicles.(24) Only with these reinforcements were the
UNFICYP units capable of protecting themselves and carrying
out their emergency tactical tasks. As the Cyprus example
indicates, the principal requirement is not for troops but for
the equipment to extricate peacekeeping troops and to defend
key installations. Thus, the equipment which a force may
require in an emergency must be available within the force,
even though it may not be required for routine day-to-day
use.

Tactics Summation

This discussion of peacekeeping tactics has not revealed any
major problems. Rather, there are a number of lesser
problems which require attention but which are not critical,
except under emergency conditions.

The two problems of use of force and freedom of movement relate to the force mandate. Understandably, many
argue that, for political reasons, the mandate must be
ambiguous. However, it is essential that either the mandate,
or an amplifying document, specify the circumstances under
which the force may be used and to what degree. Similarly, a
document, formally accepted by all parties, must specify the
degree of freedom of movement to be accorded to the peacekeeping force on land, in the air, and on the water. While
such an agreement should provide the peacekeeper with the
greatest possible freedom of movement, the realities of the host
nation's military security should not be overlooked.

Considerations regarding the chain of command and the
composition of a headquarters are related. As any headquarters will be international and multilingual, if at all
practical, it is best to have only one headquarters - that of
the force commander - and to have a simple chain of command
directly to units. Contributing nations must provide force
headquarters personnel at the time of deployment, and it would
be an asset if these personnel had some training in peacekeeping staff procedures.

The remaining problems concern the capabilities of the
operational elements of the force. The requirement for units
to have the strength, training, and equipment necessary to
perform their mission has been proven. Well-trained operational units have little difficulty adapting to peacekeeping even
in the tense situation which usually accompanies the formation
of a new force. The opportunity to redeploy experienced
peacekeeping units from a neighboring force must not be
overlooked. Also, in the embryo stage of a force, political

pressure for the deployment of national units, whose training or equipment states are unacceptable, must be guarded against. Such units can be a liability rather than an asset to the new force. While infantry battalions are the standard peacekeeping unit, geographic factors may dictate a requirement for specialist naval, land, or air units. Finally, if a commander is to develop tactics for the emergency situations which his force might encounter, he must not be deprived of the equipment required to meet such contingencies.

LOGISTICS

The sections on "Strategy" and "Tactics" revealed few military problems because peacekeeping operations are simple in comparison to wartime military operations. In a military operation, such as an attack, numerous elements require precise coordination, often at brigade, divisional, or higher level. In a peacekeeping task such as interposition even a section post may act independently, and coordination is seldom required above company level. But what of the logistical support required in peacekeeping? Because of the multinational nature of the force and other factors which will be discussed below, it is often more complex than in many military operations. Especially in the deployment stage, logistics and administrative considerations may have a greater effect on the peacekeeping operation than strategic and tactical factors.

Contingency Planning

When UNIFIL was launched in 1978, the greatest logistics lesson learned was that the UN had not learned the lessons vividly demonstrated during the deployment of the earlier forces, namely, that a logistics contingency plan, even in outline, is required for the deployment of a peacekeeping force. In war, an operational contingency plan takes precedence. But in peacekeeping, little operational planning can be done before the force mission is defined and, as line units operate independently, military proficiency will enable each to comply with the force commander's hastily devised plan. Conversely, materiel requirements are predictable. Precise volumes may not be known until the force size is determined, but requirements, their sources, and movement can be planned in advance. This will ensure that the materiel requirements of the force are met and avoid the diseconomies of crisis purchasing.

Administrative and logistical contingency planning, at the force level, has been virtually nonexistent during the history of UN peacekeeping. As the military headquarters of a force does not exist prior to its inception, the contingency planning task must fall to the civilian staff of the Office of General Services at UN headquarters, which is established to support only existing UN commitments. Further, although an attempt has been made, the General Assembly has never agreed to provide resources for advance planning and its Committee of 33 has not determined what advance planning could be authorized for peacekeeping.(25)

This absence of contingency planning resulted in the initial logistical support for UNEF I, II, ONUC, and UNIFIL being arranged on an ad hoc basis. A few of the most serious resultant problems were:

1.   Operations were suspended or jeopardized due to a lack of materiel.

2.   UN troops had insufficient rations or ate food bordering upon being unfit for consumption.

3.   Large quantities of materiel were destroyed in transit because the ad hoc plan did not include a check on packaging and stowage.

4.   Misunderstandings and "panic" ordering saw goods delivered which bore no semblance to those demanded.

5.   Faulty estimating resulted in major stock level problems.

6.   Unscrupulous entrepreneurs dumped substandard goods on the UN, knowing there was no quality control prior to receipt in the force.

7.   Little thought could be given to economy, as goods were required immediately to meet an emergency.

Although there were other contributing factors, the logistical system in ONUC never fully recovered from this initial shock. In UNEF I, the logistics required almost two years to recover from the initial emergency period. UNEF II was phased out in its sixth year without stock levels being brought under complete control, and UNIFIL is still struggling to establish a smooth-running replenishment system.

As the deployment of UNFICYP and UNDOF did not present major logistics problems, a word of explanation is in order. Prior to the formation of UNFICYP, British units were maintaining the peace in Cyprus and were logistically supported by the British system, with its two sovereign bases on the island. When UNFICYP was formed, the UN negotiated the transfer of this British support to UN units. Some adjustments were necessary, but no overall contingency plan was required. The transition proceeded smoothly, and today the British sovereign bases continue to support UNFICYP in much the same way as they did fifteen years ago.(26) UNDOF is the one UN peacekeeping force for which some contingency planning took place prior to deployment. This occurred because there were indications that the force would be authorized and formed as the stepchild of UNEF II. Consequently, while on the staff of UNEF, this writer prepared logistics contingency plans and orders for the deployment of UNDOF and for its initial support from UNEF installations.(27) These plans and orders contributed to the setting up and initial functioning of UNDOF with a minimum of logistics disruption. It is interesting to note that no communication was received from UN headquarters concerning this contingency planning.(28)

The future of logistics contingency planning looks bleak indeed. The fortunate circumstances of UNFICYP and UNDOF occur more by good luck than good management. There is no mechanism whereby military contingency planning can be undertaken; and, more than twenty years after the first ad hoc efforts, the UN headquarters staff has not been provided with either the resources or the authority to undertake it. Consequently, some other solution must be sought.

The UN Procurement System

The UN Office of General Services is responsible for the support of peacekeeping operations, including all actions required to meet materiel needs. This organization is manned at a level commensurate with current commitments and, therefore, can easily be overextended by an emergency.

The local authority for the support of a peacekeeping force is vested in the civilian chief administrative officer (CAO). Although officially responsible to the force commander, the CAO acts as a local extension of the Office of General Services in New York. His principal areas of responsibility are the procurement of the materiel needs of the force and the financing of these activities. Stated simply, the CAO's function is to vet the requirements submitted by the military and, within his financial authority, either let a contract locally or recommend action by the Office of General Services. After the fact, the CAO arranges local payment or recommends payment by New York. Obviously, this allows the CAO to control, in large measure, the standard to which a force will be supported.

Although UN field officials use elaborate titles such as "Chief Procurement and Supply Officer," the UN does not have a supply system. It procures materiel on the world market and utilizes international transportation to ship directly to the force area. When materiel cannot be obtained on the open market, the UN uses a supplementary system of purchasing from member nation governments.(29) Again, shipment is made directly to the force area. Consequently, the supply system begins within the force and is the responsibility of the military. Thus, the UN procurement system differs greatly from the systems which support most military forces. This creates several problems which can be grouped under "quality control," "regulations and procedures," and "staff considerations." In analyzing these problem areas, examples will be cited from UNEF II.

The quality control problems in UNEF II coincided with the sequence of obtaining goods - requisitioning, contracting, and receipt. The accepted military procedure in requisitioning materiel is to state the quantity required and to provide a description or general quality statement. Precise specifications are the purview of the procurement agency. When military officers began requisitioning in 1973, they wrongly assumed that, as the UN had been purchasing for peacekeeping forces for twenty-five years, the UN procurement system would have specifications for most military items. Thus, long delays were experienced in obtaining urgently needed items as procurement agents in UNEF, in New York, or both requested the military to amplify most requisitions. Time and experience, plus national specifications provided by the military, were needed to bring this problem within manageable proportions. Initially, the procurement system had no quality control at the place of purchase. A contract could be let and goods shipped to UNEF II without a UN procurement representative being on the same continent. Needless to say, many contractors did not justify this blind trust. In 1975, improvement was seen following the stationing of a UN procurement (quality control) officer in north-west Europe - a major source area.(30) Lack of quality control at the source created greater problems in the receipt of goods in the force area. As the military received all goods, the responsibility for quality control shifted from the UN procurement system to the military. When the wrong or inferior quality goods arrived at the force seaport or air terminal, the military officer was on the horns of a dilemma. He could reject the goods knowing that the force would be deficient until a replacement arrived some six months later, or he could accept the shipment and immediately provide the force with some materiel, albeit unsatisfactory.

UN administrative, logistical, financial, and procurement regulations and procedures cause the military more frustration than any other aspect of the system. UN officials might argue that strict regulation has resulted from instances (extremely isolated ones) when military officials violated the trust placed in them in the handling of UN resources.(31) This is not the case, but there are two main reasons for the frustration. First, these regulations tend to be antiquated and inflexible. The Canadian experience best illustrates this point. In 1956, most support regulations were written by the first Canadian officers of UNEF I. In discussions today, it is frustrating to a Canadian to be told that "such-and-such" is the UN regulation as written by Major X of Canada in 1956 - especially when UN officials disregard the counterargument that the Canadian forces have amended it five times in the interim. As a group, UN officials tend to look upon regulations as unalterable edicts rather than guidelines requiring amendment when a better way has been found. Second, the UN system's attitude toward a balance between responsibility and authority is incomprehensible to the modern military logistics officer. While the modern officer expects the procurement of the materiel for which he is responsible to be controlled by his civilian masters, he demands sufficient financial authority to make those minor local purchases which will enhance the efficiency of his operation in the eyes of his customers. When these customers are peacekeeping units from other nations, the desire for this authority is that much greater. Thus, the UN procurement system should delegate greater financial authority to the military and, through this and greater flexibility in regulations, exhibit a trust in the military officer responsible for the handling of UN resources.

Staff considerations relate to the civilian personnel requirements and appointments in a peacekeeping force headquarters. The UN experiences periodic difficulty in filling key positions because the posts are often not in an attractive locale, especially for the family man, and the requirements of international recruitment limit the breadth of talent available. This presents the following scenario (admittedly stereotyped). On the one hand, the UN has older officials, probably ex-military, who understand military requirements but cannot manage a complex operation because they are either past their prime or have been promoted beyond their level of competence. On the other hand, the UN has dynamic young executives who are good managers but, because they have spent all their service in headquarters or in one of the UN's diverse organizations, have no appreciation of military peacekeeping requirements. In all forces, the UN has established civilian appointments which duplicate the military staff in both title and responsibility. Examples are the civilian Chief Communications Officer, Chief Transport Officer, and Chief of Movement Control, whose functions overlap the military Chief Signals Officer, Staff Officer of Transportation, and Force Movement Control Officer, respectively. Lastly, the attitude of some UN civilian staff members upsets the military. An example is the senior official who stated, when discussing a military requisition, "Beds! What do they want beds for? They are soldiers, aren't they?" At the same time, this official and his UN civilian staff were billeted in the best international class hotel in the force area.

From the above discussion, it appears that the UN civilian procurement staff holds all the cards and intentionally stacks them against the military. This is not the case. Many UN member nations play international politics by preying upon the financial resources necessary to support peacekeeping forces.

Thus, it is incumbent upon UN officials to devise regulations and procedures which will keep the entire system, civilian and military, as free from criticism as possible. All that is needed is a proper balance between this requirement and the prime purpose - the effective support of the peacekeeping force. This can be achieved by improving quality control, updating antiquated regulations, and mutual military-civilian understanding.

Administrative and Logistics Functions

As UN forces have experienced innumerable support difficulties, only sample problems in the major functional areas will be cited.

Because airlift has been the main function performed by the air units of all peacekeeping forces, it is categorized within logistics. There are many requirements in the provision of efficient airlift but none approaches the importance of air safety. All UN peacekeeping forces have had an acceptable air safety record, except ONUC. Not only was the safety record in ONUC poor - so bad that it cost the lives of a secretary-general and his party(32) - but the maintenance, serviceability, and scheduling were unsatisfactory as well. This occurred because the air transport operation in all forces, except ONUC, was provided by the regular air force of a member nation. In the Congo, airlift was provided by a mixture of military and civilian operators from several countries operating such a wide variety of aircraft that it proved impossible to set standards of aircraft maintenance, crew competence, and flight safety.

The signals unit must have competent operators proficient in the official language(s) of the force. English has been the official language of UNEF I and II, UNFICYP, and UNDOF. In ONUC and UNIFIL, both English and French were accorded official status. Partially because of this bilingual requirement, Canada has provided a signals contribution to all six forces. Exceptions to exclusively Canadian responsibility are that the United Kingdom, with Canadian assistance, handles the function in UNFICYP, India supplemented the Canadian unit during most of the tenure of UNEF I, and Canada provided the UNIFIL signal unit for the first mandate period only. Obviously, the basic language(s) of the signals unit must parallel the force's official requirement.

An inadequate appreciation of the engineering tasks in peacekeeping has caused problems in the force area. The requirement is for a changing balance between a "field" engineering and a "construction" engineering capacity. While the field capability to lift land mines, clear routes, and remove obstacles is vital when a force is deploying or redeploying, the need swings quickly to the construction, modification, or repair of camps and installations.   The Polish engineering unit in UNEF II presents one example.   The original unit performed effectively in the field role but did not have a construction engineering capability sufficient to meet the force's earliest needs.   This necessitated extensive local contracting for construction work on UN camps and a proliferation of con- tingent self-help projects to improve their accommodation.

Transportation, maintenance, and supply problems are interrelated and have been alluded to when discussing the UN procurement system.   In addition to UN procured vehicles, most national units bring their own vehicles to a new force. In UNEF II, within the first three months, there were over fifty different types of vehicles in use.   The repair expertise and the tools required for this range of equipment are major maintenance considerations.   The supply problem of obtaining a full range of spare parts often appears to be beyond solution. In UNEF II, an early problem was that there were no manu- facturer's repair manuals for most of its vehicles.   Only with great difficulty was the UN hierarchy convinced that these manuals were the key to a repair program and to the indentifi- cation of spare parts.   Other major problems include: the procurement delays and quality control problems mentioned earlier; the transportation and movement control problems associated with using resources and facilities controlled by the host nation; and the maintenance problems encountered because there is no major rebuild (in military parlance, third or fourth line) workshop and little civilian contract capability in the force area.

In the medical field, the requirement is simple - a competent professional force hospital.   As the operation is peacekeeping, not war, there is no requirement for a complex military casualty evacuation system.   Both the air and road transport units, covered above, have the capability of moving emergency cases to the force hospital or, as is the case in UNIFIL, the force hospital can have an integral ambulance fleet.

Unit Capabilities

Greater care must be taken in the selection of national units to perform support functions than in choosing units for opera- tional tasks.   As there are a number of similar operational units (e.g., infantry battalions), the force commander can assign the more difficult tasks to the stronger units or he may hold a weak unit in reserve.   This is not possible with support units as there is only one unit of each functional type in a peacekeeping force and, if one of these is incapable of doing its job, there is no other unit which can be called upon. Therefore, it is essential that effective support units be selected when the force is formed.

If a peacekeeping force is to function and be domiciled in the territory of the disputing parties, all of the support units must be acceptable to all such parties. The force hospital is probably alone in being able to function effectively when accepted by only the one party on whose territory it is located - and this only if the other units have the capability of evacuating patients to the hospital. For example, in UNEF II, the Polish contingent was politically unacceptable to Israel and could not enter Israeli-held territory. Thus, every time an engineering or road transport task arose in Israeli-held territory, an ad hoc solution had to be found. Examples were borrowing vehicles and drivers from nontransport units, implementing unit self-help building projects, and obtaining host country assistance. Given the circumstances of a dispute, certain nations may be acceptable contributors of support units but not operational units. As in the past, future peacekeeping operations may require Warsaw Pact or NATO nations be involved solely in peacekeeping support roles.

An obvious criterion is that the national unit selected must be capable of performing its designated support function. A review of the six peacekeeping deployments indicates that there have been numerous occasions when stand-by operational units have been dispatched, but the Norwegians in UNIFIL constitute the only instance of stand-by support units being contributed.(33) Instances of the UN requesting nations to substitute a support contribution for an operational one indicate that there are ample operational contributions but support units are in short supply. The reason for this is that many developing nations, acceptable as peacekeepers, do not have suitable support units. The ONUC deployment, which originally intended to avoid the use of experienced Western units, proved that the field support units of developing nations could not perform many of the technical and managerial tasks required in support installations. Even with the functions split between several nations - both developing and developed - there is evidence of poor logistics support in ONUC.(34) The scarcity continues and developed nations have contributed the great majority of peacekeeping support units. Excellent units are also required because peacekeeping support tasks are often more difficult than national ones. The peculiarities of the UN system have been explained. The multinational situation brings with it a great variety in equipment, tastes, languages, customs, and expectations concerning logistical support. All these peacekeeping exigencies combine to make the support tasks more complex.

The next criterion is the establishment and maintenance of competence within the support units. That is, the units must have the skilled technicians and competent supervisors required to give full support to a force. This can be achieved by accepting support units from only those nations which offer regular, rather than reserve or short-term conscript, units. It takes several years to train support technicians, especially at the supervisory level, to the degree of competence required in a peacekeeping force. Reservists and conscripts do not normally serve long enough to reach this level of training. To maintain this competence, the contributing nation must also agree to a man-for-man rotation system. That is, the support unit, per se, remains continuously in the force, but a number of personnel are replaced at regular intervals, as often as weekly. This provides the continuity necessary to maintain competence.

Although adequate support can be provided to a force when the units involved are contributed by two or three nations, a higher standard can be achieved when all support units are from one nation. This final criterion represents an ideal from two aspects: (1) the contingent headquarters can double as the "logistics base" or "maintenance area" head-quarters for the force; and (2) the interface between functions can operate more smoothly because it does not cross national lines. Examples of these interfaces are: signals, engineering, and road transport with maintenance for the repair of equip-ment; maintenance with supply for spare parts; and supply with road and air transport for the movement of goods. Although the medical function depends to a degree on the others, it has the least interface and would be first choice for assignment to another nation if a one-nation support policy was not possible. Next in line for similar assignment would be engineering and signals, particularly if these national units contained some "in-house" maintenance and repair capability.

The scarcity of support units for a peacekeeping force is aggravated by the necessary criterion of political acceptability to all parties to the dispute. It is essential that these units be fully capable of carrying out their task in relation to field support and to peacetime technical and managerial functions. Also, the many complexities of the peacekeeping situation and the UN system make the tasks more difficult. Thus, it would be ideal if one developed nation could contribute all of the regular administrative and logistics units to a peacekeeping force but, if this were not possible, the medical, engineering, and signals functions, in that order, could go to a second nation.

Logistics Summation

Though operational peacekeeping tasks are less demanding than those encountered in war, the discussion above demonstrates that the support of peacekeeping is an extremely complex undertaking. The analysis of the problems resulting from these complexities points to two groups of recommendations:

one applies to the UN secretariat, and the other relates to the arrangements for military units which perform the support function.

UN experience in supporting peacekeeping forces has resulted in several documented recommendations. Examples are: standardization of force equipment;(35) establishment of UN stores depots; establishment of a UN staff college to train officers in support functions as well as operations; and establishment of a skeleton UN field headquarters which could do some advance planning and, as the need arises, deploy as the headquarters of a new peacekeeping force.(36) These recommendations have merit, but with political and financial constraints in the UN likely to persist for some time, there is little chance of their implementation. Thus, the UN must look elsewhere for assistance in contingency planning, and should concentrate on more mundane innovations which would improve cooperation and understanding between UN officials and military support personnel in the field. Specifically, the secretariat should continue to improve materiel specifications and quality control, eliminate civilian force headquarters appointments which duplicate military functions, delegate a level of financial authority to military officials which would be more in concert with their responsibilities, and update outmoded UN regulations.

The examination of military support functions and units indicates a preference for regular, as opposed to reserve or conscript, units which are competent to perform their assigned task from deployment onward. The following are suggested as additional criteria for the selection of competent regular support units which may be available:

1. Units must be politically acceptable to all disputing parties.

2. Selection should be restricted to countries whose military activities include the modern peacetime management of activities and installations comparable to peacekeeping force levels.

3. For continuity, staff and units should be selected from countries willing to implement a man-for-man rotation system.

4. Preference should be given to the selection of all administrative and logistics headquarters staff and units from the same country.

5. With regard to specific functions, airlift must be provided by a unit with an excellent safety and maintenance record, the national language(s) of the signals unit must be compatible with the force official language(s), and the engineer unit must contain an appropriate balance of field and construction engineering capabilities.

One criterion which might be added is that the support units be a portion of a national UN stand-by commitment. This would open the possibility for a future peacekeeping force to benefit from some national administrative and logistics contingency planning. Although no such planning has taken place due to the ad hoc nature of most peacekeeping administrative and logistics deployments, some benefits might accrue. National stand-by support units could be trained and equipped for peacekeeping deployment. More orders, guidelines, and procedures could be made available, possibly as a result of liaison with the Office of General Services. These and other measures would contribute to improved support of a peacekeeping force, especially during the deployment phase - the time when the most serious problems have occurred in the past.

This analysis envisages the ideal situation whereby the complete spectrum of support would be provided by the regular armed forces of one developed nation. As any one nation's units might not be politically acceptable or available in a given peacekeeping situation, more than one potential contributor is required. Therefore, the secretary-general should let it be known that military stand-by commitments of administrative and logistical support units are required from a number of competent nations. Having so committed themselves, these nations would then undertake national contingency planning and, as a result, a new level of UN administrative and logistics effectiveness might be attained in the future.

RECOMMENDATIONS

The preceding sections describe and analyze the military problems of peacekeeping and offer basic recommendations for their solution. Because of the natural overlap of operational recommendations dealing with the sections on "Strategy" and "Tactics," these are summarized under the categories of mandate, command, and the selection of operational units, with a final summation of the major recommendations on matters of "Logistics."

The political requirement for ambiguity in a mandate for a peacekeeping force is understood and appreciated; but, as has been demonstrated, this runs counter to the force commander's requirement for clear political direction confirmed by all interested parties on which he can base his strategy and tactics. The requirement is to establish the authority of the force with respect to all former combatants, give broad guidelines as to its routine functioning, and make provision for emergencies. Two important aspects are the use of force and freedom of movement. When political considerations are paramount and specifics cannot be included in the mandate, at least two other avenues remain open. The secretary-general can issue an <u>aide-memoire</u> to the force commander giving additional direction not contained in the mandate, as has been done on several occasions. Also, the UN should negotiate a Status of Forces Agreement with the host nation(s) that includes such matters as freedom of movement. It is recommended, therefore, that the official peacekeeping force mandate or amplifying documents establish the authority of the force, give broad guidelines for the selection of a strategy, make provision for both routine operations and emergencies, and specify the degree of force which may be used and the freedom of movement to be accorded.

It has been demonstrated that difficulties in command occur primarily when deviations have been made from accepted UN peacekeeping practice. Thus, it is recommended that the force commander be directly responsible to the secretary-general; the force commander be the sole and the supreme commander of the force; and, if at all practicable, there be no intermediate headquarters between that of the force commander and the operational units. In the overall context of command and control, there are several other matters of importance. There is a requirement for a single system of staff procedures to be followed in the commander's headquarters, and that potential staff officers receive some training in that system. As formation of a UN staff college is so remote, it is recommended that the UN select a staff system and make arrangements with an appropriate independent agency to conduct a series of international staff seminars on the system selected. Finally, so the force commander can effectively exercise all aspects of his command, it is recommended that he be provided with methods of obtaining all possible information regarding the relevant political and/or military developments which involve the disputing parties or factions.

Examination of the performance of operational units indicates that virtually all have been capable of performing routine peacekeeping tasks. This applies to regular, non-regular, conscript, or volunteer units provided from highly developed nations at one end of the scale, and to the less militarily sophisticated at the other. Two exceptions are noteworthy. First, operational units contributed by member nations which adopt political policies in opposition to UN objectives may create difficulties in the operational fulfillment of a mandate - a hazard that should be avoided. Second, the stage of initial deployment is the moment of the greatest need for completely effective and, if possible, experienced peacekeeping units. After the deployment phase, it is possible to accept less effective units, as their effectiveness can be increased by the issue of UN equipment and/or by local peacekeeping training. Thus, it is recommended that, during the initial six months, only operational units which are capable of immediately assuming peacekeeping duties be deployed.

Furthermore, the physical geography of an operation must be taken into consideration in the formative stage as some specialist units may be required. And, upon consideration of emergencies which may result from hostile action by former combatants, it is recommended that peacekeeping forces be so constituted and provided with such equipment as may be required, within reason, to meet such contingencies.

The analysis of "Logistics" shows both a scarcity of support units and a requirement for a level of competence more demanding than that which applies to operational units. This is so because there is only one functional support unit available to perform each function, and each initial function is made more difficult by international conditions, the lack of contingency planning, and additional constraints associated with the UN procurement system. The latter could be overcome by recommending that the UN secretariat improve its contracting and quality control practices, eliminate appointments which duplicate military positions, take the initiative in amending its procurement and financial regulations, and delegate greater financial authority to the military.

Each support unit must have an accurate appreciation of its task and be capable of performing it from the day the force is formed. Because administrative and logistics units must support all units of a force, regardless of physical location, it is recommended that the UN accept support units only from countries which are politically acceptable to all parties involved. Lastly, it is recommended that all support units be provided from one nation - a developed nation - which would earmark for UN peacekeeping regular administrative and logistics units, skilled in modern technology and management, and subject to a man-for-man rotation system when in the field. Implementation of this recommendation would allow the coordination of all support by a single headquarters - that of the national contingent concerned - and facilitate the necessary interface between functional units. It could also be the method by which a national administrative and logistics contingency plan could be provided where no such plan has as yet been devised by the UN.

The dedication of military personnel from the many nations which have and will contribute to peacekeeping operations can overcome many obstacles. But the future success of peacekeeping could be better assured if some of the matters suggested here could be implemented.

NOTES

1. B.H. Liddell-Hart, Strategy: The Indirect Approach (London: Faber and Faber, 1954), pp. 333-72.

2. Lieutenant-General E.L.M. Burns, Between Arab and Israeli (Toronto: Clark, Irwin, 1962), p. 188.

3.   United Nations, General Assembly, Question Considered by the Security Council at its 749th and 750th Meetings Held on 30 October 1956. Canada's Draft Resolution, A/3276, 3 November 1956.

4.   United Nations, Security Council, Resolution Adopted by the Security Council at its 873rd Meeting on 13 July 1960, S/4387; Resolution Adopted by the Security Council at its 879th Meeting on 22 July 1960, S/4405; and Resolution Adopted by the Security Council on 9 August 1960 (886th Meeting), S/4426.

5.   United Nations, Security Council, Resolution Adopted by the Security Council at its 942nd Meeting on 21-22 February 1961, S/4741.

6.   United Nations, Security Council, Resolution Adopted by the Security Council at its 982nd Meeting on 24 November 1961, S/5002.

7.   United Nations, Security Council, Resolution Adopted by the Security Council at its 1102nd Meeting on 4 March 1964, S/5575.

8.   United Nations, Security Council, Resolution Adopted by the Security Council at its 1781st Meeting on 20 July 1974, S/RES/353 (1974); Resolution Adopted by the Security Council at its 1789th Meeting on 1 August 1974, S/RES/355 (1974); and Resolution Adopted by the Security Council at its 1793rd Meeting on 15 August 1974, S/RES/359 (1974).

9.   United Nations, Security Council, Resolution Adopted by the Security Council at its 1747th Meeting on 22 October 1973, S/RES/338 (1973); Resolution Adopted by the Security Council at its 1748th Meeting on 23 October 1973, S/RES/339 (1973); Resolution Adopted by the Security Council at its 1750th Meeting on 25 October 1973, S/RES/340 (1973); Resolution Adopted by the Security Council at its 1752nd Meeting on 27 October 1973, S/RES/341 (1973); and Resolution 425 (1978) Adopted by the Security Council at its 2074th meeting on 19 March 1978, S/RES/425 (1978).

10.   J. King Gordon, The United Nations in the Congo (New York: Carnegie Endowment for International Peace, 1962), pp. 25-28.

11.   For an appreciation of both sides of this controversy, see the arguments of the central figures as contained in Ralph J. Bunche, "The UN Operation in the Congo," in The Quest for Peace, edited by Andrew W. Cordier and Wilder Foote (New York: Columbia University Press, 1965); and Major-General Carl von Horn, Soldiering For Peace (London: Cassell, 1966).

12.   D.W. Bowett, United Nations Forces (New York: Frederick A. Praeger, 1964), pp. 208, 209 and 379-81; and von Horn, Soldiering For Peace, pp. 155, 187 and 188.

13. United Nations, Security Council, Report by the Secretary-General on the United Nations Operation in Cyprus, S/11137, 1 December 1973, pars. 14-22; and Report by the Secretary-General on the United Nations Operation in Cyprus, S/11294, 22 May 1974, pars. 10 to 14.

14. United Nations, General Assembly, United Nations Emergency Force - Report of the Secretary-General, A/3943, 9 October 1958, par. 70. Hereafter cited as UN Document A/3943.

15. Burns, Between Arab and Israeli, p. 373.

16. United Nations, Security Council, Note by the Secretary-General, S/5653, 11 April 1964, attached "Aide-Memoire concerning some questions relating to the function and operation of the United Nations Peacekeeping Force in Cyprus," pars. 16-19.

17. James A. Stegenga, The United Nations Force in Cyprus (Columbus: Ohio State University Press, 1968), p. 127.

18. Lincoln P. Bloomfield et al., International Military Forces (Boston: Little, Brown, 1964), pp. 159 and 160.

19. There are several sides to this controversy. In addition to Conor Cruise O'Brien, To Katanga and Back (London: Hutcheson, 1962), see R. Simonds, Legal Problems Arising from the United Nations Military Operations in the Congo (The Hague: Martinus Nijhoff, 1968), pp. 89-91; and Ernest W. Lefever, Crisis in the Congo: A United Nations Force in Action (Washington: The Brookings Institution, 1965), pp. 84 and 85.

20. Gordon, The United Nations in the Congo, pp. 126-133.

21. Lefever, Crisis in the Congo, pp. 94-99.

22. United Nations, Security Council, Report of the Secretary-General on the United Nations Emergency Force, S/11248, 1 April 1974, par. 15. (j).

23. UN Document A/3943, pars. 70 nd 71.

24. Captain Ian Nicol, "Cyprus," Sentinel 10 (1974/8): 15-19; 10 (1974/9): 16-21; and 11 (1975/1): 22-24.

25. Exchange of letters, Lieutenant-General Ensio Siilasvuo, Force Commander UNEF, 12 February 1974, and Mr. Kurt Waldheim, Secretary-General, 14 March 1974.

26. Stegenga, The United Nations Force in Cyprus, p. 101.

27. The writer, as Assistant Chief Logistics Officer (Canadian) at headquarters UNEF, Cairo, with the assistance of a small Canadian and Polish staff, prepared the "Movement" and "Administrative and Logistics" orders for the deployment and initial support of UNDOF. The writer then deployed with

headquarters UNDOF, Damascus, as the first Chief Logistics
Officer of the Force.

28.   If UN headquarters had any knowledge of this contingency planning, it was provided through "closed" personal communication from the force commander or one of his principal staff
officers.   Certainly, no direction or guidance was forthcoming
from New York.

29.   The UN does have a small supply depot in Pisa, Italy,
which handles a few vehicles, radios, and technical spare
parts.   In the overall materiel support of a peacekeeping
force, the volume of goods provided from the Pisa depot is
insignificant.

30.   Discussions with Colonel E.R. Brost, Chief Logistics
Officer, headquarters UNEF from April to October 1975.
Ottawa, May-June 1976.

31.   Edward H. Bowman and James E. Fanning, "Logistics -
Experience and Requirements," in Bloomfield et al., International Military Forces, pp. 161 and 168.

32.   Simonds, Legal Problems Arising from the United Nations
Military Operations in the Congo, p. 151; and Bowman and
Fanning, "Logistics - Experience and Requirements," p. 171.

33.   Nordic Stand-by Forces in United Nations Service, 2nd
ed.   (Stockholm: UN Department, Swedish Army Staff, 1978),
p. 28, and discussions with Lieutenant-Colonel B. Skoland,
Deputy Chief Logistics, UNIFIL, 1978, at the Joint Canada/Nor-
way Workshop on UN Peacekeeping, Kingston, 11-14 June 1979.

34.   Arne Holm-Johnsen and Odd Oyen, "Experiences Relating
to Logistics in Gaza and the Congo," in Per Frydenberg,
Peacekeeping Experience and Evaluation - The Oslo Papers
(Oslo: Norwegian Institute of International Affairs, 1964), pp.
165-67; Bowman and Fanning, "Logistics - Experience and
Requirements," pp. 151-61; and Lefever, Crisis in the Congo,
p. 105.

35.   Bowman and Fanning, "Logistics - Experience and Requirements," pp. 162-71.

36.   Lieutenant-Colonel R.B. Tackaberry, "Keeping the
Peace," Behind the Headlines 26 (September 1966): 18-23.

9
The International Peace Academy and
the Development of Training for Peacekeeping
Clayton E. Beattie *

INTRODUCTION

Are we to go from crisis to crisis improvising in haste? Or can we now pool our experience and our resources, so that the next time we, the governments and peoples whom the United Nations represents, will be ready and prepared to act.(1)

For more than thirty years, the United Nations has had military observers deployed to monitor and report on the maintenance of cease-fire and interim peace settlements. For more than twenty years, at least one and frequently several United Nations peacekeeping forces have been placed in areas of international conflict. In each case, planning, mounting, deployment, and employment of these United Nations elements have been characterized by ad hoc preparations, made by contributing countries and a small team of experienced diplomats and international civil servants who try to serve the secretary-general as a kind of tactical staff for international crises. The prior military training of the contingents is done by the countries contributing to United Nations' peacekeeping operations and varies in quality and extent. The United Nations itself does not conduct training, although the higher level of training of officers and diplomats, both inextricably involved in the process of peacekeeping, has been available from the International Peace Academy.

---

*The observations and opinions expressed in this paper are those of the author, and do not necessarily represent the views or policy of the Canadian Department of National Defence.

ELEMENTS OF THE TRAINING PROBLEM

The vital activity of peacekeeping has been perpetuated in its
present ad hoc form from the inadequacy and inappropriateness
of provisions in the United Nations Charter to foresee and
meet: "the changing pattern of international politics,
international Third World decolonization and development,"
long-standing international conflicts, and the switch from an
original concept of enforcement by major powers to one of
pacific third party initiatives to achieve peaceful settlement.
Further, the inability of the United Nations military staff
committee and the Committee of 33 (originated in 1964) to
develop the political, legal, and military guidelines,
procedures, and methods of financing have hampered the
United Nations organization itself from taking progressive
initiatives in the field of "prior planning" and in the
coordination of international training programs. Hence,
development of a capability to prepare and train for the
conduct of peacekeeping operations has had to be developed
outside the formal structure of the United Nations organization.(2)
    However, the training process itself is complex because of
the several unique "characterisitics" of a peacekeeping mission
or force. The first of these is its international character.
This requires an appreciation of the fact that there will be
differences in cultural, social, and professional attitudes
affecting the melding of the composite of national representa-
tions into a single force. (See Appendix for lists of states
which have contributed to United Nations peacekeeping operations.) The modular construction of a force also presents a
problem where national contributions form part of a functional
group, but continue to retain individual unit and national
identity. Of course, there are advantages in such groupings,
where national identity fosters high morale or esprit de corps
and, often, a healthy competitive spirit which promotes
efficiency. However, these remain as practical challenges
related to cultural attitudes, language, and professional or
disciplinary standards that must be resolved in order to forge
a peacekeeping team possessing unity of purpose and a high
standard of operational efficiency.
    Then there is the second characterisitic element of
"semi-permanancy." A three or six-month mandate may be
regularly renewed to last for years, as in Cyprus, or it may
come to an abrupt halt, as the withdrawal of UNEF I. Because
of uncertainty about duration, there is a logical reluctance to
deploy a large force, or to leave a mission in the field any
longer than absolutely necessary. Thus, in the name of
economy and alleged administrative efficiency, support services
are slow to materialize. The absence of advanced logistics

planning can complicate and delay this process even further; and, when the deployment of logistics staffs are first delayed and then hastily added, they must adapt to an unfamiliar system which is peculiar to United Nations' needs and does not resemble traditional military concepts of logistics support in the field. Thus, without benefit of a standardized United Nations concept for logistics support in the field, each operation is launched precariously, with its cast of players being required to write the script as the play proceeds, without any indication as to the form of the final act or the duration of its run.

In all missions, the semi-permanent character of a force is influenced by contributing country policies of contingent rotation. These are, in turn, influenced by the recurring renewals of a specific mission mandate.

As a rule, unit rotations are carried out every six months while key appointments in force headquarters, with the exception of the force commander and chief of staff, are rotated annually. This discontinuity together with the requirement to be constantly familiarizing and upgrading newly arrived elements of a force are problems which could be reduced significantly if standardized United Nations forces concepts of operations and doctrine were to be agreed and published for the preparatory training of national contingents.

The foregoing are only some of the key elements which contribute to the training challenge. But perhaps most important is the realization that the major challenge begins when national elements arrive in the mission area where they are often required to function immediately and efficiently as a team, under difficult circumstances. Clearly, any prior familiarization or standardization of training and operational procedures can only have positive results. It must also be accepted that, no matter how well trained individual contingents might consider themselves to be, there is a continuing requirement for "in theatre" training and the practice of force operational procedures if the military, political and, where applicable, police elements are to be melded into an effective team so as to exploit strengths and minimize weaknesses.

In addition, there are problems related to the different national military standards and procedures which follow from policies governing recruitment, terms of service, and operational training goals. This important aspect will be considered in greater detail later. It should be noted, however, that despite the ad hoc nature of peacekeeping operations, precedent has built upon precedent to the point where discernible guidelines have evolved and are followed as appropriate in the implementation of each new operation. Also, in formal and informal ways, the International Peace Academy has contributed to correlating and synthesizing this experience, making the results available for the training of peacekeepers and for their practical use in the field.

THE INTERNATIONAL PEACE ACADEMY: TRAINING,
RESEARCH, AND DEVELOPMENT

The International Peace Academy (IPA) was founded in 1970 to
fill the vacuum in international training and research in
peacekeeping. For political reasons, the United Nations was,
and is today, unable to launch such programs on its own. In
response to the crises at the United Nations deriving from the
Congo experience (ONUC) and the problems of financing
peacekeeping operations, and as a forerunner in the development of United Nations practice, the Committee of 33 was
established by the General Assembly in 1964 to develop agreed
guidelines on the political, legal/constitutional, and financial
aspects of peacekeeping. Though it has labored hard and long
and has gained consensus on several aspects which have
influenced United Nations' practice, there is no final agreement
in sight. There has been no movement at all with regard to
training programs and basic research, although a great deal of
precedent and accumulated experience is lodged in the offices
of the under secretary-general for special political affairs and
field operations. To fill this void, the International Peace
Academy has drawn upon the vast array of United Nations and
national diplomatic, military, and academic experiences in the
preparation of training programs for mid-career officers and
diplomats to enable them to comprehend the complexities of
peacekeeping and to serve ably in the field. Many graduates
have done so since participating in the academy's programs.
     The academy is concerned with and is close to the nego-
tiations on major international issues, formally or informally,
on the agenda of the United Nations which may give rise to
peacekeeping operations. Therefore, it can work in close
harmony with the diplomatic community in "off-the-record-
workshops" dealing with these issues, such as the Middle East
and Namibia. From this has evolved a second thrust of the
academy in the field of international negotiations including
third-party roles, and work on regional conflict resolution as
with the Organization of American States (OAS), the Organization of African Unity (OAU), and the League of Arab States.
     The commendable progress made by the International
Peace Academy since its inception is evident in that 114
countries have sent military and diplomatic officials to its
series of unique international training seminars in peacekeeping
and peacemaking hosted by the government of Austria. In
addition, the governments of Finland, Japan, France, Nigeria,
Peru, and Venezuela have hosted special seminars, as have
private educational institutions in the United Kingdom, Canada,
India, the United States, and regional bodies such as the OAS
and the Inter-American Defense Board. A specific example of
its research and publication is the Peacekeeper's Handbook,(3)

the basic manual on peacekeeping doctrine and practice in use
by some 55 military and diplomatic academies and by schools
and institutes of international affairs in some 90 countries.
The special task force of the IPA has also done innovative
work on the application of remote sensing technology to
peacekeeping as a means to improving effectiveness and extending confidence in the process and in one another by the
host countries in a peacekeeping operation.

The fundamental aims of the Academy training programs
for peacekeeping and peacemaking are, in the final analysis, to
train military and diplomatic personnel at the national level
and, in effect, to develop multinational competence for the
creation of United Nations peacekeeping forces mandated by
the Security Council for the restoration and preservation of
peace within a designated mission area. The complexity of the
programs requires an international and interdisciplinary team
of experts. It involves a consortium of professional and
technical groups, and a range of occupational and social experience which is as broad as the United Nations organization
itself. They are drawn from the:

United Nations Secretariat

○   Full-time international political, administrative, and legal
      staffs; and

○   The Field Service Organization, which is made up of full
      time specialists.

The Military

○   Professional soldiers; and

○   Reservists or part-time personnel.

Diplomatic Corps

○   International diplomats who might reasonably be called
      upon to intervene in a confrontation situation to help
      restore peace and possibly establish peacekeeping opera-
      tions.

UN Civilian Police

○   Nonmilitary national police elements skilled in techniques
      for the maintenance of law and order and for safeguard-
      ing civil rights and freedom by peaceful means.

Other International Agencies

°   The United Nations, the OAS, OAU, Commonwealth, and
        other agencies that might become involved in independent
        peacekeeping situations or those requiring close coop-
        eration with a United Nations force.   Other organizations
        are: International Red Cross (ICRC) and the United
        Nations High Commissioner for Refugees (UNHCR).

The Academic Community

°   Specialists in the field of conflict resolution, peace-
        keeping, and negotiations.

Each brings to bear its special area of expertise and must, at
the same time, be prepared to collaborate with different professional perspectives and approaches.   Mutual understanding
of the issues and of one another and a determined effort on
the part of all to work in harmony are essential to the production of effective training programs.   As well, the programs
must be designed in such a way as to invoke military and
diplomatic personnel participation in the further development
and   refinement   of   peacekeeping   doctrine   and   procedures.
Consideration must also be given to innovative methods and
structures for peacekeeping and conflict resolution.
        Fortunately, time and experience have permitted improve-
ments in the ability of nations to prepare standby elements, to
institute special training programs, and to pursue multinational
or   transnational   cooperative   training   and   readiness   programs.(4)   It is against this background that the role of the
International Peace Academy as a catalyst and facilitator has
been   valuable   and   in   which   it   can   perform   an   even   more
important service in the future, providing it continues to
receive the encouragement, cooperation, and support of all
governments pledged to reinforce the United Nations peacekeeping capability.

THE SPECIAL TRAINING REQUISITES FOR PEACEKEEPING

        It is recognized that peacekeeping operations are
        highly political in nature but their actual conduct
        must conform to military norms and practices.(5)

Assuming that peacekeeping forces are going to be drawn from
a pool pledged by contributing United Nations member countries, and that such countries already maintain military forces
to meet an ascending scale of national security or development
needs, it follows that national armed forces will have been

trained to deal with a variety of conflict situations. This means also that, in most cases, contingents should be capable of dealing with a higher intensity of confrontation or conflict than that normally found in a peacekeeping mission.

Having troops available who are trained and equipped to deal with "worst case" situations is a condition that should promote "peace of mind" in any force commander. However, having been assured of the operational competence of troops in a combat situation, there remains a need to make certain adjustments in national tasking and to emphasize specific peacekeeping techniques not normally associated with traditional combat roles.

At the national level, elements placed on standby are normally "dual tasked" and, therefore, must pursue at least two types of training programs. Since peacekeeping operations emphasize the limitation or cessation of conflict, there is also a natural desire to limit the equipment of such troops to "light weapons" in order to further emphasize the pacific nature of their mission. While desirable, this rationale has not proven valid in certain situations in recent years such as in Cyprus and Lebanon where United Nations troops have required the increased capability provided by antitank and indirect fire support weapons to prevent intimidation or to assure their own security.

In the preparation of a mission, tasking changes and adjustment of equipment scales can be easily implemented. However, training, which could better prepare troops for their peacekeeping role, is more demanding and requires careful planning, familiarization, and practice. The first of these involves the psychological change from an adversary to a pacific role, from confrontation to third party interposition. In peacekeeping, there is no enemy: the objective is to avoid hostilities, to improve communications between the parties, and advance the process of reconciliation. This necessitates a full understanding of the causes of the conflict - political, military, and economic - as well as the social and cultural environment. It demands a fair-minded and impartial approach while operating within an atmosphere of distrust and suspicion among the protagonists, often under difficult and provocative conditions.

To be fully effective in such a situation, United Nations troops must have a thorough knowledge of United Nations organization and procedures, the role of their contingent within the larger force, and with the operational and administrative functioning of the force in the field. Having mastered these basic requirements, emphasis must then be placed on the necessity of being familiar with the political situation and the sensitivities of the parties involved. Also, United Nations troops who are in frequent contact with the protagonists must develop communication skills to improve performance in medi-

ation and negotiation, in developing good will, and in handling
situations in which it is necessary to resolve difficult
humanitarian problems. Beyond these fundamental peaceful
pursuits, United Nations troops must also be prepared to meet
any military confrontation or escalation of tension with courage
and determination, standing by the principles and purposes of
the force mandate; and they must be prepared, if necessary,
to use force in self-defense.

IMPACT OF THE POLITICAL FACTOR

> While it can be debated whether war is a negation of
> diplomacy or a continuation of diplomacy by other
> means, there can be no argument that peacekeeping
> exists as a reinforcement to diplomacy for the pur-
> pose of facilitating a continuance of, or a revision
> to, diplomacy. Peacekeeping is not an end but a
> means to an end.(6)

The political character of peacekeeping operations is paramount. After all, the primary purpose of such operations is
to restore peace and create stable conditions within which
peacemaking can proceed. It should, therefore, not come as a
surprise to members of a peacekeeping force that they must be
fully aware of political and diplomatic sensitivities of their
mission and that they must train to function within the force
as members of a close-knit military/political team.
      While all members of the force must be aware of this
requirement, those most affected and upon whom greater
demands will be made are personnel holding senior appointments at contingent and force headquarters levels. It is at
these levels that it will be most apparent that almost every
incident or tense situation, whether it be military, economic,
or humanitarian in nature, will involve political implications
which reflect in some way the attitudes of the parties toward
one another and hence on final settlement of the dispute.
Thus, members holding senior appointments must recognize
that there are "differences" in the functioning of a United
Nations force headquarters and that they should train to cope
with practices, and sometimes frustrations, not normally found
in the functioning of a traditional military headquarters.
      The first difference arises from the special political/mil-
itary character of such operations. Since peacemaking
negotiations will normally be underway (often conducted by the
secretary-general's special representative in the field), almost
every significant incident or military development can have an
effect on the tenor or progress of "peace talks." Thus, it is
necessary to coordinate closely political and military peace-

keeping efforts on a daily basis. Because political negotiations
are normally "high profile" in nature, United Nations headquarters must be kept informed and consulted in areas where
its influence can be brought to bear in resolving controversy
or facilitating a solution.

Military members must, therefore, be prepared to work
closely as a team with their political counterparts and to be
involved in the preparation of reports or exchanges of correspondence and message traffic. A thorough knowledge of
United Nations' staff and communications procedures is
essential. Within the normal course of events, senior staff
members should also be prepared to negotiate with or mediate
between the parties to the dispute and to keep United Nations
headquarters fully informed on the current state of affairs.
In this regard, close monitoring and sometimes seemingly
abnormal degrees of control of all contingents and members of
the force must be exercised by higher headquarters. This is
because sensitive situations or minor incidents can frequently
escalate to major proportions, either inadvertently as the
result of a spontaneous development of events or through a
deliberate initiative of one of the protagonists seeking to
resolve a situation in his favor or gain some short-term
advantage.

In sensitive areas of policy relating to finance, personnel
security, welfare and logistics support, and, especially where
practical, on the use of force, there are frequently matters
which must be resolved either between force headquarters and
the United Nations in New York, or clarified for the benefit of
national contingents by force headquarters. These and other
subjects have emerged as problem areas over the past thirty
years and their importance has marked them as special subjects
for study by any officer anticipating a senior appointment in a
United Nations force headquarters. Fortunately, such problem
areas have been addressed in recent seminars conducted by
the International Peace Academy. This treatment has recognized the sensitivity of these policy areas and their
importance in peacekeeping operations, but study in greater
depth would still prove valuable.

THE NEED FOR DOCTRINE

A good deal has been researched and written on the subject of
peacekeeping operations over the past twenty years; and,
while it has added to the valuable store of "military history"
and drawn attention to some "lessons learned," it has not
contributed significantly to the store of peacekeeping "doctrine." In recent years, countries such as Austria, Canada,

Denmark, Finland, Norway, and Sweden have produced peace-keeping doctrine on a national basis or on a joint basis, as in the case of the Nordic countries, but there have been no concepts of operations or doctrine produced and agreed on for publication by the United Nations organization. The only text which has approached such status as a widely read and accepted peacekeeping manual has been the Peacekeeper's Handbook, published by the International Peace Academy in 1978.

If contributing countries are to become better prepared to participate in peacekeeping operations, and if the ad hoc character of such operations is to be redressed, then a more serious effort must be made to research past operations and to review all previous publications with a view to the development of a body of international doctrine for the conduct of peace-keeping and peacemaking. Training manuals which might be published as a result of such activity would include:

- the United Nations organization - policies, procedures, and practices in the conduct of peacekeeping operations

- Peacekeeping operations

- Peacekeeping techniques:

    internal pacification
    establishment of a buffer force
    establishment of a border patrol
    observation of armistice or cease-fire lines
    enforcement action
    use of force

- Truce supervisory and observer missions

- Peace restoration operations

- Administrative and logistics support for United Nations operations in the field

- Preparation for and conduct of negotiation and mediation to restore peace

There is already much experience available in the foregoing areas, but some central agency is required to initiate, collate, and edit the project so that new personnel can take over where no experienced personnel are available. Up to the present time, approximately twenty countries have contributed "formed units" to United Nations forces and could, in all likelihood, assist in such a project. With broad cooperation in the preparation of a manual on peacekeeping doctrine, it would undoubtedly receive a certain de facto recognition and perhaps adoption by other members of the United Nations.

NATIONAL PREPARATION AND TRAINING OF TROOPS

One of the most difficult areas in which to achieve a uniform international standard is in the training of formed units of field troops, be they combat arms or support elements. This problem derives from several causes, some of which are related to the various perceptions of what United Nations soldiers are or should be and how they should be employed. However, the most important determinants of the type or caliber of soldier one finds in the field are:

1. the type of national service system from which the candidate is drawn; and

2. the method of contingent rotation adopted by national contributors.

The system of national service chosen by any contributing country is a predetermined factor and obviously cannot be changed with regard to United Nations service. Generally, there are two "type" systems. The compulsory selective service requires an individual to give a relatively short period of up to two years of active training and service after which he reverts to a reserve status to be called in the event of a national emergency. This system also normally provides for a small base cadre of full-time professionals to provide stability and continuity. In some instances, a voluntary option can be taken for United Nations service, in which case the individual would go on standby until such time as he is called up for service in the national United Nations standby unit for a specified period or until completion of a fixed tour in a United Nations field force. This system generally produces a younger, perhaps less experienced soldier, but the system is flexible, economical, and additional specialist training can be provided as and when required. The second system is that of voluntary full-time service in which an individual undertakes career service in his national armed forces and may find that as a member of his battalion, regiment, or squadron he is committed to a tour of United Nations service. In this system, the individual has the advantage of continuity of service and experience in his chosen career and is more likely to proceed to advanced trade qualification and rank within his chosen field. He has the benefits which flow from regimental training, identity, and esprit de corps.
   Both of the above systems require a period of basic and advanced or specialty training and, where possible and practical in the event of United Nations service, an additional short period of peacekeeping familiarization training. The Nordic countries have further developed their preparations to

the extent that they jointly have the capability to provide up to 5,000 troops comprising the Nordic Stand-by Force "NORD-BFERFN," a pool grouping of battalions and specialist or support units, observers, and headquarters staff personnel.(7)   There are evident advantages and disadvantages in these two basic systems.   But one thing that will not change is that, when forced to function under fire or in other confrontation situations, a force commander wants the best trained, most highly disciplined, and professional a soldier it is possible to produce.

One of the many problems to be faced by a force commander is that he is unaware of the degree and quality of training of contingents when they first arrive in the field, regardless of which system under which they were trained.   This makes it difficult to decide on "in-theatre" training that should be conducted if all are to work together as an effective team.   This consideration is important when two or more contingents are to share a support capability such as logistics or armored personnel transport, or be mutually reliant in terms of support weapons or other capabilities.   What is needed is a careful evaluation of strengths and weaknesses in order to ensure, where possible, that essential training is completed prior to departing for the mission area, and if not possible, then as a matter of priority upon arrival.

Each operation will have specific characterisitics at the outset which may alter over time.   Not every contingency can be provided for, but should be anticipated within realistic limits.

In the early days of United Nations operations, emphasis was placed on the fact that troops should be lightly armed so there were no extensive field defenses or security measures taken to "harden" United Nations installations.   The events in the Congo, and in Cyprus in 1974, quickly brought home lessons on the necessity to assure the safety and security of United Nations troops.   It was soon appreciated that, in the confusion of war, it is often impractical to debate the impartial status of United Nations troops.   Combat capability and protective "sand-bagging" are more effective than blue paint in stopping bullets.   Unfortunately, this lesson had to be relearned in Lebanon in the summer of 1979, and again later in 1980-81 as hostile action against the United Nations force escalated.

The method of contingent rotation is the second factor which affects the efficiency of a United Nations force and relates to the national system of service.   In the first case of formed units on full-time service, one entire unit replaces another, with some exceptions for specialist support services or headquarters staffs.   This method requires a system of reconnaissance and advance parties to carry out necessary familiarization and handover activities prior to the arrival of the main body. Other than some contact or continuity which is possible for troops between aircraft chalks, a completely new unit finds itself responsible for a sector or zone of operations.

An example of the second case, based on the compulsory service system, is the Austrian procedure for maintaining its contingent in UNFICYP. In this case, only one half of the contingent in the mission area is changed in one rotation and there are two rotations per year. It is carried out by two flights carrying personnel from the standby pool having completed two weeks of refresher training in peacekeeping duties. On the first plane, the key appointments who require briefing and handover are transported to the mission area while the return flight carries riflemen. The key personnel have one week handover and the second flight which carries riflemen to the mission area returns with the replaced key appointments who have just completed briefings and handover. The tour of the commanding officer has recently been of one year's duration, and it is not unusual for members of the cadre of full-time service officers to complete successive tours in different appointments.

This latter approach provides advantages of continuity for the contingent in the mission area, but newly arrived personnel do not have the advantages of the continuity and identity provided by full-time service in a parent battalion. Also, personnel are not screened for the mission by the senior officer who will command them, and each arrives as a "new face" in the contingent.

The foregoing underlines some of the problems related to training systems and rotation arrangements. Having only scratched the surface of these problem areas, there is much scope for investigation and analysis, if not by the United Nations, then by an agency such as the International Peace Academy. In any event, there is a need to investigate the possible standardization of training methods and the systems of rotation in order to ensure that techniques are developed to exploit advantages and counter shortcomings. Though it may not be possible to standardize national rotation systems, perhaps it is feasible to plan contingent deployment and rotations in such a way as to minimize the adverse effects of the latter in a mission area.

CONCLUSION

It is evident that peacekeeping requires specific skills for its effective performance. However, because of the ad hoc implementation of UN operations, and the failure of the members of the UN to agree on the need for special training, the task has been left to individual nations to do what training they will on their own, and to the International Peace Academy to design and provide training programs for international participation. But, despite the successful work already being done, the gap between what is needed and what is being accomplished is still very large. It would be preferable if the UN itself could coordinate these activities. But, for political reasons, this is unlikely to occur; this, despite the fact that the UN is making increasing appeals to member states to contribute personnel and contingents to a growing number of peacekeeping operations, often under varying conditions and circumstances.

There are basic training requirements that can best be done only on a multilateral basis. Diverse units with varied degrees and types of training are assembled on extremely short notice and required to work together immediately as a coordinated team. This means that an efficient headquarters staff of officers unfamiliar with the situation and with one another must function as a unified team immediately on arrival in a mission area. To do so, they must have a common appreciation of the tasks and limitations of their mandate, a common understanding of the political and military context of the operations, and a measure of the capabilities of the various national units assigned to the operation, for their most effective deployment and employment.

Haste is essential. What is not done properly and to best advantage in the first days and weeks of an operation may be impossible to accomplish at a later time. One of the unfortunate characteristics of UN peacekeeping is that the pattern established at an early stage becomes entrenched, and the host country(ies) may be extremely reluctant to consider any change.

The best way to offset these problems is to establish the facilities and methods for multinational studies of past, current, and possible future practice. Much more can be done through the development of common doctrine, instruction, and appreciation of the special political skills and requirements of peacekeeping. Preplanning, research, and design of future operations of different types, as they may be applied to varied political and military conditions, must be pursued if only for the purpose of drawing lessons and ideas from such hypothetical studies.

Such training could go a long way toward improving the current and future practice of peacekeeping. Provision of this kind of training could also encourage states that have not as yet contributed contingents to peacekeeping to do so in the future. In fact, one might expect that successful international training as proposed above would also encourage national staff colleges to replicate the courses of study at the national level. Nor is it too much to hope that it would foster a climate of heightened appreciation of the utility of peacekeeping in po-

litical quarters at the national and international levels. This
would generate more preplanning and imaginative development
of new modes of peacekeeping in the maintenance of international peace and security.

The International Peace Academy has, since 1970, played
a vital role in these developments. It is an institution which
calls on the resources of many states and has been endorsed
by the 114 states that have already participated in its
programs.

It has already contributed significantly to research,
training in peacekeeping, a greater understanding by states
and international organizations of the utility and potential of
peacekeeping, and, hence, to improvements in peacekeeping
operations in the field. There is, as we have argued, much
more that needs to be done. Some of the tasks may be taken
up by individual states and regional organizations, if not by
the United Nations itself. But, until such time as the
international situation may make it possible for new international institutions to evolve, every effort should be extended
to the support and enhancement of the work of the Academy.
In the words of Clausewitz: "It is our aim to keep the peace
as secure as possible. To achieve this goal no sacrifice can
be considered to be too much."

NOTES

1. Lester B. Pearson, "Force for UN." Foreign Affairs 35,
(April 1957): 404.

2. Brig. Gen. C.E. Beattie, Books-critiques - "Peacekeeper's Handbook," Canadian Defence Quarterly 9 (Summer 1979):
61.

3. Peacekeeper's Handbook, edited by Brig. Michael Harbottle, International Peace Academy, New York, 1978, pp. 356.

4. Brig. Gen. C.E. Beattie, "Preparation for Peacekeeping
at the National and International Level," Canadian Defence
Quarterly 8 (Autumn 1978): 26.

5. Maj. Gen. Indar Jit Rikhye (ret.), The Sinai Blunder
(New Delhi): Oxford SIBH Publishing Co., 1978, pp. 155.

6. Brig. Gen. F. Leslie, "Some Thoughts on International
Peacekeeping," Canadian Defence Quarterly 7 (Winter 1978):
18.

7. Nordic Stand-by Forces in United Nations Service, 2nd
ed., Stockholm, 1978.

10
Technology and the Future of Peacekeeping
William M. Stokes *

The astonishing growth in electronics and remotely manned systems in the 1960s gave rise to thoughts of electronic battlefields on which many missions performed by men might be turned over to sophisticated materiel. The peaceful uses of such technology had been less evident, though it has been suggested for years that advances in information, communication, and monitoring systems might lead as well to greater harmony among nations. Some interest was aroused with the advent of the Sinai field mission(1) which, manned by United States civilian personnel and equipped with modern surveillance and communications equipment, has provided strong evidence of the utility of technology in peacekeeping and in the enhancement of the confidence of invaded parties, in this case Egypt and Israel, in their reliance on the disengagement of forces.

Further interest in the application of technology to peacekeeping was generated at the 1978 UN special session on disarmament. The precedent and interest therefore exist, but subsequent study and political development have not kept pace. This study, in consequence, is meant to contribute to the process through examination of the potential utility and limitations of the instruments of technology in international peacekeeping and to chart the path for further interdisciplinary analysis. If it evokes political interest, all the better. The well-planned and imaginative use of advanced technology may broaden political options and contribute to more effective and efficient peacekeeping. Technological capabilities may offer opportunities for confidence building between antagonists

*The views expressed in this paper are those of the author and do not necessarily reflect positions of the US Government.

218

that appear well suited to the resolution of potential conflicts of the decade ahead. Indeed, the nature of conflict in the 1980s will demand the technological upgrading of peacekeeping capabilities if international forces are to serve as effective third-party instruments in containing conflict. The very credibility of international peacekeeping forces will depend, in part, upon their capabilities with technologies which, in the past, have been viewed as intrusive from the standpoint of national sovereignty, but which now may be regarded as essential to the effectiveness of third party surveillance along demarcation lines or buffer zones established by cease-fires. The challenge for the peacekeeper is to incorporate and apply these capabilities, while operating under considerable, but not insurmountable, political and economic constraints.

Multinational peacekeeping is highly complex, involving political, military, economic, and ideological interactions on the local, regional, and international levels. In recognition of these complexities, the salient factors are the integration of technology into peacekeeping and mediation activities, the nature of collective arrangements which might enhance the utility of technology in peacekeeping, the need to reconcile technological capabilities with the needs for autonomy and flexibility of the parties in dispute, as well as those of supplier and participant states.

Discussions of technology and peacekeeping trigger visions of exotic materiel, of satellites peering into every corner of the globe or permitting instantaneous communications in support of conflict resolution, and sophisticated sensor devices on the ground, leaving no movement unreported. The case for advanced technology should be kept in perspective, however. There are clearly political and economic constraints. Consequently, the rational design of peacekeeping forces should take all these factors into account. It is essential to determine the potential peacekeeping requirements, the manner in which the requirements will influence the structure of the forces and the identification of the requisite capabilities, doctrines, and training. Further, the nature of future conflicts will have a direct bearing whether or not they may be amenable to the application of peacekeeping in association with other forms of conflict resolution.

While conflicts of the 1980s can be expected to have political, economic, and social roots primarily, tension leading to warfare may also arise from pressures or changes in military balances resulting from arms acquisition. Indeed, activities in outer space and maritime areas, made possible by technological achievement, may generate conflicts in new environments. Of special interest to the peacekeeper is the possibility that technology may affect the frequency, duration, scope, and intensity of conflict.

With regard to frequency, it is often argued that modern weapons have made major conflicts too costly for the super-powers and their allies, yet their arsenals remain. For less developed states, technology serves as a source of symbolic power, military capability to counter perceived threats, and support for other political and social aims. Possession of advanced military technologies may embolden military leaders to take military action. Paradoxically, it could also become a factor in restraint of aggressive action. Modern technology may even be introduced to create more balanced military capabilities among parties in conflict in the hope that more stable conditions will evolve. The continued explosion of capabilities in communications, data handling, and surveillance offers potential for influencing the way in which states handle their disputes. But, overall, there seems to be little evidence that technology alone will alter the frequency of conflicts in which third-party peacekeeping forces might be used. Trends do suggest that international conflicts of limited scope will occur throughout the next decade; such conflicts may or may not have potential for third-party peacekeeping.

In the years ahead, military technologies may well affect the duration of conflict. If significant technological disparities exist among parties' capabilities, open hostilities may be short, although conflict may continue on a smaller scale. This possibility suggests that peacekeeping forces may be required to be put in place rapidly, if they are to play an immediate interposition role. In other situations, where the antagonists' motives and capabilities do not facilitate immediate third-party interposition, surveillance technology may provide early warn-ing to the international community, which may in turn bring pressure to bear on the parties to restrain or minimize the hostilities. In the event that peacekeeping forces would be called upon, the alert would provide a longer period of time to plan, organize, and equip a peacekeeping force. Interestingly enough, it may be that seemingly intractable conflicts offer the greatest opportunity for applying new techniques to peace-keeping. Parties to a conflict and third-party peacemakers may be able to use technology in more innovative ways during drawn out conflicts, since other confidence building measures would have failed and frustrations would be exacerbated.

The scope of conflicts in the 1980s can also be expected to influence peacekeeping requirements. Today, any inter-national crisis has global implications. In this interdependent world, virtually all crises quickly involve other states, either as supporters of opposing parties or in third-party peace-making roles. Revolutionary advances in communications and transportation provide opportunities for increased cooperation and communication, but, at the same time, may enlarge small conflicts into global security issues. In such cases, the geographic areas of conflicts will also be extended, requiring peacekeeping activities well beyond the more traditional border-oriented ones, particularly where core areas become involved. Buffer requirements may increase in depth because of increased ranges of aircraft, artillery, and missiles. The speed, day/night capability, and mobility of technologically advanced military forces may allow them to be marshaled for combat well to the rear of boundaries, beyond the direct observation capability of border-oriented peacekeeping forces.

The intensity and potential destructiveness of warfare are clearly on the rise. The increased accuracy, target coverage, rates of fire, and lethality are facts of life. Weapons range from small arms to nuclear devices. Setting aside the nuclear extreme or war between major powers, in cases where peacekeeping forces are introduced, the ideal should be that, in the aggregate, they employ capabilities nearly as modern as the opposing forces in order to provide credibility to their presence and the ability to fulfill their mandates and to protect themselves from harassment. This is not to suggest, however, that peacekeeping forces should be so heavily equipped that they become or appear as a threat to the opposing parties. But it is an argument that the armament and technological capabilities of peacekeeping forces should be upgraded from traditional levels.

SURVEILLANCE REQUIREMENTS AND CAPABILITIES

With the changes in scope and intensity of conflict, and the introduction of new technologies in warfare and in peacekeeping, some nontraditional peacekeeping functions may evolve. But the basic functions of peacekeeping forces are unlikely to change radically in the 1980s, e.g., conflict isolation and management, fact finding, observation, supervision, and the maintenance of law and order. These functions result in tasks which generate, in turn, specific surveillance requirements: border surveillance, buffer zone maintenance, maritime peace management, limited airspace management, assessment of conflict preparation, and physical security of peacekeeping contingents. The notion of surveillance and verification (actions taken to ascertain compliance with certain provisions) is tied to three major objectives: first, to raise the probability of detecting and correctly classifying violations so pressures for conformity to agreed rules can become operable; second, to reduce misinterpretation in mediation and contribute to confidence building and stability - an environment in which peacemaking can take place more effectively; and third, to contribute to crisis management.

Fundamentally, improved technologies seek to extend the eyes and ears of the peacekeeper so that surveillance and verification can be accomplished more satisfactorily and reaction, if required, expedited. The naked eye and unaided ear provide only limited capabilities during the day and virtually no surveillance capabilities at night. Surveillance technology will allow the peacekeeper to extend his senses and verify events by close inspection when required. Such capabilities have potential for overcoming such human problems as boredom, frustration, and fatigue, as well as allowing the introduction of pertinent information about things and places to which the peacekeeper has no immediate access.

It is against these requirements that a number of ground-, air-, space-, or sea-based systems can be applied. Such systems, fixed or mobile, could incorporate photography, television, radar, thermal imaging, light amplification, and sensor systems with magnetic, electro-optical, seismic, acoustic, pressure-sensitive, or infrared capabilities. Information drawn from intercepted electronic signals could be used as well to complement other means of surveillance and verification (Fig. 10.1). Beyond detection and classification, of course, is the requirement for supporting command, control, communications, and information systems to make data available in a useful form to parties to the conflict and to the peacemakers. Such capabilities clearly have the potential for reducing mistrust through documentation and hence contribute to confidence building.

We are concerned with an integrated system consisting of tactical subsystems in the area of confrontation and deep surveillance subsystems designed to identify violations, provide early warning, help control entry and exit from buffer zones, count force levels in specified areas, and pass information on to evaluation centers in as near real-time as possible. Surveillance systems may also be used to assist in the demarcation of buffer areas or demilitarized zones. To ensure the fullest coverage possible, a surveillance system should provide overlapping coverage to ensure that the temporary loss of any system component will not imperil the mission. In areas where topography limits the effectiveness of surveillance equipment, barriers, patrols, or illumination might be used to steer would-be intruders into areas where identification and interception can be made more easily.

SURVEILLANCE TECHNOLOGY - NEED FOR A REGIME

The successful application of surveillance technology to peacekeeping (acquisition of technology, effective use of technology, and ability to cope with the consequences of technology) will require rules, processes, and structures with prescribed procedures for the management of the technological capabilities

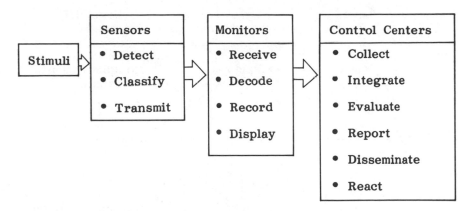

Fig. 10.1.   Simplified Remotely Monitored Sensor System

and the distribution and evaluation of the acquired data.   One form of regime for applying surveillance technology to peacekeeping might consist of:

1.   the parties to a conflict relying on their independent facilities, with an arrangement for the exchange of data;

2.   the joint bilateral management of common facilities - apart from such facilities which the parties might independently maintain;

3.   third party management of facilities, with specific arrangements for evaluation and concurrent distribution of the data to the parties and the third party international political center, e.g., the United Nations.

The extent to which the parties may be able to cooperate will depend upon their perceptions of their independent interests and of the benefits they may derive, domestic support for such cooperative efforts, and the ability of a third party (organization or state) to bring a collective effort to fruition.

Whatever form of cooperation may be achieved (these could be variations or combinations of the above), it should function on three levels in conjunction with the peacekeeping operation: (1) the field operational level in direct management and use of the facilities, (2) interparty national level arrangements for reception and evaluation of the data, and (3) third-party political evaluation of the received data and consultation with the parties (see Fig. 10.2).

Parties to a conflict may or may not possess equivalent levels of technological surveillance capability.   Where there is

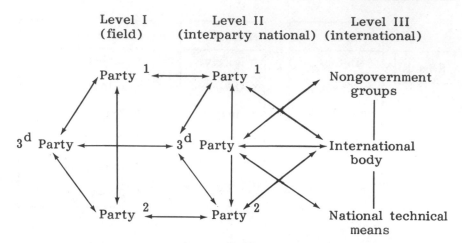

Fig. 10.2.   Framework for Applying Surveillance Technology

an imbalance, then the party with the greater capability
(Nation A) may not wish to lose this advantage by sharing
data with the other party (Nation B) or allowing a third party
(Nation C) to install an equally or more sophisticated
technology and share the data.   Nation B, on the other hand,
would prefer the third of the structural regimes, involving
Nation C, thereby gaining equivalency in surveillance data
and, of perhaps greater importance, an early warning of arms
build up by Nation A.   Hence, in conflictive situations,
opposing parties should, in the first instance, be encouraged
to use their independent surveillance technologies to monitor
compliance in coordination with peacekeeping initiatives in
order to raise the probability of their own detections of
violations and provide national early warning.   But they
should be discouraged from using their national technical
means in ways which might be viewed as overly intrusive by
the other or which are especially provocative; either baiting
the other side to the effect of causing to continue, or of
allowing the other side to perceive the surveillance operation
as preattack reconnaissance.   Yet, to be realistic, nations in
conflict are likely to press for information through whatever
technical or human means are at hand.
        Either the first or second structural regimes, exchanging
independently acquired data or jointly administered surveillance, is preferable to strict reliance on their independent
capabilities.   Cooperative interaction and information product-
sharing, stemming from joint partrols, joint facility usage, or
voluntary data exchanges, while not likely to be a suitable

basis upon which a party might take critical security decisions could, nevertheless, provide a forum for dialogue contributing to mutual understanding.

The most desirable structural regime is the third which adds the tactical surveillance capabilities of a third party to the surveillance capabilities of opposing parties. Through such a structural regime, a higher degree of confidence may be achieved through third-party detection, identification, correlation, analysis, interpretation, and neutral reporting. The competent performance of these tasks could reduce tension and make possible early mediation of minor incidents at the lowest feasible level in the field. Confidence in this framework would depend heavily upon perceptions among conflicting parties to the effect that they were simultaneously receiving the same information from third-party surveillance systems.

However, even if identical data are provided simultaneously to opposing parties, their capabilities for using such information in decision making are likely to be asymmetrical. At the level of interaction and consultation between opposing parties and third-party mediators, the regime should permit the detailed planning for the use of more intrusive forms of surveillance - such as overhead surveillance systems and signal intelligence - provided by the third-party, more complete mutual evaluation of data received from all sources, dissemination of data to both the field and international levels, and the settlement, when feasible, of issues stemming from surveillance in the field which cannot be resolved at that level. It should be noted that some surveillance systems can be operated effectively by third parties without the consent of the conflicting parties. The initial linkage of tactical and strategic surveillance capabilities might occur on this level. It is on this level as well that surveillance products (written reports, data printouts, photographs, or films) might be injected directly into the formal mediation process and, perhaps, into the regular policy processes of participants where they may contribute to the development of norms supportive of peace efforts. Further, activity on this level of the regime potentially contributes more directly to confidence building by influencing threat perceptions on a broader scale, reducing the likelihood of deception by opposing parties, and maintaining the capability to provide more complete early warning of war preparations to all concerned parties. Information systems are critical on this level, as they are in the field. At the international level, rules, processes, and structure must contribute to even broader requirements of conflict resolution. Over time, the institutionalization of technology in the function of peacekeeping may affect the norms of conflict resolution, ultimately leading to the establishment of more meaningful practices for the peaceful settlement of international disputes.

But there are pitfalls. Would a decision to use sophisticated surveillance technology have to be indicated and
affirmed in the Security Council mandate, the UN being the
most likely source of future peacekeeping? There may be real
or imagined objections raised on issues of data sharing and
sovereignty, or the fear of some states that the UN might
evolve its own independent peacekeeping or surveillance
capability. There would also be the question of costs and
willingness of states to pay the additional requisite assessments. Such factors might produce a mandate difficult to
interpret in practical terms and, thereby, hamper the
operation and reduce interest in what otherwise could and
should be a valuable contribution to international peacekeeping. But despite such possible problems, the introduction
of special technical surveillance capabilities at an international
organization level in peacekeeping operations is advisable
where it can reduce the elements of uncertainty and contribute
to international stability.

From time to time, the idea of an international surveillance information pool surfaces as a matter for consideration.
Under such a scheme, existing international surveillance
capabilities could feed directly and unfiltered into an
information reservoir. States with significant national technical
means would provide information, filtered for their own
national security purposes. Other states would be expected to
contribute to the data base as well, or draw from it information which might contribute to the peaceful settlement of
conflict. The use of such capabilities might help prevent
conflicts, before the deployment of peacekeeping forces is
required, where parties to a potential conflict are confronted
with evidence which allows or induces them to seek mutual
accommodation bilaterally or through third-party mediation.
Such a framework would be no panacea. Without adequate
political endorsement, capabilities for a full range of
operational support, and adequate training, any international
regime would be essentially useless. But fuller examination of
such a regime would be desirable in terms of its special
utility, operational functions, and contribution to norm creation
and rule observance.

FACTORS AFFECTING FEASIBILITY

Even if requirements can be articulated clearly, there remain
significant factors which will influence the applications of
technology to peacekeeping in the 1980s. General acceptability
of surveillance technology in international peacekeeping will
depend on many factors, including perceptions of autonomy
and sovereignty, perceptions of motives, materiel availability,
costs, and political bargaining.

With regard to the sovereignty issue, the establishment of surveillance systems in mutually agreed buffer areas may pose relatively few problems. Systems of limited range and capability likewise may not be controversial. More likely to be controversial, however, are those systems capable of deep penetration of sovereign areas or those which require support facilities in geographic areas not under control of third-party mediators – particularly strategic systems that operate at great altitudes or speeds and are capable of collecting information without the consent of the nation observed. Data control would be an especially sensitive issue. Further, the desire by some parties for a collective response may well clash with national views of autonomy. The use of intrusive technical systems poses interesting international legal questions, including those of the ownership of data captured through remote sensing. But it can be argued that, over time, politics and technology will adjust to one another. Surveillance technology may help convert intractable political issues into more manageable technical ones, thus supporting mediation efforts. Technologies at the national and international levels with potentially intrusive applications have already been applied to the collective good – land satellites and seismic sensors in land resource use and earthquake detection roles come readily to mind. The bottom line here would seem to be that some applications of technology previously viewed as excessively intrusive may be viewed less so in the future, as their utility becomes evident.

Perceptions of motives will play an important role in the acceptability of new technology. Opposing parties may view the use of surveillance technology from several perspectives: (1) as a means of early warning against attack, (2) as a means to increase stability, (3) as a means of power redistribution, (4) as a means to encourage relationships with the provider of technology, or (5) as an attempt by a third party to dominate local events. Supplier states may seek a more stable world for economic or security reasons or to enhance their image and prestige and, hopefully, their political influence within the international community. Among peacekeeping forces which lack organic field-level surveillance capabilities, acceptability may stem from a desire to do a more effective job, interest in greater safety, or interest in the use of new technology. In short, acceptability will depend heavily on norms and expectations of the parties affected, the relative advantages they perceive in surveillance technology, and complexities of employment. All too frequently, the rapid introduction of advanced technological capabilities depends, for psychological impetus, upon crises of the moment. For the purposes of peacekeeping, such conditions are precisely those that should be avoided – hence, the necessity of prior planning and general political agreement, so that when the need does arise, rapid and effective implementation would be possible.

Another factor that must be considered is availability. How much surveillance equipment will already be in the inventories of the parties concerned? The very criteria by which peacekeeping forces are selected to fulfill UN mandates (geographic balance and acceptability to the parties) will mean that serious asymmetries continue to exist in the surveillance capabilities of the deployed contingents. Can surveillance hardware be procured commercially in a timely fashion by international organizations, or introduced by other third parties? Hand-me-down material - material that is in widespread use - and systems on the shelf are likely to be more acceptable as instruments of international procurement and management in the eyes of supplier states than equipment of limited density. The idea of stockpiling tactical surveillance systems for peacekeeping has, at first blush, wide appeal, since the early deployment of such equipment might reduce the likelihood of a wider conflict and help avoid the piecemeal application of material which would hamper system integration. But the cost of establishing and maintaining national or UN stockpiles of decade-old surveillance equipment for future operations which cannot be clearly foreseen limits the practicability of the notion. The international use of surveillance hardware will also depend upon supplier states which might be reluctant to release advanced surveillance technology.

A key limitation on the use of sophisticated surveillance equipment is the factor of cost. While the experience of the Sinai field mission suggests that peacekeeping under some conditions can be made less manpower-intensive through the use of surveillance systems, potential cost benefits from more technology-intensive peacekeeping forces in more difficult and varied terrain differ from scenario to scenario. Technicians acknowledge that comprehensive surveillance systems which are integrated into peacekeeping operations at an early stage tend to drive up initial costs, but they also argue that such capabilities will allow manpower savings and reduced operational costs over time without reducing (and potentially improving) effectiveness and efficiency. Others suggest that peacekeeping efforts must be militarily manpower-intensive to affirm a UN presence and to create conditions under which peacemaking may take place. Once peacekeeping forces are deployed under mandate, however, the alteration of their composition and introduction of new technologies are difficult to accomplish. Thus, manpower savings may be elusive. In attempting to weigh the cost benefits of technology in peacekeeping one must, of course, take into account the unmeasurable contributions of multinational peacekeeping contingents in the field, structural alterations that would be required of their forces, and the potential impact of reducing peacekeeping opportunities for less technically advanced nations which may wish to serve and are politically acceptable.

All the factors above have an impact on the feasibility of applying surveillance to peacekeeping. That feasibility, however, will be greatly enhanced over the long run, if a common international understanding emerges regarding the application of surveillance technology to peacekeeping, and if clear-cut objectives are established for the use of such systems. Nevertheless, the need to optimize the limited use of particular technologies rather than extensive general use will probably be a fact of life in determining how technology may be used in future operations.

As we examine peacekeeping requirements in light of potential conflicts, we note a wide array of surveillance capabilities which could contribute to confidence building and early warning. Operations and cost-benefit analyses will have to be conducted to determine if, when, where, and how surveillance systems may be used. It is essential that surveillance systems be given targets which provide reliable indications of activities that affect stability and mutual trust. Effective information storage and distribution systems will be key factors in ensuring that surveillance products are appropriately shared in the field and at interparty national and international levels.

The next steps in considering the role of surveillance technology should be those which directly examine its feasibility and utility in peacekeeping. Acceptability, cost, and availability should be analyzed in considerable detail. The greatest problem associated with the integration of surveillance technology into peacekeeping may be one of changing traditional political attitudes. It is essential, therefore, that opposing parties fully recognize the benefits which might flow to them from the addition of third-party surveillance technology.

Another important hurdle that must be overcome before tactical surveillance material can be widely adapted to peacekeeping will be the requirement to train peacekeeping forces to accept, employ, and maintain equipment made available to them. The training of both surveillance equipment operators and processors of information within the system will be required. Simulations and seminars at the policymaking level could as well profit from discussions of surveillance-related issues. But, the most critical need is for a demonstration in the field that will show whether peacekeeping forces are more effective and efficient when equipped with and supported by modern surveillance capabilities. Such a demonstration might be designed to test the ability of contributing countries to operate and maintain sophisticated surveillance capabilities. Further, the demonstration should help to identify the advantages and disadvantages associated with centralizing control of surveillance equipment under the force commander or decentralizing all or a part of the employment down to the contingent level.

The foregoing discussion has suggested the potentially advantageous use of surveillance technology in future peace-keeping operations and identified some of the hurdles which must be overcome before it is internationally recognized and applied. The experience of the Sinai field mission also provides evidence that surveillance technology can effectively and efficiently direct and classify activity within buffer zones and border areas under certain conditions. But we need further evaluation of the Sinai experience and its applicability to other scenarios before broad generalizations can be drawn from that experience. Beyond this, we need to carefully assess potential peacekeeping requirements for the 1980s, determine how surveillance technology might be applied against those requirements, examine the roles of international organizations and potential supplier states, and seek ways to integrate surveillance technology with peacekeeping and peace-making.

As we discuss the role that technology might play in surveillance and verification, it is important to bear in mind that the effective exploitation of technology depends largely on a number of nontechnical factors, including political accept-ability, resource allocation, doctrine, training, and the degree to which technology would alter the power relationships among the parties in conflict.

The possibility and desirability of the greater use of surveillance technology in peacekeeping operations should be apparent from both national and international perspectives. Those nations and international organizations which play third-party roles in various forms and configurations must be vigorous in safeguarding and preparing for the most appropri-ate applications of international peacekeeping.

NOTES

1. See Watch in the Sinai - The United States Sinai Support Mission, June 1980, Department of State Publication No. 9131; and The Weapons of Peace, How New Technology Can Revitalize Peacekeeping, A Report of the International Peace Academy Task Force on Technology (Bournemouth, U.K.: Bourne Press, 1981).

IV
Regional Peacekeeping

Introduction to Part IV

Though the greatest development and concentration of peace-keeping has taken place within the UN, it also has been employed by regional organizations and by unique ad hoc arrangements. Furthermore, there are indications of growing interest among regional organizations and evidence of special multinational arrangements, as that between Egypt and Israel following the withdrawal of UNEF II in April 1982. For these reasons, any analysis of international peacekeeping must reach beyond the UN itself.

Latin America possesses one of the oldest and most highly structured regional organizations. In "Peacekeeping Within the Inter-American System," Paz-Barnica describes the legal and structural arrangements of the Organization of American States (OAS) which provide for the establishment of peacekeeping operations, and the cases where it has been employed, such as the conflicts between Costa Rica and Nicaragua, Honduras and El Salvador, and within the Dominican Republic. A thorough analysis details the unique procedures and characteristics and the problems and accomplishments of OAS peacekeeping, and "demonstrates that peacekeeping operations are feasible and practical within the framework of the organizational structure and the legal terms and arrangements which regulate the inter-American system." Yet it is also pointed out that there are major differences in the application of peacekeeping between those conflicts which are purely bilateral and those which are internal in nature, however aggravated and compli-cated by international ideological, economic, and strategic factors. The OAS is very zealous of avoiding external inter-ference in its affairs and of managing affairs in its own region without UN intervention. Examination of the Latin American historical experience is vital for the assessment of what forms of conflict resolution might be applied to the grave national

and binational conflicts in Latin America in the decade of the
1980s and beyond.

Africa is a continent composed largely of new nations
which formed the Organization of African Unity (OAU) modeled
on the OAS. Yet, for reasons special to Africa, as Pelcovits
states in "Peacekeeping: The African Experience," the OAU
"was never designed as a hemispheric alliance" nor was it
envisaged as a "collective security arrangement." He contrasts
the OAU with the OAS, shows that its constitutional structure
lacks a strong, central, political, decision-making body and
that it functions predominantly by "negotiation, mediation,
conciliation, or arbitration." Furthermore, the OAU secretariat
is limited in size and political discretion, severely restricting
its peacekeeping capability. Pelcovits offers a detailed
analysis of the OAU showing that, though the preferred procedure is to consult the OAU first, in practice, the UN and
other external bodies are frequently called upon to manage
crises. The historical background and case studies, such as
Chad, are carefully analyzed showing the variety of factors,
political and military, which hinder effective regional
peacekeeping. In consequence, Pelcovits prescribes what
measures would be required to improve the OAU peacekeeping
capability, were it politically feasible to do so.

David Cox, in "The International Commission of Control
and Supervision In Vietnam, 1973," argues that any examination of peacekeeping efforts in Vietnam, as established in 1954
(ICSC) and 1973 (ICCS), must conclude that they were, more
or less, failures. The problems were legion. But precisely
because they were functionally constituted to perform the tasks
of observation and reporting of cease-fire arrangements similar
to those performed by UN operations, and because of the
emerging practice of other non-UN "multilateral" peacekeeping
arrangements, as in the Sinai in 1976, the Vietnam operations
are immensely important experiential lessons for any like
endeavor in the future. By contrast, moreover, they point
out the many advantages of UN or well structured regional
peacekeeping arrangements, despite their inherent difficulties.
As Cox points out, with particular emphasis on the ICCS of
1973, the Vietnamese operations totally lacked any overriding
and continuing political authority of control and coordination,
they suffered from political disagreement among the participant
members (the 1973 operation was initially comprised of forces
from Hungary, Canada, and Poland), and they failed to receive the cooperation of the parties in conflict. It proved
impossible to monitor the 18,000 violations of the cease-fire.
Was the ICCS expected to function effectively, or was it
primarily a necessary piece of the tactics of negotiating the
1973 Paris agreements?

Cox analyzes the ICCS within the full context of those
agreements and the renewal of hostilities which followed,

pointing out, especially from the Canadian point of view, that the members of the Commission were forced to mediate among themselves and were unable to function collectively in an objective fashion.   Contrasting experiences are an essential ingredient for broad understanding of the practice of peace-keeping and of assessing its future.   An appreciation of the operations in Vietnam is a prerequisite to that understanding.

11
Peacekeeping within the Inter-American System

Edgardo Paz-Barnica *

GENERAL OVERVIEW

Specific peacekeeping operations have been carried out within the inter-American system for the explicit purposes of maintaining peace. These have been of two types: international action of a regional nature, or political action on the part of member states whenever deemed necessary to attain or restore peaceful coexistence.

The principal body within that system, the organization of American States (OAS), is also one of the regional organizations within the United Nations system. Consequently, peacekeeping operations are generally carried out within that regional structure but with the support of the appropriate legal structure within the universal system, i.e., the United Nations. The Charter of the United Nations provides the mechanism for this type of coordination by stating that the UN does not oppose the existence of regional pacts or organizations dealing in matters of the maintenance of international peace and security by means of regional action. However, these pacts or organizations, and the activities they pursue, must be compatible with the purposes and principles of the United Nations. Any UN member participating in such pacts or organizations must make every possible effort to settle conflicts by means of said pacts or organizations before

---

*The author of this chapter was an international official of the Secretary-General of the Organization of American States in Washington, D.C. The opinions expressed herein are of a personal nature and are not necessarily those of the Organization of American States.

submitting them to the UN Security Council. It is only then that the Council may seek a peaceful settlement, based on such regional pacts or organizations, either at the initiative of interested states or at the suggestion of the Security Council itself.(1)

The Charter of the Organization of American States as well as other international juridical mechanisms within the regional system adhere to principles of maintaining the peace which are compatible with peacekeeping operations. Among these are: the guarantee of peace and security in the hemisphere; the prevention of possible causes leading to disputes and the assurance of peaceful settlements of conflicts; the condemnation of wars of aggression; the assertion that any act of aggression against any American state constitutes an act of aggression against all American states; and the condemnation of the use of force or the threat of force. All of these principles aim at "achieving an order of peace and justice, promoting solidarity, strengthening collaboration, and defending state sovereignty, territorial integrity and independence."(2)

Experience has shown that peacekeeping operations within the inter-American system have rendered positive results, although some have led to frustrations as well as polemic and controversial judgments. In any event, peacekeeping operations, whether at the universal or the regional level, have become - as stated by Galindo Pohl - one of the essential ingredients in the complex procedures utilized by our modern international community to maintain the peace and security of the world. The term peacekeeping operations has become part of the international lexicon, and implies specific ways to deal with international differences that may lead to and/or involve violence. Extensive political and juridical literature, as well as important UN actions, have bestowed solid foundations on this peaceful process. Its similarities and differences, when compared with other methods used to solve conflicts, have also been stressed. It might be true that the pertinent articles in the UN Charter deal at greater length with juridical context than with political expediency. However, we are certain that the members of the international community agree unanimously that the peacekeeping process has provided the United Nations with a useful, and even irreplaceable tool, in order to carry out its responsibilities in matters of peace and security. These operations are sufficiently flexible for adaptation to peculiar circumstances, and those countries who have criticized them occasionally have later found them ideal for preventing the outbreak or escalation of violence.(3) According to General Indar Jit Rikhye, President of the International Peace Academy, "the term peacekeeping, within the UN context, implies the consent to mount a type of operation that does not entail coercive action."

STRUCTURAL NORMS FOR PEACEKEEPING

The structural norms for peacekeeping within the inter-American system consist of a series of international juridical mechanisms which determine the conduct of the member states of the regional organization in the fulfillment of mutual objectives and in the pursuit of the maintenance of peaceful coexistence in the hemisphere.

The Charter of the Organization of American States was adopted at the Ninth International Conference held in Bogota, Colombia, in 1948. It was amended by a Protocol of Reforms signed in Buenos Aires, Argentina, in 1967. Within the basic purpose of guaranteeing the peace and security of the hemisphere, the OAS charter affirms the principle of collective security when it states that any act of aggression on the part of one state against the integrity, territorial inviolability, sovereignty, or political independence of any American state shall be viewed as an act of aggression against all other American states. Thus, in the event of an armed attack, aggression, extra- or intrahemispheric conflict, as well as any act or situation endangering the peace of the Americas, the states have the right to apply those measures and procedures set forth in the special treaties dealing with such matters. Also, the OAS charter provides for the peaceful solution of international conflicts between the states of the hemisphere by means of peaceable methods prior to submitting them to the UN Security Council. When a conflict arises between two or more states which, in the opinion of one of them, cannot be resolved through traditional diplomatic channels, then the parties must agree on such other peaceful method that will permit its resolution.

The American Treaty for Peaceful Solutions, signed in Bogota at the 1948 international conference, implants and implements the entire system for the solution of conflicts at the diplomatic and juridical levels with technical precision. Thus, it regulates the processes of good offices and mediation, investigation and conciliation, judicial processes via the International Court of Justice, and arbitration for the settlement of any differences whether juridical or otherwise.(4)

The Inter-American Treaty of Reciprocal Assistance (signed in Rio de Janeiro in 1947 at the Inter-American Conference for the Maintenance of Peace and Security in the Hemisphere, and amended by the Protocol signed in San Jose, Costa Rica, in 1975) introduces several very important innovations, such as the right of every state to freely choose its own political, economic, and social organization. The Rio de Janeiro Treaty, conceived when the superpowers were engaged in the so-called cold war during the post-World War II era, provided both the legal foundations for collective action and consultation and a scale of sanctions in cases of aggression or rejection of peaceful methods. The contractual parties voiced their condemnation of war, and pledged to refrain from the use or threat of force in their international relations as violation of the charters of the OAS and UN or of the stipulations contained in the treaty itself. They promised to resolve their conflicts peaceably, and to make every possible effort to do so by means of the processes and mechanisms provided by the inter-American system. In the event of a conflict between one or more American states, without detriment to the right of self-defense and in accordance with Article 51 of the UN Charter, the parties to the Rio de Janeiro Treaty pledged to meet as a consultative body in order to exhort the warring states to cease hostilities and restore the situation to the status quo ante bellum. They further pledged to take any other necessary steps to restore or maintain inter-American peace and security, and to solve any conflict through peaceable means; the rejection of such peaceful means by either party to be taken into account when determining the aggressor, with measures adopted by the consultative body considered to be of immediate effect and application.(5)

INSTITUTIONAL MECHANISMS

The juridical structure of the inter-American system provides the institutional mechanisms required for settling problems relating to the maintenance of peace and security in the hemisphere. These are found within the competent bodies responsible for setting up peacekeeping operations. Said bodies, as provided for in the OAS charter, are as follows:

The General Assembly is the supreme body of the Organization of American States. It is mandated to determine the general activities and policies of the organization, to determine the structure and functions of its bodies, and to deliberate any matter relating to the coexistence of the American states.

The Consultative Meeting of Foreign Ministers is held for the purpose of considering problems of an urgent nature and of mutual concern to the American states, as well as to serve as a consultative body. Any member state can request a meeting by addressing such a request to the Permanent Council.

The Permanent Council acts provisionally as a consultative body under the circumstances stipulated in Article 63 of the OAS charter. It is responsible for overseeing the friendly relations of the member states and, to that effect, assist them in seeking effective and peaceful solutions to their conflicts. The parties to a conflict may appeal for assistance to the Permanent Council. Any party to a conflict for which no negotiations are being conducted through peaceful diplomatic or juridical channels may come before the Permanent Council to discuss the situation. Based on a report submitted by the Inter-American Commission for Peaceful Settlement, in accordance with the charter, the Permanent Council can suggest a rapprochement between the parties and encourage them to prevent actions that may aggravate the situation.(6)

The Consultative Defense Committee was created by the OAS charter to counsel the Permanent Council on the problems of military collaboration that may arise as a result of the application of existing special treaties dealing with the question of collective security. Its membership is composed of senior military officials of the American states, who also participate in the Consultative Meeting of Foreign Ministers. The General Assembly, the Consultative Meeting, or the governments may request technical studies or reports on specific subjects to be prepared by the Consultative Defense Committee.

The Inter-American Commission for Peaceful Settlement acts as a subsidiary body of the Permanent Council and assists in the exercise of its powers with regard to the peaceful settlement of conflict. The Permanent Council, with the consent of the parties involved, may submit a controversy directly to this commission and, through its auspices, may investigate events related to the conflict, including on-site investigations within the territory of any of the parties by prior consent of the respective governments.

The Inter-American Defense Board is a technical body responsible for the preparations of plans and recommendations for legitimate matters of collective defense. It is not an integral part of the institutional structure of the inter-American system as defined in the OAS charter, but is associated as a specialized body of a peripheral nature. It communicates directly with the governments of the member states via their respective delegations. It has no military forces under its command. Besides the advisory functions based upon its own expertise, the board is responsible for similar functions as may be

requested by the Consultative Defense Committee. The board
carries out its duties with the assistance of the chairman, the
council of delegates, the chiefs of staff, the secretariat, and
the Inter-American Defense College.(7) On several occasions,

> Discussions have dealt with the questions of incor-
> porating the Inter-American Defense Board into the
> OAS and of establishing an Inter-American military
> force. Neither of these proposals have won suffi-
> cient support to warrant further action. The
> Inter-American Defense Board therefore continues to
> be the body responsible for plans and recommenda-
> tions on matters of the legal collective defense of the
> Hemisphere until such time as the Member States
> acknowledge the need to expand its mandate, or
> until such time as two-thirds of the Member States
> dissolve its Charter.(8)

The board was created by Resolution XXXIX of the Third
Consultative Meeting of Foreign Ministers held in Rio de
Janeiro in 1942. It has continued to exercise its duties by
means of Resolution IV of the Inter-American Conference on
Problems of War and Peace, held in Mexico in 1945; Resolution
XXXIV of the Ninth International American Conference, held in
Bogota in 1948; and Resolution III of the Fourth Consultative
Meeting of Foreign Ministers, held in Washington, D.C. in
1951.(9).
  In the opinion of experts on such matters, governments
may place matters before the Inter-American Defense Board
either by resolutions of the OAS, or directly through their
delegations to the board. "The legal structure of the Inter-
American System does not provide of itself a doctrine for
Hemispheric Security; consequently the approaches for such
planning must be of a general nature, yet must cohere to
specific characteristics."(10) The system whereby the board
is directly dependent on its participating governments, which
is occasionally invoked, provides the framework for the operational modality, being compatible with the existing organic link
between the board and the OAS.(11)

CHARACTERISTICS OF PEACEKEEPING OPERATIONS

Within the scope of activities of contemporary international
organizations, peacekeeping operations have a definite link
with political decisions aimed at preventing conflicts that may
endanger international peace and security. This is evident if
we consider, as Galindo Pohl has pointed out, that the objec-

tives of such activities are to locate, anticipate, and moderate conflicts while, at the same time, creating the conditions necessary for satisfactory solution by means of the diplomatic and legal channels recognized by international law.

This holds true as well in the universal context of the United Nations as it does in the regional context of the Organization of American States. According to Mr. Pohl, two types of peacekeeping operations have been identified: missions of observers, and missions of peace forces. The former have been initiated as a type of assistance offered by the states to the United Nations, while the latter have been based on voluntary contributions and the consent of the states. General Gaston Ibanez O'Brien, who served as the commander of the Peruvian contingent to the UN Disengagement Observer Force on the Golan Heights in 1974, believes that the peace forces have been so efficient that, on several occasions, they have contributed to the cessation of hostilities and restoration of peace in trouble spots throughout the world, with tremendous sacrifices and even loss of lives of their members.

There are measures within the inter-American system which, based on the relevance of numerous criteria, allow for the execution of peacekeeping operations. The General Assembly of the OAS may consider any matter relating to the friendly relations among American states. The goal of the Permanent Council is to consider problems of an urgent nature and of mutual interest to the American states; it has the right to make decisions or issue recommendations; and any assistance it agrees to provide to a state (party in a conflict) cannot be implemented without the consent of said state. The Permanent Council may assist the states (parties in a conflict) and recommend the procedures deemed appropriate for the peaceful settlement of the conflict. Also, via the Inter-American Commission for Peaceful Settlement, it may investigate the facts related to the conflict, even within the territory itself of any of the parties, with the prior consent of the respective governments.

Zelayo Coronado, a distinguished diplomatic expert in inter-American matters, believes that, given the nature of the regional organization, the mandates related to peacekeeping activities which throughout history have been given to designated commissions have revealed, in general, characteristics of great usefulness. The amplification of those mandates have allowed them to function either as fact-finding commissions reporting back to the political body from which the mandate originated and to the higher body when such has been the case; or as commissions of observers with the added and explicit power not only to observe the peace, but also to monitor the observance of the resolutions dictated by the Permanent Council when the application of the Inter-American Treaty for Reciprocal Aid has been invoked. The mandate "to monitor" has often included also that of "supervision."(12)

Within that context, the inter-American system has various models, each with its own characteristics, for the execution of peacekeeping operations. Based on the history of the conflicts that have arisen between states within the international American community, these models may be classified as follows:

- Inter-American organizations or forces, of a military nature, to avert an international conflict between states;
- Commissions of Observers, of a civilian nature, for the purposes of gathering information, verification, and even investigation;
- Commissions of Observers, of a military nature, for the purposes of gathering information, investigation, and verification; and the prevention, supervision, and settlement of disputes in areas of conflict, including supervision of force withdrawals, demilitarization, and establishment of cease-fire zones.

These models of peacekeeping operations have embodied special characteristics to carry out specific tasks of a technical, logistical, operational, and/or administrative nature, as dictated in each particular case. They have also had specific built-in mechanisms for management, integrated procedures, concrete regulations, methods of financing, and processes for the periodic reporting of their activities to the competent body within the inter-American system. And, because of their objectivity and impartiality, they have tended to acquire a quality of conviction to the effect of guiding the adoption of subsequent measures leading to a satisfactory and peaceful solution.

PAST EXPERIENCES

Conflicts between Costa Rica and Nicaragua from 1948 to 1979

In December 1948, immediately after Costa Rica charged that its territory had been invaded by Nicaraguan armed forces, the Consultative Meeting of Foreign Ministers appointed a commission, the so-called "Fact-Finding Commission," to investigate the facts on site. Based on this commission's report, the Permanent Council urged the governments of the conflicting states to refrain from any type of hostile action and to observe the principle of nonintervention. An Inter-American Commission of Military Experts was subsequently appointed to travel to both countries and oversee the effective compliance of the agreed-upon measures. The actions of both commissions contributed to the fact that Costa Rica and Nicaragua signed a Friendship Pact on 21 February 1949.

In January 1955, Costa Rica charged that its sovereignty was being threatened by Nicaragua. The OAS Council appointed a commission to investigate the pertinent facts on-site and to report back on its findings. Based on the commission's report, the Permanent Council condemned the acts of intervention to which Costa Rica had been subjected; called upon member states of the OAS to respond quickly to the Costa Rican request for planes; and asked the Fact-Finding Commission to implement a plan for the effective monitoring of the common border by its military advisors. The commission set forth the measures for the movement of land forces and established a security zone on the international border of both countries. Subsequently, the Permanent Council, by resolution, issued an appeal to the governments of both countries to designate their respective representatives to the Commission for Investigation and Conciliation in an effort to resolve the conflict, in accordance with the American Treaty for Peaceful Settlement; to create a special commission of the OAS Council to extend its cooperation in the execution of the adopted resolutions, recommending that military observers be maintained without interruption in the zone of conflict; and to keep said special commission in force during the course of the negotiations for a bilateral agreement, in accordance with the Friendship Pact previously signed by both countries.

In June 1959, Nicaragua charged that it was the victim of an armed invasion perpetuated with the assistance of Costa Rica. The OAS appointed a commission to gather data related to these charges. The commission held several meetings in Washington, D.C. and then moved to Nicaragua and neighboring countries. It submitted a detailed report on the activities of anti-Nicaraguan elements in Costa Rica and Honduras. According to the report, the governments of these two countries declared their neutrality regarding the events taking place in Nicaragua, and that they had taken adequate steps to prevent their territorial borders from being used as charged.(13)

In October 1977, the OAS Permanent Council was informed of the border incidents between Costa Rica and Nicaragua. The Council appointed a three-member ad hoc commission to verify the claims and to investigate the measures adopted by both governments. It further authorized the OAS secretary-general to make such expenditure of funds as required by the commission. In November 1977, the Permanent Council heard the commission's report and, based on its conclusions, terminated the proceedings. However, the Council issued several calls to the governments of both countries, one of them recommending that the government of Nicaragua reiterate its precise instructions to its armed forces in order to prevent incidents which could violate Costa Rica's sovereignty. In the treatment of this conflict, the Permanent Council invoked the principles contained in articles 2 and 82 of the OAS charter; in particular, the latter which calls upon the Permanent Council to maintain a vigil over the friendly relations among member states, and to that purpose effectively assist them in the peaceful settlement of their disputes.

On 15 September 1978, the Permanent Council of the OAS was informed of charges by Costa Rica that Nicaragua was violating its sovereignty, and, by resolution, appointed an ad hoc committee to verify and report the facts.   Three days later, in accordance with article 59 of the charter of the OAS, Venezuela requested a meeting of the Consultative Meeting of Foreign Ministers to learn of the "serious events occurring in the Central American region," and of the human suffering endured in Nicaragua where a civil war had broken out.   The Permanent Council thereupon resolved, among other measures, to request the Inter-American Commission on Human Rights to launch an ad hoc commission of observers to investigate the situation.   The Permanent Council also made reference to the "friendly cooperation and conciliatory efforts that might be offered by several Member States of the Organization in order to establish, without delay, the conditions necessary for a peaceful solution to the situation."   On 16 October the Permanent Council heard the report of the ad hoc commission of observers, and censured the deliberate violation of Costa Rican air space and other acts committed by the Nicaraguan air force which had bombed and fired upon civilians in Costa Rican territory.   On 22 November, the Permanent Council appointed a further ad hoc commission under its own juris- diction to investigate on-site the charges made by Costa Rica, and also appointed a commission of civilian observers to monitor the border zone and submit periodic reports.   The governments of both countries were asked by the Council to guarantee and facilitate the work of both committees, stip- ulating that the expenditures of the commission of civilian observers must be defrayed by the governments of Nicaragua and Costa Rica.   The expenditures of the ad hoc commission were financed from the budget of the OAS.   On 29 December 1978, the Permanent Council called another meeting of the Consultative Meeting of Foreign Ministers at the request of Costa Rica, who charged that the government of Nicaragua had adopted an attitude which implied a serious threat to the peace of Central America and to the sovereignty and territorial integrity of Costa Rica.   This meeting was called in accordance with article 6 of the Inter-American Treaty for Reciprocal Assistance.   The advisory body reaffirmed the principle of the proscription of any threat and/or the use of force in inter- national relations, and called upon the Permanent Council to activate the establishment of a commission of civilian observers, whose terms of reference and duties were approved by the Permanent Council on January 8, 1979. (14)

The commission of civilian observers submitted its first report on 17 March 1979, stating that it "considered it had effectively fulfilled its task in spite of the difficulties encountered, on the one hand due to the nature of the mandate and, on the other hand, the complexity of the general situation existing in the border zone." It added that the situation had improved and that there was better monitoring and control of the zone as a result of the clean-up operations conducted by the Costa Rican National Guard. The second report, submitted on 17 May 1979, stated that the performance of the commission continued to be useful, and that the governments of both countries "had stated that the general situation along the border zone had improved due to the presence of the Commission of Civilian Observers." In June, however, the work of the commission was made virtually impossible due to the escalation of the civil war in Nicaragua. Nevertheless, the commission continued to render its services.(15)

On 17 June 1979, the government of the United States requested a Consultative Meeting of Foreign Ministers for the purpose of considering "the critical situation in Central America, particularly the extremely serious events of a political and human nature taking place in Nicaragua which constitute a problem of urgency affecting the common interests of the countries of the Hemisphere." On 23 June 1979, the Consultative Meeting of Foreign Ministers adopted an historic resolution which declared that the solution to the serious problem rested exclusively with the Nicaraguan people; and that such a solution must be based "on the immediate and definitive replacement of the Somoza regime"; on the establishment in Nicaragua of a democratic government with the participation of the principal anti-Somoza groups; on the guarantee of respect for human rights; and on the prompt implementation of free elections leading to the establishment of a democratic government with guarantees of peace, liberty, and justice. The member states of the OAS were urged (while respecting the basic principle of nonintervention) to assist in the negotiation of a lasting and peaceful solution to the Nicaraguan problem. They were also asked to pledge their efforts to promote humanitarian assistance to the population, and to contribute to the social and economic restoration of the country.(16)

Conflict in the Dominican Republic - 1965

In 1965 and 1966, the Permanent Council and the Consultative Meeting of Foreign Ministers were apprised of the "serious situation created by the armed struggle in the Dominican Republic." As a result, the mechanisms of the inter-American system were invoked and the following measures were adopted:

(1) an initial resolution was approved to achieve the establishment of a cease-fire and a neutral international zone; (2) a special fund was established to finance the costs of transportation, food, and administration, and, as well, to defray the costs of a program of emergency aid; (3) a special commission was appointed to promote the restoration of peace and normalcy, and to this purpose negotiated the signing of the "Act of Santo Domingo," which ratified a cease-fire agreement; (4) the OAS secretary-general was called upon to make his good offices available to the parties in dispute for the purpose of achieving a climate of peace and reconciliation that would be conducive to the functioning of democratic institutions; (5) an Inter-American Peace Force was established, subject to the authority of the Permanent Council, for the purpose - in accordance with the related resolution - of "collaborating in the restoration of normalcy in the Dominican Republic, of assuring the maintenance of security of the population and the inviolability of their human rights, and foster the spirit and climate of peace and reconciliation that will allow the functioning of the democratic institutions within the Republic." The member states of the OAS were asked to provide land, air, naval, or police contingents to make up the peace force. In that regard, a united command, made up of representatives of the national contingents, was established to carry out the instructions of the Permanent Council and, as well, an agreement was negotiated among the chiefs of staff of each state and the OAS secretariat for the provision of the technical requirements for the performance of its tasks; and (6) an ad hoc commission was established whose principal objective was to bring about the "Dominican Reconciliation and Institutional Act," which culminated in September 1966 in the establishment of a provisional government that, in turn, promoted the resurgence of democracy to the Dominican Republic.

The Inter-American Peace Force was established by the 6 May 1965 resolution of the Permanent Council. The 24 May 1966 resolution, also passed by the Council, ordered its withdrawal from the territory of the Caribbean country in accordance with the following conditions: (1) that the withdrawal begin before 1 July 1966 and be concluded within a maximum of ninety days from that date; and (2) that the ad hoc commission, in concurrence with the government of the Dominican Republic, issue to the Inter-American Peace Force the necessary instructions regarding the dates and methods for the execution of the said withdrawal. It was also resolved to inform the Security Council of the United Nations on the substance of the resolution.(17)

The dispatch of an Inter-American Peace Force to the Dominican Republic has been the subject of lengthy debate within the inter-American system, as many believed that all that was accomplished was to use collective action to endorse the military intervention of the United States which took place at the outbreak of the civil war in that country. The resolution itself, formalizing the establishment of the peace force, specifically stated in one of its clauses "that the establishment of an inter-American force shall constitute, ipso facto, the transformation of the forces at present in Dominican territory into another force which will not belong to one State or to a group of States, but rather to an interstate organization, namely the Organization of American States, directly responsible for interpreting the democratic will of its Members."

General Rikhye, who is an expert on peacekeeping matters with vast experience in UN affairs and as the military adviser to the secretary-general, was sent to the Dominican Republic to assist Dr. Jose Antonio Mayobre, the secretary-general's special representative. He has stated that the OAS and the UN were informed of the U.S. military intervention only after the fact, and that the Security Council considered the OAS action as a violation of article 53 of the UN Charter which stipulates that "no coercive action shall be carried out by means of regional agreements without the authorization of the Council." He has further stated that lessons were learned about the capability of regional organizations and the United Nations to work in concert for the resolution of interstate and intrastate conflicts, and, though many difficulties had been encountered, both the OAS and the UN learned more about the process of collaboration, thus strengthening their efforts.(18)

Conflict between Honduras and El Salvador, 1969

The conflict between Honduras and El Salvador, arising from an armed confrontation between these two countries in 1969, was the cause of the most prolonged and highly effective action of OAS military observers in the execution of peacekeeping operations. In this situation, the OAS, in progressive stages, has demonstrated its capacity to serve in the restoration of peace between two member states of the American community. On 4 July 1969, the Permanent Council appointed a seven-member commission to study the prevailing situation on-site; and urged both governments to cease hostilities, restore the situation to that existing prior to the armed confrontation, and to take measures conducive to the restoration and maintenance of peace and to a peaceful solution of the conflict. Four days later, arrangements were made for the cessation of hostilities and the immediate dispatch of peacekeeping troops. At the same time, the commission was requested to name observers to monitor the implementation of the measures adopted by the Permanent Council and to order the surrender of the towns occupied by the armies of the states in conflict, either to the commission or to the observers. The latter, at the request of the commission, were appointed by the secretary-general who, in this regard, solicited the expeditious collaboration of member states.

The Consultative Meeting of Foreign Ministers met on 26 July and ordered the immediate withdrawal of troops; and instructed the commission to strictly monitor the situation in accordance with the reports submitted by the military observers who were being kept in the zone for as long as necessary. Once these measures were carried out, the Consultative Meeting of Foreign Ministers then adopted a further series of resolutions regarding various aspects of the conflict to the purposes of achieving a peaceful solution. These related to peace and associated treaties, free transit, diplomatic and consular relations, demarcation of borders, the Central American Common Market, claims, and issues of human and family rights.(19)

On 9 June 1970, in consequence of the above, the Permanent Council took note of the agreement concluded by the foreign ministers of Honduras and El Salvador by virtue of which a "plan for the establishment of a security zone for the purposes of peace" was approved. The plan was adopted under the auspices of the OAS, to be implemented with the supervision of military observers (land, sea, and air components) to prevent incidents along the border.

The Permanent Council also authorized the continuing presence of the group of military observers for a further period of time. When armed confrontations between the two countries recurred in 1971, the San Jose-Costa Rica Agreement was invoked on the basis of the above mentioned plan, by virtue of an agreement approved at the Consultative Meeting of Foreign Ministers and Central American Chiefs of Staff held on 29 July 1976 in Guatemala, and by the Act and Protocol of Managua of 9 and 12 August 1976, signed by the chiefs of staff of the armies of Honduras and El Salvador and the group of military observers. These two acts conferred on the OAS military observers significant powers relating to the supervision of the cease-fire, the withdrawal of troops, the prevention of incidents, the control system for the return of displaced civilian staff, the supervision of the administration and maintenance of public order in the areas of conflict, and a control system for the disarmament of civilians.(20) On 10 November 1976, the Permanent Council, by resolution, extended the presence of the military observers, and reiterated that their expenses would continue to be borne in equal parts by the governments of Honduras and El Salvador.(21)

It is important to emphasize that coincident with and complementary to the difficult and effective tasks carried out periodically by the OAS military observers, the two countries in dispute focused their efforts toward a peaceful settlement through diplomatic means; at first through direct negotiations and then through mediation based on the Mediation Convention signed by both countries in Washington, D.C. before the secretary-general of the OAS on 7 October 1976.

The mediation efforts under the auspices of the OAS and the direct negotiations by the parties based on the earlier agreements culminated in the signing of a General Peace Treaty by both countries in Lima, Peru, on 30 October 1980. This treaty was later ratified by both governments in accordance with their respective constitutional requirements, and took effect between them in accordance with the practice of international law upon exchange of the instruments of ratification.

The General Peace Treaty dealt with the various aspects of the controversy and, technically, resolved them. With specific reference to the demarcation of borders, the treaty stipulates the demarcation of the traditional lines in those zones upon which there is agreement and which are not the object of a dispute. However, with regard to the controversial areas, a Joint Border Commission was appointed to study the claims of the parties in order to solve problems of a technical nature, whereas cases of a political nature were to be relegated by the commissions to the foreign ministers for their study and solution by means of direct negotiations.

In the last analysis, disputes of a persistent nature, which cannot be resolved by those means stipulated above, are to be submitted to the International Court of Justice for a definitive decision, but only after the treaty has been in force for a period of five years.

The General Peace Treaty concluded by Honduras and El Salvador is generally considered as substantive testimony to the effectiveness of the juridical and mediatory mechanisms operative within the OAS. It is important to point out, however, that the compromise agreement, reached between the parties to provide for the continued presence of the OAS to monitor the border zones, is independent of the General Peace Treaty.

THE FUTURE OF PEACEKEEPING OPERATIONS WITHIN THE OAS

This analysis has presented an examination of the organizational and functional aspects of peacekeeping operations within the OAS. It demonstrates that peacekeeping operations are feasible and practical within the framework of the organizational structure and the legal terms and arrangements which regulate the OAS.

However, it is necessary to point out that there is a difference in the effectiveness of such peacekeeping operations as between those cases of clear international conflict or controversy (that is, a conflict between two or more member states) and those of internal conflict within a state, even when such a conflict has clear international implications due to its effect on the maintenance of peace and security in the hemisphere.

In the former cases, the peacekeeping operations have been well developed and effectively implemented through various types of OAS commissions for the purposes of providing information, investigation, supervision, and verification, as well as for the execution of special tasks within an international juridical context.

In the latter cases, the peacekeeping operations have eventually run into difficulties. These peace forces have not had the decisive support of the deliberative bodies of the OAS, since experience has shown that they contradict basic principles, particularly that of nonintervention, which is a fundamental principle of the OAS. This was the case of the Inter-American Peace Force sent to the Dominican Republic in 1965, even though it resulted in the restoration of a democratic and representative government via peaceful negotiations.

The consequences of that experience became evident at the deliberations at the Thirteenth Consultative Meeting of Foreign Ministers held in Washington, in June 1979, to deal with the matter of civil strife in Nicaragua. The secretary of state of the United States, Cyrus Vance, proposed a draft resolution which envisaged creating a special delegation to assist the Nicaraguans to reach a political solution, and recommended that the governments of the member states (if requested by the special delegation) "be willing to provide an OAS peacekeeping presence, in order to contribute to the maintenance of public order as required by the circumstances attendant to the political process."(22) This was interpreted as an attempt to put into place an Inter-American Peace Force, and the resolution was not well received by the foreign ministers. In consequence, other measures relating to a cease-fire and blockade on the movement of arms were also not accepted. As noted earlier, a resolution was adopted by the required two-thirds majority declaring that "the resolution to the serious problem rested exclusively with the Nicaraguan people; and that such a resolution must be based on the immediate and definitive replacement of the Somoza regime."

The historical experience clearly leads to the conclusion that observer missions, civilian or military as the case may be - intended for the identification of the source of conflicts, their verification, supervision, and settlement - are the appropriate mechanisms, as adapted to circumstances, for the peaceful resolution of conflict through diplomatic means.

These types of operations have rendered satisfactory results in cases of prolonged or chronic conflicts, or in sporadic disputes in which the motivating causes have disappeared within a reasonable period of time.

These operations for the management of conflict and the maintenance of peace, in the light of the beneficial role they have played as means of collective persuasion and dissuasion within the regional context, must be further improved and perfected in the future. They can then be implemented as necessary if adequate consideration is taken into account of the prevailing political realities and the interests of the particular moment. In order to do so, however, we must also keep in mind that the passage of time will bring an increase in the desire to strengthen general political awareness with regard to safeguarding all the fundamental principles of the OAS; particularly the principles of nonintervention, the peaceful settlement of conflicts, the prohibition against the use of threat or violence, the respect for the political sovereignty and territorial integrity of the member states, and the self-determination of peoples.

NOTES

1. This measure, contained in Article 52 of the UN Charter, in no way affects the application of Articles 34 and 35 of the Charter which grant to the Security Council the power to investigate all conflicts and situations which may lead to international friction or give rise to a controversy, and grant every member state of the UN the right to bring any situation of this nature to the attention of the Security Council or the General Assembly of the United Nations.

2. Articles 1, 2, and 3 of the Charter of the Organization of American States.

3. Reynaldo Galindo Pohl, "Juridical Aspects of Peacekeeping Operations," address given at the seminar on said subject held in Lima, Peru, in 1977.

4. Article IX and subsequent Articles of the American Treaty for Peaceful Solutions.

5. Articles 1,2,3,5,7, and 8 of the Inter-American Treaty tor Reciprocal Assistance and Protocol of Reforms.

6. Article 63 of the OAS Charter states that, in the event of an armed attack on an American state, territory, or the security zone delineated by existing treaties, a consultative meeting shall be held without delay, immediately convened by the chairman of the Permanent Council, who, at the same time, must also convene a meeting of the Council itself.

7.   Articles 1 and 2 of the Bylaws of the Inter-American Defense Board.

8.   Inter-American Defense Board, "Juridical Sources and Present Status of the Inter-American Defense Board, 1975," A report submitted on May 25, 1948, to the Inter-American Defense Board by its chairman, Lt. Gen. M.B. Ridway, regarding the Bogota conference, stated: "Finally, and so that it can exercise its present consultative functions more efficiently, as well as such other similar duties delegated to it by the Consultative Defense Committee, the Board is authorized to implement whatever reorganization it deems necessary to carry out said duties."

9.   At the Ninth International American Conference held in Bogota in 1948 to approve the OAS Charter, Resolution VII was adopted which stated: "The budget referred to in Article 53 of the Charter shall include, besides the expenditures for the Panamerican Union, the Council, and the Council of Bodies, those expenditures required by the Secretariat of the Inter-American Defense Board."

10.   Chief of staff of the Inter-American Defense Board, "Basic Elements of the Inter-American System for the Security and the Legal, Collective Defense of the Hemisphere Against Aggression," Washington, D.C., 1972.

11.   Permanent Council of the OAS, "Status of the Inter-American Board vis-a-vis the Organization of American States."

12.   Jorge Luis Zelaya Coronado, "Operations for the Observance of Peace," address given at the Seminar on the subject held in Lima, Peru, in 1977.

13.   Secretary-General of the OAS, "Inter-American Treaty for Reciprocal Aid, Applications," Volume I: 1948-1959-1973.

14.   The "Terms relating to the incorporation and duties of the Commission of Civilian Observers" were approved by Resolution 263.   They contained detailed aspects of the mandate, incorporation, technical and secretarial advisory services, duration of the mandate and its prolongation, scope of activities, and insignia.   The obligations of both governments consisted of the supply of transportation, communications, health services, clothing, food, offices, financial arrangements, liaison, privileges and immunities, identification, and security measures.   The mandate consisted of monitoring the border zone and submitting reports, with orders to travel to the site where an armed conflict had broken out and to remain while it lasted, but to abstain from interfering with or reporting about the internal affairs of either state.

15.   The first report is contained in Document 973/79, and the second report in Document 966/78 of the OAS Permanent Council.

16. Seventeenth Consultative Meeting of Foreign Ministers, Resolution 40/79, 23 June 1979. The Nicaraguan problem was discussed at two meetings of this body: the Seventeenth requested by Venezuela in accordance with the OAS Charter; and the Eighteenth requested by Costa Rica in accordance with the terms of the Inter-American Treaty for Reciprocal Assistance.

17. Tenth Consultative Meeting of Foreign Ministers, Document 461/27 of June 1966.

18. Indar Jit Rikhye, President of the International Peace Academy, "The Dominican Republic," address given at the International Seminar on Peacekeeping Operations, Lima, Peru, April 1978.

19. Thirteenth Consultative Meeting of Foreign Ministers, Report to the OAS Assembly, Document 653/75, 13 May 1976.

20. Act signed at the 29 July 1976 meeting in Guatemala, Document 144/76 of 11 August 1976; and Act and Protocol signed in Managua on 9 and 12 August 1976, Document 147/76 of 16 August 1976.

21. Documents 155/76 and 166/76 of 27 August and 10 November 1976.

22. Draft resolution submitted by the delegation of the United States to the Thirteenth Consultative Conference of Foreign Ministers, Washington 1979 Document 33/79.

12
Peacekeeping: The African Experience
Nathan Pelcovits

By the time the Organization of African Unity (OAU) appeared on the scene in 1963, certain arrangements for collective management of conflicts, including modes of what came to be called peacekeeping, had been practiced by the United Nations for over a decade. Apart from regional alliances like NATO, which were legitimated by the collective self-defense provision of article 51 of the UN Charter, just one regional security organization, the Organization of American States (OAS), was really in business both as a collective defense arrangement and as a mechanism for containing internal quarrels.(1) So it was the experience of the OAS that proved instructive as to the uses and limits of regional peacekeeping in Africa.

In fact, the founding fathers of the OAU consciously patterned certain features of its charter and institutional modes for dealing with intra-African disputes on the OAS model. The Ethiopian draft, which was the basic negotiating paper, was based largely on a text prepared by a Chilean consultant and modeled on the OAS charter. At the same time, the drive for regional integration emanated from native African concerns, particularly to cope with security problems and to provide a mechanism for economic and political cooperation. Thus, when the Nigerian delegation left for the Addis Ababa summit in May 1963 to help draft the OAU charter, it carried a brief calling for adherence to the principles which, with few changes, ended up as article III of the charter.

Virtually without exception, in both continents the institutional arrangements for management of regional conflicts did not take the form of peacekeeping in the stricter sense. Constitutional and political constraints restricted "regional arrangements and agencies for dealing with such matters relating to the maintenance of international peace and security

256

ERRATUM

Chapter 12. "Peacekeeping: The African Experience" by Nathan Pelcovits — page 277, line 5 from the bottom: *for* "General Gebre-Egziabher Dawit of Ethiopia who had been designated force commander" *read* "Mr. Dawit Gebre-Egziabher of Ethiopia, Special Representative of the Secretary-General of the OAU, and Major General Geoffrey Ejiga of Nigeria, who had been designated force commander."

ISBN 0-08-027554-0   Wiseman PEACEKEEPING: Appraisals and Proposals

as are appropriate for regional action" - to recall the cautious language of article 52 of the UN Charter - to low-intensity and unintrusive modes of conflict management.

It is hard to find a clear-cut case of regional peace-keeping by the OAU, or more accurately under OAU auspices, before the ill-starred and abortive "peacekeeping group" (only one unit actually arrived) sent to Ndjamena early in 1980 to police the civil strife in Chad. The OAS record is fuller, though there, too, the regional involvement rarely went beyond mediation. In only two instances was a regional military presence engaged. One is at best an impure case of peacekeeping: the Inter-American Peace Force, which in essence legitimated the American military presence in the Dominican Republic in 1965. The other, a true regional action, was the OAS peacekeeping venture in the "soccer war" between Honduras and El Salvador four years later.

REGIONAL AND UN AGENCIES: RIVALS OR PARTNERS?

From the beginning, the relation of global to regional agencies was both complementary and competitive. As Haas points out, regional security organizations did not challenge the con-stitutional supremacy of the UN in the maintenance of peace and security, which is anchored in the UN Charter. But left somewhat obscure was whether and in what respect such institutions and the world organization were rivals or partners, especially whether regional disputes had to go through a prior stage in the regional forum before being cleared for UN action.(2)

What really determined the possibilities and modes for egional as against international conflict resolution was less constitutional niceties or even institutional capacity than the political dynamics of the crisis. Overall, two cardinal rules or norms governed: the rule of prior reference to regional agencies before going to the UN; and the principle of non-invervention or, in OAU terminology, "non-interference in the internal affairs of states." Both these guiding principles, particularly the second, operated in a manner that set bounds to UN and regional intervention in certain regional disputes.

First Use of Regional Mechanisms

The legalities were that the preservation of peace and security s entrusted to the UN Security Council, but regional orga-nizations were competent to act either through collective self-defense under article 51 or through regional security arrangements, employing "collective measures," or pacific settlement procedures under articles 52 and 53. In fact, the

UN was under an obligation to encourage the first use of
regional arrangements. Article 33 encouraged disputants to
exhaust regional possibilities before invoking UN measures.

In practice, regional agencies, and particularly their
politically dominant members, served as gatekeepers in allowing
regional crises to be subjected to Security Council scrutiny
and determining what conflict-resolution mechanisms were
acceptable. "Prior reference" came close to giving the
dominant regional powers, and, in Africa, the political
grandees among heads of state, a de facto veto over UN
involvement. In Latin American, this rule of the game
legitimated, for the first two postwar decades, America's role
of continental policeman. In Africa, ironically, regional
primacy came to mean that intra-American disputes that might
have been contained or managed by the UN were in effect left
untreated.

Occasionally, a party in regional disfavor would slip
through the gate and compel an airing of its cases in UN
forums. Thus, in 1977, Benin (formerly Dahomey) brought to
the Security Council its complaint against France, Morocco,
and certain West African states alleging complicity in an
attempted coup. Still, the powerful caucus and regional voting
bloc in the end pronounced how far the UN could go. Asserting a political monopoly over regional issues and the prerogative of subjecting African problems to African solutions, the
OAU effectively kept crises like Angola and the Ogaden out of
the UN, even though the regional agency was not equipped to
handle them.

There were exceptions. Algeria successfully broke the
rule and has kept the UN involved in the West Sahara issue,
on the plausible ground that the problem is an outgrowth of
the Spanish Sahara question with which the UN has been
concerned since 1963. By the same token, in the case of
Namibia - where a key party to the conflict, South Africa, is
not a member of the regional body - the African political
consensus naturally favors internationalizing the crisis and the
African political effort operates to mobilize UN involvement.
Following the World Court opinion in 1971 declaring South
Africa's mandate over Southwest Africa terminated and its
continued occupation illegal, Africa enlisted the Security
Council behind an "internationally acceptable" plan to assert
UN authority over Namibia and to hold free elections under UN
supervision and control. In the plan for Namibia, the regional
organization as such was assigned no role at all. Instead,
African consensus backed the Western-sponsored UN plan for a
UN Transition Assistance Group (UNTAG) to supervise the
elections and internal order during the transition. Moreover,
in a compromise proposal (to which South Africa continues to
raise objections), the UN peacekeepers would not only monitor
the election and oversee the transitional administration, but

join with forces of Angola and Zambia to police a 50-mile wide demilitarized zone on either side of the border to assure against infiltration by SWAPO (South West Africa Peoples Organization) guerrillas. But whether to handle a regional dispute locally or "internationalize" a crisis hinged largely on political crosscurrents in the region at the time of the crisis.

For the OAS, the rule of prior reference turned on how the Latins coped with their ambivalence about the U.S. role - protector or intervenor - and how the U.S. perceived the OAS (as against the UN) as supportive of is security concerns. From the outset, the OAS was seen primarily as a hemispheric alliance, article 3 of the Rio Treaty of 1947 (Interamerican Treaty of Reciprocal Assistance) declaring in classic terms that "an armed attack . . . against any American state shall be considered an attack against all American states." Article 6 called for consultation and "collective measures" to meet both external and intracontinental threats. Hemispheric disputes consumed much time of the institution, but well into the 1960s dispute settlement and "conflict management" of this kind took second place to maintaining the solidarity of the alliance.

U.S. dominance in the OAS ensured that hemispheric disputes were kept out of the UN through the 1960s. Guatemala in 1954, Cuba in the early 1960s, and the Dominican crisis in 1965 are obvious examples, though in the last the U.S. acquiesced in the dispatch by the Security Council of a UN representative to "observe and report" on what the Inter-American Peace Force was doing.

Inevitably, perspectives change over the years. At San Francisco in 1945, the Latins took the lead in advocating regional primacy so that the UN Charter (and later the Rio Treaty and the OAS charter) had enshrined the doctrine of prior reference of regional disputes to regional arrangements. Some 28 years later, the Mexican delegate to the UN General Assembly, reflecting a different outlook on the world in which the external threat appeared to diminish and some Latins viewed their basic political affinity not to the region but to the Third World, urged repeal of the once sacrosanct principle of prior reference. A measure of the decline of its power in the OAS is that the United States no longer enjoys a commanding voice in determining whether the UN is brought into regional crises. Now, world politics rather than regional solidarity largely determine which disputes are reserved for regional treatment.

Try the OAU First

In contrast to its Latin American counterpart and model, the OAU was never designed as a hemispheric alliance, though it is sometimes referred to as such; there is no equivalent to the provision in the Rio Treaty that an armed attack against any African state shall be deemed an attack against all. Nor was the OAU viewed primarily as a collective security arrangement. The closest the OAU charter comes to institutionalizing the idea of collective defense is the provision for a defense commission as one of several special commissions in the OAU structure; its mandate was left obscure and it remained dormant until the very end of the 1970s.

By and large, the OAU showed neither political inclination nor institutional capacity to undertake peacekeeping. Rather, the declared principle of "peaceful settlement of disputes" was to be implemented through traditional diplomacy and by "negotiation, mediation, conciliation, or arbitration." While the OAU insisted on keeping family quarrels out of the UN, political and ideological division and sheer lack of institutional capacity and resources, as a rule, limited its own action to diplomatic measures often of only cosmetic effect. And the inclination was to employ not the OAU as an institution but personal diplomacy, a mode more in line with African cultural preference for "palaver" as a way of seeking reconciliation.

Despite (or perhaps because of) limited institutional capacity to manage crises, the OAU insisted on the norm of "try-the-OAU-first." In practice, this meant excluding UN involvement at any stage unless and until there was a continental consensus to engage the UN. The regional leaders could not stop a determined member from airing complaints; but, in disputes between members, the African leadership neither sought nor accepted Security Council recommendations for peaceful adjustment (Art. 36) or proposals for settlement (Art. 37), much less a mandate for peacekeeping. OAU resolutions stressed the need to seek regional remedies first and interpreted the principle in the broadest manner.(3)

It was observed at the Kingston Round Table of the International Peace Academy in 1979 that UN peacekeeping has been beneficially engaged in instances where no regional organization embraces all the adversaries, as in Namibia and the Israeli-Arab conflict. But bringing the UN into these disputes has less to do with the reach of the regional agency than with the Arab-African strategy of reciprocal support for enlisting international media and agencies in their respective conflicts to isolate the adversary. The lesson is not, as might be inferred, that in intraregional disputes the regional peacekeeping option obviates the need to turn to the UN.

Though jealous of its primacy, the OAU (in contrast to the OAS) has on occasion reached out to the UN for complementary action even in intra-African disputes. Sometimes this reinforced deadlock. Thus, concurrent OAU and UN investigations of allegations that Morocco and Gabon (purportedly at French instigation) were behind the mercenary raid on Cotonou in January 1977 just served to exacerbate division and tension. Morocco temporarily withdrew from OAU proceedings and the ministers referred both the UN and OAU reports to the heads of state. Benin, however, pressed its case for compensation before the Security Council, accusing Morocco, Gabon, Togo, Ivory Coast, Senegal, and France of complicity in the raid. The Libreville OAU summit reasserted control of the issue (partly because Benin boycotted the meeting) only to sidetrack it to an ad hoc commission.

Other times, the UN has been enlisted for supportive action. In rival claims to territories given up by former colonial rulers, such as French Somaliland (Djibouti) and Spanish Sahara (Western Sahara), complementary UN action has been sought not only to reconcile political differences but to monitor and certify the validity of elections and to legitimize the succession. International authority for the referendum and elections in Djibouti in 1977 flowed from parallel OAU and UN resolutions which mandated that observers from both would monitor the referendum and elections to ensure that "the principle of self-determination" would be carried out "smoothly and in the most democratic manner." In practice, this was a tripartite exercise since responsibility for arranging the referendum and elections remained with the French administering power.

The UN had been involved in the Western Sahara problem as a decolonization issue, and in 1975 sent a commission of inquiry to the territory which found overwhelming sentiment for independence and called for a United Nations referendum. When the OAU became directly involved in the dispute, however, the UN's role was downgraded. An OAU ad hoc committee of wise men, meeting in Monrovia in December 1979, assigned to the UN a carefully-defined supporting role: to help its own secretary-general conduct studies on technical details of conducting the referendum. More significant, the decision of the heads of state at the Freetown summit in 1980 to seek UN assistance if the OAU proved unable to finance a regional peacekeeping effort in Chad on its own may adumbrate a lessening of traditional OAU misgivings about non-African involvement in African conflicts.

In any event, such readiness to involve the UN in African quarrels has been rare. The rule of prior reference, indeed of exclusivity, has been jealously guarded. And this precedence has been encouraged by the UN. As Stremlau notes, Secretary General U Thant endorsed recourse to the OAU in the Nigerian civil war of 1967-70 and affirmed the belief that regional organizations should provide the first and foremost forum for assessing the international significance of a local dispute, strongly implying this would preempt UN involvement in the Nigerian crisis.(4) Throughout the conflict, he took the position that, so long as the regional body

remained united in its approach, neither the UN political
organs nor for that matter the secretary-general could be
actively engaged.

OAU: Institutional Shortcomings

Ironically, this jealousy of OAU prerogatives stems not from its
effectiveness but from the opposite - that the regional agency
could be trusted not to overstep the carefully circumscribed
political bounds of authority as defined in the OAU charter.
The built-in weakness and incapacity of the OAU flows from its
political origins. The common purpose of the founders was to
give body to an almost mystical concept of Pan-Africanism,
even more than to institutionalize political and economic
cooperation. True, a primary political goal was to help
safeguard hard-won independence and territorial integrity, to
promote economic development, and to keep from being drawn
into the magnetic field of external powers.(5) Functionally,
the OAU was designed as coordinator of African policies within
the limits of agreement, not as a defensive alliance; at most,
an instrument for conflict mediation, not for collective
measures to contain or stabilize conflict.

The main cleavage within the OAU ran along subregional
and ideological lines. Two rival camps - the Casablanca and
Monrovia groups - emerged in 1961. Divergent outlooks on
handling the Congo crisis of 1960-65, the conflict over Algeria
and the future of Mauritania, and differing visions of the
design of unity polarized the continent.

Centrifugal tendencies were aggravated by a legacy of
imperial languages and continuing economic, political, security,
and cultural dependence on the former metropole. Internal
quarrels, insurgencies, secessionist movements, and well-
founded fears of subversion by aggressive neighbors further
eroded unity. When tested in crisis, the OAU political bond
often could not withstand the strain of contending national and
subregional interests.

A weak structure and strict limits on executive authority
in intra-African conflict were an inevitable consequence of this
political geography. The OAU provided an insufficient basis
for legitimizing regional peacekeeping. If the consent doctrine
inhibited the scope of UN peacekeeping, it was construed so
strictly in the African region as to give the parties a veto not
only on whether to invoke the OAU but on the modalities of
regional involvement.

Non-intervention--the Supreme Principle

Paramount, however, in constraining the possibilities for regional peacekeeping in continental disputes was the sanctity ascribed to the principle of nonintervention. In Africa, dedication to the norm of "non-interference in internal affairs" in the OAU Charter is reinforced by fears of seismic instability that would follow attempts to change by force the frontiers inherited from colonial days or to challenge the legitimacy of sitting governments.

Nonintervention is in constant tension with the principle of settling regional disputes peacefully, but there was never any doubt as to which took primacy in the case of Latin America.(6) This sensitivity about any form of intervention makes the OAS Council resistant to any regional security action in interstate disputes beyond their immediate pacification.(7) Even mediation is rarely invoked, and only once did the OAS inject even a rudimentary form of peacekeeping in such disputes.(8)

Unease about intervention, whether in a UN or regional context, stems partly from small-power suspicion that "conflict control" can become a euphemism for ganging up by large powers to dictate terms of settlement. Naturally, the small powers, who too often are the objects of peacekeeping, view it from a different perspective than strategic planners in international organizations or in the capitals of the larger regional powers. It is precisely the intrinsically unstable condition of so many small countries in Africa, coupled with linguistic, political, and ideological divisions on the continent, that have constrained OAU peacekeeping capacities.

On the African scene, the norm of noninterference has been aimed - in principle if not always in practice - against both great-power intervention and interference and subversion by neighbors. As a corollary, and despite Africa's fierce adherence to self-determination for colonies, when it came to relations among African states themselves, the right of self-determination was subordinated to the overriding principles of territorial integrity and respect for established boundaries. Given the vulnerability to subversion and separatism, Nigeria's leaders were not alone during the late 1960s in declaring stability of the state as transcending any claim to self-determination. Granting that self-determination "underlies our efforts to secure decolonization of those parts of Africa still under the colonial yoke," a Nigerian paper in 1966 sounded "a word of caution: the principle of self-determination in its purely theoretical context may be at variance with the other important principle of territorial integrity . . . " and sections of existing states may not claim the right to self-rule on the ground of self-determination.(9) National unity of African states could not countenance any regional interference on behalf of claimants to self-rule by separatist movements within African states or, as in the case of the Ogaden, by neighboring states on behalf of their kinsmen.

Historically, the noninterference doctrine has been most successfully asserted by regional powers like Nigeria to block OAU peace efforts. The consent factor extended even to denying the OAU the right to consider a dispute without the consent of the parties or, in the case of civil struggle, the approval of the sitting regime. In the Biafra secession, the Nigerian delegation at the Kinshasa summit in the summer of 1967 insisted that the issue not even appear on the agenda without its full consent, and threatened to walk out if it was inscribed on terms other than its own. Nigeria effectively dictated that the ad hoc committee of African heads of state be constituted not as a mediatory body but as a "consultative committee" in support of Nigerian aims.

Regional Intervention in the Name of Nonintervention

In practice, the nonintervention principle has been flexibly interpreted and, especially in the 1970s, was often inoperative and overridden by other "principles." Doctrinally honored in OAU rhetoric, in practice, noninterference neither inhibited regional involvement in policing the Chadian internal crisis in 1979-80 nor was it a key determinant of the political acceptability of external forces to bolster either internal or external security.

Both the Nigerian peackeeping initiative in Chad in the spring of 1979 and the successor regional peacekeeping operation early in 1980 were, admittedly, undertaken with the consent of the government and contending factions. But the consent factor was not the paramount reason given to justify regional intervention. Rather, a novel exegesis on the doctrine of nonintervention was articulated by Nigeria at the Monrovia summit and has apparently caught on: regional intervention by African peacekeepers is justified as a countervailing force to foreign intervention (and not necessarily because of the consent of the parties).

The background is instructive. As part of its assertion of regional leadership, Nigeria had for some time taken a strong stand against intervention by African states in each other's affairs (e.g., Tanzania in Uganda) on the ground that this would invite extracontinental intrusion.(10) And, the new logic was invoked to explain and justify the Nigerian peacekeeping initiative in Chad early in 1979.(11)

Earlier, in 1977-78, Nigeria had vainly tried to muster an African consensus for regional action in Shaba province to obviate the need for Zaire's recourse to outside forces. Concern about Soviet-Cuban presences in Angola and Ethiopia were not far from the surface of African consciousness. And, to counter Soviet influence, Nigeria would in early 1980 enter into a defense agreement with Benin.

In any event, in expounding the new creed at the Monrovia summit, Gen. Olusegun Obasanjo, then head of the Nigerian state, denounced the Tanzanian invasion of Uganda earlier that year and charged that such acts create a dangerous precedent.(12) He called for engaging African regional peacekeepers in internal conflicts so as to deter the weaker, vulnerable states from being driven "into the laps of extra-African powers for defense and security." The "neocolonialist" (i.e., French) presence in Chad, said Obasanjo, constituted a greater threat to Africa than any African intervention. Black Africa was also disturbed at the neocolonialist fashion in which French paratroopers had dethroned "Emperor" Bokassa of the Central African Empire, despite his unpopularity.(13)

To a certain extent, then, unease about growing foreign intervention in Africa was the spur for the unprecedented regional involvement in the internal conflict in Chad. But, apart from skepticism about is effectiveness, the OAU peacekeeping ventures in Chad in 1980 did not signal a reversal of national policies about relying on outside protectors. Africans remained ambivalent about calling on external forces for security, about what kind of intervention was legitimate and acceptable. In fact, despite lip service to nonintervention and regional self-reliance, as noted below, far from renouncing the option of external protection, the 1970s saw an increase in reliance on external forces. Sensitivity and concern about intervention is not likely to inhibit recourse to the foreign option so long as no reliable regional peacekeeping option is available.

While Obasanjo and others at the Monrovia summit (1979) called for structural reforms to strengthen OAU peacekeeping, these were not expected to materialize soon. For the near term, economic and military weakness and a pervasive sense of regional impotence seemed likely to reinforce the underlying political and institutional constraints on developing a reliable regional peacekeeping capacity. Forms of OAU conflict management for the foreseeable future - at least through the 1980s - are likely to follow the pattern of the past. So, the record of previous efforts at conflict control continues to be instructive about future possibilities and future limits. The failure of the second OAU peacekeeping operation in Chad in 1982, due to the lack of clarity of mandate, difficulties of implementation, and the renewal of civil war is indicative of OAU weaknesses in the practice of peacekeeping. So, the record of previous attempts at conflict control continues to be instructive about future possibilities and future limits.

THE OAU RECORD: LIMITED PEACEMAKING

Given the cautious consensus about the extent of OAU authority at the time of its founding, it is not surprising that
nothing like the constitutional and institutional base of the
OAS is to be found in the OAU structure.

What the OAU provides is not an alliance but an organizational framework for concert diplomacy, a mode and
institutionalized procedure for discussing matters of common
interest. Conflicts may be considered at regular or emergency
meetings of the Assembly or Council which usually provide a
means for mediation "under an umbrella of broad consensus on
norms and identities."(14)

The architects of the OAU did recognize the need for
more permanent machinery in article XIX of its charter which
provided for a Commission on Mediation, Conciliation, and
Arbitration, whose terms of reference were defined in a
separate protocol signed at Cairo on 21 July 1964. The
commission of 21 members is elected by the Assembly on the
basis of "recognized professional qualifications" but with an
eye to equitable geographic representation.

Initially, expectations were high that the commission
would play a significant role in resolving boundary disputes
and, invoking either customary African law or OAU principles,
pronounce judgment. These hopes never materialized. From
the outset, there emerged a preference not only for the soft
option of good offices and conciliation but for more flexible, ad
hoc mechanisms. At most, the commission served as a panel of
candidates for ad hoc committees.

In recent years, African leaders have been far from
insensitive to the flaws in the OAU machinery for dealing with
political crises that might flare into open conflict, but have
found that political constraints on strengthening the OAU
peacemaking structure are formidable. At the Council of
Ministers meeting in Freetown in June 1980, Sierra Leone
proposed establishment of a Political Security Council to serve
as a "permanent security organ within the OAU for the speedy
and effective resolution of situations which endanger the
security and stability of Africa." But the institutional design
of such a council was left unclear. According to the West
Africa correspondent, the proponents had in mind "a small
group of either ambassadors or ministers who could be swiftly
called into session to react to an emergency." The ministers
cautiously welcomed the idea and referred the proposal to
experts for further study.(15)

Effective OAU peacemaking was further inhibited by the
restricted competence of the secretariat. Explicitly subordinated to the Assembly and the Council, the administrative
secretary general was granted no power of political initiative

or latitude to intervene on his own authority in disputes. With distrust of a strong secretary general heightened by the assertive and controversial role of UN Secretary General Dag Hammarskjold in the Congo crisis, the drafters were careful not to place real power in the hands of his OAU counterpart. In fact, as Woronoff notes, at the Addis Ababa constitutional convention in 1963, an already cautious Ethiopian draft was further watered down so as to deny the secretary general the right to participate in the deliberations of OAU institutions even without a vote. Pointedly reminded that his role was "administrative," the secretary general was surrounded with assistants independent of his will.(16)

All this reflected African determination to keep a tight rein on regional executive and institutional power, particularly in dealing with disputes which the parties judged as affecting their vital interests. On decolonization, nonalignment, and economic cooperation, members could agree; but, while the founders were mindful of the urgency to maintain peace and security on the continent, the authority and capacity to prevent or settle disputes were narrowly circumscribed. The mandate, whether in the form of resolutions of the Assembly or Council or as agreements reached on an ad hoc basis,(17) tended to be hedged not only by a fragile consensus and hypersensitivity to the consent of the parties but by aware-ness that is implementation was not necessarily to be relied on.

Despite these constraints, during the honeymoon years (1963-65) the OAU structure helped contain certain disputes, mainly by fostering a climate for conciliation and nudging the parties to negotiate. Diplomatic-consultative modes rather than "collective measures" was the regional style. The OAU started off with verve and some success in the Morocco-Algerian territorial dispute of 1963, mainly in prodding the parties themselves to negotiate a settlement, and in the Ethiopia-Somali wars of 1963-64 which ended less conclusively and continued to fester. A let-down followed in the second half of the 1960s as the Congo crisis polarized Africa, and the OAU emerged from the Biafra crisis uncertain about its peacemaking role.

Five crises

Of the five major African crises in which the OAU intervened as peacemaker in its formative years, the Algeria-Morocco conflict proved the high water mark in scope and precedent. After Morocco rejected intervention by the OAU Council of Ministers in its boundary dispute with Algeria, a heads of state meeting in Bamako (30 Oct. 1963) agreed on a cease-fire, troop withdrawal, and a demilitarized zone to be supervised by a commission of officers from Algeria, Morocco, Ethiopia, and Mali. But the Bamako agreement fell apart. An ad hoc commis-

sion for good offices and mediation, set up by the Council in
November, had little effect on the situation on the ground.
Disengagement was slow; no suitable mechanism to supervise
demilitarization had been provided; and the parties refused to
evacuate positions. More than a year later, in February 1965,
another agreement for a cease-fire, withdrawal, and demilitarization of a buffer strip proved abortive. In the end, it was
the parties themselves, rather than the OAU or any intermedi-
ary, that achieved settlement.

Though unable to come up with an operative solution or
effectively to engage the institution in peacekeeping, the very
process of seeking solution through the OAU was hailed as a
victory for African unity and a harbinger of a significant OAU
role in future conflict management. This was illusory for the
lasting impact was less to advance peace than to underscore
the primacy of the OAU principle of inviolability of inherited
boundaries. The Algeria-Morocco dispute also established the
precedent of institutionalizing personal diplomacy of heads of
state (and not necessarily through the OAU Assembly) and of
preference for ad hoc bodies to supervise implementation (or
lack thereof) of the Council's mandate.

The Ethiopia-Somali crisis in 1964 reinforced these
lessons. While the dispute remains on the OAU docket and an
ad hoc commission holds an inactive watching brief,(18) the
earliest stage of OAU involvement set the political and
institutional limits of its OAU action. When full-scale fighting
broke out in February 1964, the Council of Ministers ordered a
cease-fire. Somalia also proposed a demilitarized zone to be
supervised by neutral observers and, at a later meeting, a
border peacekeeping force. These proposals were rejected by
Ethiopia which wanted a free hand against the insurgent
shiftas who could readily filter through any observer net.
Apart from political reluctance to assume the task, the Council
was dissuaded by the length of the frontier and the size and
cost of supervisory machinery. The Council settled for a
shrunken mandate: African diplomatic missions to the two
warring states were requested "to do their best and to assist
in the implementation of the cease-fire."

After a futile effort to bring the dispute to the UN
Security Council (which bucked it back to the OAU), Somalia
vainly asked the OAU secretary general to appoint an investigative commission. For all practical purposes, the OAU was
unable to take effective peacekeeping action. While providing
a useful forum for airing the dispute, it was clear that the
OAU could neither effectively mandate a cease-fire nor provide
border monitoring machinery. The end result was to reinforce
the lesson that, for all practical purposes, disputes involving
challenge to existing boundaries were outside the effective
reach of OAU peacemaking.

If the Algeria-Morocco case showed certain limited
possibilities for regional peacemaking, the Congo crisis of
1964-65 demonstrated how very restricted were the OAU's
options in an ideologically-charged conflict. As rebellion
spread in the months following the withdrawal of UN troops at
the end of June 1964, African states called for OAU action to
settle the civil war. Radical African countries called on the
OAU to find a "political solution," a code word for granting
legitimacy to the rebels. As Woronoff notes, Prime Minister
Tshombe (who had been brought out of exile in a vain attempt
to restore order) did not oppose a meeting but rejected any
idea of offering the Congo "as an experiment" in African
peacekeeping.(19)

In a tenuous compromise, the UN Security Council in
September (1964) appointed an ad hoc commission (the Congo
Commission) to supervise a cease-fire and devise a plan for
national reconciliation. Whatever hope there may have been
for reconciliation was shattered by the Stanleyville affair of
November-December 1964. When rebels took foreign hostages
and Belgian paratroopers were flown in by U.S. aircraft on a
rescue mission, African indignation turned against the West.
Tshombe rejected a Congo Commission plan for a cease-fire,
withdrawal of mercenaries, and OAU supervised elections as
one-sided. Ideological lines were soon sharply drawn as the
radical bloc openly supported the rebels (Algeria pledged arms
and "volunteers") while the moderates declared their support
for the legitimate government.(20)

The OAU was discredited as impartial arbiter and peacemaker. At the Council of Ministers meeting in Nairobi in
February 1965, a bitter confrontation ensued between supporters of the legal government and of the rebels. No action was
taken. The OAU played no further role in the Congo and the
final resolution was a military one.

If the Algeria-Morocco and Ethiopia-Somali disputes
showed at least limited possibilities for enlisting the OAU in
conflict containment, the Congo crisis of 1964-65 revealed the
geological fault in the OAU's peacemaking structure. When
Africa is ideologically polarized, the OAU's peacemaking
mechanism is rendered immobile. Regional retreat from peacemaking, lasting from the mid-1960s to the closing years of the
1970s, can be traced largely to the Congo trauma.

Other facets of the political and institutional limitation on
effective OAU peacemaking were exposed in the OAU effort in
1965 to curb Ghana-inspired subversion against neighboring
states and the frustration of attempting to mediate the Nigerian
civil war of 1967-70. The founders were deeply troubled by
the disruption to African order stemming from "political
assassination as well as subversive activities on the part of
neighboring states" and condemnation of such action became a
central principle of the organization. In keeping with this

principle, Nkrumah's Ghana was widely condemned at the Lagos session of the Council of Ministers in June 1965 and the issue was put on the agenda of the Assembly at Accra in October (an occasion not without irony since the meeting had been planned by Nkrumah as a gala affair in his honor).

Given the divisiveness of the issue, however, the sole action the heads of state could agree on was to adopt a Declaration on the Problem of Subversion (acceptable to all as it named no names) whereby the heads of state agreed "not to tolerate the use of our territories for any subversive activity directed from outside Africa against any Member States . . . [and] to oppose collectively and firmly by every means at our disposal every form of subversion conceived, organized or financed by foreign powers against Africa, the OAU or its Member States individually." Patently, a resounding declaration which few took seriously could make little impact on curbing externally inspired subversion; and the OAU, in effect, concluded that such disputes were to be handled by accepted diplomatic processes rather than institutionalized conflict management through the OAU.

In the fifth case, the Biafra crisis which erupted in 1967, the inhibition on OAU peacemaking arose partly from African fear of secession and partly from acquiescence in Nigeria's insistence that, in an "internal matter," the legitimate sovereign government could dictate the limits of regional intervention. As noted earlier, when the Kinshasa Assembly met in September, Nigeria successfully insisted on defining the terms in which the item would be inscribed on the agenda as well as the terms of the OAU's mandate. An ad hoc committee of heads of state was constituted as a "consultative" mission "to assure" Nigeria "of the Assembly's desire for the territorial integrity, unity and peace of Nigeria."

As the conflict intensified, several initiatives were pressed for mediation in a Commonwealth forum, but the OAU stepped in again partly because it feared loss of prestige if it abdicated on an African issue of this magnitude, and partly because four African states had recognized Biafra in April and May 1968. The OAU consultative committee did persuade the two sides to resume talks in 1968, but no progress was made. And, when the Assembly met later that year in Algiers, it gave emphatic support to the position of the federal government.

AFRICA'S SEARCH FOR OTHER OPTIONS

By the end of the 1960s, the OAU's attempts to engage its institutional mechanisms in conflict management thus showed a record of very modest achievement. Given the ideological split (exposed particularly in the Congo crisis) and reluctance of disputants to have recourse to the OAU, the organization entered a decade of inactivity. Ad hoc commissions set up to deal with perennial issues - such as the Ethiopia-Somali dispute - for the most part marked time. Third party mechanisms established in more recent crises, such as the commission on the Gabon-Benin dispute, were intermittently active.

In key crises, however, the OAU was dormant. It adopted a neutral and uninvolved position when Ugandan forces in October 1978 invaded and occupied some 700 square miles of Tanzanian territory north of the Nagera River. Rebuffed in its efforts to resolve the civil wars in the Congo and Nigeria in the 1960s, the OAU was almost demonstratively passive in the bloody internal strife which erupted during the 1970s into massacres, mistreatment of ethnic minorities and other gross violations of human rights in the Sudan, Equatorial Guinea, Burundi, Uganda, and Ethiopia. The organization paid a heavy price in the erosion of its moral authority and in acquiring a reputation for ineffectiveness, indeed of irrelevance, in addressing the security concerns of its members.

African states, with low expectations of the OAU's security role, turned to other options. As noted, the UN was enlisted in preparation for peacekeeping and quasi-peacekeeping operations to manage the transition to majority rule in Namibia and was also asked to help supervise the referendum in Djibouti. But the more ideologically-charged the issue and the more vital the perceived interests, the less acceptable was that option.

Although politically embarrassed and ambivalent about the practice, African regimes increasingly turned to outside protectors. Former metropole powers were looked to as peacekeepers as well as protectors. Recognizing a residual responsibility from colonial days, Britain was the political catalyst and principal element of the British Commonwealth Monitoring Force that supervised the transition to independence in Zimbabwe early in 1980. France maintained a strong military presence in Djibouti after independence (1977), and several francophone states - Senegal, Ivory Coast, Gabon, Tunisia, Chad (until May 1980), Mauritania, and the Central African Republic - continued to accept the shelter of the French security umbrella. Early in 1980, France responded to a Tunisian call for military help (transport aircraft and units of the French navy to patrol its waters) to help defeat a Libyan-supported rebel attack. France also allied itself with Morocco and other African states in support of Zaire against Shaba raiders in 1978.

Cuban troops backed by the Soviet patron and arms were introduced into the Angolan civil war and reportedly supported the invasion of Shaba province by Zairean exiles. Ethiopia's leader, Mengistu Haile Mariam, called on Cuban troops and

Soviet advisers and arms to bolster its own forces in the struggle over the Ogaden and in suppressing the revolt in Eritrea. Mengistu's failure to end the separatist wars presaged a long stay.

Various theories and rationalizations were invoked to explain acceptability of such outside intervention. The Commonwealth force was welcomed to help Zimbabwe navigate to majority rule because it was judged reliable, fair, and acceptable to all factions. The Soviet-Cuban military role in Mozambique was explained as legitimate assistance in a liberation struggle; some rationalized the Cuban presence in Angola by the same reasoning. Though uneasy about Soviet-Cuban power in the Horn, it was justified by some as a legitimate response to Mengistu's appeal to help Ethiopia defend an established border. Senegal, Cameroon, Gabon, and other francophone governments needed French economic and military support to counter Soviet-supported North African intervention and influence in the Sahel and parts of West Africa; though hardly likely to say so publicly, certain francophone leaders put more trust in the former metropole than in their fellow Africans.

Thus, a growing sense of economic and military impotence and lack of trust in the will or ability of African regional powers to assure security drove vulnerable states into the arms of foreign protectors. The OAU was perceived too weak or politically divided to intervene as either guardian or mediator, making a mockery of the policy of African solutions to African security problems, the talismanic formula prescribed by the Carter administration and like-minded Western advocates.(21) As noted below, it was this perception of the OAU's becoming irrelevant to Africa's security concerns that spurred the "new policy" of regional peacekeeping involvement in the Chad and West Sahara crises in 1979. But, given the collapse of the Chad peacekeeping venture in March 1980 and the doubtful beginnings of a new operation in November 1981 following the withdrawal of Libyan troops, as well as the impasse in OAU efforts to resolve the West Sahara conflict despite the "decision of the OAU Implementation Committee on Western Sahara" in Nairobi in August 1981, vulnerable African states are not likely soon to abandon the option of looking to outside powers for security.

Subregional Efforts: The Eclipse of Regionalism?

An option that gained favor in the 1970s - though it is premature to forecast its course or significance - was to extend the reach of subregional economic groupings into the defense field.

When the OAU was founded, the subregional groupings were not disbanded, and, in fact, were formed and reformed in various configurations, but there was agreement that the OAU should be the political body for Africa. However, ambiguity as to scope of subregional action remained. The organizing resolution simply omitted "political" from the list of activities allowed states in a geographic subregion that shared economic, social, and cultural interests. The Charter did not define the actual relations between the OAU and the subregions, nor was the OAU to exercise any supervisory authority over them. Still, it was clear the subregion would defer to the OAU on "political" and security matters. Thus, the Union Africaine et Malgache (UAM), popularly known as the Brazzaville group, transformed itself into a purely economic and cultural structure under the name Union Africaine et Malgache de Cooperation Economique (UAMCE). But, as political differences emerged within the OAU, particularly over the Congo crisis, the UAMCE was reconverted into a political organization, with slightly enlarged membership, and became known as the Organisation Commune Africaine, Malgache et Mauricienne (OCAM).(22)

Over the years, OCAM remained a closely knit political grouping. In its smaller and specialized configuration as the Communaute Economique de l'Afrique de l'Ouest (CEAO), this subregional francophone grouping concluded a nonaggression pact in 1977, and early in 1978 discussions were initiated on mutual defense arrangements. The immediate spurs were growing fears about the expanding Soviet-Cuban military presence in Africa and, for some, a perceived Libyan-Algerian threat against moderate regimes in the Sahel. The ability of the small francophone grouping to plan or mount a concrete defense was questioned, however, and both Togo and Senegal saw greater promise in moving onto the broader stage of the Economic Community of West African States (ECOWAS).

The ECOWAS subregional grouping had been established in 1975 by a joint initiative of Nigeria and Togo to promote economic cooperation and "collective self-reliance" among 16 West African states, embracing both francophone and anglophone countries.(23) Early hesitation of Senegal and some of its francophone neighbors about extending the ECOWAS agenda into the political-security realm because of fears of Nigerian dominance (especially since the secretariat was in Lagos) was overcome and a nonaggression treaty in the form of a defense protocol was signed in June 1978. Senegalese misgivings were also calmed by the commitment of the Ivory Coast to help finance the venture and by placing the office as well as the headquarters of the ECOWAS fund in Lome.

Terms of the defense protocol are not accessible, but apparently no institutional defense arrangements are projected. Members remain divided over whether to move ahead with these arrangements. Why did the ECOWAS economic grouping venture into the defense field? Motives varied. Nigeria, a prime

mover of ECOWAS, saw a defense relationship as creating the
atmosphere for closer political links; the defense pact was
considered in Lagos to be a valuable political by-product of
the economic relationship. Closer political ties might help wean
the francophones from French tutelage.

Senegal and Togo had other motives. In their eyes, with
a population of 150 million and significant resources, the
subregion could develop sufficient defense potential to deter
politico-military pressures from outside, particularly from
radical North African countries.(24) Moreover, some francophone leaders professed that an ECOWAS defense potential
might some day serve as the nucleus of a defense force for
Africa as a whole, a benign version of Nkrumah's Pan-African
force.

Though neither CEAO or ECOWAS have given concrete
form to the defense protocols and economic cooperation remains
their key purpose, ECOWAS has come to be valued also as a
potential security community, conceivably with a long-term
possibility of replacing extracontinental forces. A security
relationship of this kind reflects a certain consciousness of
shared political goals and values which would appear to be
lacking in the region as a whole.

Whether workable defense arrangements will materialize
appeared to depend largely on Nigeria: as the preeminent
military power, is it ready to assume a leading role in a
subregional community? On the other hand, would the Ivory
Coast and like-minded francophone countries overcome their
misgivings about Nigerian dominance of the ECOWAS community? As of the end of 1982, the way these cross-currents
would impact on ECOWAS remained clouded.

Irrespective of how this matter comes out, clearly the
drive toward subregional political-security cohesion reflected a
vote of no confidence in the OAU's capacity to provide a
reliable security option or to undertake peacekeeping. Subregional proponents grant the OAU primacy in collective
regional diplomacy (including good offices and mediation in
low-intensity disputes) but doubt that the OAU will soon be
capable of effective peacekeeping either in intrastate boundary
disputes or internal conflicts in which ideological differences or
political ambitions by regional powers lie at the heart of the
conflict.

The Monrovia and Freetown Summits, 1979 and 1980

The OAU's institutional ineffectiveness as peacekeeper, and
particularly its inability to cope with the continent's grave
human rights and security problems, was on the minds of many
at the Monrovia summit in the summer of 1979. Despite bitter
division (particularly between Tanzania and Nigeria) over the

legitimacy of Tanzanian military action in Uganda (which deposed Amin) and Morocco's concern about the direction of OAU policy on Western Sahara, a measure of unity was achieved on certain security-related issues. Nigeria's peacekeeping initiative in Chad was regionalized and by the end of the year the Chad peacekeeping operation had been put into an OAU framework; momentum was apparently generated toward a negotiated solution for Western Sahara; and the idea of a defense force was endorsed.

The Freetown summit the next year, however, exposed the limits of the OAU's capacity to deal with the Chad and West Sahara crises. A bitter dispute over admitting the Saharan Democratic Arab Republic (SDAR) threatened to break up the OAU as Morocco and its allies were poised to walk out if this happened; the paper compromise referred the West Sahara dispute back to the ad hoc committee. The decision to appeal to the UN for assistance in Chad if the OAU failed in an effort to restore the all-African peacekeeping presence (which had been withdrawn on the outbreak of factional fighting in March) signaled a realistic assessment of the limits of OAU institutional power.(25) By year's end, however, the prospect of devising an acceptable joint UN-OAU force (or an OAU force for that matter) did not look promising as will be noted below. Monrovia and Freetown also underlined the reality that an OAU operational peacekeeping capacity in the form of a defense force still lay in the future.

Civil War in Chad

Though success looked doubtful from the start, the Chad case is significant as the first (and so far only) clear-cut peacekeeping venture under OAU auspices. At the outset, the regional link was tenuous. Following overtures late in 1978 from the Chad foreign minister and key leaders among the warring factions and some neighboring states, Nigeria convened a series of conferences in Kano and Lagos to negotiate a cease-fire and (in later conferences) to establish a government of national reconciliation. With the consent both of other neighboring states and of the regime then in power in Ndjamena, Nigeria on 7 March 1979 sent a force of 150 men (later reinforced to 800) to assist in the maintenance of a cease-fire and assure stability in the Ndjamena area while negotiations for a national unity government proceeded. Nigeria's concern was both for stability of the area and fear of possible spillover of Chad internal strife into its own ethnically-fractionated society. (Libya and certain others also saw this move as a step toward nudging Chad out of the French orbit.)

Though initially welcomed, and despite early success in helping pacify the situation, the Nigerian force was abruptly withdrawn early in June ostensibly because its mission was accomplished: the cease-fire was holding and a transitional unity government was being formed. The Nigerian government's press release of 5 June 1979 merely noted that Nigeria had "found it necessary" to withdraw the troops from Chad though it remained "committed to assist in Chad." The Lagos Daily Times (June 6) said the withdrawal had been ordered by the northern-dominated transitional government of Chad which "accused the Nigerians of behaving like an army of occupation." Animosity between some of the northern leaders in power in Chad and the Nigerian peacekeepers reported by diplomatic observers were attributed partly to suspicion that Nigeria would be tempted to extend its influence (and perhaps its borders) at Chadian expense and partly to a traditional feeling of ethnic superiority among northern Chadians toward Nigerians whose authority as peacekeepers they did not comfortably accept.

Views differed on whether the venture had been technically successful: some claimed the troops did not comport themselves well, and linguistic and cultural differences hopelessly complicated the peacekeeping task. It was an uncommonly difficult assignment at best, given the complex local politics of eleven rival factions, reflecting old ethnic and religious-communal antipathies (Moslem versus Christian and adherents of tribal religions). Many of the factional leaders were proteges of outside powers and some had links to Libya and other contiguous states which trained and secretly supported the warring factions. These same political cross-currents and cultural animosities were destined to frustrate the successor OAU peacekeeping force the following year.

Following deliberations at the Monrovia summit, an accord was reached at Lagos in August 1979 between leaders of the various Chadian parties and representatives of ten African countries, including Chad's neighbors. While the conference was held outside the OAU framework, it was attended by the organization's secretary general, and the institutional link became closer over time as the OAU secretariat helped organize logistics and funding of the "neutral force" called for by the accord. Though not initially authorized by the OAU, the force came to be termed the "Neutral OAU Force in Chad."

The Lagos Accord proclaimed another cease-fire, declared that the area around Ndjamena should be demilitarized, and required that arms be deposited with the neutral force. The force (or peacekeeping group as it was sometimes called) was to be composed of troops from countries not having common borders with Chad, a condition regarded as crucial for impartiality in view of the close links between the warring factions and some neighboring states. The Lagos conferees agreed that the force would be composed of units from Guinea, Congo (Brazzaville), and Benin, totaling 1,500 men.(26) Though the make-up of the force could not be considered ideologically balanced, it proved acceptable to Senegal and certain other moderates as an African instrument for restoring stability. Airlift and logistical support would be provided by Algeria and Nigeria, with costs reimbursed out of a special OAU fund to which members were asked to contribute $50,000 each. Only five paid up - Cameroon, Liberia, Libya, Niger, and the Sudan. Algeria airlifted the Congolese unit, the first and (as it turned out) only contingent to arrive, early in January 1980; it was reported that when reimbursement was not forthcoming from the OAU Algeria sent the bill to Brazzaville.

Alongside the "neutral force," the Lagos Accord provided for a monitoring commission headed by the OAU secretary general and under the "moral authority" of the chairman (or president as he came to be called) of the transitional national union government. It was composed of two representatives from the participating countries and one each from the 11 Chadian political factions that were to share power. The commission's mandate was to ensure application of the "conditions of the cease-fire" and its "effective maintenance," as well as to oversee implementation of all provisions of the accord.

The mandate of the OAU Neutral Force derived not from any OAU authority but from the Lagos Accord itself and from the monitoring commission. It was wide-ranging and soon exposed as unrealistic: to supervise the cease-fire; ensure freedom of civilian movement throughout Chad, while disarming the population; restore and maintain law and order; and help organize and train an "integrated armed force." Its mission would end when such a force was in being. The accord also contained a section declaring that the Chadian parties unanimously recognized that continued presence of French troops in Chad "is an impediment to finding a peaceful reconciliation and solution to the Chadian problem" and that the transitional government when formed "shall effect the withdrawal of the French troops."

This ambitious mandate encountered formidable obstacles from the start. The 500-man Congolese unit was the sole contingent to show up; the Guinea unit was delayed, purportedly because Nigeria refused to airlift them until the French departed. Functions of the mission, including the command structure and the status of the force, were supposed to be worked out between the Chad government, the monitoring commission, and General Gebre-Egziabher Dawit of Ethiopia who had been designated force commander. (Dawit had left for Addis Ababa on an unrelated mission before the breakdown of the cease-fire in March and never returned to Ndjamena during the fighting.) Because of factional division in the Chad government, no consensus could be reached on the command structure or functions of the peacekeeping group, the status of the force, whether it could interpose to separate warring factions, where it would be deployed, how it might supervise and police the cease-fire, or what law-and-order authority it would exercise.

The stay of the Congolese troops was short-lived. Except for its officers ensconced in a hotel, the contingent was, for all practical purposes, confined to the Ndjamena police barracks and kept from contact with the mainly-northern local population (which showed a certain hostility and harbored ethnic and cultural prejudices against the Congolese) so as to avoid incidents. During the fighting in March among rival northern factions, the "peacekeeping" force did not intervene (one Congolese soldier was killed by a stray bullet); and the unit was evacuated by the French on March 26 without having engaged in any peacekeeping duties.

The fight for Ndjamena in March was mainly between two rival Moslem factions led by transitional president Oueddei Goukouni (temporarily allied with southern forces and backed by Libya) and by then defense minister Hissene Habre. Goukouni's effective authority was confined to the "European" and "administrative" sections, while Habre's force held the African quarters to the east and north. The French military presence had little effect on the fighting, and the last of 400 French civilians were evacuated with the last of 1,200 French troops in May. (Later in the year, several francophone leaders voiced concern about the removal of French protection from the area.)

The Chad peacekeeping operation was aborted and whether it could be restored depended largely on Nigeria's success in revitalizing the Lagos Accord. In April, OAU Secretary General Edem Kodjo vainly tried to arrange a meeting with Goukouni and Habre, and a Nigerian delegation to Ndjamena appealed to them to observe a cease-fire "so that the path for the rapid implementation of the Lagos Accord could be cleared." During the OAU Economic Summit in Lagos on 29-30 April 1980, Nigeria convened the Lagos Accord participants and a decision was taken to renew efforts to reactivate the peacekeeping operation but with a significant change. At the initiative of President Leopold Senghor of Senegal, it was decided that "if by the OAU Summit in Freetown no solution is found to the Chadian drama particularly with regard to the dispatch of peacekeeping forces, the OAU would appeal to the United Nations to intervene through the dispatch of its 'Blue Berets' to Chad."(27)

Many African leaders were reluctant to involve the UN in an intra-African conflict. But, as the civil war dragged on and the OAU's inability to end the fighting became embarrassingly manifest, a consensus emerged in the Council of Ministers, at its Freetown meeting, which served as prelude to the summit, to ratify the proposal to seek UN assistance if the OAU force could not be restored within two months.

As endorsed by the summit on 4 July, the resolution affirmed the validity of the Lagos Accord on the formation of a Transitional National Union Government, the establishment of a cease-fire, the "arrival of the Neutral OAU Force in Chad," and the holding of elections within 18 months; (28) recalled that the Council of Ministers had approved the dispatch to Chad of "an OAU Peace-Keeping Force composed of contingents from Benin, Congo and Guinea"; and decided to make "one further attempt" to find an African solution to the crisis by reactivating the OAU force. African states in a position to do so were requested to provide forces at their own expense, "it being understood that logistic and operational costs be met from voluntary contributions." Further, it was decided that "in the event of failure by the OAU to raise the necessary funds of the Peace-Keeping Force by its own effort after a period of one month [the Council of Ministers had proposed two months], the UN Security Council will be requested, through the African Group, for assistance, particularly the necessary financial means to enable peace to be restored in Chad."(29)

The nature of the peacekeeping assistance to be sought from the UN was left deliberately vague because of differences among the African heads of state and government. Most wanted a UN role limited to financial and management help for an all-African force under OAU control; some (notably Cameroon and Senegal) favored a mixed force and UN command, partly out of concern for efficiency and partly out of anxiety that an OAU force would become ensnared in the crosscurrents of ethnic antagonisms which permeated the Chad conflict.

From the start, it was clear that collaboration with the UN would be no easy matter. Chad itself (the Goukouni regime) and its patron Libya opposed "internationalizing" the conflict and involving non-African powers in an African dispute. At bottom, they opposed any peacemaking effort (including the OAU) since outside involvement could only hamper whatever designs Libya had for extending its influence in the area. In the Chad debate at Freetown, Libya's military intervention in Chad - viewed as part of a campaign to extend hegemony over the Sahel and destabilize governments in neighboring countries - was widely condemned. And, in an unprecedented action, a provision was included in the Chad resolution denouncing interference by foreign and African (emphasis added) powers in the conflict, interpreted correctly as a rebuke both to France and Libya.

Moreover, the UN would have its own terms for collaboration. Talks at the United Nations on 28 October 1980 between the OAU Secretary General Kodjo and UN Secretary

General Kurt Waldheim revealed differing perspectives on acceptable terms of collaboration. The Africans preferred a hybrid arrangement: an all-African force controlled by the OAU but supported financially and operationally by the UN. Waldheim countered that establishment of a UN peacekeeping force in Chad would require, as usual, a decision by the Security Council. The operations would then be implemented and managed under established terms of reference, presumably including a geographic balance in composition of the force. At year's end, African leaders were reportedly divided over the extent of acceptable UN involvement and particularly over the acceptability of non-African contingents.

Meanwhile, the need for a peacekeeping decision became more urgent as Libya's military intervention on the side of Goukouni transformed the situation on the ground. Habre was driven out of Ndjamena on 15 December and withdrew his troops to the mountainous region of eastern Chad bordering the Sudan. Despite denials that Libyan combat troops were involved (Goukouni admitted only to "technicians" and "experts"), Libyan troops taking part in the conquest of Ndjamena were estimated at from 1,000 to 4,000 (some accounts put the figure for Libyan troops in all of Chad at 7,000).(30) Habre signed a cease-fire on 16 December, 1980 and Libya and the Goukouni government contended there was no further need for peacekeepers since all was quiet and the government was in control.

But Habre's force was still intact and fighting could erupt at any time. To states neighboring Chad, it appeared vital to restore order in Chad and remove the pretext for the Libyan military presence.(31) Nigeria, which earlier in the year made common cause with Libya against the French presence in Chad, was becoming increasingly anxious about the Libyan threat to dominate the Sahel. Reportedly, Nigeria was now in favor of UN involvement if this proved to be the price of restoring the Lagos Accord.

It was under such unpromising circumstances that the Lagos Conference (of August 1979) participants, joined by President Siaka Stevens of Sierra Leone as current chairman of the OAU, met in Lagos at the end of December 1980. This group was now constituted as the OAU Ad Hoc Committee on Chad and its purpose was to consider measures for implementing the Freetown decision, including reactivating the peacekeeping effort. Prospects for moving ahead with this effort suffered a setback when the conference closed on December 24 (the second day) without reaching consensus on how to deal with the issue of Libyan intervention. The depth of the split was demonstrated by the refusal of 7 of the 12 participants to approve the final communique because it did not call for the "unconditional withdrawal of all foreign troops from . . . Chad."(32) Instead, the communique ambiguously urged that "no foreign troops should be stationed" in Chad except in accordance with provisions of the Lagos Accord. While the validity of the Accord was affirmed as "the basis for the establishment of permanent peace in Chad," no specific reference was made to a renewed peacekeeping effort or to seeking UN peacekeeping assistance. Instead, the communique called for an OAU monitoring force to oversee future elections in Chad, and the UN came into the picture only as the object of an appeal for "all possible assistance" to help the transitional government in its program of reconstruction.

The outcome of the Lagos conference left Libya in control and the OAU in disarray. A year later, the picture had changed. In a surprise move, Libya withdrew its troops from Chad in October 1981, thus paving the way for a renewal of the OAU peacekeeping effort. At a mini-summit in Nairobi the end of November 1981 assembled by Kenya's President Daniel arap Moi, chairman of the OAU, an agreement was reached with Goukouni's transitional government to send a Pan-African peacekeeping force to Chad to "ensure the defence and securi- ty" of the country and to help Chad "integrate" its forces in accordance with the resolution adopted at the summit the previous summer. Six African states pledged troops. The OAU summit also revived the idea of seeking UN assistance. By year's end, units from Nigeria (which also supplied the commander) were in Ndjamena and some troops were deployed in northern and eastern prefectures.

Though a good beginning had been made and the OAU had enlisted three of its larger members in a substantial peacekeeping operation (4,000-5,000 troops were projected), success was far from assured. Operating with an uncertain mandate - Goukouni wanted OAU peacekeepers to help him drive Habre from eastern Chad while the OAU pressed for a cease-fire as a prelude to elections - the "Pan-African" force was dependent on outsiders, mainly France and the U.S., for logistical sustenance. Clashes among factional armies con- tinued. And, President Moi's request to the UN baffled UN headquarters as to what was wanted and what arrangement would be mutually acceptable. Still, the venture was a serious and unprecedented commitment by the OAU to enlist regional peacekeepers in helping settle an infra-African dispute.

Western Sahara

In another peacemaking action, the Monrovia summit in the summer of 1979 endorsed the plan of the OAU Ad Hoc Commit- tee of Wisemen on Western Sahara (Guinea, Mali, Nigeria, the Sudan, and Tanzania). Affirming the right to self- determination of the people of Western Sahara, the summit called for a "general and immediate cease-fire" as a prelude to a "general and free referendum."

The summit endorsed the plan despite the opposition of Morocco which questioned the impartiality of two committee members (Tanzania and Mali). The Monrovia resolution indicated which way the political wind was blowing. By early 1980, some 36 countries, including 18 in black Africa, had recognized the Polisario Front as the legitimate representative of the Saharan people, and it appeared only a matter of time before a majority of the OAU would follow suit. Prevailing African opinion saw the Western Sahara as a colonial-liberation issue to which self-determination applies, and appeared little bothered by further balkanization of the continent. Most African opinion had turned against Morocco following Mauritanian withdrawal of its forces and renunciation of claims to the territory it had occupied in the southern sector, an area which was then taken over by Morocco. (Mauritania continued to claim and hold the territory around the Saharan city of La Guera to protect its most important seaboard outlet.)

Despite Moroccan refusal to attend and a boycott of the meeting by Guinea in support of King Hassan, the ad hoc committee met with Algeria and the Polisario in Monrovia in December 1979 to carry forward implementation of the summit's resolution. The late President Tolbert of Liberia, as chairman of the OAU, warned of the "threat of internationalization of this conflict" and the danger of intervention by outside powers if the OAU failed to act. Agreement was reached that Morocco should withdraw its troops and administration from that part of Western Sahara which had been evacuated by Mauritania (but, significantly enough, not from the part of the territory it had previously taken); contending parties should immediately effect a cease-fire in all of Western Sahara to permit a "free and fair referendum"; and "an OAU peacekeeping force [should be set up] for the purpose of monitoring the cease-fire." The secretary-general of the OAU was instructed to study, in cooperation with the UN secretary general, the technical details of holding a referendum.

But the plan could not be implemented without the cooperation of Morocco and its backers. Rather than a referendum, they urged a negotiated solution leading to partition and satisfaction of some of Morocco's territorial claims as well as sharing revenue from the rich phosphate deposits. A referendum might follow as symbolic endorsement.

The fragility of the consensus reached at Monrovia became all too evident at the Freetown summit in 1980. Discussion of the report of the ad hoc committee degenerated into an acrimonious debate over admission to the OAU of the Polisario movement as the Saharan Democratic Arab Republic (SDAR). With the help of Algeria and Libya, the SDAR lined up the necessary majority (26 out of 50 members) for admission. Its bid failed when nine states (Cameroon, Egypt, Gabon, the Gambia, Ivory Coast, Senegal, Somalia, the Sudan, and Tunisia) were reported ready to join Morocco in a credible threat to leave the OAU if the SDAR were admitted. Given the strong opposition, and in order to preserve the integrity of the OAU, the application for admission was turned aside, and a special committee came up with a compromise formula which was quickly adopted by the summit. The ad hoc committee was directed to reconvene in three months to try to reconcile the parties and seek a "peaceful and lasting solution." The other side of the bargain (which persuaded many to go along with the deferment of a substantive resolution) was Morocco's commitment to "engage in discussions will all interested parties and to participate in the work of the ad hoc committee."

This vague and "astonishingly anodyne" resolution contained neither a call for a cease-fire nor reaffirmation of the referendum.(33) It was accepted by certain states only because of Morocco's promise to negotiate seriously. Still, the decision to refer the issue back to the ad hoc committee was a temporizing measure and demonstrated the softness of support for the Polisario when balanced against a threat to the integrity of the OAU.

The outcome of the committee's meeting in Freetown in September did not promise to move the conflict closer to resolution. The wisemen met separately with each delegation; Morocco refused to talk directly with Polisario representatives and paraded before the committee 10 separate groups of "their" Saharans to show local support. The committee's report, while noting the widely divergent positions of the parties, called for a cease-fire by December to be policed by a United Nations peacekeeping force (an idea never broached before nor previously endorsed by any OAU organ) and for a referendum to be conducted by the OAU "with the assistance of the UN."

As of the end of 1980, the impasse over the West Saharan conflict continued despite a political victory for the Polisario at the United Nations. In November, the General Assembly, by a striking majority (86 to 6, with 44 abstentions), reaffirmed the previous year's call on Morocco to withdraw and allow the West Saharans to exercise their right to self-determination. Morocco and the Polisario were urged to enter into direct negotiations to this end.(34)

It is too early to assess the impact of the Chad and Sahara cases on the OAU's future peacemaking capacities. In Chad, the OAU's role has been essentially to provide institutional cover and support for an enterprise undertaken by a coalition of Chad's neighbors. When this effort aborted, the OAU recognized the realities of its limited power and declared itself ready to seek UN assistance if this proved necessary to ensure renewal of the peacekeeping operation. And, while certain African leaders and OAU secretariat officials had reservations about the wisdom of bringing the UN into the effort, the African consensus backed President Moi's appeal for

UN assistance in organizing and financing the renewed OAU peacekeeping operation at the end of 1981. The Sahara venture can come into play only if there is a precedent negotiated solution. At his stage, both efforts are significant not as tests of the OAU's institutional capacity to undertake peacekeeping but as signaling a turn toward political readiness for active regional involvement as peacekeeping in intra-African conflicts, if and when existing political and institutional constraints can be overcome.

A Pan-African Defense Force

Monrovia also revived a long-dormant interest in a Pan-African Defense Force, which actually antedated by several years the formation of the OAU; but, in the end, the proposal of the Defense Commission was remanded to a Committee of Experts for further study but without expectation of quick progress.

At the OAU organizing conference at Addis Ababa in 1963, the heads of state had opposed Nkrumah's proposal for a joint defense structure. Even the idea of a board of chiefs of staff as an embryo OAU military staff was turned aside. Nor did the conference consider the eventuality of the OAU engaging in peacekeeping operations. The OAU Charter did, however, provide for a Defense Commission (one of the "special commissions") to serve as an institutional base for meetings of defense ministers. At the first session in Accra that fall, Ghana renewed the proposal for a "union high command" with a military staff, subject to the orders of a "union government"; until it was established, orders would come from the OAU Assembly. The plan was opposed at the Lagos Council of Ministers in February 1964.

The first serious discussion took place in Freetown, Sierra Leone, the next February (1965) when the Defense Commission considered suggestions for cooperative military training, exchange of officers, joint maneuvers, and a common military academy. A plan for an African Defense Organization was accepted for later consideration: a voluntary force, with contingents earmarked for and placed at the disposal of the OAU for specific operations. The force would be used only at the express request of member states, even the modalities for action requiring the consent of the parties concerned. It would be activated by the Council of Ministers, presumably serving like the UN Security Council to authorize and be the ultimate supervising organ for a peacekeeping operation. Operational plans were to be prepared by the secretariat and a Committee of Defense experts to be established for the purpose.

The Freetown meeting proved a high-water mark. Interest in an African defense force waned and the Defense

Commission met in formal session just three times in the next 15 years. It was not until the end of the 1970s that the idea stirred serious political interests again, its proponents arguing that African unity and political maturity had reached the stage where a continental army could be effectively engaged in restoring peace and managing conflicts without the need to enlist foreign protectors. For some, the primary object was to help liberate southern Africa; others were concerned about the Soviet-Cuban presence; still others were disturbed that Zaire had to call in French troops in Shaba and that certain francophone states continued to rely on French forces d'intervention. The Defense Commission set in motion a study designed to develop a set of guidelines for debate at the sixth session of the Defense Commission in Addis Ababa in April 1979.

It is not too speculative to conclude that the Defense Commission action was at least partly spurred by the Western (principally French) initiative soon after the Shaba affair to promote formation of a continental peacekeeping force. At a Paris meeting in June 1978, the United States and four Western allies discussed backing a multinational African force that could respond to situations like the rebel attack in southern Zaire the previous month. Africans split on the proposal, with almost all francophones approving the general aim, while Angola, Algeria, and Uganda termed it a form of Western intervention. Liberia's Tolbert was opposed. Kenya unofficially declared the idea might be appropriate, but there was something wrong with discussing such a proposal in the absence of Africans. The United States adhered to its long-established position that any force must be under OAU aegis.(35)

Whatever the influence of this Western initiative, the Defense Commission, at its sixth session in Addis Ababa on 28 April, 1979, accepted a proposal of its experts to establish a Pan-African Force and appointed a committee to prepare an "organizing proposal" and guidelines for review at the Monrovia summit in July. As it came before the Defense Commission and in large measure was passed on to the summit, the proposal envisaged a force both for collective defense against outsiders and as a peacekeeping mechanism in "internecine conflicts" provided the states involved consented to engage it. It thus retained the Freetown concept of 15 years earlier of a consent-type peacekeeping force.

The structure would consist of a Defense Council made up of ten heads of state operating through their chiefs of staff as an advisory committee. National contingents would remain at home on a standby, on-call basis. Size of budget, formal structure, and financial details were to be clarified at Monrovia. In what was probably a conscious parallel to the UN design, the secretary general was to be assisted by a "military counselor" and would name the commander after consultation with the Defense Council. The military counselor would be assisted by "political counselors" from various geographic "theaters of operation." An interesting feature was that the Defense Force would "cooperate with the United Nations" in defense and security of member states.

What the drafters may have contemplated was that such a force would be employed not for the intractable, lingering territorial conflicts, as in the Ogaden, but in two other kinds of situation. One, probably most prominent in their minds, was that it might take over the stabilizing function of external security forces, such as the French, in internal (or as the guidelines put it "internecine") wars as in Chad or any replay of Shaba; and ultimately, perhaps, take over from the Cubans in Angola. The second would be to provide an integrated African component to serve in UN peacekeeping operations, including ventures like UNTAG for monitoring transitional arrangements and to provide a security backstop for the transfer of authority to African majority governments.

Whatever the drafters had in mind, when the OAU secretary general presented the report at Monrovia he received a tepid welcome. As observers had predicted at the time of the Addis Ababa meeting in April, given both political differences and unsolved problems of financing, organization, control, and logistics, the best that could be hoped for was that the plan would be approved for further study. The cautious estimate of prospects for a defense force was reflected in the statement by OAU Assistant Secretary for Political Affairs Peter Onu, who put a respectable face on the outcome, noting (a) a consensus that in principle the idea of establishing a force was timely, but (b) the Defense Commission had to study the idea further with the aid of financial and other experts.

Apart from the fiscal implications, more thought had to be given to the structure of the force, the manner in which it would be utilized, the command structure and, more broadly, the structure of authority. During the debate, no delegation took an openly negative stance on the value of a defense force, but endorsements were so hedged by reservations about how to translate the idea into practice that the Monrovia summit temporized and remanded the proposal to the committee of experts for study of financial and legal implications. The Freetown summit in 1980 once again deferred action. The Defense Commission was requested to convene "as soon as possible," to study the recommendations of the committee of experts and report to the Council of Ministers the following year.(36) The outlook for early progress did not look promising.

Still, the first serious effort in 15 years to examine the purpose and design of a regional force explicitly intended for OAU peacekeeping suggested that the African leadership might be prepared to proceed with serious planning once the political auguries were more favorable. Much depends on the lessons Africa draws from the short-lived peacekeeping venture in Chad. But, given the OAU's structural weakness, a regional peacekeeping capacity can, in all likelihood, become a practical proposition only if Africa can draw on outside resources and institutional assets in a manner that does not compromise regional autonomy. History and political affinity may make a Commonwealth or French Community connection appropriate and attractive in some cases, as in Zimbabwe-Rhodesia. However, for most conflicts of the 1980s that might lend themselves to peacekeeping at all (as described elsewhere in this volume), the UN experience would seem to indicate that some form of regional collaboration with the United Nations would appear to hold more promise.

OAU AND UN: A PEACEKEEPING PARTNERSHIP?

Africa's relation to the UN has been ambivalent, competitive in its insistence on "try-the-OAU-first," but complementary in reaching out to the UN on issues that could advantage Africa by being "internationalized." Both political support and institutional facilities of the UN were seen as crucial for workable solutions on such issues as orderly transition in Namibia and in succession crises in former colonial areas such as French Somaliland and Spanish Sahara.

   A dramatic shift in African attitudes toward peacekeeping collaboration with the UN appeared to be signaled by the decision at the OAU summit in Freetown in the summer of 1980 to seek UN assistance if the "OAU Neutral Force" in Chad could not be restored by the OAU's independent effort. As noted above, this decision was not taken without misgiving. Some African leaders recalled with apprehension that the UN intervention in the Congo in the 1960s had polarized the continent and intensified cold war tensions even though its original purpose was precisely to insulate the area from great power confrontation. At Freetown, surprisingly little opposition was voiced to the principle of OAU-UN collaboration, but the nature of the partnership was contentious. The debate on the kind of peacekeeping "assistance" Africa would find politically acceptable is far from over. Some African leaders would accept only an all-African force under OAU command and control to police intra-African conflicts, though supported financially and logistically by UN institutional facilities. Inclusion of non-Africans as peacekeepers in Chad-type conflicts is suspect to some as inviting "European" intrusion. Others, particularly leaders of francophone countries, would accept or even welcome non-African participation in a joint operation as a warranty of operational efficiency and a better

chance of avoiding entanglement in ethnic and religious
factionalism. International relief and refugee aid, which often
becomes vital in the wake of fighting, would also be more
reliably managed.

Though by the end of 1980 it looked doubtful that the
joint Chad peacekeeping venture would materialize, or succeed
if it did, the debate around the proposal reflected a new sense
of realism about the limits of OAU power along with a new
readiness to enlist UN help in policing Chad-type conflicts
when the OAU faces insurmountable financial and institutional
problems. Peacekeeping collaboration with the UN appeared to
many African leaders as an attractive option, at least for the
near term. The reason in the minds of many was that the
political and institutional weaknesses that underlie the OAU's
"crisis of effectiveness" - to use Professor Ali Mazrui's telling
phrase - could sometimes be transcended by addressing regional conflict through the UN process and by enlisting UN peacekeepers. The UN connection could both help overcome local
rivalries and marshal international financial and logistical
resources. Prospects for OAU peacekeeping in the near term
may lie less in structural reforms than in working out procedures for collaboration with the UN. By acting jointly or in
tandem with the UN, the OAU might discover its most effective
peacekeeping role in the 1980s.

Of all regional organizations, the OAU has been most
closely linked to the UN structure and most receptive to
cooperative action. As Andemicael has noted, in the UN "the
OAU tends to act as the collective agent of its members in a
more formal way than do the OAS and the League of Arab
States . . . ; the African Group in the United Nations is regarded as a body of the OAU while the Latin American and
Arab Groups have only informal links with their respective
regional organizations."(37) This is partly because of the
OAU's modest organizational and resource capabilities and
partly that, in certain crises, a political consensus on
peacekeeping action is more readily achieved through the UN.

Institutional collaboration is facilitated by the fact that
for Africa the connection with the UN does not have the
appearance of tutelage. African leaders carry great political
weight in UN deliberative bodies; intersecretariat exchanges
are common; Africans are prominent in the higher ranks of the
UN service and as commanders of UN peacekeeping operations.
Mutuality of interest has been codified in recent years in
parallel resolutions adopted by the UN General Assembly and
the OAU summit which call for strengthening cooperation
between the UN and the OAU.(38) While the UN resolutions
are mainly symbolic - and the 1979 version was politicized into
yet another vehicle for rhetorical promotion of Third World
causes - such a formalization of the relationship reflects a
certain reality and increasing acceptance of a special institutional relationship.

While no formal agreement has been reached, the two secretaries general have agreed to cooperate in "positive, dynamic cooperation and mutual assistance," and participate in certain sessions and special committees of the other organization. Moreover, the African group in the UN is represented by the chairman of the month in many UN meetings. Joint or collaborative action in peacekeeping would be a natural outgrowth of this institutional closeness.

What is perhaps more to the point is that, while some Africans were soured by the ideological dissension that erupted during the Congo operation, the 1970s saw renewed and large-scale participation by African contingents in UN peacekeeping operations in the Middle East. The fresh emphasis on "equitable geographic representation" in the makeup of UN forces has brought several African states into the club of UN troop contributors. In 1979, infantry battalions from Nigeria (700), Senegal (591), and Ghana (300 plus 57 in headquarters command) were serving in the UN Interim Force in Lebanon (UNIFIL), and its commander was a veteran peacekeeper, Major General Emmanuel Erskine of Ghana. When UNEF II was disbanded in mid-1979, a Ghana battalion numbering 595 was manning four forward command posts and 18 buffer positions, including posts monitoring access to the Sinai passes and to the early warning stations. Earlier, contingents from Senegal as well as Ghana had manned forward command posts and outposts in the Sinai. Apart from the prestige accruing to participating nations,(39) the experience has built habits of functional cooperation and provided field training.

Despite their jealousy of regional autonomy in dealing with internal conflicts, there is reason to believe that African leaders would be receptive to the option of UN-OAU collaboration out of awareness that the OAU is not institutionally ready to cope effectively, lacking as it does "sufficient military, financial and personnel resources for such functions as border sealing, truce observation and restoring law and order," tasks which, as Andemicael has observed, "require close collaboration between the OAU and the United Nations."(40) As noted earlier, the Freetown summit highlighted a new sense of readiness to enlist UN help, particularly financial and logistical, for peacekeeping operations even in internal conflicts like Chad. Similarly, as noted above, with the renewal of the OAU peacekeeping operation at the end of 1981, overtures were made for UN organizational and financial assistance.

If the central working principle for African regional peacekeeping in the 1980s is such collaboration, progress in strengthening the OAU's institutional capacity would appear most promising for the long term by concentrating on a serious effort to explore possibilities for cooperative undertakings in training and prepositioning of regional facilities.

Collaboration in Preparedness

Collaboration in preparations for peacekeeping could provide an operational link between UN and OAU staffs, and might be the road to broader structural reforms in the OAU. The very act of engaging in planning and preparations could enhance the legitimacy of the OAU and give it renewed purpose. In particular, the Defense Commission could take on a new lease in cooperative ventures with the UN on peacekeeping preparedness.

Cooperation could extend across a broad spectrum, from planning an organization and command structure to establishment of a training college to provide advice and guidance on standby arrangements. Though its own system is flawed, the UN still has access to talent and experience which could prove beneficial to regional peacekeepers. In particular, the working group of the Special Committee on Peacekeeping Operations (Committee of 33) could serve as a clearing house and guide on training of standby contingents thus assuring logistical readiness.(41) The objective is to have trained, ready forces to be available on short notice when a regional consensus emerges.

Joint planning should both try to forecast areas of crisis and their susceptibility to conflict resolution, and prepare guidelines for complementary UN and OAU action. Correcting organizational shortcomings and defining the command structure, particularly in relation to political authority, should be on the agenda. Systematic evaluation of recent UN experience should also be a priority matter for OAU planners. In particular, the operations in Cyprus, the Sinai, and the UN Interim Force in Lebanon offer lessons on the needs and vulnerabilities of managing peacekeeping. The political tolerances and institutional capacities that determine limits of successful peacekeeping are covered elsewhere in this volume. (See especially Alastair Taylor, chap. 16).

Training

Training is probably the most promising area for collaboration. As noted, Africa is able to draw on its own experienced peacekeepers, as well as those of other nations with whom African contingents have served in UN peacekeeping operations. Among possibilities are a joint defense college and joint military exercises, which would appear to be acceptable provided national contingents retain autonomy, thus removing any suspicion that the enterprise is aimed at bringing in through the back door an African high command or centralized defense force. (See Beattie, "The International Peace Academy and the Development of Training for Peacekeeping" in this volume.)

African contingents thus trained would then be put on standby for either UN or OAU action. Units might be integrated under OAU auspices to whatever extent the political traffic would bear, and could become the nucleus of a voluntary defense force as proposed in the guidelines presented to the Monrovia summit. Such an African component would appear to be acceptable politically if it remains loosely structured in national units, though trained to operate together. Ultimately, the objective could be that Africa, through the OAU if this is feasible, contribute collectively to UN peacekeeping as does the Nordic group.

Worth exploring also would be an arrangement for UN technical assistance, to be provided through the OAU, to help train and support contingents operationally assigned to a specific African peacekeeping operation.

Standby arrangements should ideally embrace both the earmarking of national units for such dual service and, on the Nordic pattern, advance stipulation of what each would supply by way of logistical support. One formulation, suggested by Gen. L. Okai in November 1979, is that units be equipped on an agreed scale, not only to ensure their operational meshing but for ease of accounting. The same principle of "modular" contributions could apply to contributions of airlift and other services to be made available on short notice. Stockpiling necessary arms, communication and other equipment, rations and other supplies is probably beyond OAU capacity, but plans for national or subregional prepositioning, available on short notice, should be explored.

Africa might be receptive to another form of collaboration: the UN to facilitate and sanitize the flow of military assistance from major powers for regional security purposes, thus minimizing risks of foreign intervention. Logistical support, airlift, and advanced military equipment could be filtered and sanctioned through the UN. Even technical services of specialists could be funneled through the UN, and legitimated by Security Council endorsement to ensure against political manipulation. Advance arrangements could be worked out whereby the UN would both legitimize and facilitate the flow of vital goods and services which cannot readily be secured in any other manner.

Whether the Soviet Union would agree to the United Nations - which perforce means the UN secretariat - controlling the flow of arms aid for peacekeeping may be questioned. But peacekeeping history, notably experience with UNEF II, suggests that, where a regional consensus exists, a formula can be devised whereby the resources of major powers can be absorbed by an international peacekeeping operation as an acceptable risk to impartiality and effectiveness.

Obviously, preparedness and standby arrangements, even should they prove workable, are not a magic formula for

overcoming the political constraints or the structural flaws that
have blocked the emergence of an African peacekeeping capacity.   Nor will they compensate for the intrinsically unstable
conditions and social and economic weaknesses of many small
states in Africa which will continue to block the emergence of
a regional security order.   Aspirations for regional institutional structures to contain conflict certainly exist, as the
debates on human rights and on a defense force at the
Monrovia summit in the summer of 1979 demonstrate; but,
without the political cohesion and the boldness to transcend
ethnic feuds and ideological division, the OAU is not soon
likely to develop the organizational skills and institutional
capacity for peacekeeping.   Moreover, Africa's cultural
preference for personal diplomacy and low-intensity modes of
mediation and conciliation will continue to be inadequate for
coping with the continent's acute and persistent crises.
Developing skills and an institutional capacity for peacekeeping
are essential if the OAU is to become an effective regional
instrument for conflict resolution.

What preparedness can do at this stage is, first, to
signal the OAU's institutional commitment to undertake a
regional security role in crises where a political consensus for
settlement emerges and, second, to provide the beginnings of
a structural and institutional base for African participation in
UN operations as a region rather than on an individual country
basis.

For the next decade at least, Africa is likely to be
dependent on superior institutional and operational capacities
of outsiders and the UN's role could be helpful both in
assuring that resources are available and that military
assistance is forthcoming in a politically acceptable manner.
So long as the Organization of African Unity remains vulnerable to both political divisions and institutional deficiencies,
such a partnership offers the best hope of dealing with its
crisis of ineffectiveness.

NOTES

1. The Arab League's venture into regional peacekeeping in
Kuwait in the summer of 1961 proved an exceptional exercise,
though fifteen years later the League gave its blessing and
political cover to Syria's peacekeeping presence in Lebanon.
In any event, the Arab League experience, surprisingly, in
view of overlapping membership, does not appear to have
influenced OAU policies or action in conflict management.

2. E.B. Haas, "The United Nations and Regionalism," The
Evolving United Nations: A Prospect for Peace?, edited by
K.J. Twitchett (New York: St. Martin's Press, 1971), p. 124.

For regional perspectives on the UN-OAU relationship see B. Andemicael, The OAU and the UN, Relations between the Organization of African Unity and the UN (New York: Africana, 1976); and Y. El-Ayouty, The Organization of African Unity After Ten Years: Comparative Perspectives (New York: Praeger, 1975).

3. Andemicael, The OAU and the UN, p. 92. In the Algeria-Morocco border dispute of 1963, the Council of Ministers declared its determination "always to seek" a peaceful solution within the framework of the OAU Charter. The following year, in the face of a Somali move to internationalize its struggle with Ethiopia, the Council of Ministers reiterated that a solution for all African disputes should "be sought first within the [OAU]." Fifteen years later, the African states insisted on keeping jurisdiction over the Chad and Ogaden crises away from the UN, though the OAU had yet to prove that it could intervene constructively in these cases. However, the OAU has consulted with the UN on modes of cooperation notably for the peacekeeping operation in Chad.

4. John J. Stremlau, The International Politics of the Nigerian Civil War, 1967-1970, (Princeton, N.J.: Princeton Univ. Press, 1977), pp. 94-95.

5. Jon Woronoff, Organization of African Unity, (Metuchen, N.J.: Scarecrow Press, 1970), p. 39.

6. Article 15 of the Rio Treaty states: "No state or group of states has the right to intervene, directly or indirectly, for any reason whatever, in the internal or external affairs of any other state. . . ."

In Article III of the OAU Charter, members declare their adherence to the principles of sovereign equality of states, non-interference in the internal affairs of states, and respect for the sovereignty and territorial integrity of each.

7. William L. Krieg, "Peaceful Settlement of Disputes Through the Organization of American States," unpublished monograph, prepared for Department of State, 1973, p. 98.

8. In the Salvador-Honduras "soccer war" of 1969. Antagonism between the two countries flared at a football match in San Salvador when Hondurans were roughed up; in response, Honduras attacked and drove out Salvadoran settlers; Salvadoran troops invaded. An OAS committee was appointed to negotiate a cease-fire, ordered suspension of hostilities and withdrawal, and sent military and civilian observers to ensure compliance. When Salvador delayed troop withdrawal, sanctions were threatened and the threat worked. Military observers supervised the withdrawal and reported on conditions in evacuated towns. They left at the end of 1971. Thereafter, the OAS slackened its efforts and proved unable to settle the disputed boundary and economic issues.

9. Quoted in Stremlau, The International Politics of the Nigerian Civil War, p. 12. For the same reason, the OAU has supported Ethiopia's claim to the Ogaden and denied self-determination to its inhabitants. To do so would "invite the process of self-determination in Eritrea where Ethiopia's stakes are far greater. . . ." Sean Kelly, "Letter from the Ogaden," Foreign Service Journal, March 1980, p. 35. Kelly recalls that in introducing the OAU resolution declaring inviolable the inherited boundaries, Tanzania's President Julius Nyerere remarked that "Africa's borders are so absurd they must be considered sacrosanct."

10. Jean Herskovits, "Democracy in Nigeria," Foreign Affairs, Winter 1979-80, p. 333.

11. The circumstances and particulars are described later. In brief, Nigeria and neighboring states organized a series of negotiations to bring peace and national reconciliation. Nigeria dispatched a force to Ndjamena, the capital, to supervise a cease-fire and bring the parties together. Nigeria took the step after Libya blocked an earlier initiative by Sudanese President Jaafar Numeri (then chairman of the OAU) out of concern that a Sudanese-led African presence in Chad might enhance Numeri's influence at the expense of Libya and its proteges.

12. Tanzania's action had split African opinion. Though Amin's brutal treatment of his people was not condoned, the manner of Amin's downfall left much of Africa uneasy. The fear was that Tanzania's action might set a destabilizing precedent.

13. David Ottaway, "Africa: U.S. Policy in Eclipse," America and the World, 1979; Foreign Affairs, 1980, p. 651.

14. Prof. I.W. Zartman, at a conference on OAU and Conflict Management, Washington, D.C., May 1978. Concert diplomacy is most evident at the annual summit - as the Assembly of heads of states and governments is generally known. Following a tradition of consensual decision making, no action is taken against significant minority opposition. Thus at the Freetown summit in 1980, despite the requisite majority for admission of the Saharan Democratic Arab Republic (the Polisario), threats by some ten countries to join Morocco in leaving the OAU if this happened led the summit to shelve the issue and adopt a temporizing resolution on the substance of the West Saharan problem.

15. "Matchet's Diary," West Africa, July 7, 1980. The text of the Council of Ministers' resolution is in OAU document CM/Res. 789 (XXXV), 18-28 June 1980.

16. Woronoff, Organization of African Unity, p. 184.

17. According to some authorities, the summit alone has the executive power to make authoritative decisions binding on OAU members. Formally, resolutions of the Council of Ministers need to be endorsed by the summit. In practice, the Council has appointed peacemaking commissions and authorized their mandates on its own.

18. In fact in the spring of 1979, a Nigerian delegation visited the area in a mediation effort on behalf of the commission, not because of any new development on the ground or expectation of progress on the disputed Ogaden, but because Nigeria expected to have to report to the OAU summit in July on the status of mediation.

19. Woronoff, Organization of African Unity, p. 385.

20. At the founding session of the francophone Organisation Commune Africaine, Malgache et Mauricienne (OCAM) in February 1965, the OAU's "policy of partiality" was condemned and the heads of state declared that the malaise from which the OAU was suffering was due to lack of respect for the principles of sovereignty of states and noninterference in their internal affairs.

21. See, for example, Peter Jay, "Regionalism as Geopolitics," America and the World, 1979; Foreign Affairs, 1980, p. 501. Nor was the Arab League able to deal with the Libyan-Tunisian dispute when it met in Tunis at the end of February 1980.

22. Andemicael, The OAU and the UN, p. 13. OCAM was described by its founders as a "new African grouping whose aim, within the context of the OAU, is to reinforce cooperation and solidarity between Afro-Malagasy States, and to speed up their political, economic, social and technical, and cultural development."

23. On economic goals and prospects of ECOWAS see "ECOWAS' Way Ahead," West Africa, July 7, 1980. On prospects for economic cooperation in the subregion, see supplement to International Herald Tribune, Zurich, June 1980.

24. Libyan penetration of the Sahel and charges of Libyan-fomented subversion led certain African states (Senegal, Gambia, Ghana) to sever diplomatic relations during 1980 and others (Mauritania and Niger) to close down Libyan cultural centers. The perceived threat from Libya mounted with Tripoli's military intervention in Chad at the end of 1980.

25. See "OAU's Limits Recognized," West Africa, July 7, 1980.

26. The choice of the three nations designated to provide units for the neutral force was apparently not fortuitous. After the French intervention in Shaba in 1978, Libya took the lead in organizing and training forces from states considered

Guinea) so that, if the occasion arose, trained and politically reliable forces would be available for service in an African force.

27. Report of OAU Secretary General on Situation in Chad to the Council of Ministers, 35th Ordinary Session, 18-28 June 1980, Freetown, Sierra Leone. OAU document CM/1050 (XXXV).

28. At Freetown, Habre's supporters tried to derail endorsement of the Lagos Accord on the ground it was defunct and only served to legitimize Goukouni. Their attempt to dilute the language endorsing the accord was overwhelmingly defeated.

29. Resolution on Chad of the Assembly of Heads of State and Government, Freetown, Sierra Leone, 1-4 July 1980. OAU document AHG/Res. 101 (XVII).

30. Among press accounts, see "President of Chad Denies Libya Dominates Country," Reuter report in Washington Post, Dec 27, 1980; "Libyans Replace French in Chad's Battered Capital," New York Times, Dec. 28, 1980; R. Koven, "Libya Announces Merger with its Neighbor, Chad," Washington Post, Jan. 7, 1981, and "Libya Carves Niche in Chadian Chaos," Washington Post, Jan. 8, 1981. On fears of a larger Libyan design to "destabilize the region from the Sudan to Senegal," see James M. Markham, "Libya's Islamic Visions are Real Nightmare in Africa," New York Times (Sec E), Dec. 28, 1980.

31. Complicating the situation was Libya's claim to a potentially mineral-rich part of Chad. In 1975, Libya occupied a 50-mile strip of Chadian border territory, including part of the Tibesti region, claiming successor rights under a Franco-Italian treaty of 1935 (which was never ratified by France, the former colonial power to whose territory the Chadian government also claims succession).

32. See L. Dash, "Africans Split by Libya's Role in Chad," Washington Post, Dec. 25, 1980.

33. "Tense Time for the OAU," West Africa, July 14, 1980. It was the West Africa correspondent who characterized the resolution as "astonishingly anodyne." Text of the summit's decision is in OAU document AHG/DEC. 118 (XVII), July 4, 1980.

34. UN General Assembly. A/RES/35/19, 17 Nov. 1980. In August 1981, the OAU Implementation Committee on Western Sahara adopted the decision calling upon the parties to agree to a cease-fire and the holding of a referendum under "OAU and/or United Nations peacekeeping forces." Report of the secretary-general, 16 October 1981, UN A/36/602.

35. M.T. Kaufman, "Black Africans Sharply Split Over Joint Peace Force," New York Times, June 8, 1978.

36. Resolution on the OAU Defense Force, CM/Res. 815 (XXXV), 35th Ordinary Session of the Council of Ministers, Freetown, 18-28 June 1980.

37. Andemicael, The OAU and the UN, p. 16.

38. See, e.g., UNGA resolution 33/27, Co-operation between the United Nations and the OAU, 1 December 1978, and 34/21 of 9 November 1979. A recent OAU resolution is CM/Res. 782 (XXV), 18-28 June 1980, which was endorsed by the Freetown summit early in July. The resolution "requests the African Group at the UN and the OAU Secretary General to continue to take the necessary measures to strengthen co-operation at the political, economic, social, cultural and administrative levels between the UN and the OAU, particularly on matters of interest to Africa."

39. In Senegal, for example, it has been the practice for the Minister of the Armed Forces to address the departing contingent in ceremonies that emphasize that the troops are going on a mission of "peace and honor" and in the national interest. Peacekeeping experience is weighed in career advancement.

40. Andemicael, The OAU and the UN, 165.

41. See report of the Special Committee on Peacekeeping Operations, UN General Assembly, A/34/592, 19 October 1979.

13
The International Commission of Control and Supervision in Vietnam, 1973
David Cox

The International Commission of Control and Supervision in Vietnam (ICCS) was created by the Paris agreement of January 1973. When the Canadians withdrew from the Commission at the end of July of that year, they were replaced by Iran, an interesting footnote to modern events. But it is perhaps not too ethnocentric to suggest that with the Canadian withdrawal went all efforts at a vigorous and painstaking approach to international supervision.

The disappearance of the ICCS was unlamented. The United States, having achieved its military withdrawal, was indifferent to the Canadian decision, as were the Vietnamese protagonists. The Canadians saw their withdrawal as the culmination of a successful diplomatic campaign, in which they had demonstrated their willingness to help American withdrawal, had conscientiously attempted to implement the protocol on international supervision, and retired in the knowledge that they had done their best to accomplish a task which they had known to be impossible from the outset. As to "the international community," the relevant cross-section of which had met in Paris in February 1973 to ratify the agreement,(1) it had shown no desire to be informed of the post-agreement state of the cease-fire, and failed to stir when the commission ceased to function.

This general indifference reflected in part a belief that peacekeeping - or peace monitoring - outside the United Nations was unlikely to succeed and, in any case, was undesirable. This was a view, of course, based in good measure on the experience of the former commission in Vietnam (the ICSC) which had progressively atrophied but failed to die. It had become a commission, in the words of one senior Canadian diplomat, which was not international (here drawing attention to the commission as a meeting of three national delegations rather than as an international body per se), could not control, and would not supervise. It had become, in the words of Mitchell Sharp, "a farce."(2)   No better fate was expected for the second commission despite some strenuous efforts to improve its conditions of operation.   The conclusion was fairly easily reached, therefore, that such ad hoc authorizing arrangements were antithetical to successful peacekeeping, whatever the complexity of the political situation.

A decade later, that conclusion is not quite so obvious. In Zimbabwe, a Commonwealth observation force was considered more appropriate than a UN force; in the Middle East, President Carter offered the Israelis and Egyptians a "multinational" force if the UN could not provide an international presence to monitor the Israeli-Egyptian treaty,(3) and the negotiations over Namibia suggest that a Western-oriented rather than a strictly UN presence may eventually be used there.

These prospects, therefore, make it useful to consider the experience of the ICCS, notwithstanding the peculiarity of the circumstances in which it was created and operated.   I shall begin with a brief account of the circumstances surrounding the establishment of the ICCS.   The organization and pattern of behavior of the commission form the middle part of the chapter.   In the conclusion, I seek to balance the story – largely favorable to the Canadian position to this point – by explaining the political viewpoint of the Polish and Hungarian delegations regarding the commission.   The chapter concludes with some general reflections on the dilemmas of the commission.

THE MAIN PRINCIPLES OF THE PARIS AGREEMENT(4)

On first reading, the Paris agreement signed on 27 January 1973 is a confusing and ambiguous document, in its apparent haste and carelessness remniscent of its 1954 predecessor.   In fact, the logic to the agreement is predicated on a fundamental political assumption, namely, the ability of the two South Vietnamese parties to reach agreement whereby the future of South Vietnam could be settled in a noncoercive manner.   It is tempting to note that, but for this trifle, the agreement could have been both implemented and supervised.   But to dismiss the agreement in these terms is to ignore the elements of substance in the negotiations, and to blur the distinction between those parts which lent themselves to implementation and supervision and those which, in the nature of the disagreement that they represented, were certain to be difficult to implement, and therefore not susceptible to international supervision.   Just as in 1954 there were important elements of

the disengagement between the French and the Vietminh which
were facilitated by the presence of an international body, so in
1973 there were certain hard agreements which were more
likely to be implemented if they could be independently
verified.

In brief, the integral character of the January agreement
might be summarized in the following terms:

o   By acknowledging the 1954 Geneva agreements (Articles 1
     and 15), the United States conceded in principle the
     North Vietnamese goal of ultimate reunification of Vietnam.
o   There followed a specific agreement on the cessation of
     hostilities and the withdrawal of U.S. and other foreign
     troops, the future noninvolvement of the United States in
     the affairs of South Vietnam, and the release of American
     prisoners of war, which was not conditional upon the
     settlement of the fate of the political prisoners in South
     Vietnam, but was linked in time, and by implication on a
     quid pro quo basis, to U.S. troop withdrawal. This is
     the "hard" part of the agreement, and, strictly from the
     point of view of the use of international forces, it is
     important to remember that the implementation of this part
     of the agreement provided specific tasks for a superviso-
     ry commission.
o   Basically in exchange for this agreement, North Vietnam
     allowed an (indeterminate) status to the Thieu regime,
     and to South Vietnam as a political entity whereby, put
     simply, the South Vietnamese parties were to settle the
     political affairs of South Vietnam before the process of
     unification with North Vietnam was to begin. In short,
     both the United States and North Vietnam were to refrain
     from imposing any political settlement on South Vietnam,
     although in reality this was a rather one-sided self-
     denying ordinance, since the North Vietnamese forces
     were allowed to remain in South Vietnam by virtue of not
     being mentioned in the Agreement. Although in principle
     the ICCS had a part to play in this political process, in
     practice there was only a remote possibility that a third
     party could promote a reconciliation which was desired
     neither by the Saigon regime nor by the Provisional
     Revolutionary Government of the National Liberation Front
     (PRG).

Since the ICCS did not exist during the negotiations in Paris,
and since there was no international body to speak for a
prospective commission, the only party to intervene in the
negotiations was the government of Canada. Well aware that
they were likely to be asked to serve, and seriously concerned
at the prospect of a continuation of the futility of the ICSC,
Canadian Secretary of State Mitchell Sharp pressed the Cana-

dian view as vigorously as possible in Washington, though with
limited success. For the record, Sharp identified certain
conditions which had to be met if Canada were to serve. They
included the following:(5)

1. Sharp argued that, taken as a whole, the provisions
for the new commission should be such as to offer "real prospects of being effective."
2. The four present belligerents should be bound by the
new agreement which the commission would be required to
report upon. Possibly this condition reflected a fear on the
part of the Canadians that the United States and North Vietnam might conclude an agreement without the support of
Saigon and the PRG, but it may have been designed to emphasize that, as far as the old commission (ICSC) was concerned,
three of the four belligerents were not signatories, nor did
they consider themselves bound by the 1954 treaty.
3. Mr. Sharp reiterated the need for a continuing
political authority, "which would assume responsibility for the
settlement as a whole and to which the Commission or any of
its members would have access through reports or consultations." This was the critical condition laid down by Mr.
Sharp, and the most difficult one to achieve in the ambiguous
circumstances where the legitimating body was either the
belligerents themselves as signatories to the treaty or an ad
hoc group of governments as happened in 1954. Recognizing
the difficulty of establishing such a political authority, Sharp
softened the requirement by stating that, although the Canadian government would prefer the political authority to be
established by the agreement, it was prepared to wait for the
proposed international conference to convene, and that it
would be prepared to serve for a minimum of sixty days while
it awaited the outcome of the conference deliberations. Thus,
the Canadian government agreed to participate while avowing
its intention to leave if the conditions of its participation were
not met within some reasonable period of time. This position
had the logical effect (for it is difficult to say what its actual
effect was on the parties to the dispute) of making the stated
conditions of Canadian participation something short of actual
conditions. One is tempted to the conclusion that the government did not wish to have its freedom of decision too rigidly
circumscribed by its own conditions. To the same effect, but
in a novel departure, Sharp also suggested that Canada might
participate for some purposes, but not for others.

> The government is conscious of the fact that there
> are several possible forms of response open to it
> between a simple refusal to take part at all to a full
> and unconditional involvement. The government's
> assessment of the relevant texts will also take into

account the importance of contributing to a scaling down of hostilities in Vietnam and to the disengagement of American forces and the return of their prisoners of war. It is conceivable that the result of this examination might suggest a participation limited to certain aspects of the agreement or a participation for a limited period of time rather than an outright refusal or an unqualified undertaking to serve. If so, the parties concerned will be so advised, and if they found this acceptable Canada could take part on a limited basis.

4. Sharp's statement repeated the Canadian insistence that the peacekeeping force should have freedom of movement and observation in both South Vietnam and the demilitarized zone. In the outcome, the protocol was ambiguous on this point, allowing the commission "such movement for observation as is reasonably required for the proper exercise if its functions." (The practical limitations to freedom of movement are discussed below in the account of the work of the commission.)
Despite strenuous efforts by the Canadians to direct the attention of the Paris negotiators to the importance of the commission, failure was inevitable. Securing the support of the Saigon government and the reconciliation of differing influences and points of view in Washington inevitably assumed priority. When the Paris agreement was signed on 27 January, Canada agreed to participate on the commission before Mitchell Sharp had seen the agreement or the protocol. The Poles and Hungarians were even more in the dark - the Hungarian ambassador was given a copy of the agreement and protocol to read on the plane to Saigon - and the Indonesians were new to the task and the least experienced of all the commission members.

ORGANIZATION OF THE COMMISSION

The organization, deployment, and support of an international commission of 1,000 men, drawn from four very different countries, and thrust into an alien environment, all in the space of a week or so, is a task of major proportions. Almost literally at the doorstep lay the example of the old ICSC - by-passed and bankrupt, with its heat and water cut off by the city of Saigon for the nonpayment of bills. The initial steps taken to organize the ICCS, then, are significant not simply for the insights into the practice of supervisory commissions, but also because the actions of the respective delegations in the early days did much to set the tone and direction of the commission's work.

Initiatives in the early period rested almost entirely with the Canadians, who took full advantage of the passivity of the other delegations - including, surprisingly, the Poles, who, despite their experiences on the ICSC, showed no inclination to assert themselves or exercise leadership. The Canadians, by contrast, were determined to lead the way. In doing so, they had several advantages over the other delegations. First, whatever the ultimate intent, the immediate goal of the Canadians was to take every possible step to ensure that the ICCS did not recapitulate the travesty of the ICSC; therefore, their purpose was to act quickly to organize and deploy the commission so that there could be no suggestion of inactivity. The other delegations did not share this urgency of purpose, and, as a consequence, they surrendered most of the early initiative, being content to accept or react to Canadian proposals on organizational and housekeeping matters. Secondly, the Canadians had the benefit of their experience in Vietnam from 1954, both of the country and of the operating procedures of the old commission, which only the Poles could match. Interestingly, the Poles throughout made little effort to take an active part in the commission; and, of the two communist delegations, it was the Hungarians who proved to be the more active and vocal, particularly in countering Canadian efforts to make the dealings of the commission as public as possible. Thirdly, Canada turned the happenstance of the alphabet to good use by suggesting that the chairmanship of the commission rotate alphabetically (C-H-I-P), thereby allowing their ambassador, Michel Gauvin, to exercise an early dominance publicly and privately that might otherwise have been contested.

Finally, the Canadians had close ties with the Americans, particularly at the military level. This liaison provided a number of advantages. First, although the Canadian government had been unwilling for political reasons to allow a sizeable advance party to go to South Vietnam (they were unwilling to act in any way that would suggest, de facto, that they had accepted participation in the commission), an unofficial reconnaissance had taken place in December 1972 with the cooperation of the American Military Assistance Command (MACV) in Saigon. While this reconnaissance was too brief and limited to establish as much contact with civilian contractors and South Vietnamese authorities as the Canadian military might have liked, it undoubtedly helped to give the Canadians a quick start at the end of January.

Similarly, knowledge of U.S. army procedures and logistics systems was certain to give Canada an advantage over the East European members of the commission. This was particularly important since the American military provided almost all material support to the commission for the first six weeks. It did this - at American expense - through its support contractors, primarily Pacific Architects and Engineers (PAE), who were responsible for supplies of equipment, consumables, and vehicles; for the operation and maintenance of vehicles including the provision of drivers; for the delivery of equipment to team sites; for the accommodations provided to the commission, and for other engineering needs. When direct American support ended, on 16 March, PAE continued to provide support services to the commission on the basis of a letter of intent. The Canadian member of the Administrative and Financial Committee was given the task of drawing up a proposal for competitive contracts. The other delegations showed no interest at all in the resulting proposal, despite the fact that it would have diversified the supply services and made them less obviously under the control of the Americans. For what seem to have been reasons of bureaucratic inertia, the proposal lagged, and PAE continued to be the primary support contractor.(6)

In these circumstances, then, the administrative initiatives of the Canadians began with the mundane business of letting contracts and setting up house. In themselves of no importance, the possible exception was air support, where a $14 million contract was awarded to Air America with the active support of the Poles and Hungarians, who surprisingly emphatically rejected a competitive offer from the French. At a general level, however, the letting of these contracts for communications, accommodation, etc., which are normally provided by military personnel, was critical to the effective functioning of the commission.(7) The Canadians had been planning these programs since mid-November 1972, and were successful not only in implementing them but in maintaining a reasonable measure of control of the organization throughout their tenure.

The significance of this control goes beyond points of detail. The organization of the commission as outlined in figure 13.1 was also a Canadian proposal, modified somewhat by four-party discussions, but not in any major way. The organization chart draws attention to a number of important points about the functioning of the commission, but it also tends to conceal the reality of the organization, particularly the secretariat, which is that it never acted as "a single body."(8)

Neither the Paris agreement nor the protocol made any provision for a secretariat - a fundamental omission, of course, and one which again draws attention to the limitations of ad hoc international supervisory commissions. The four delegations agreed at the outset that there should be a secretariat, and thus accepted the principle that there should be a single support organization for the commission. The differing objectives of the delegations, however, made it extremely difficult to implement this intent, and exacerbated the problem;

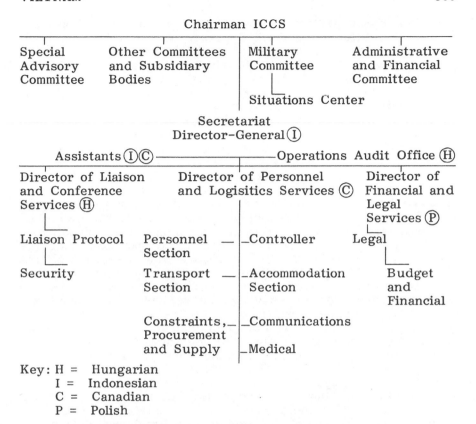

Fig. 13.1   Organization of ICCS Headquarters

the staffing requirements of the secretariat could not be met
by the individual delegations.   The protocol limited the total
number of personnel from each delegation to 290.   The commission members were unable, consequently, to man the various
inspection teams, service their own delegations (though, of
course, this need would have been much less if the secretariat
had been effective), and provide skilled staff officers to the
secretariat.   Where the initial plan for the secretariat called
for more than fifty staff officers, the delegations provided
only six or seven each.   The result was that the secretariat
was slow to organize, and a number of weeks passed before it
started to report.   It was forced to employ local personnel, an
unsatisfactory arrangement for it necessarily detracted from
the influence and effectiveness of the secretariat; and, since
the locals were from Saigon, it certainly did not satisfy the
requirements of political balance.

The administrative failure of the secretariat, therefore, tended to reinforce the divided nature of the commission itself whereas an effective secretariat might have absorbed some of these divisions. The manner in which it operated is evident in some of the implications of the organization chart.

The allocation of tasks in the key offices of the organization reinforced the Canadian grip on day-to-day operations.(9) Symbolically, the willingness of the Poles and Hungarians to accept an Indonesian as director-general of the secretariat marked the unique position of the Indonesians – pro-Western, but also Asian, and as such the closest thing the commission had to a neutral member. Nevertheless, the secretariat did not function successfully, and tasks which ought to have been performed in the secretariat seem to have gone either up (to the commissioners) or sideways (to the individual delegations). Therefore, the individual activities of nationals within the secretariat assumed greater proportions. In the day-to-day operations, for example, the activity of the Canadians in the post of Director of Personnel and Logistics Services served to entrench the Canadian control of deployment activities. As we shall see below, this bore upon some critical arguments of principle about the conduct of investigations – specifically, the Canadian insistence on investigation of incidents immediately after the lodging of the complaint – and on the capacity to prevent the absence of transportation or other support services being used as an excuse to avoid investigation. Needless to say, the Canadian delegation had set out to obtain control of that critical post.

By contrast to the premeditated concern of the Canadians with logistical services, the Polish and Hungarian delegations did not appear to gain any overwhelming advantage from their own positions. For example, the apparently attractive position of Director of Conference and Liaison Services – in principle, one might have thought the vantage point from which to control and influence the public relations of the commission – tended to be superseded by individual press briefings and releases – particularly by the ubiquitous and garrulous Canadian ambassador, M. Gauvin. Whether he was speaking as chairman of the month or head of the Canadian delegation was never clear, but it is certain that he did not speak to the press with the approval of the other delegations, nor, necessarily, on the basis of information common to all delegations. M. Gauvin's press arrangements, moreover, were made by the Canadian delegation, not by the Hungarian Director of Liaison and Conference Services. The latter was located in relative isolation on the fourth floor of the ICCS building at Tan Son Nhut, while the Canadians maintained a twenty-four hour highly accessible post on the main floor.

The importance of public relations is better appreciated if one remembers that immediately after the cease-fire there were more than 500 foreign correspondents in Vietnam; and, at the same time, the South Vietnamese government was clamping down on the press, making it more difficult for them to gain access to the field, impeding contacts with the North Vietnamese and PRG delegations, and carrying out close surveillance of press activities.(10)   Only belatedly did the communist members of the commission react to the Canadian grip on the media, protesting with increasing passion within the commission at the propensity of the Canadians to represent themselves as the commission and, finally, in the case of the Hungarians adopting what might be called a "counter-mouth" policy of their own.(11)   In the international press, however, the Canadian profile remained high and favorable (in itself an objective of Canadian policy), and declined not with adverse publicity, but only as the international press lost interest in Vietnam after the successful withdrawal of the American troops and the repatriation of the prisoners-of-war.

The failure to achieve any collective purpose in the activities described above might be noted in one further important area of the work of the secretariat.   For the commission to function successfully, the commissioners ought to have received continuous intelligence from the secretariat on military activity in Vietnam.   In principle, this was to have been provided by the military committee.   Within the military committee, the Situations Centre was envisaged as a forum in which, each day, the respective military representatives would pool their information on the military scene, out of which would come a composite intelligence report for the commissioners.   The Situations Centre was unsuccessful - according to the Canadians, because the East European delegations showed no interest in pooling information - and the delegations again went their respective paths in regard to their assessment of the cease-fire and its aftermath.

Once again, it must be added that the Canadians probably came out best from this situation, for they had access, as the Poles and Hungarians certainly did not, to American and South Vietnamese intelligence sources under the auspices of MACV. Could it reasonably be expected that the Canadians would be sufficiently impartial as to share this knowledge with their East European colleagues in the Situations Centre, and conversely, would not the liaison with MACV suggest a quid pro quo in which the Canadians passed on appraisals of the tactics, policies, and activities of the other delegations?   It is difficult to believe that such exchanges did not take place.   One must remember also the contrast between the Canadian position and that of the East Europeans, who suffered from the lack of an infrastructure in South Vietnam, particularly in communications.   (They were, of course, without the usual communications facilities provided by diplomatic services for they had no embassies in Saigon.)   This was true not only of the Polish

and Hungarian delegations, but also of the PRG and North
Vietnamese delegations to the Four Party Joint Military
commission.

The Poles to some extent remedied this defect by bringing
high powered communications equipment which provided them
with communications links to PRG headquarters in South Vietnam (at Loc Ninh, near the Cambodian border) and to Hanoi.
Whether this was an activity appropriate to a member of an
international commission was debatable, but so, of course, was
the very close relationship between the Canadians and Americans. In any event, it emphasized the unequal positions of
the respective delegations. There can be little doubt that the
Canadians were the most fully informed (or most fully
misinformed, depending on one's perception of the merits of
American intelligence), and that the sources of their information inhibited free and open exchanges with the Poles and
Hungarians. Whatever tactical benefits resulted from this
advantage must be balanced against one of the declared
objectives of the Canadian military delegation which was "to
conduct a joint-operation with the Military Components of the
Hungarian, Indonesian and Polish military delegations."(12)
The failure of the Situations Centre was the clearest indication
that the joint military operation was not to be, but the
circumstances of the failure suggest that not very much
thought went into the problem of how to make it a success.
Moreover, where military intelligence, albeit of a general
nature, was concerned, the division in the commission was
apparent: no matter how much they might have wanted to be
impartial, the Canadians in the end were bound to recognize
their association with the United States and thus the Saigon
regime; the Hungarians and Poles, for their part, made no
bones about their task, which was to represent the interests
of the two communist parties to the Paris agreement.

Finally, a brief reference may suffice here to another
area of Canadian enterprise, this time in the workings of the
commission itself. The commission, of course, had no procedures of any kind, from those basic matters which might in
other situations be covered by a Status of Forces Agreement to
rules of procedure for the commission itself. The Canadians
offered a draft set of rules to the commission, which became
the working document for the Special Committee on Operating
Procedures. In the following section, critical elements in the
draft proposal are discussed in conjunction with the discussion
of the commission's activities. The general point to be made
here is that the draft proposal incorporated many of the points
of substance which the Canadians had initially proposed to the
Americans in the period October-January 1972. They were
remarkably successful in reintroducing these issues into the
commission itself in the guise of operating procedures, although, as we shall see, they were not always able to gain
acceptance of them.

The organization of the commission, then, was of more than passing administrative significance. First, the principle of selection to the Commission - representing the conflicting parties in some sense, despite Canadian insistence that they represented nobody - was in general incompatible with the concept of an international commission. This well-worn truth about the ICCS is nicely illustrated in the administrative details discussed above, for it is apparent that its organization must be understood in terms of the adversary relationship among its members. The first criticism of the Canadian policy must be that they went imbued with a sense of this adversary relationship, which they acquired from their experience in the ICSC, and were equipped with a technically admirable bag of tricks designed to give them the tactical advantage. There is no indication of any thought in Canada's Department of External Affairs directed toward techniques of cooperation with the East European delegations.

Second, the structure and work of the commission secretariat emphasized the need for loyalties beyond those to the component delegations. Whatever may be said of the failings of a United Nations peacekeeping force, it is a body which claims the loyalty of the national contingents. This is true both for international civil servants and for soldiers, as, for example, in the apparent ability of commanders-in-chief of UN forces to fully support and commit their allegiance to the international body. In such circumstances, there is the opportunity to contain and control politically diverse national contingents. In UNEF II, for example, the Canadians and Poles accepted a division of labor determined by UN authorities, and achieved the necessary minimum level of cooperation. In Vietnam, by contrast, not only were the adversaries required to work closely together in the field - unlike UN operations, where the respective contingents are generally kept together and assigned a sector responsibility - but they had to compete to form the rules and procedures of the commission itself. In such circumstances, the chances of achieving a coherently functioning commission were bound to be slender, and the actual outcome - the breakdown of the commission into its component parts - easily predictable.

Third, it should be recognized that without the initiatives of the Canadian delegation it is extremely unlikely that the commission would have deployed on schedule, and one might doubt whether it would have deployed at all, given the lack of preparedness and experience of the other delegations. The commissioners had to worry about where to sleep, what to eat, and so on. That they were able to perform the necessary housekeeping activities, organize the teams for deployment to the field, convene meetings of the "South Vietnamese parties," and chide the four party JMC for failure to move quickly enough in its own deployment was due to the Canadians, who came committed to the view that the obligations of the commission were to be fulfilled strictly according to the letter of the protocol and, thus, with the logistics planning that they knew would be necessary if the commission were not to lapse immediately into confusion.

The converse, however, was that the Canadians came committed to the belief that the commission would operate in an adversary manner. No doubt, the subsequent history of the commission could be cited by the Canadian delegation to support their presumptions; in turn, these were based on the experience of the first commission (ICSC), which had soured the attitudes of members of the Department of External Affairs to a surprising degree.(13) Such an approach, nevertheless, placed Canada in an awkward position. By defining the situation in adversary terms, Canada was bound to find itself, all protestations to the contrary, as lending itself to the side of the American and the Saigon governments. Determined not to do this (in principle, that is), and having insisted that Canada represented not one side but the international community, the delegation tended to focus on revealing why the commission could not work. In this they were extremely successful, but it was a success achieved at a price, for, as the following pages show, not only were there some convenient omissions from the policy of strict legality, but there was also a neglect of opportunities to provide the commission with a more positive role.

THE WORK OF THE COMMISSION

The ICCS met in session 82 times during the six months that Canada participated. Technically, there were no sessions in the month of May – M. Gauvin was chairman for the second time, and adjourned the 66th Session sine die in order to force a resolution on an investigative report – but, on average, the commissioners met twice a week or more. The amount of time spent in discussing relatively trivial matters, however, was remarkably great. No doubt, questions of pensions or disability allowances have their place, and occasionally the trivia touched on intriguing questions – the Hungarians claimed $200 per day allowance for their officers, for example, while the Canadians came in with the low bid of $7 per day – but an extraordinary amount of time was wasted on such matters. The explanation lies in the divisive character of the commission discussed above. Since it was difficult or impossible for the committees of the commission to make decisions, most questions, great and small, were referred to the commissioners. One consequence of this was that the mechanics of the commission tended to assume far too prominent a role, for often the intramural points at issue seemed to be more important than the larger conflict in Vietnam. One of the great disappointments, therefore, is that one looks in vain for evidence that the ICCS sought to carry out its tasks in the context of an ongoing political appraisal of the situation in South Vietnam after the Paris agreement.

Instead, the main substantive work of the commission focused on questions arising from investigations which raised issues about the investigative process itself. Sometimes, though not always, these questions (such as the obligation to investigate, freedom and security of movement, or the disposal of an investigation report) bore upon major issues in the conflict, as, for example, when investigations produced evidence of fresh North Vietnamese troop movements into South Vietnam. But generally speaking, with the Canadians again setting the pace, it was the ground rules of international observation missions that were the primary issue, not the resolution of Vietnam's problems.

In this context, discussions were often tense and sometimes abusive. For the most part, the ICCS divided two and two, but there can be no question that the main conflict was between Canada on the one hand and Poland and Hungary on the other. Indonesia, interestingly, was less willing to support Canada as time went on, and there were occasions when the latter was isolated within the commission. Equal to the occasion, the Canadian delegation, protesting strenuously from first to last against the principle of unanimity, was willing at those points to prevent the other three from speaking for the commission.(14) It is fair to add that these tactics were never employed to defend the South Vietnamese or the Americans per se (as the East European delegations defended the PRG) but, rather, to defend the Canadian view of what the commission should and should not do. Nevertheless, as time went on, the Canadians became more isolated within the commission; their ultimate withdrawal was timely in the sense that, had they continued, they would have been obliged to choose between a policy which was increasingly unproductive and an attempt to make the commission work which would of necessity have meant accepting the mediatory role espoused by the Poles and Hungarians. In short, the Canadians left before it became necessary for them to identify themselves as the representatives of the South Vietnamese in a bargaining or mediating process.

These themes are most clearly revealed in the efforts of the commission to investigate alleged violations of the cease-fire. Although not their only function, nor the one most successfully performed, almost every major issue coming before the commission related to an investigation or a request for one. It is to complaints of violations of the cease-fire, therefore, that we turn next.

VIOLATIONS OF THE CEASE-FIRE

In the six months following the cease-fire agreement, there were more than 18,000 "incidents" in South Vietnam involving more than 76,000 casualties. As Loomis points out, this approximates the estimated 80,000 casualties for the six months preceding the cease-fire.(15) Moreover, with the exception of Tet and the rapid increase in fighting in June, the level of incidents from day to day is relatively consistent. Particularly, it might be noted that the cease-fire did not produce a steady decrease in the fighting, as was implied by spokesmen for the U.S. government who suggest that the incidents in the first weeks of the cease-fire were a necessary "tidying-up" of the cease-fire in place. Rather, the decrease in fighting immediately after the cease-fire reflected the unusually high levels of fighting preceding the cease-fire, as both sides sought to improve their territorial positions in anticipation of the cease-fire in place.

As time passed after the cease-fire, a clear pattern of conflict emerged. The North Vietnamese and PRG forces exerted strong pressure on the northenmost province of Quang Tri, from the north across the demilitarized zone, and from the northwest across the Laotian border. In the central areas of South Vietnam, and to the northwest of Saigon, the struggle for control produced many incidents and full-scale military conflicts. Further south, in the delta, most military activity appeared to center on the so-called rice road to Saigon, particularly in the area of Cai-Lai, while in the extreme south military activity was sporadic and consisted largely of isolated incidents. Similarly, large areas of the eastern part of the country were relatively peaceful.

In this military context, objectives of the two South Vietnamese sides were logically different. The PRG, one can only surmise, was interested primarily in securing recognition for its political position in South Vietnam. It addressed very few complaints to the ICCS and maintained poor liaison with it.(16) The Saigon government, on the other hand, had some obvious points to bring out into the open in regard to the military situation described above. First, it wanted to establish the flagrant resupply of men and material that made possible the PRG/North Vietnamese pressure along the lines described, and to draw attention to the continued use and improvement (all-weather surfacing) of the Ho Chi Minh trail. Secondly, of course, it wanted to establish that the PRG was at fault in the individual complaints; that is, that the PRG was the "aggressor."

The total number of investigations ordered by the ICCS (1,081 in the six month period under consideration) might have constituted perhaps one-twentieth of the total incidents in the period. Nor were the commission teams overworked, since, with 47 teams deployed, investigations averaged about one per week per team. In the most direct sense, therefore, the ICSC neither controlled nor supervised the cease-fire, nor was there a meaningful cease-fire. But if one asks the more realistic question, namely, did the activities of the ICCS permit it to control (that is, monitor) the state of conflict between the parties, the answer is qualified, but more encouraging. First, the rate of requests for investigation through the six months suggests that the ICCS did not become irrelevant, as the ICSC had. Of course, the overwhelming number of these requests came from the DRVN, but the rapid increase in the number from the PRG in the last month, whatever the reasons, indicates that the PRG may have thought twice about its earlier neglect of the commission.

Moreover, the pattern of investigation by region and time roughly corresponded to the overall pattern of military activity. While the overall number of requests remained reasonably consistent month by month, the critical regions III and V (Pleiku and Bien Hoa), where PRG and North Vietnamese strength flowed across the Cambodian border, showed a marked increase as time passed; Region VI, (My Tho) to the immediate south of Saigon, was also very active. This picture is confirmed in the analysis of investigation by type of incident. In Regions IV (Phan Thiet) and VII (Can Tho), the preponderance of incidents were conventional, and in Region VI conventional and terrorist attacks were approximately half and half. If we accept that in Regions I and II, adjoining the demilitarized zone, there was a situation in which conventional battles were fought, then it is reasonable to conclude that the ICCS did indeed have a sample of cases before it which reflected the military realities of the ongoing conflict in South Vietnam.(17)

Reflecting on the principal substantive issues which the ICCS faced would support this analysis. For the most part, the routine incidents of a "terrorist" nature occasioned few protracted debates within the commission; on the other hand, the incidents discussed below - An Loc, Khe Sanh, Tong-le-Chan, Lao Bao, and the issue of places of entry for the PRG - can be related to the central conflict outlined above. Yet, within the ICCS, there was barely a mention of these incidents in the broader strategic context. Instead, perhaps because of the tactics adopted by the Canadians, the context of discussion was invariably the rules of investigation of the commission itself. This, of course, was because the Canadians were determined either to investigate with scrupulous attention to the rules, or to establish that other parties were obstructing the investigative process. The following analysis, therefore, concentrates on the process of investigation. In doing so, however, the political context of what might at first sight seem to be purely procedural issues is stressed. This has the advantage of introducing the viewpoint of the East European delegations, as well as suggesting the limitations of both the commission itself and specifically the Canadian approach to international supervision in Vietnam.(18)

FIELD INVESTIGATIONS

In the conduct of field investigations, two aspects are of interest. First, from the viewpoint of the development of international observation techniques, the actual conduct of the investigation merits comments. Secondly, partly from the internationalist perspective and partly as a commentary on the politics of the commission itself, the procedures governing investigation, beginning with the initiation of the complaint and ending with the submission of a report to the parties to the agreement, are of critical importance.

Tri-Ton - A Field Investigation(19)

Tri-Ton was a subregional team site in Region VII, in the south of Vietnam. Tri-Ton itself is located in the border province of Chan Doc, some 25 kilometers from the Cambodian frontier. It was the first complaint received in Region VII – submitted by the RSVN – and it involved an alleged PRG rocket attack upon a schoolhouse, with several casualties. The Canadians and the Indonesians were anxious to investigate immediately, the Poles and the Hungarians less so. In the outcome, the investigation was belated but, reluctantly, the East Europeans went along.
The casualties, of course, had been removed, and merely seeing victims in a local hospital did not suffice to establish that they were indeed the casualties from that particular attack – it certainly did not meet the standards of verification required by the Poles and Hungarians. In regard to the spent rocket case, however, the Canadians utilized equipment necessary to establish verifiable evidence. Every officer deployed to a team site was issued with a tape-recorder and camera; they took photographs of the victims and the damage, interviewed witnesses, and subsequently transcribed their testimony. In the case of Tri-Ton, they were able to go further. Using experts at the military delegation in Saigon, the Canadians claimed to be able to calculate the distance of the plate of the rocket from the point of impact. This information was transmitted to the investigating team, which then established the presumed location of the firing. Since, in the case of Tri-Ton, it was in territory occupied by North Vietnamese

regulars, the RSVN liaison officer was unable to guarantee the security of the investigating team if they decided to look for further evidence at the site of the firing; the PRG liaison officer denied that the area was occupied by North Vietnamese regulars (there were no North Vietnamese regular forces in South Vietnam according to the official position), but did not undertake to guarantee security.   The investigating teams were under instructions not to investigate if their security was not guaranteed; therefore, the investigation concluded at this point.

In their reports, the Canadians and Indonesians present-ed the evidence obtained, and concluded that the PRG was guilty of a violation of the cease-fire.   The Poles and Hun-garians disputed the evidence presented, arguing that there was no evidence that the victims seen were actually the casu-alties of the alleged rocket attack, and that there was no sure way of knowing how long the rocket casing had lain impacted in the ground.   The dissenting reports were duly forwarded to the   commissioners.   With   some   delay,   the   commissioners agreed, without discussion of the substance of the reports, to forward the findings to the four parties.   Since the report was not unanimous, the report does not have the status of a commission report, but was forwarded as the views of indivi-dual members of the commission.   At this point, the incident at Tri-Ton disappeared from sight.   There was no indication that the parties to the agreement made any further use of the Tri-Ton report, nor any sign that the matter was raised again in the commission.

Several comments may be made about this "typical" inves-tigation.   The most obvious one is that, more so than any other delegation, the Canadians had the technical competence and means to carry out such investigations.   They brought highly trained personnel – selecting officers with the best career records rather than simply choosing those it might be convenient to send – and looked for previous experience in peace observation missions among the officers chosen.   The cameras and tape recorders indicated an awareness in the planning process of the necessities for complete investigation. Providing the investigators with such equipment reflected the developing awareness in Canada that the act of investigation requires military knowledge (the investigator has to be familiar with weapons systems, troop deployments, the military signifi-cance of incidents, etc.), combined with interrogatory skills, the sensible collection of information, the capacity to approach civilians, and other "nonmilitary" skills.   Although they had the added advantage that the working language of the ICCS was English, there is no doubt that field reports submitted by the Canadians were considerably more detailed and thorough than those of the other delegations.

It would be a mistake, however, to conclude that the apparently hard evidence accumulated at Tri-Ton was typical of ICCS investigations. In many cases, highly trained ballistics experts and sophisticated equipment would have been necessary to determine whether a given projectile had actually impacted, and at the time stated, or whether it had been planted there in order to stage an incident. The Poles and the Hungarians constantly complained that the RSVN rigged incidents, and that the so-called witnesses were simply hostile to the PRG. It is doubtful if the RSVN needed to rig incidents, but, on the other hand, it is also clear that the RSVN sought to take greater advantage of the commission in order to gain propaganda advantages over the PRG than vice-versa. (When one remembers that the Americans accused the PRG of air-lifting the wreckage of an ICCS helicopter some 15 miles in order to claim that it was off course, the allegation that the RSVN might be planting used rockets or persuading war victims to give a revised account of their wounds takes on the dimensions of only a small paranoia.)

In other situations, what might be reasonable to surmise hardly constituted proof. For example, one investigation was of an ICCS complaint that its helicopters had been fired upon, even though they had received the necessary flight approval.(20) While nobody doubted the attack, there was a disagreement among the teams on board as to the origin of the small arms fire. The Canadians and Indonesians claimed that it came from one side of the river bank which was PRG controlled; the Poles and the Hungarians, not surprisingly, held that it came from the other. Narrowly construed, there must have been plenty of room for doubt strictly on the basis of observations from the helicopter. (In reality, it was well understood that, not having any aircraft of its own, the PRG tended to shoot at anything in the sky; while, conversely, the RSVN was equally likely not to shoot at anything.)

Such problems tended to place a premium on uncontestable evidence, but the conclusion is inescapable that the matter was not to be judged strictly in terms of the evidence. With every allowance for reasonable doubt, it is clear that the Poles and Hungarians were under instructions not to file reports critical of the PRG. What is more to the point, therefore, is the politics of the conflict in South Vietnam, and particularly the nature of the cease-fire. In their defense, it can be said for the Poles and Hungarians that they did not view isolated violations of the conflict as germane to the overall political nature of the cease-fire. The Canadians, however, abetted for the most part by the Indonesians, were determined to carry out the task assigned to them in the protocol. This they did with a persistence which was at times comic as it became increasingly divorced from the military realities of the situation. For Canadian diplomats, the torturous process of investigation was rigorously adhered to in order to establish that the investigative process was impeded by the political motives of the communist members of the commission, and by at least some, if not all, parties to the agreement. The political corollary of the military attempt to investigate without restriction, therefore, was an insistence within the Commission on procedures which would guarantee that all complaints would be investigated without constraints imposed from within or without the commission.

Expediting the Process of Investigation

A clear indication of the concerns of the Canadians is the draft document produced by the working group in November 1972.(21)   As suggested earlier, this document comprised in effect a summary assessment of the Canadian experience with the shortcomings of the ICSC, together with some general principles drawn from other peacekeeping experiences.   Unsuccessful in gaining American support for the incorporation of these ideas into the protocol of the Paris agreement, the Canadians introduced essentially the same set of proposals on procedures into the ICCS as a "Memorandum of Understanding" which served as the working document of the Special Committee on Operating Procedures.   Insofar as the commission itself was concerned, the thrust of the Canadian proposals was to preclude any possibility that the ICCS might serve to provide the veneer of supervision while in reality its composition produced a willful stalemate.   In part, then, the "Memorandum of Understanding," different items of which appeared before the plenary sessions of the commission throughout February and March, proposed that:

1.   The Commission should meet when necessary, and in any case not less than once each week.   Meetings were to be held within twenty-four hours of the request of any single delegate, and in a situation deemed "urgent" by any single delegate, or by the chairman, within two hours;

2.   The nonattendance of any delegation was not to invalidate the meeting, or to preclude the possibility of a unanimous report;

3.   The agenda was to be drawn up the morning or afternoon before the next meeting, and, by unanimous agreement, items might be added at the meeting itself.   (This was an effort to forestall procedural excuses for refusing to consider an issue.)

4.   The minutes of the commission were to be forwarded to the parties in accordance with articles 18(b) and (c) of the protocol, until or unless the Paris Conference made other definitive arrangements.

These proposals passed through the special committee, and were accepted by the commission itself, on February 19th.(22)

The emphasis on urgency in investigation was reinforced by another Canadian proposal which came to the commission via the Special Committee on Operating Procedures, and was accepted by the commission on March 21st:

> Except as otherwise provided by the unanimous agreement of all National Delegations, the teams shall report the results of all observations and/or investigations provided for under the Agreement and Protocols to the Commission as follows:
>
> a)   promptly, and not later than twenty-four hours after the conclusion of the observation and/or investigation;
> b)   in the case of observations and/or investigations which are prolonged for more than twenty-four hours, after the beginning of such observations and/or investigations and subsequently every twenty-four hours until a final report is made.(23)

By such procedures, the Canadians hoped to avoid the pitfalls, particularly the scope for procedural delays, that had hampered the ICSC. As is partially evident in the case of Tri-Ton, and more so in the cases discussed below, no such procedures could ensure immediate action in the field, yet the acceptance of all the proposals seeking to remove constraints in the commission marked again the capacity of the Canadians in the early days to carry the other delegates along on the strength of their initiatives.

While the Canadians were quite successful in creating procedures to prevent procrastination in the ICCS, they were somewhat less so in their pursuit of open hearings. The intent here, of course, was to allow any delegation to be completely outspoken on matters coming before the commission, and on all matters within the purview of the commission, and to make public disagreements among the delegations, thereby forcing greater awareness of blatant violations of the agreement, or revealing the unwillingness of certain delegations to recognize glaring transgressions. The original Canadian proposals within the special committee were that the sessions of the commission should be public, and that the minutes of the commission and its committees and the investigating team reports should be public documents. On the first point, the Canadians compromised (effectively, they surrendered the point), and it was agreed that sessions of the commission would be open if the delegations agreed unanimously that they should be. On the second point, the Poles and Hungarians asked for time to consult their respective governments. Subsequently, the matter was quietly dropped; the status of all documents except unanimous reports, which it was agreed would be public documents, remained undetermined.(24)

These efforts at publicity were, of course, paralleled by the "open-mouth" policy of M. Gauvin. Since the open-mouth policy began from the time of the arrival of the Canadian delegation in Vietnam, it is clear that in itself it was an attempt to obtain the substance of the proposals of the working group after their proposals had died in the negotiations prior to the Paris agreement. Whereas in the ICSC the Canadians had abided by the rules and accepted the policy of unanimity, in the ICCS, they intended to circumvent the procedural shortcomings, if necessary at the cost of orthodox diplomatic conduct. The open-mouth policy, therefore, reflected Ottawa's willingness to turn the ICCS into a contest rather than to accept it as a passive instrument, and to incur the hostility of the East European delegations rather than to accept the constraints of a politically divided commission. In doing so, they also settled for a limited period of tenure, for the utility of the Canadian approach predictably declined as the opposition mounted, so that, even without the consideration of external political factors, by the end of July 1973, it was clear that the Poles and Hungarians would have been more disposed to find mutually acceptable solutions with some other pro-Western state than they were with Canada.

Initiating Investigations

Two issues were of significance in the initiation of investigations. The first was the question of who could initiate investigations; the second, and more important one in the context of the commission's work, was the matter of whether all requests for investigation had to be acted upon. The protocol allowed requests for investigation from the two JMC's, from "any party," and from the National Council of National Reconciliation and Concord in respect to matters concerning the holding of elections, and also permitted the commission itself to initiate investigations where it deemed that there were "adequate grounds."(25) It did not, however, prescribe the procedures whereby investigations would be initiated. The Poles and the Hungarians insisted that all investigations require the approval of the ICCS itself. The Canadians proposed that all commission teams have the right to receive a complaint and initiate an investigation, including the subregional teams. The Canadian formulation in the special committee aimed both to devolve and expedite the investigative process:

> When a request is received by one of the teams
> referred to in Article 4(c) of the Protocol [on the
> ICCS], that team will despatch or assign an inves-
> tigating team within 12 hours of the receipt of such
> request. . . . (26)

This formulation, which was supported by the Indonesians,
was modified by the Poles and Hungarians so that, while
accepting the obligation to act quickly, the approval for an
investigation would be communicated to the local team from the
regional headquarters. Whether this amendment meant that the
regional headquarters would make the decision to investigate is
not clear; but, in general, it is evident that the East
Europeans were unwilling to allow the investigative process to
be apolitical. This matter was never formally settled, but
regional headquarters as the source for approval appears to
have been accepted in practice by the commission. Even on
the matter of hastening the investigating process, a persistent
Canadian complaint (repeated by one after another of the
Canadian members in the field) is that, quite apart from the
foot-dragging tactics exemplified above in the case of Tri-Ton,
the East European representatives showed bad faith in refusing
to facilitate field investigations.
       Typically, two incidents in Region I, near the former
demilitarized zone, illustrate the Canadian view of the
thwarting of the commission's work. An RVN complaint concerning an incident in the Cua-Viet area had been received on
30 January.(27) The investigation had been unable to proceed
because of the failure of the PRG and the RSVN to provide
liaison officers, and thus guarantee the security of the investigating team. Several weeks later, a PRG complaint was
received concerning another incident at Cua-Viet, which
became known as the "Vinh-Hoa incident." The commission
agreed to investigate both incidents. The Vinh-Hoa investigation was completed within the week, and the field report
passed to the commission on March 20th, the investigation
having received the full cooperation of the PRG and DRV.
The Cua-Viet incident remained uninvestigated, as the Canadians alleged, because the PRG and DRV liaison officers
refused to assist, and "even refused to ask their superiors in
Saigon for instructions."(28)
       The Canadian ambassador drew the obvious conclusion
from this - that the level of cooperation from the PRG depended upon whether or not it considered that the outcome of the
investigation would be to its advantage. The Hungarian
ambassador defended the disparate efforts in the two investigations. The instruction from the commission in the Cua-Viet
complaint, he said, was "to ask the team to report on its
ability to investigate this complaint in the light of its contacts
with the regional JMC. That meant that the team's task had

been to report on its ability to investigate a complaint and there was quite a difference between reporting on an investigation and reporting on the team's ability to investigate."(29)

In partial defense of the Hungarian position, it might be said that the discussions of the commission were marked on all sides by this kind of sophistry, which was clearly designed to defend a position rather than to enhance the supervision of the cease-fire. On the other hand, it is simply indisputable that the Canadians never veered from their policy of strict and even-handed treatment of complaints received,(30) whereas the East European delegations pursued a highly discriminatory policy in the matter of investigations. On this point, perhaps one more example will suffice.

On February 20, M. Gauvin made a statement to the commission complaining about the situation in Region VI.(31) As of that date, he claimed, 22 requests for investigations of alleged cease-fire violations in Region VI had been received, but the commission had been able to agree to start investigations in only five of them. M. Gauvin argued that the reasons for the delay rested entirely with the other side. In two cases, the PRG had failed to provide safe passage for the investigating teams; in two others, the Hungarian chairman of the regional ICCS had failed to initiate the investigations. More fundamentally, however, the chairman had claimed that investigations could not proceed without liaison officers and guarantees of security from all four parties to the cease-fire. It was precisely this procedural stalemate of the commission that the Canadians had set their minds to preventing, and M. Gauvin thus argued that not only was this condition a violation of the ICCS protocol, but that in reality such a rule would preclude any possibility of investigations taking place. In the specific case, the PRG representatives in Region VI claimed that they were only an advance party for the PRG delegation, and had authority only to procure accommodation, while the DRVN delegation, again closing the circle, had announced that they would participate in investigations only if all four parties were represented.

Nothing if not persistent, M. Gauvin directly accused the Poles and Hungarians: "Since the Hungarian and Polish delegations were aware of the fact that the PRG would not respond to the request, the Canadian delegation can only conclude that the Hungarian and Polish insistence on liaison officers from all four parties constituted deliberate obstructionism."(32) More interesting than the charges and countercharges (the Record of Decisions notes that "the Polish and Hungarian delegations objected in strong terms to what they called the general attack made by the Canadian delegation"), was the broader policy of the East European delegations. On March 14th, while Region VI accumulated a backlog of investigations, a complaint was received from the PRG which the Canadians and Indonesians agreed to investigate. The Poles and Hungarians, however, argued additionally that complaints ought to be investigated in order of their seriousness, and since the PRG complaint alleged that a major violation had taken place, they considered that it ought to be investigated first.

Such shifts in direction placed considerable strain on the Canadian policy of strict adherence to the protocol. As in the first commission, disputes such as this tended to drive the Canadians to a position which they did not want: championing the rights, as it were, of Saigon. Their response, as the above account shows, was to vigorously attack the opposing delegations for failure to implement the protocol. This attack was predicated on the assumption that the Poles and Hungarians did not want violations to be "internationally" supervised, and that their approach to the commission was based on expediency and "Machiavellianism."(33) It is worth noting that this example of apparently crude opportunism in Region VI is somewhat mitigated by a consideration of the sequence of complaints. The first seven complaints were initiated by the RSVN and the United States. In sum, they concerned incidents in which two civilians had been killed and five wounded; 23 military personnel had been killed and 92 wounded; additionally, one hamlet chief had been killed. The eighth incident was the one initiated by the PRG: it alleged that 300 civilians had been killed, and 1,288 houses and large amounts of rice had been destroyed. The ninth incident was initiated by the RSVN and concerned an obvious retaliation by the PRG: 8 civilians were killed, 29 wounded, and 229 houses and a temple were destroyed. Thereafter, the remaining incidents, all RVN or American initiated, were of the same pattern as the first seven.

It can be said for the East Europeans that, if one assumed that a certain low level of conflict would inevitably accompany the settlement process, the task of the commission was to draw the attention of the parties to major violations which threatened the basis of the cease-fire itself. The PRG complaint was just such a case. On other occasions, the Hungarians in particular complained bitterly that the commission was being asked to investigate incidents which ought to have been referred to the police or other civilian authorities. To allow the same significance to a sporadic outburst of firing at a military outpost as to a major military attack on a civilian target may indeed seem a distortion. On the other hand, it could hardly have been lost on the Hungarians that small-scale attacks, intimidation, or assassination of government administrators, and so on, were the stock-in-trade of the antagonists at the local level. There are two points to be made here. The first is that the Hungarian position was not quite as indefensible as it first seems: there is some merit to the argument that the Commission ought to have have discriminated according to the severity of the incident. The second point is, however, that, if the East European delegations were genuinely interested in a creative role for the commission, they were hardly likely to realize it by pursuing a policy which was so evidently one-sided. The question, then, is what, if anything, their delegations wished to achieve in the commission other than the negative policy of preventing it from being used against the PRG.

While the Canadians sought to establish practices to ensure that the investigating teams could respond promptly and efficiently, they also argued fiercely within the commission itself to prevent complaints dying in the commission, and to forestall any suggestion of passivity or neglect on the part of the commissioners. The earliest and critical indication of this was sparked by the incident at Khe Sanh in the west of Region I, about 15 miles south of the demilitarized zone.

General Woodward, the chief U.S. delegate to the four party JMC, entered a complaint on February 28th to the effect that the North Vietnamese had violated the agreement by building a surface-to-air missile site at Khe Sanh. Khe Sanh was astride the new all-weather road system which the North Vietnamese were building into South Vietnam, and the missiles were clearly intended to protect the road and its users. (Ironically, the same road played a part in the shooting down of the ICCS helicopter at Lao Bao in May, for the new road was not marked on maps, and was the source of the navigating error that led the helicopter far away from its flight path.)

Predictably, but particularly in the light of the seriousness of the occasion, the Canadians, supported by the Indonesians, called for an immediate inquiry. The Poles and Hungarians, however, expressed the view that, in order to make "a decision on the investigation" (the decision, that is, on whether to hold an investigation), the Commission should first seek the views of the PRG delegation to the four party JMC. This the Canadians resolutely opposed, maintaining that the ICCS had never in the past sought the views of one party on the complaint of another before deciding to investigate, and clearly having in mind that this procedure, if accepted as a precedent, could be used to prevent action on any matter which was unpalatable to one party.(34) The discussion ended in a deadlock, as did a subsequent discussion in the commission on March 2nd. Three days later, M. Gauvin again introduced the matter, stating that his government "had taken a very serious view of the failure of the ICCS to investigate the Khe Sanh case."(35)

There is no doubt that the Canadians saw the Khe Sanh case as the thin end of the wedge for the return to practices that would reduce the ICCS to the inactivity of the old ICSC. The critical change in the operating procedures of the ICCS, however, was the provision that individual members of the commission could send reports to the parties, though such reports did not have the standing of a commission document. Combined with the Canadian decision to "go public," M. Gauvin exploited this opening with considerable success in the case of Khe Sanh. On March 9th, he presented a statement to the chairman of the commission (M. Estergalyos, the Hungarian ambassador), requesting that it be forwarded to the four party JMC under article 3(b) of the protocol. In a parallel move, he took great care to attract maximum publicity to the Khe Sanh issue.(36) The political environment at the time, moreover, was conducive to such pressure. The Paris Conference of late February had focused attention on some of the problems of the cease-fire; the prisoner-of-war exchange was continuing, but was surrounded by recriminations; and the American military presence in South Vietnam was still sizeable, so there was point to General Woodward's assertion that, if the missiles were not removed, the United States reserved the right to take "appropriate action."(37)

The first consequence of this policy was to draw out the opposing members of the commission. They argued strongly against Gauvin's statement of March 9th insofar as it purported to summarize their position, and on March 12th the Polish delegation produced a statement of their own - also with a request that it be forwarded to the four party JMC. The Polish statement addressed itself to two questions: the basis of the Polish opposition to an investigation, and the conduct of the Canadian delegation. Both points raised issues which went beyond Khe Sanh:

> The Head of the Canadian Delegation in his statement distorted the stand taken from the very beginning by the Polish Delegation. This distortion consisted in extracting from the context only part of the reasoning as well as in leaving aside essential parts of our stand. It omits in particular basic legal arguments, presented by our Delegation, that aerial photographs, because of evident reasons, cannot constitute proofs in the case. The more so that the deliverer of these photographs admits by the same that he has violated the sovereignty of the other party as well as the Agreement and the Protocols.
>
> Moreover, the Head of the Canadian Delegation, in spite of the reached understanding, on his own and in a non-objective way informs the public about the work of the Commission, particularly about details of sessions and stands of the respective delegations. The Head of the Canadian delegation is not a spokesman of this Commission, hence he is not entitled to speak on behalf of the Polish Delegation, which has not authorized him to do it.(38)

In raising the issue of the violation of sovereignty, the Polish argument touched upon a point which was central to their approach to the cease-fire. As an argument for not investigating, however, it was based on a rather fine legal argument. In a later reply, M. Gauvin made the most of this, arguing that, on the basis of the Polish position, there was an argument for two investigations - of the allegation concerning the missile site, and of the possible illegality of the photographic evidence - but that it was not an argument for no investigation at all. On the other hand, if one accepts the view that the Poles and Hungarians saw their task as one of defending the interests of the PRG and North Vietnamese, then there is a relatively straightforward explanation of their refusal to allow an investigation at Khe Sanh.

First, Khe Sanh was unlike previous investigations in that it involved not two parties to an act of violence, but one part violating the agreement. Whereas other complaints could be argued to and fro, and, as we have seen, some room found for argument, at Khe Sanh, either there was a missile site or there was not. In short, an investigation might have produced undesirable evidence. If this reasoning holds good, then the minimum objective of the Poles and Hungarians must have been to give the North Vietnamese an opportunity to remove the missiles, as in fact, according to the Americans, they did.

Secondly, the North Vietnamese maintained strict security insofar as their new road system into South Vietnam was concerned. They demonstrated this very clearly in the helicopter incident at Lao Bao, and again at the ICCS team site near the demilitarized zone in Region I. In the latter case, they refused to allow the ICCS team to deploy to the designated site, but, a short time after, offered an alternative site some miles away from the original, which they said would be more congenial to the team. The Canadians in Region I believed that the original site was too close to construction work being carried on by the North Vietnamese and, at least pro forma, they did not want it to be witnessed by the Commission. Such considerations, then, not only explain at least in part the communist reluctance to investigate Khe Sanh, but begin to throw light on the circumstances in which the issue of freedom of movement must be understood.

As for the second part of the Polish argument, it is clear evidence that, for a time at least, the "open-mouth" policy brought problems out into the open which otherwise would have lain dormant in the privacy of the commission. The Canadian needling on the Khe Sanh matter forced a Polish response, although it did not produce an investigation. In a sense, therefore, Khe Sanh was a victory for the Canadians. In his reply to the Polish statement, M. Gauvin reiterated the Canadian position:

> To my knowledge, it had never been questioned in
> this Commission that a member has the right to
> speak publicly about Commission activities and its
> involvement therein. It should now be quite clear to
> all members of the Commission, after nearly two
> months of public statement, that I am carrying out
> Canadian policy in doing so.(39)

The "reached understanding" that the Polish statement referred to was apparently the understanding that delegations
would not reveal publicly the positions of other delegations as
expressed in the commission. Of course, in substance, it was
nigh impossible to do otherwise, as M. Gauvin himself was well
aware, for to give an account of a dispute within the commission necessarily involved revealing the positions of the
disputants: "I will admit," said M. Gauvin, "that it does not
take much perspicacity to identify delegations without naming
them; correspondents must have been using their own knowledge about which Delegations were likely to take the positions
that I had carefully refused to attribute to any particular
delegation."(40)

On March 11th, the U.S. secretary of state, William
Rogers, announced that the missile site had been removed from
Khe Sanh, and General Woodward credited the Canadians for
being a decisive influence in forcing the removal. On March
13th, in Tokyo, Mr. Sharp made a significant change in
direction in Canadian policy. On the first leg of his trip to
Saigon, Vientiane, and Hanoi, the minister for external affairs
stated that, while the government still saw the willingness of
the parties to respect the cease-fire as a critical point, "the
overriding factor in deciding the future of the Canadian force
is whether the Canadians are effective and playing a 'useful'
role."(41) The role in the Khe Sanh affair was, of course,
useful, but its success was also its failure, for it was a major
example of, on the one hand, the tendency of the situation to
drive Canada into the role of defender of Washington and
Saigon, and, on the other, of the inability of the ICCS to act
as a genuinely supervisory body. In this respect, Khe Sanh
exemplified the Canadian diagnosis of the shortcomings of the
Commission and the political hazards of serving as a Western
member.

CONCLUSIONS

To emphasize the field work of the ICCS is to put the Canadian case in the best light and the Polish and Hungarian case
in the worst. It must be stated frankly, moreover, that the
Record of Decisions of the commission allows no other conclu-

sion. But this reflects, in turn, a difference in approach between the two sides.

The Canadians, aided for the most part but not invariably by the Indonesians, sought to establish that "peacekeeping" involved certain functions and behavior. Central to the task was the objectivity of investigation and reporting. All their efforts in the commission may be seen as directed toward the realization of this approach. Their unconcealed view of the Poles and Hungarians was that the latter were not committed to objectivity; hence, the Canadians made great efforts to expose their alleged obstructionism.

The East Europeans had a different view of the ICCS. They saw it not as a value in itself, or as constituting an international element in the situation, but as a very small part of a political situation which was still out of control. In what was for them a hostile environment, their task was to ensure that the PRG did not lose ground. Hence, the question of sovereignty in South Vietnam was central to their concerns. The inescapable weakness in the Paris agreement was that it allowed the PRG a status in South Vietnam, but did not clarify the point as to whether, after 27 January 1973, there were two governments - by implication, of equal standing in their relationship to the ICCS.

The East Europeans, of course, insisted that there were, and saw the Canadian tendency to treat the PRG as a party to the agreement and Saigon as the sovereign government of South Vietnam as highly discriminatory. In turn, the Poles and Hungarians accepted that the conflict continued, and saw no advantage in identifying the guilty party incident by incident - "to point fingers at one another," as the Hungarian ambassador argued. Instead, they thought that if the commission had an effective role it would be in persuading the parties to lessen tensions - in short, to mediate.

Both these arguments were unacceptable to the Canadians. The question of sovereignty they ignored, for it was clear that on the part of the Americans this was a deliberate ambiguity designed to maintain the last vestiges of Saigon's claim to legitimacy in South Vietnam. The prospect of mediation they resisted vehemently, convinced that this was simply a maneuver to prevent investigation, and consequently inhibit fulfillment of the basic functions of the commission described in the protocol.

In this fundamental conflict of views, one comes to the demise of the ICCS. Lacking a political authority to which to report, hampered by the parties to the agreement, required to oversee a cease-fire which was not a cease-fire, it would be reasonable to suppose that the ICCS could never have functioned effectively. But its ultimate undoing was that its members could not find the common ground which would have permitted them to speak and act in a concerted manner.

Lacking this prerequisite, an essential element was missing in Vietnam - that of a genuine international presence.

NOTES

1. In accordance with Article 19 of the Agreement, the Paris Conference met from 27 February to 2 March , and was attended by the four parties to the Agreement, the four members of the Central Commission, four outside great powers (the Soviet Union, China, Britain, and France), and the secretary-general of the United Nations. Intended as the forum in which the deficiencies of the Agreement would be connected, the conference was an echo of the 1954 Geneva Conference, but its actual contribution was insignificant. It certainly did not constitute the international political authority hoped for by the Canadians.

2. In an interview with Charles Wasserman, CBC Weekend, 23 February 1971.

3. For President Carter's letter on this question, see the New York Times, 8 April 1979, p. 8.

4. The principal secondary sources for the negotiation culminating in the agreement are: H.A. Kissinger, White House Years (Boston: Little, Brown, 1979); Gareth Porter, A Peace Denied (Bloomington, Indiana: University of Indiana Press, 1975); Allan E. Goodman, The Lost Peace (Stanford, Calif.: Hoover Institution Press, 1978); Marvin and Bernard Kalb, Kissinger (Boston: Little, Brown, 1974).

5. In a speech to the House of Commons, Commons Debates, January 5th, 1973, pp. 29-31.

6. PAE well illustrates the danger of what might perhaps be called "bias by logistic association." In a 1980 advertisement, the firm explained: "[Our] geographic scope of activity has extended to Afghanistan, Greece, Ethiopia, Germany, Iran, Japan, Korea, Taiwan, Laos, Cambodia, Malaysia, Vietnam, Thailand, Indonesia, Singapore. . . ." The roll call of American political and military involvement in the rim countries of the Eurasian land mass is no doubt inadvertent but well illustrates the association of the firm. (1981-1982 ENR Directory of Design Firms, New York: McGraw-Hill, 1980, pp. 178-79.

7. See Colonel D.G. Loomis, "An Expedition to Vietnam: The Military Component of the Canadian Delegation 1973," Canadian Defence Quarterly, Spring 1974, p. 36.

8. Article 9(a) of the Protocol Concerning the International Commission of Control and Supervision states: "The Interna-

tional Commission, and each of its teams, shall act as a single body comprising representatives of all four members."

9. The following section is based on interviews with key personnel who served on the commission. The Canadian Department of National Defence produced a comprehensive but restricted assessment of their part in the ICCS operation, entitled "Project Gallant" - a precise reflection, incidentally, of how the department saw its role. A number of the details that follow are derived from that report.

10. See, for example, the survey of these restrictions and the protests by American news agencies, in Editor and Publisher, 10 February 1973.

11. M. Gauvin became even more outspoken after the Canadian decision to stay beyond the first 60 day period. For example, he expressed strong public support for an American charge that North Vietnamese troops were infiltrating South Vietnam (Ottawa Citizen, April 14). In commenting on the crash of the ICCS helicopter on April 7, Gauvin not only linked the attack with North Vietnamese infiltration, but came dangerously close to supporting the American claim that the wreckage had been moved. The Poles and Hungarians appear to have taken the decision to "go public" themselves around April 7th, when in a briefing to reporters they directly attacked the Canadians as arrogant and contentious. "It took us nearly two months to adjust to the situation here," said one senior official," . . . in every case, the Canadians have picked out the point that divides." (Globe and Mail, 7 April 1973). Gauvin's comments on those responsible for the helicopter attack brought a strong response from Hanoi Radio on April 15th which, among other things, challenged Gauvin's impartiality. Thereafter, there were numerous public charges and countercharges.

12. The objective is defined in Operation Gallant, p. 3. Precisely how a joint operation was to be conducted is not made clear, except to note the need to "exchange information concerning operations and support arrangements." Perhaps more to the point, in one of the summary conclusions of Gallant: "Many [Canadian officers] found themselves unprepared for the unique nature of the adversary negotiations they were required to conduct with the Polish and Hungarian delegations to the ICCS. Some training in this would be beneficial. . . . A discussion of adversary negotiating techniques should also be included in pre-deployment orientation briefings for operations in which we again find ourselves associated with Communist nations" [p, 46].

13. See Paul Bridle, "Canada and the International Commissions in Indochina 1954-1972," Behind the Headlines, Toronto: Canadian Institute of International Affairs, Vol. 4, 1973. For

a highly critical assessment of the Canadian role in this
regard, see Charles Taylor, Snow Job. (Toronto: Anansi
Press, no date). The official account of Canada's role in the
ICCS may be found in Mitchell Sharp, Vietnam: Canada's
Approach to Participation in the International Commission of
Control and Supervision, October 25, 1972 - March 27, 1973.
(Queen's Printer, May 1973).

14. The Canadian veto was most prominently seen in the
proposal by the Indonesian delegation to mediate an end to an
ongoing confrontation between the PRG and Saigon at Tong-Le-
Chan, a Saigon-held outpost. The Poles and Hungarians, who
believed that the commission should play a mediatory role,
were enthusiastically in favor; the Canadians, determined that
the commission's task was investigation not mediation, refused
to cooperate. See Record of Decisions, 40th Session, 5 April
1973; Globe and Mail, 6 April 1973.

15. Loomis, "An Expedition to Vietnam, p. 37.

16. Of the 1,081 complaints made to the ICCS as of 31 July
1973, 1,039 were from the RVN, 38 from the PRG, and 4 from
both. (Figures compiled from Record of Decisions.) Various
explanations have been given for the failure of the PRG to use
the commission. First, the PRG may not have considered the
ICCS to be sufficiently important, although since they lodged
more complaints as time passed it may well be that they recon-
sidered the public relations element involved. Secondly, they
did not deploy teams to regions and team sites as prescribed
in the protocol, and were not in a position to lodge complaints
at the local level. Some members of the commission believe
that this reflected the officer shortages of the PRG, but there
were also numerous reports, unsubstantiated but acknowledged
by commission members, that PRG representatives were killed
by RVN army elements, or, at best, were severely harassed
when they tried to deploy.

17. The allocation of ICCS teams to the seven regions, with
additional teams to control and supervise the exchange of
prisoners and points of entry into South Vietnam, is described
in Article 4 of the Protocol concerning the International
Commission of Control and Supervision.

18. I have commented at length on certain issues concerning
the ICCS which reflected the approach of the Polish and
Hungarian delegations in "Helpful Fixing in Vietnam: Some
Views from the Other Side," in The Canadian Image Abroad,
edited by Dennis Stairs and Donald Munton, (New York:
Pergamon Press, 1982).

19. I am grateful to a number of civilian and military members
of the Canadian delegation to the commission, who discussed
this and other incidents at great length with me. I also had

the opportunity to discuss the general operation of the commission with members of the East European delegations, who were
extremely helpful, but even more anxious not to receive personal acknowledgments.

20. There were a number of accounts of firing on ICCS
helicopters, and other hostile acts against commission personnel, including the detainment of two Canadian officers by
the PRG.   Incidents concerning helicopters were particularly
important to the Canadian delegation, however, because they
most visibly challenged the principle of freedom of movement,
and were easily attributable to the PRG.   Not having aircraft
of their own to worry about, local PRG units tended to treat
all aircraft as hostile.   A measure of the local autonomy in this
matter was the shooting down of the ICCS helicopter on April
7th, which contained two PRG liaison officers.   (See Globe and
Mail, 12 April 1973, for a lengthy account of the incident by
Canadian survivors.)   In this case, the helicopter was totally
off-course, but in subsequent incidents, where a flight path
had been carefully cleared with the PRG, the latter were still
unable to prevent local small arms fire against ICCS aircraft.
(See, for example, Press Communique Number 45 from the
Canadian Department of External Affairs, 3 May 1973.)

21. The working group was drawn from the Department of
External Affairs and National Defense.   It was put together
after it became clear that Canada would be called upon to form
part of a supervisory commission, and the strictness of the
operating procedures that it proposed reflected the defensive
nature of Canadian policy - genuinely unhappy at the compromised position that Canada had fallen into in the first
commission, the group was indirectly establishing the grounds
for a decision not to participate.   Taylor, Snow Job, pp.
146-47, offers a somewhat different version of the origin of the
group, noting that their "draft protocol" was received with
little enthusiasm in Washington, but comes to essentially the
same conclusion: "For most of the Canadians, their draft
protocol was designed to give Ottawa an honourable and
compelling reason for saying 'no'. . . ."

22. Record of Decisions, 17th session, 19 February 1973.

23. Record of Decisions, 32nd session, 21 March 1973.

24. Record of Decisions, 17th session, 19 February 1973.
The indeterminate status of the Record of Decisions had at
least one beneficial consequence.   The Canadian records, being
unclassified by virtue of the Canadian argument in the commission, were placed initially in the public library of the
Department of External Affairs.   Not for long, however.   Away
from the heat of battle, it was soon decided that they were,
after all, confidential documents, and they were removed for
classification.

25. Article 2, Protocol Concerning the International Commission of Control and Supervision.

26. Record of Decisions, 23rd session, 28 February 1973.

27. Apparently at the regional level, for it is not referred to in the Record of Decisions of the commission.

28. Record of Decisions, 37th session, 30 March 1973.

29. Ibid.

30. The Canadians were not as conscientious about other possible violations which they chose not to raise in the commission. These concerned, for example, the transfer of military bases and supplies from the United States to South Vietnam, the overflying of PRG-held territory by the United States and South Vietnam, and the legal status of the PRG in the light of the Paris agreement. For comment on some of these issues, see Tad Szulc, "Behind the Vietnam Ceasefire Agreement," Foreign Policy, no. 15, Summer 1974.

31. Record of Decisions, 18th session, 20 February 1973.

32. Ibid.

33. The characterization is that of Bridle, "Canada and the International Commissions," p. 25.

34. Record of Decisions, 23rd session, 28 February 1973.

35. Record of Decisions, 26th session, 5 March 1973. In this case, the Canadians were supported by the Indonesians, but the Polish and Hungarian delegations reiterated their opposition to an investigation.

36. It should be noted that this was still at a time when there was international media coverage of the work of the commission. The difficulty with Gauvin's strategy, however, was that, regardless of the merits of the case, he appeared to be engaged in a public campaign coordinated with General Woodward - as Hanoi Radio said later, echoing "the bad intentions of the Washington and Saigon governments" (Canadian Press, 25 March 1973).

37. General Woodward drew attention to the alleged missile base in public comments which were widely reported in the press on 28 February 1973, and thereafter.

38. Record of Decisions, 29th session, 12 March 1973.

39. Statement by the head of the Canadian delegation to the commission, 32nd session, 21 March 1973.

40. Ibid.

41. Canadian Press, March 16th. It should be noted that the report attributed Mr. Sharp's change of direction not to the

Khe Sanh incident, but to pressure from the Japanese government.   The Japanese were anxious that an "international
presence" be maintained while they were canvassing the possibilities of some form of regional international organization in
Asia.   Sharp returned to this argument in his speech to the
House of Commons explaining Canada's decision to participate
for a further 60 days after March 31st.   However, he then
rejected the idea of "an international presence as an indication
of the continued involvement of the world community in the
Vietnam situation," and based the decision to continue simply
on the grounds that more time was needed for the two South
Vietnamese parties to begin the process of political negotiations.   See House of Commons Debates, Tuesday, 27 March
1973, pp. 2629-31.

V
Peace, Law, and the Future

Introduction to Part V

The authors in this section firmly believe that peacekeeping, for all its faults and limitations, is a well-established feature of the international system. Their task here is to extrapolate historical practice to demonstrate continuing incremental growth and development; to pose the basic normative, philosophical, legal, and political questions that must be considered to ensure that this growth will occur; and to offer a broad gauge conceptual and theoretical vision of the evolution of the nation-state system and the contradictory pressures at work upon it at a critical stage of change and transformation.

In "Peacekeeping: The Dynamics of Future Development," Wiseman adopts the perspective of the "art of the possible." He views peacekeeping as a contemporary third party conflict control mechanism subject to incremental development, and as the foundation blocks for the transformation of the existing international system to a different and more peaceful system some time in the future.

Notwithstanding the ad hoc nature of each peacekeeping operation and the lack of political will in the UN to create a full-fledged institutional and military peacekeeping contingency regime, the procedures have become highly institutionalized. Grave disagreements over authorization, command and control, and financing, which threatened to wreck the UN in 1964 and became the subject of negotiations in the Special Committee on Peacekeeping Operations, to a considerable extent have been resolved in practice with the mandate for UNEF II. Furthermore, successive peacekeeping operations exemplify a broadening of mandates in response to intrastate as well as interstate conflicts which encompass the diversity of disputes typical of the international system: territorial, neocolonial, strategic, ideological, civil strife, and national self-determination, which may include governmental as well as nongovernmental parties.

337

As a result, peacekeeping operations are increasingly required to perform a wider and more complex range of functions.

On the political level, there is also evidence of growing political support for peacekeeping and a greater realization of its utility in the management of conflict in its potentially constructive relationship to the processes of arms limitation and Third World development. Wiseman also marshals the available evidence which suggests increasing general propensity to understand and appreciate the practical significance of employing third party measures for the management of international conflict which necessarily require the strengthening of international structures for peacekeeping and peacemaking.

"The international community has finally come to recognize, in principle, the concept of 'collective security' and its attendant notions of 'common responsibility' for the maintenance of international peace and security." Yet what role should the UN now be playing? Raman, in "UN Peacekeeping and the Maintenance of World Order," examines the legal basis and charter principles which form the basis of support for UN peacekeeping and which mark the signposts for future development. He shows commensurate progress in the evolutionary development of the norms and practices of other important segments of the UN, such as UNCTAD, ECOSOC, and Law of the Sea, symbolized by the last in the principle of "the heritage of mankind." While acknowledging that peacekeeping is "still a fragile and voluntary process," and that cold war factors tended to inhibit its expanded usage, he argues that many of the Third World and small states have a vital stake "in a strong UN-based security system." They play an important role in contemporary practice, and it is in their interest to strengthen the institutional structures of peacekeeping to enable the UN to expand its future usage. Raman elaborates further on the criteria and principles of the charter for such a course of action. In doing so, and based on actual cases and political development, he also asks the fundamental political and philosophical question about the rights of states to expect the UN to respond to their security needs in the anticipatory stages of conflict, as well as in the advanced stage of crisis. This is a profound question imbedded in the philosophy of the UN Charter and in the established legitimacy of peacekeeping. A more effective and prominent role for UN peacekeeping in the future may well depend on how states respond to this challenging question.

In "Peacekeeping: A Component of World Order," Taylor adopts a threefold approach to the analysis of contemporary anarchical international society: an historical investigation of the evolution and conditions of the present state system, alternate directions of its future development, and consideration of the moral imperatives involved in the choice of which alternative direction to follow. He asks, "What has been happening to our nation-state system?" and to what extent is the present anarchical society "capable of transforming its political institutions so as to be able to cope with an accelerating change in the nature of conduct of warfare?"

He presents three historical geopolitical paradigms partly derived from theoretical scientific models of space, time, and matter. The first, the Ptolemaic paradigm, represents the emergence of the nation-state system in a Machiavellian-Hobbesian type world of struggle and competition between autonomous state units, "the logic of Westphalia." The second is the Copernican paradigm of the eighteenth and nineteenth centuries where states evolve a sophisticated system of international diplomacy and the practice of the balance of power, both of which coincide with the evolution of profound ideological divisions and the exponential increase in the technology and destructive capability of warfare. The third is the force field paradigm, a concept in which every particle "becomes involved with every other in a complex of overlapping fields." Science has brought this international system into being, but not the organizational structure to make it work. The dilemma is caused by the dual tensions of Hobbesian struggle and Kantian cooperation.

Taylor thus provides a penetrating and powerful picture of the condition of the nation-state system and of the necessity to utilize the interactive elements of the "interdependent" force field to evolve further and functionally integrate peacekeeping and peacemaking as operative components of world order. If this fails to take place, the advance of technology and the persistence of Hobbesian conflict will inexorably push the nation-state system into self-destruction. Taylor thereby succeeds admirably in taking peacekeeping out of its narrow, postwar context and placing it into the larger picture of the dynamics of the international state system. "Peacekeeping: A Component of World Order" is a provocative look into the historical evolution of human civilization.

14
Peacekeeping: The Dynamics of Future Development
Henry Wiseman

From the hesitant and elementary beginnings of UN observer and reporting functions in the nascent period, 1946 to 1956, peacekeeping has been extended in use and expanded in function, complexity, and legitimacy. It has become the most prominent feature of UN capability in the management of conflict. The evidence is well established in the historical record (part of which is treated analytically in the chapters in this volume), in its contemporary importance in UN considerations, in its use by regional organizations and ad hoc arrangements, and by the emphasis it receives among statesmen and academics in their aspirations and projections for a more orderly world.

Is it reasonable to assume that the UN, regional organizations, and novel ad hoc structures will employ peacekeeping to restrain, contain, and/or resolve current or future conflicts? Would this be a desirable course to follow? From a normative point of view, any such means are better employed than allowing conflicts to persist or escalate without restraint in their destruction of humanity and resources and to threaten to engulf the world in chaos. There are many prescriptive models for the achievement of a peaceful world as it crosses the threshold of the year 2000 and beyond. Some are based on existing political historicist ideologies, Marxist or capitalist, which are locked in the struggle for dominance. Others are conceived de novo, as systems models designed primarily to manage international conflict. The latter area is a relatively new field of inquiry, though the literature is provocative and already abundant.(1) Two central questions of these inquiries are whether the state system as it is presently known can be more effectively managed or should be fundamentally restructured, and whether the transition process of either course can or should be a gradual process or a radical transformation.(2)

These questions considered, the point of view adopted here is that a disciplined regard for the association of theory and practice, of what is as well as what ought to be, calls for a realistic assessment of the art of the possible in the use of conflict control mechanisms within the structure of the contemporary state system, and the incremental development of such mechanisms as foundation blocks for the transformation of the existing system to a different and more peaceful world some time in the future. The argument is that the structures and practice of peacekeeping are a sound basis for the management of conflict in the immediate future and for the eventual transformation of the system itself, while readily acknowledging that it can be only one component of the multifaceted global management of conflict.

There are several compelling reasons why peacekeeping is on the current and will be on the future international agenda throughout the 1980s and beyond. The first are the innumerable grave crises which threaten international peace and security and which cry out for resolution; the second is that much still needs to be done to improve the political, structural, and operational capability of peacekeeping. It is one of the few viable, effective, and available instruments of conflict management. As well, there is considerable evidence from the historical experience of peacekeeping and of contemporary political proposals and academic commentaries to sustain this line of reasoning.

Accordingly, the following is a presentation of: (1) an historical analysis of UN peacekeeping showing its progressive development to its present state of institutionalization, including an examination of the deliberations of the Special Committee on Peacekeeping Operations (the Committee of 33) to determine agreed formulations and guidelines for the organization and administration of peacekeeping operations (see Wiseman, "UN Peacekeeping: An Historical Overview" chap. 2 in this volume); (2) the analysis of the progressive development of UN peacekeeping; (3) analysis of regional and ad hoc arrangements; (4) contemporary affirmation for the strengthening of peacekeeping; and (5) theoretical considerations of the third party characteristics of peacekeeping, namely in a relative sense, neutrality, objectivity, and the pursuit of the peaceful resolution of conflict. From this perspective, peacekeeping is a transnational regulatory process suitable for the management of conflict in the contemporary international state system as well as for any conception of a transformed international system that presupposes the existence of conflict and the requirement of conflict management.

ANALYSIS OF THE PROGRESSIVE DEVELOPMENT OF
UN PEACEKEEPING

The Legal and Political Parameters

Though conceptually peacekeeping belongs somewhere between Chapter VI and Chapter VII of the UN Charter, those who framed the Charter did not anticipate its use and made no provision for it. Each operation, from first to last, has been mounted on an ad hoc basis, frequently within a matter of hours or days of the tabling of a crisis on the agenda of the Security Council and without reference to the Charter; being a subject for post hoc attribution or speculation by scholars of international law. And the numerous meetings of the Special Committee on Peacekeeping Operations, the Committee of 33, established in 1965 to examine these and related questions, have failed to reach ultimate agreement, though some progress on specific issues has been reported.

This history of "adhocracy" and the failure of the Committee of 33 convey the impression that UN peacekeeping has a very tenuous existence. In retrospect, however, the contrary is true. The practice of peacekeeping has become highly institutionalized. Security Council, as well as General Assembly, resolutions demonstrate clarity of purpose enhanced by precedent after precedent, though there is lack of functional precision, that being best left to consultations and definitions by the secretary-general. And the structural apparatus that manages these operations, the undersecretaries for special political affairs, has evolved vast experience, astute judgment, and quick reflexes in mounting operations with the support of the field operations division. There are still many serious problems that have to be overcome (see chapters herein by Brian Urquhart, Clayton E. Beattie, and J.D. Murray). Nevertheless, peacekeeping is firmly implanted in the politics and performance of the United Nations.

Important elements of the original controversy between the USSR and the United States, which came to a head in 1964 over the constitutional control and direction of peacekeeping, persist; but in a sense they are dormant, and do not affect Security Council procedures to mandate peacekeeping operations. They are discussed annually as questions of principle in the Committee of 33 without result, in contrast to the active agreement in the Security Council on the practical arrangements, or at least acquiescence, to allow new operations to be implemented, as with UNEF II and UNDOF where both the United States and the USSR voted in favor of the respective resolutions, and with UNIFIL approved with a United States vote in favor and a Soviet abstention.

In fact, several of the key divisive issues were quickly and satisfactorily resolved in the establishment of UNEF II and replicated in UNDOF and UNIFIL. These were matters of Security Council oversight and the commensurate level of organizational and administrative discretion of the secretary-general; the selection of a force commander, equitable geographic composition, and the mode of financing.(3) The USSR, however, has stated that, the agreed procedures adopted for these operations notwithstanding, they should not be considered as precedents.

Differences on matters of principle are, therefore, still important questions, and continue to forestall agreement in the Committee of 33, though for the time being they do not affect operations. But any attempt in the future to buttress the legal and organizational structures of peacekeeping will have to consider and resolve these matters of principle. The core question is constitutional. The USSR insists on the "exclusive competence of the Security Council"(4) which in effect means that "having authorized a peacekeeping operation, the Security Council shall continue to exercise supreme control with regard to all aspects of the establishment of this operation and the direction of it throughout the entire operation."(5) The United States, however, puts the matter differently, i.e., "there is no question about the prerogative of the Security Council to exercise supervision over the implementation of the mandate after an operation has been launched."(6) The USSR demands exclusive and continuous Security Council control and direction whereas the United States implies, in the interpretive phrase used by Canada, "general control and overall direction."(7)

In practical terms, there is a wide difference between the two positions, particularly in respect of the functions performed and political discretion of the secretary-general. The USSR continues to insist that the exclusive competence of the Security Council derives from and is a function of article 43 of the Charter which should regulate all agreements and aspects for the provision and deployment of peacekeeping forces. This position overrides the difference between the use of military contingents for enforcement action under Chapter VII and the pacific interposition of peacekeeping forces based on the principle of consent. At the core of the Soviet position is the insistence that no action of either type be taken or effected beyond the grasp of the Soviet veto, in effect denying the UN as an organization any inherent theoretical or legal quality of third party independence. This principled or, more accurately, political position is in contrast to that of the parties in conflict which consent to receive peacekeeping forces as an independent nonpartisan third party interposition.

These contrasting points of view, quite apart from prevailing partisan political pressures which reflect the normal condition of the UN, have not, with noteworthy exceptions, affected the general practice of UN peacekeeping. The present pattern of adhocracy has, therefore, the advantage of avoiding what could very well be political hindrance and restrictive interference were the parameters of Security Council control to be formally resolved.

Nevertheless, the Committee of 33, in compliance with its mandate, has attempted to determine organizational structures that would balance exclusive Security Council competence with operational discretion of the secretary-general. These range from the use of the military staff committee for the conduct of operations, the establishment of a suborgan of the Security Council with the core composition of the five permanent members that would function as an intermediate organ between the Security Council and the secretary-general, to the establishment of a suborgan of the Security Council which would act only in an advisory capacity to the secretary-general. But none of these proposals have been able to bridge the gap between the positions of the USSR and the United States. Since the Committee of 33 has adopted a total package approach, agreements on lesser but important guidelines on such matters as standby arrangements, training, and logistics arrangements are held in abeyance.

There were moments of progress in 1969 with the preparation of Model 1, a typology for housing all the questions at issue;(8) in 1973, with the production of a document containing the agreed language or diverse positions of the members on all matters under discussion;(9) and several subsequent attempts by third world countries, Canada, Scandinavian countries, Austria, and others to find a middle ground acceptable to all, but to no avail. General frustration and malaise set in, and by 1975 both the USSR and the United States, believing that no agreement between them was possible except their mutual conviction that would deny any General Assembly competence to mandate peacekeeping operations (neither believed they could control or trust the General Assembly to do their bidding), they informally agreed to terminate the Committee of 33. When this became known to other members of the Committee they rallied and succeeded in keeping the committee alive because they were convinced of the great importance of peacekeeping, and because the committee, as a suborgan of the General Assembly, is the one means to assure that the General Assembly itself, would continue to have an opportunity to deliberate on the future modalities of peacekeeping.

There are, broadly stated, two choices of approach to the general question of the future modalities of peacekeeping. The one is to continue negotiations in the hope that a satisfactory agreement can be achieved, with the advisory caution that any agreement which prescribes peacekeeping in constitutional

terms may be inhibitory and restrictive. The other is to
continue along the pragmatic path of adhocracy which historically has proved to be the more flexible, adaptive, and
constructive course to follow.

Whichever course is followed in the future, there is ample
evidence to demonstrate that peacekeeping has historically
progressed in incremental fashion. Furthermore, despite their
controversies the USSR and the United States have both
enabled peacekeeping operations to be mounted during the most
intense periods of the cold war as well as at times of detente,
a matter of essential importance in the consideration of the
future viability and utility of peacekeeping. The historical
record also shows that peacekeeping has been applied to a
broad and expanding spectrum of types of conflict, and that
mandates have become more extensive in scope and varied in
their functional implementation.

Types of Conflict Resulting in Peacekeeping Operations

Conflict has been a constant feature of the global system since
World War II, with the incidents ranging somewhere between
200 and 300, depending on definition of conflict adopted by
different researchers. The matter becomes even more complex
in attempting to formulate a typology in which to categorize
events defined as conflicts. These problems are considerably
simplified in the context of UN peacekeeping because of the
limited number of cases. But the problems cannot be avoided
altogether because of the question of the extent to which they,
as a group, typify the full range of conflicts that have
occurred in the international system in the period under
study. A subjective analysis suggests two broad overlapping
categories: the first category, based on the systemic nature of
the action involved, which may be interstate or intrastate, the
latter necessarily and the former at times including nonstate
parties; and the second based on the causal offensive or
defensive objectives of the parties in conflict which may be one
or a combination of more than one of the following: ideological,
territorial, strategic, imperialistic, class, neocolonial,
decolonial, and/or national self-determination.

Assuming that this paradigm is adequately representative
of postwar conflicts, how representative are those that have
engendered UN peacekeeping? To begin with the first systemic category, the peacekeeping cases are both inter- and
intrastate. UNMOGIP (1948) and UNIPOM (1965) were created
following the wars between India and Pakistan. The Middle
East cases UNEF, UNEF II, and UNDOF were all interstate as
between Israel and its neighbors, with other extremely important intrastate components regarding Palestinian rights. The
Congo case, ONUC (1960-64), and Lebanon, UNIFIL, begun in

1978, defy exclusive categorization. The Congo conflict stemmed from the entry of external Belgian and mercenary troops into the territory, internal destabilization, and provincial attempts at secession. Lebanon is even more complex, but also essentially the same – interstate as between Israel and Lebanon; and intrastate in terms of the containment of ad hoc military forces in Lebanon and the restoration of Lebanese military control in the areas under UN supervision.

In regard to the category of causal offensive or defensive objectives, most of the early peacekeeping cases derive from the process of decolonization and of national self-determination. These are, for example, the UN Commission of Indonesia (1948), necessitated by the struggle for Indonesian independence from the Netherlands, hence, also imperialistic in character; and UNFICYP, begun in 1964 following the withdrawal of the United Kingdom and decolonization, when Cyprus disintegrated into communal strife between the Greek and Turkish communities. All the Middle East cases, in one way or another, also stem from the period of the withdrawal of the colonial powers from the area, but have since been complicated and overburdened with other political, ideological, and territorial factors; and, from the Arab point of view, Israeli imperialism. Ideology was a factor of the Yemen case, UNYOM (1963), where right and left wing factions were struggling for the control of the territory, both with the active support of foreign powers. The problem in the Balkans (UNSCOB) was also inherently ideological in terms of the civil war between the left and right in Greece in the aftermath of World War II. A minor UN peacekeeping event in the Dominican Republic, DOMREP (1965), was also necessitated by a clear case of ideological and class struggle with the left wing forces trying to regain control of the government which had been seized by a right wing military junta, and United States intervention which introduced the element of imperialism.

One type of conflict that has been withheld from UN involvement, with the exception of the Dominican Republic and the Balkans cases, is that which occurs in the direct or declared strategic spheres of influence of the two superpowers. The UN was excluded from intervening in the Soviet invasions of Czechoslovakia in 1968 and of Hungary in 1956, and from the United States military engagement in Vietnam, though in the latter case (discussed in David Cox "The International Commission of Control and Supervision in Vietnam, 1973," chapter 13 in this volume), a hybrid form of peacekeeping was introduced by the Geneva Accords of 1954 and again by the Paris Agreement of 1973, both unsuccessful. Nonetheless, the strategic rivalry between the USSR and the United States has certainly been a major factor in the Balkans case, it was imported into the internal struggle for power in the Congo case, and was inherent in the Yemen case (depending on interpretation or degree, or whether the concept of surrogate conflicts is an accepted category), and in the three wars in the Middle East, all of which have resulted in peacekeeping operations.

In the early period, peacekeeping was viewed as a phenomenon largely related to the process of decolonization. But over time, as the cases became more numerous and complex, member states of the UN came to regard peacekeeping as a conflict control mechanism per se, and not attached to any particular type of conflict, always with the proviso that a veto of any of the permanent members could prohibit an operation from taking place.

Because peacekeeping has demonstrated its utility in a wide variety of conflict situations is not to presuppose that it should be applied in all similar situations. But it does mean that the future of peacekeeping will not be confined to a limited type of conflict. The Lebanese situation since 1978 is one of the most complex crises in terms of the number of parties and issues involved that the UN has ever attempted to contain and resolve. The peacekeeping operation is extraordinarily difficult, but it is maintained because no other interim arrangement is available. In anticipation of the later discussion of non-UN peacekeeping, the Rhodesian/Zimbabwe case is also one that mirrors a multitude of characteristics typical of contemporary crises - interstate, intrastate, ideological, political, and economic, as well the numerous regional and global parties which have had a hand in supporting one or another of the indigenous parties and/or in the attempt to resolve the situation. Yet, the peacekeeping operation, fully integrated with the peacekeeping process, was a strikingly successful affair.(10) In all, there can be little doubt that the types of conflict which have engendered peacekeeping operations represent most of the systemic, political, economic, and ideological types of conflict which have occurred since the end of World War II.

Peacekeeping Mandates

As might be expected, UN peacekeeping mandates and functions have evolved commensurately in response to the variety, complexity, and intensity of the conflicts to which they have been applied. Yet all the mandates, and renewals thereof, are characteristically expressed in clear and sparing language, conveying the essential intent of the Security Council, or the General Assembly, without elaboration. It has been left to the secretary-general to outline the objectives, principles, and functions within the parameters of the language of the mandate,(11) generally upon consultation with the interested states. There is great advantage, indeed necessity, in this process. The political negotiations required to formulate acceptable language for a mandate are generally difficult, at times rancorous. Any attempt to amplify or detail a mandate in the process of formulation might be impossible, particularly in the midst of a crisis where immediate action is necessary to bring a halt to ongoing hostilities.

Yet, even within these contraints, mandates do denote the type and level of action to be taken. During the nascent period, 1946-56, when peacekeeping evolved as a process for the observation of specific conflict situations, the mandates effectively expressed this intent; in the Balkan Case, UNSCOB was established as a "Commission of Investigation to ascertain the facts relating to the alleged border violations along the frontier";(12) in Indonesia, career consular representatives were called upon "to cover the observance of the 'cease-fire' orders and the conditions prevailing in areas under military occupation,"(13) and later military observers were called for to carry out these duties; UNTSO in the Middle East was created inferentially by the Security Council "to supervise the observance of the . . . provisions" dealing with the terms of a cease-fire;(14) and UNMOGIP observers were established for the purpose of "supervising the observance of the cease-fire" between India and Pakistan.(15) In each case, the clear intent was to observe the situation, though the actual process varied according to the specific conditions.

With the beginning of the assertive period, 1956-67, mandates prescribed actual interpository military forces with a greater degree of authority and responsibility. Following the invasion of Egypt by Israel, the United Kingdom, and France in 1956, the General Assembly established "a United Nations command for an emergency international force to secure and supervise the cessation of hostilities."(16) For the first time, the words "United Nations command," "emergency force," and "secure" as well as "supervise" a cease-fire appeared in a UN mandate. UNEF was clearly a military operation authorized to use force only in self-defense, but with a special responsibility with respect to the maintenance of the cease-fire. The case in Lebanon, UNOGIL, where the mandate provided for the dispatch of "an observation group to proceed to Lebanon so as to ensure that there is no illegal infiltration of personnel or supply of arms . . . across the Lebanese border,"(17) is more closely related to the observation and reporting missions of the nascent period. Yet, it also went beyond them in the language "to ensure," though ensure was not meant to actively guarantee that no infiltration would occur.

The several mandates required to complete the peacekeeping operation in the Congo (ONUC) are particularly symptomatic of the general incremental enlargement of the authority and responsibility prescribed in successive UN mandates from 1946 to 1978. The first mandate of ONUC "calls upon the Government of Belgium to withdraw their troops from the territory of the Republic of the Congo . . . [and] Decides to authorize the Secretary-General . . . to provide the government with such military assistance as may be necessary."(18)   The fourth resolution "requests the Secretary-General to take vigorous action in accordance . . . with the aforesaid resolutions to assist the Central Government of the Congo in the restoration and maintenance of law and order."(19)   The fifth mandate later "urges that the United Nations take immediately all appropriate measures to prevent the occurrence of civil war in the Congo including arrangements for cease-fire, the halting of all military operations, the prevention of clashes, and the use of force if necessary, in the last resort,"(20) a mandate unusual in explicitness of language.   But, as the situation did not improve, even this mandate required reinforcement in a new resolution which "authorized the Secretary-General to take vigorous action, including the requisite measures of force,"(21) for the immediate apprehension and/or deportation of all foreign military and paramilitary personnel.   As D. W. Bowett has commented, this resolution "authorized the Secretary-General to use a degree of force which surpassed the limits of self-defense and involved police action,"(22) which represents a qualitative change in the development of peacekeeping, and involved the UN forces in serious fighting to overcome the secession of the province of Katanga.   Because peacekeeping is a pacific and not an enforcement action, there had to be a great deal of provocation before ONUC engaged in hostilities. Yet, there have been other occasions since where UN forces were involved in hostilities.   UN forces were overrun in the Israeli attack on the Sinai in 1967.   In July 1974, UN forces controlling the airport in Nicosia were attacked by the invading Turkish army.(23)   And, since 1978, UN forces in Lebanon have been subjected to offensive action by ad hoc forces and have taken strong counteraction to defend themselves and to maintain their positions.

Whether this is indicative of a pattern that may continue into the future is difficult to predict.   Yet these events, and the fact that UN forces in Lebanon are more heavily armed than in any previous operation, suggest the need for further study of the question of the use of force and of the level of armament required in anticipation of the use of force in self-defense.   Peacekeeping has been, and is, the pacific interposition of impartial third party military forces.   But, because of their deployment in critical military situations where they have become involved in direct military action, there is some danger that the pacific character of peacekeeping may be slowly eroded, or that the function of UN peacekeeping will come to be regarded as ineffectual.

Returning to the examination of the evolutionary growth of mandates, the first occasion to include "the tasks of maintaining law and order"(24) was in West Iran (UNTEA), which stems from the agreement between the parties. This phrase reappears in the Cyprus case (UNFICYP) where the UN force, upon entering an area of violent communal conflict, was called upon "to use its best efforts to prevent a recurrence of fighting and, as necessary, to contribute to the maintenance and restoration of law and order and a return to normal conditions."(25) The situation on the island clearly required a broad-ranging mandate if the peaceful conditions for a political settlement were to be achieved. The operation in India-Pakistan in 1965, UNIPOM, is similar to previous ones in calling upon the secretary-general "to provide the necessary assistance to ensure the supervision of the cease-fire and the withdrawal of all military personnel."(26)

The massive war in the Middle East in 1973 was one of the most serious threats to international peace and security that had occurred since World War II. The Security Council became the focus of intense negotiations and the demand for a cease-fire. The creation of a new peacekeeping operation followed. The resolution read: "Demands that immediate and complete cease-fire be observed and that the parties return to the positions occupied by them . . . on 22 October 1972 . . . and decides to set up, under its authority, a United Nations Emergency Force."(27) The relationship between these two paragraphs of the resolution were linked by the secretary-general in his follow-up report, which stated that the terms of reference of the force would be the implementation of the first paragraph, beginning "Demands."(28) Because the situation was so dangerous, the language of the mandate could very well have been much stronger. But, because the USSR and the United States held opposing views on the causes of the conflict, the wording of the mandate was the maximum to which they would agree. In any event, compliance with the mandate was dependent on the will of the parties in conflict and the extreme pressure put upon them by the USSR and the United States.

The Lebanese operation of 1978 was the last peacekeeping mandate prior to 1981 (and, thus, the last to be discussed here). The mandate established a UN force "for the purpose of confirming the withdrawal of Israeli forces, restoring international peace and security and assisting the government of Lebanon in ensuring the return of its effective authority in the area"(29) - formidable tasks in an extremely dangerous and confusing situation.

Field Operational Functions

It is apparent from the foregoing that, while there has been a continuity of the basic principle of pacific interposition, the nature of peacekeeping mandates has expanded in response to new and difficult situations. It is not surprising, therefore, that there has also been an extension in the kinds and complexity of functions performed by the forces in the field.

The operations in the nascent period, 1946-1956, were basically the observation and reporting of the infiltration of armed personnel and supplies and of border clashes, and the supervision of cease-fire lines. These tasks require continuous patrols, liaison with the parties, determining the occurrence and source of violations, mediating local conflicts and preventing their escalation, and numerous related activities. Each operation is unique and functions common to all require special forms of application, as in the case of Indonesia where the cease-fire lines were fluid, difficult to ascertain and gain agreement between the parties, and to patrol effectively.

The advent of UNEF in 1956 introduced the requirement to patrol vast areas of the Sinai to ensure the nonentry of Egyptian forces; in effect, giving UN forces special jurisdiction in the area under its control. Then the West Iran case gave UN forces the civil responsibility of maintaining law and order. In the Congo case, UN forces had to maintain the territorial integrity of a state without a functioning government and with the noncooperation of the other governmental and ad hoc parties in conflict. Reference to the numerous and diverse mandates, as noted above, gives an indication of the varied and changing functions that had to be taken with each new operation.

In Cyprus, the fundamental functions were to prevent the recurrence of fighting, contribute to the maintenance and restoration of law and order, and contribute to the return of normal conditions. In practice, this required patrols along narrow lines geographically separating the two feuding communities, ensuring the safety of people conducting such normal tasks as tending to their fields, monitoring and preventing the infiltration of arms and military supplies, mediating disputes at the local level to avoid escalation, and the provision of humanitarian assistance.(30) Invariably, the objectives designated by UN mandates are considerably extended and amplified when translated into practical actions in the field of operations.

UNEF II in 1973 is a further example of the mandate referring only to the maintenance of the cease-fire; whereas, in practice, the UN force had to assist in arrangements for the supply of Egyptian troops in Israeli-held territory, participate in the negotiations for disengagement, supervise the disengagement, patrol the exclusive buffer zone under UN control and the adjacent limited armament zones on either side, and then repeat the procedure in 1975 when all the lines were moved east with the partial withdrawal of Israeli forces from the Sinai. This list is not exhaustive, nor is it so intended. It is meant to show how each operation develops its own modalities of implementation, thereby adding to the vast store of functional competence of UN peacekeeping forces.

One further example is cited to demonstrate this process. In Lebanon, the principle functions of UNIFIL were to confirm the withdrawal of Israeli forces, supervise the cessation of hostilities, and take all necessary measures to effect Lebanese sovereignty in the area under UN jurisdiction. To show how these were carried out, notwithstanding that UNIFIL's functions have been drastically curtailed since its area of operations were overrun by the Israeli invasion of Lebanon in 1982, it is instructive to quote at length, in UN language, what methods are used "to carry out its responsibilities":

> It establishes road blocks and checkpoints throughout the area of operation along all the main and secondary road networks and, assisted by a battalion of the Lebanese National Army and Lebanese gendarmes, checks and inspects vehicles and personnel and military equipment and supplies. Uniformed or armed personnel and military equipment are not allowed to enter the UNIFIL area.
>
> Foot and mobile patrols are conducted day and night. These patrols move and operate along the key highways and in villages to ensure maximum UNIFIL visibility to the local population. They also operate in the remote wadis to keep any unauthorized armed personnel away from the area. Any unauthorized personnel detected are escorted out of the UNIFIL area.
>
> Random night-time posts are also established to detect unauthorized armed movement. These listening posts are relocated frequently.
>
> A UNIFIL presence is established in as many populated areas as possible. One method to achieve this with the limited troops available, is to assign a 10 man detachment to a given village for a one to three day period and then to move this detachment to another populated area. This has proven effective in providing the population with a measure of assurance and safety.
>
> In addition to the above, and particularly since July 1979, UNIFIL has introduced a number of operational

measures in order to better control attempts at infiltration or incursion. In accordance with a new perimeter-oriented concept, troops have been redeployed in greater density along the perimeter of the UNIFIL area. Further, UNIFIL has steadily tried to augment its surveillance and detection capability, keeping in mind the difficulty of the terrain, the limited number of troops and the increasing number of civilians moving freely in densely populated areas. Thus, the number of night vision binoculars and strong search lights has been increased, while sophisticated ground surveillance radars have been introduced in order to provide UNIFIL with an early warning system at medium range. As a further measure to improve UNIFIL's operational capacity and its reaction time to incidents, armoured personnel carriers have been introduced into a number of contingents.

Despite these measures, serious incidents occurred in the UNIFIL area in April 1980. The de facto forces (Christian and associated militias), having established four armed positions in the UNIFIL area in 1979, attempted to establish a fifth such position. Their attempt, which was firmly resisted by UNIFIL, led to serious confrontations resulting in the death of UNIFIL soldiers, including the murder of two soldiers. In addition, UNIFIL headquarters in Naqoura was subjected to heavy bombardment resulting in extensive damage to its installations and equipment, while the freedom of movement of the Force was severely restricted, particularly along the vital coastal road (S/13888 and Addenda 1 to 3). Following these incidents, the Security Council, in its resolution 467 of 24 April 1980, commended UNIFIL for its great restraint in carrying out its duties and also called attention to the provisions of its mandate that would allow the Force to use its right to self-defence. On the basis of a careful review of the situation, steps have been taken to enhance the military presence and defence capability of UNIFIL headquarters and to make a series of planned measures should Naqoura appear to be threatened in the future. Further, procedures have been refined in order to enable the contingents of UNIFIL to react firmly and consistently to threats or actions designed to interfere with the discharge of the duties of the Force. It remains evident, however, that the use of force in self-defence will not by itself achieve significant progress in the implementation of UNIFIL's mandate. While consolidating UNIFIL and taking all necessary steps to render its position as strong as possible, the main road to full implementation of the UNIFIL mandate lies in political and diplomatic efforts.

Despite the difficulties encountered, UNIFIL has continued in its endeavour, in cooperation with the Lebanese Government, to maintain the peaceful character of its area of operation and to increase and make more effective the Lebanese presence in this area. To this end, UNIFIL, has, since its inception, remained deeply engaged in humanitarian activities related to relief and reconstruction.

In the first months of its mandate, UNIFIL assisted the villagers of southern Lebanon to deal with the tragedy of their dead, wounded and missing. Emergency measures were also taken to provide the civilian population with temporary accommodation, household stores, medical treatment and supplies. In addition, major mine and bomb clearance programmes were undertaken. To achieve these purposes, UNIFIL worked closely with the Special Representative of the Secretary-General for humanitarian assistance in Lebanon. A humanitarian section was established at UNIFIL headquarters and each contingent assigned a liaison officer to assist in humanitarian tasks.

Since then, UNIFIL has continued to carry out humanitarian activities, in close cooperation with the Governor of southern Lebanon and the United Nations Co-ordinator of Assistance for Reconstruction and Development of Lebanon, who has in the meantime replaced the Special Representative of the Secretary-General for humanitarian assistance. UNIFIL has also cooperated with United Nations programmes, particularly UNICEF, in efforts aimed at assisting the Lebanese Government in the normalization of socio-economic conditions in southern Lebanon.

The Force has participated, on a continuing basis, in projects involving the restoration of water and electricity services, the distribution of supplementary food supplies, the rebuilding and repair of houses, schools and roads, and providing help, as required, in resolving cases of kidnapping. Of particular significance have been UNIFIL's contributions in the fields of education and of health. Thus, in July 1979, at the request of the Lebanese Ministry of Education, UNIFIL made arrangements for

the holding of intermediate and baccalaureate exam-
inations for more than 1,000 students from the
districts of Bint Jubail and Marjayoun, the first to
take place since 1974.   In the health sector, the
local population have had the facilities of the UNIFIL
hospital in Naqoura and of four dispensaries established with UNIFIL assistance.

The foregoing examination of the history of UN peacekeeping
shows it to be a dynamic incremental process that has achieved
a high level of international legitimacy and competence.   In
political terms, it has evolved beyond mere survival of the
damaging controversy between the USSR and the United States
in the 1960s over the control, direction, and financing of
operations, and the ignominious demise of UNEF I.   Moreover,
the very same superpower protagonists jointly supported or
withheld opposition to Security Council resolutions to mount
peacekeeping operations during periods of the cold war, as
well as during the emergent period of detente, even to the
point of employing UN peacekeeping in the Middle East where,
in October of 1973, the interests of the two superpowers
collided as each heavily supported opposing sides in the war.
       Furthermore, though peacekeeping developed in its initial
stages as a phenomenon closely related to the process of
decolonization, in subsequent stages it was applied to a broad
range of types of conflict, to a considerable extent representative of the general conflicts which have affected the
international system since the advent of the UN itself; save for
those conflicts occurring directly in the orbits of superpower
domination where all external efforts at conflict management are
prohibited entry.   This application of peacekeeping to diverse
types of conflicts has necessarily brought about a greater
elaboration in the mandates with consequent extension in the
range of responsibilities and functions performed by the forces
in the field of operations.   UN peacekeeping has reached a
stage of internationally recognized maturity and competence
that can well serve the future needs of the international
system in the process of conflict resolution.   Before probing,
however, into additional matters which support this contention,
it is important to examine, though briefly, non-UN practices in
peacekeeping.

REGIONAL PEACEKEEPING

Chapter VII of the UN Charter states that "Nothing in the
present Charter precludes the existence of regional arrangements or agencies for dealing with such matters relating to
international peace and security as appropriate for regional

action. . . ." and further, "The Security Council shall encourage the development of pacific settlement of local disputes through regional arrangements." Regional peacekeeping as a third-party mode of interposition undoubtedly comes within the parameters of this chapter. But because, until recently, the only regional practice of peacekeeping has been by the regional organization subject to the dominance of the United States (the OAS), most analysts of the UN have considered it to be outside the mainstream of UN peacekeeping. However, since the successful application of "Commonwealth" peacekeeping together with peacemaking to Rhodesia/Zimbabwe in 1980 and the subsequent endeavor of the OAU to conduct peacekeeping operations in Chad, there is a general reexamination of the regional practice of peacekeeping.

The Commonwealth

The Commonwealth is a very loose association of states from all parts of the world bound together by common historical association to the United Kingdom and therefore with one another. But it is without institutional structures designed for the organization of peacekeeping forces or the performance of electoral supervision. Yet both were conducted in Rhodesia and the latter in Uganda with great skill and impartiality, demonstrating a political and organizational competence greater than theretofore considered by its member states. It may well be that future situations will arise where the Commonwealth would be the most appropriate international organization to perform similar roles. The established precedents add to the probability that such occasions will occur.

The Commonwealth Monitoring Force and the Commonwealth Observer Group were unique components of the cease-fire and supervised electoral process adopted at Lancaster House for the attainment of black majority rule in Southern Rhodesia. The principal actor in these events was the United Kingdom. But the Commonwealth was instrumental in convincing the United Kingdom to take the leading role in the negotiations leading to and participation in the settlement process, and the Commonwealth also participated in the monitoring force and set up a distinct observer group. At the outset, spokesmen for the United Kingdom argued vehemently that the operation was definitely not peacekeeping. Afterwards, however, Lord Soames, who was appointed governor of Southern Rhodesia to ensure the cease-fire and conduct free and fair elections, did refer to the process as peacekeeping.(31)

Functionally, the monitoring force, numbering no more than 1,500, was established to ensure that the parties adhered to the cease-fire, but was clearly not intended for, nor was it capable of, enforcing the cease-fire. The Commonwealth

Observer Group, together with several other governmental and nongovernmental groups, was free to observe every aspect of the election. The situation was continuously volatile throughout the two month transition period, but the cease-fire held and the election was judged free and fair. It was a remarkable process from start to finish, and there are many lessons to be derived for the future application of both UN and regional peacekeeping arrangements.(32)

The Commonwealth was so taken by this success that it agreed to accept Uganda's invitation to witness its elections in December 1980. This would not be a function within the parameters of peacekeeping. But since electoral supervision had been part of the Rhodesia/Zimbabwe settlement arrangements, and the task in Uganda was clearly to be a third-party nonpartisan role, the Commonwealth took the opportunity to serve as an independent international witness. As noted by the Commonwealth, "It is unique in the annals of democracy for a sovereign nation to invite an international group to observe its national elections and report whether they were free and fair. Our role, which was endorsed by all four political parties, is without precedent."(33)

There were many doubts about the process before and after the election took place. A group of nine Commonwealth observers, assistants, and a secretariat working in Uganda under most difficult and at times provocative circumstances carefully scrutinized every aspect of the elections and polling procedures, and concluded that "despite all deficiencies, the electoral process cohered and held together even if some of its individual strands were frayed. Surmounting all obstacles, the people of Uganda, like some great tidal wave, carried the electoral process to a worthy and valid conclusion."(34)

The Organization of American States (OAS)

The Organization of American States has a long history of conflict resolution that is well documented, requiring only short comment here. (See Edgardo Paz-Barnica, chapter 11 in this volume.) Its charter, in existence since 1948 and as later amended, provides the machinery and specific judicial, political, and military procedures for conflict resolution. The OAS itself is a well organized, functional institution zealously determined to manage any Latin American conflict within its own operational parameters and deter "interference" from any outside power. It has, over time, engaged in conflict resolution in numerous cases, as in Costa Rica-Nicaragua in 1948-1949, and in Honduras-El Salvador in 1967-1971 and again in 1976 where mediation, observation, and peacekeeping were employed.

The more famous case of OAS third party intervention was in the Dominican Republic in 1965-66. But there the United States was the first to intervene "unilaterally" by landing substantial numbers of troops before obtaining OAS authorization and support.(35) The Dominican Republic is, as well, the only case where the UN was permitted to play a role through the presence of two military observers.

Otherwise, the UN has been studiously excluded from OAS "security affairs." In its own terms, the OAS can be considered as very successful; though profound ideological divisions in Latin America and dominance by the United States acting in its own interest are matters viewed by some observers as overriding what might otherwise be a more balanced third party interposition. Yet, even with these and other in-built countervailing factors, the OAS will certainly continue to play a salient role in the process of conflict resolution in Latin America, a role that may as well in the future reflect the growing reaction to the dominance of the United States and an assertion of "collective" independence.

The Organization of African Unity (OAU)

The OAU was founded in 1963 on the vision of Pan-Africanism to foster political and economic cooperation. Its operational philosophy is based on the principles of nonintervention in the internal affairs of member states and on the peaceful settlement of disputes. It is without a formal institutional structure capable of translating decisions of the heads of states into immediate and practical action, such as the launching of peacekeeping operations. The OAU depends largely on the processes of negotiation, mediation conciliation, and arbitration. (See N. A. Pelcovits, chapter 12 in this volume.)

Nonetheless, in 1980, seventeen years after the OAU was formed, it launched its first peacekeeping attempt to contain and resolve the civil war in Chad after Nigeria attempted but failed to do the same. Nigeria had convened a series of conferences among the warring parties in the country in 1979 at Kano and Lagos, where agreement was reached on a cease-fire under the presence of a Nigerian military contingent meant to assure the stable conditions necessary for reconciliation among the parties and negotiations to achieve national unity. The initial Nigerian contingent of 150, which arrived in March, was later increased to 800. But internal strife persisted; the Nigerians were accused of being partisan and undisciplined, and withdrew in June with the situation in Chad as volatile as it had been before.

The OAU then took up the matter and a new attempt was launched, founded on the Lagos accord of August 1979. The accord called for several complex functions which the OAU

could not accomplish. These were basically the supervision of
the cease-fire, the demilitarization of the capital of Ndjamena
and the surrounding territory, the maintenance of law and
order, and the provision of assistance for the integration of
the competing military factions – functions identical or very
similar to those prescribed by UN peacekeeping mandates. A
force of 1,500 was to have been established, composed of
troops from Guinea, Congo Brazzaville, and Benin. Only the
Congolese contingent arrived. There were severe problems of
logistics, command, coordination, deployment, and financing.
The entire operation was an abject failure.(36)

Despite, or because of, this failure and the future complications arising from the intervention of Libyan troops in
1980, the OAU was determined to overcome past deficiencies
and undertake a second attempt. In July 1980, the OAU
assembly of heads of states and governments decided:

> to make one further attempt to find an African
> solution to the crisis, particularly with regard to the
> provision of the Neutral OAU Forces by requesting
> African States which are in a position to provide
> Peacekeeping Forces at their own expenses in accor-
> dance with conditions to be determined at the
> Summit, it being understood that logistic and
> operational costs be met from voluntary contribu-
> tions; (and further decided) that in the event of
> failure by the OAU to raise the necessary funds of
> the peacekeeping force by its own effort after a
> period of one month, the United Nations Security
> Council will be requested, through the African
> Group for assistance, particularly the necessary
> financial means, to enable peace to be restored in
> Chad.(37)

The complexities of the situation did not lend themselves to
easy solution. Off-the-record discussions were held with the
UN secretariat without concrete result. Yet, in January 1981,
the heads of states of the OAU reaffirmed their earlier decision
"to send without further delay, with the assistance of the
United Nations organization, the Monitoring Force, as established by the Lagos Accord, as an African Peacekeeping Force
composed of troops from Benin, Congo, Guinea and Togo," and
mandated the secretary-general of the OAU to organize free
and fair elections in Chad under the auspices and control of
the OAU by the end of April 1981.(38) Several months
elapsed before arrangements could be made for the peacekeeping troops to arrive in Chad. But, by then, the civil war
had resumed and the role of peacekeeping was cast in serious
doubt. This entire episode reveals the inherent weakness of
the OAU to move beyond its traditional practice of reconcil-

iation and mediation by heads of state and to adopt the more formidable procedures of peacekeeping. Nonetheless, while exposing the grave problems, it does not negate the validity of the concept of regional peacekeeping, nor warrant, at this stage, the assumption that these problems cannot be overcome.

Notwithstanding the enormous difficulties in respect to Chad, the OAU is apparently determined to find a solution to the war in Western Sahara, a problem possibly even more intractable than the situation in Chad. In August 1981, the Assembly of Heads of State and Government decided to establish a cease-fire among the parties and states contending for control of Western Sahara and to conduct a referendum of "self-determination which will enable the people of Western Sahara to express themselves freely and democratically on the future of their territory" based on a choice of "Independence or Integration with Morocco."(39) The operational aspects of the OAU resolution optimistically call for "structural requirements" whereby the UN would collaborate in the organization and conduct of the referendum and the maintenance and guarantee of the cease-fire, and assist an interim administration over the territory during the period of the cease-fire and referendum.

This is a very ambitious program and will require the full support of the parties, including Morocco; will depend on collaboration with the UN; and will require extensive resources and well organized machinery to put the operation in place and bring the issue to a successful conclusion. The intentions of the OAU in Chad and Western Sahara demonstrate that African states realize the utility of peacekeeping as a modality for the containment and/or resolution of conflict, which is indicative of a general trend. But, at the same time, the members of the OAU are aware that the structure of the organization and its manner of work make it extremely difficult to play a strong role in conflict resolution and particularly in the practice of peacekeeping. The excessive reliance on pragmatism, personal diplomacy, and ad hoc procedures has been detrimental to the development of regular mechanisms and effective measures. Failure in Chad and/or in Western Sahara could, possibly, be ruinous to future OAU prospects for peacekeeping.

The OAU has, therefore, taken note of a proposal by Sierra Leone for the establishment of an OAU Political and Security Council as a principal and permanent organ to deal with serious situations.(40) The matter has been placed on the agenda of the Council of Ministers and there is active exploration of what new means, cooperative measures, and acquisition of resources are necessary for the strengthening of its competence in conflict resolution. There is, however, little indication that the members of the OAU are willing to embark on such a drastic revision of the OAU Charter and modes of procedure. Unless events in Africa cause a change in attitude, or it becomes possible to establish innovative cooperative arrangements with the UN, which would be a major develop ment, prospects for enhanced OAU competence for launching effective peacekeeping operations must at this stage be regarded as limited.(41)

Contemporary Affirmation of Peacekeeping

An assessment of regional experience does not by itself offer assurance for the future growth, competence and operational utility of peacekeeping. However, when considered together with UN experience in a broader context, which includes current negotiations on the question of Namibia, proposals that are made in regard to contemporary crises, diplomatic endeavors to strengthen UN peacekeeping capability, and noteworthy recommendations to that effect, then there is cumulative evidence of positive progression.

The arrangements for a cease-fire and political settlement in the decolonization of Namibia, the United Nations Transition Assistance Group (UNTAG), based on Security Council resolution 435 of September 1978, is still very much alive. Notwithstanding the intransigence of South Africa and the shifts in United States policy that have reinforced that intransigence, the contact group of five Western states, including the United States, is being pressed by the front line states of Africa and others to negotiate on the basis of UN peacekeeping arrangements for a supervised cease-fire and election of a constitutional assembly as the ultimate process of national self-determination for the peoples of Namibia. These negotiations are ongoing and past experience suggests further roadblocks before there is agreement. But choosing to be optimistic about the eventual outcome, the final resolution of the Namibian issue could prove to be a milestone in the history of UN peacekeeping and peacemaking.

The ideological and territorial war between Iraq and Iran bears no resemblance to the process of decolonization. It is a war, however, that poses the gravest threat to nations in the region and to international peace and security. When considered by the Security Council in September 1980, the United States put forward the idea of a peacekeeping force as part of an interim arrangement for the cessation of hostilities, but the Council was prepared to do no more at the time than call upon Iran and Iraq "to refrain immediately from any further use of force . . . (and) to accept any appropriate offer of mediation or conciliation or to resort to regional agencies or arrangements or other peaceful means of their own choice that would facilitate the fulfillment of their Charter obligations."(42) Then, in March 1981, a proposal by an Islamic peace mission included provision for an Islamic peacekeeping force to guarantee the freedom of navigation in the disputed Shatt-

al-Arab waterway pending adjudication of the disputed border.(43)   All these mediative efforts failed, but they are
nonetheless noteworthy in the political diversity of the
proponents for the neutral third party interposition of military
forces as a means of achieving and securing a cease-fire.

In June 1981, there was a proposal from an entirely
different source in another region. The Association of
Southeast Asian Nations (ASEAN) "called for a United Nations
peacekeeping force in Cambodia (Kampuchea) as part of a
three-point proposal for an end to hostilities in that
country."(44)   Though such a proposal if implemented would
be fraught with difficulties, the Canadian secretary of state
for foreign affairs, who attended the meeting, stated that
Canada was "favorably disposed" to such a notion.(45) Equally speculative is the behind the scenes discussion of a political
settlement of the civil war in El Salvador. No specific
proposals for a combined peacekeeping and electoral process
for that troubled country have, to our knowledge, been put
forward.   But it is known that, during President Reagan's
conversations with Prime Minister Trudeau in Ottawa in July
1981, Trudeau suggested that a Rhodesian-type settlement
might be appropriately applied to the El Salvador situation.
The suggestion was not pursued, though it is a reasonable
speculation that, had a peacekeeping electoral model been
applied to El Salvador, it would have resulted in a more
equitable and peaceful solution than what actually occurred.

In addition to these specific cases which brought forth
proposals for peacekeeping operations, positive affirmation of
the concept of peacekeeping is amply demonstrated by recommendations and declarations of policy that have been expressed
by prestigious statesmen and prominent governmental quarters.
One of the cornerstones of the Report of the Independent
Commission on International Development Issues of 1980,
chaired by Willy Brandt, was the conviction of the relationship
between peace, security, and development:

> A globally respected peacekeeping mechanism should
> be built up - strengthening the role of the United
> Nations. In securing the integrity of states, such
> peacekeeping machinery might free resources for
> development through a sharing of military expen-
> diture, a reduction in areas of conflict and of the
> arms race which they imply.(46)

An outcome of such manifold benefit is to be much desired,
even though the historical differences between East and West
suggest that the creation of an effective UN peacekeeping
mechanism of the kind implied in the report is not in the
offing. The recognition of need is nonetheless evident and the
recommendation does not stand alone. It clearly reflects

initiatives from other quarters, in particular, that of the European Community, launched in the spring of 1978 and culminating in the General Assembly debate in December of that year. A working paper circulated among the EC member states asserted that "peacekeeping is a central function of the United Nations. . . . The support$_*$ of UN peacekeeping reflects the common policy of the Nine."(47) Together they sponsored a draft declaration with the basic aim of bringing into focus the importance of peacekeeping operations in the maintenance of international peace and security and of strengthening the support for such operations by member states, the international community, and international public opinion. No doubt, they were deeply concerned with the very difficult situation of UNIFIL in southern Lebanon, as witnessed by the participating contingents from France, Ireland, and the Netherlands. Specifically, the draft expressed the conviction that "peacekeeping operations are an essential function of the United Nations," and it appealed "to all Member States to further strengthen the peacekeeping capabilities of the United Nations by supplementary assistance to peacekeeping operations in particular, through logistic support, and through making available to the United Nations any other peacekeeping potential to the best of their means. . . [and] to consider the creation of training facilities for United Nations peacekeeping personnel."(48)

At the UN, the European Community expanded into a "core group" of some 24 states with favorable consultation with approximately 78 countries in all. There was positive forward movement. Modest as these proposals seemed to be, if adopted, they would have been an advance in principle beyond the repetitious and unlimited progress of the Special Committee on Peacekeeping Operations.

But the USSR was strongly opposed to any action on the subject of peacekeeping in the General Assembly and engaged in a vigorous lobbying campaign against the draft resolution. Though, in part, the Soviet lobbying proved counterproductive, it succeeded in convincing the General Assembly to return the negotiations by resolution to the Special Committee on Peacekeeping, there to "work for an early completion of agreed guidelines which will govern the conduct of peacekeeping operations of the United Nations in accordance with the Charter." Nevertheless, the paragraph from the draft of the EC, "Appeals to Member States further to strengthen the peacekeeping capabilities of the United Nations by supplemen-

---

*Ed. note: Belgium, Denmark, the Federal Republic of Germany (West Germany), France, Ireland, Italy, Luxembourg, the Netherlands, and the United Kingdom. The membership of the EC increased to ten in 1979 with the accession of Greece.

tary assistance to peacekeeping operations, in particular through logistic support and through making available to United Nations any other peacekeeping potential to the best of their means," was incorporated into the above resolution, which was passed by a vote of 100 in favor, 11 abstentions, and 19 opposed, the last including the members of the socialist group of states.(49) Under Soviet pressure, the European Community retreated from its main objective of action to strengthen UN peacekeeping. But the purpose is most likely to persist to find expression once again at an opportune moment. In the meantime, the "discussions" will be maintained within the Special Committee on Peacekeeping Operations.

THEORETICAL CONSIDERATIONS

The dynamics of national survival in an interdependent world require a set of corresponding international values to guide the behavior of states and the function of international regulatory practices of interdependence. The Charter of the United Nations and its numerous regulatory bodies, the World Bank, the General Agreement of Tariff and Trade, and the persistent international efforts to gain agreements on the Law of the Sea and to formulate mutually productive relations between North and South are all examples of the evolutionary development of international regulatory practices.

Chapters VI and VII of the Charter and corresponding sections of the charters of regional organizations are the central regulatory components for the maintenance of international peace and security. They are, however, seldom if ever invoked. Consequently, peacekeeping has evolved not as a replacement but as a more moderate and acceptable form of international action. States, nevertheless, prefer to rely for their security on the defense capability within their own sovereign domain or on military alliance structures among like-minded states with common strategic concerns. They place little dependence for their security on regional or universal organizations which encompass members holding a wide variety of national, ideological, political, economic, and strategic values. Consequently, alliance structures tend to have a greater degree of ideological or strategic cohesion than do universal structures with a minimum base of consensual values. In a general sense, alliance-type structures are based on a coherence of specific national interests over a period of years or decades, whereas universal structures are committed to long-range objectives for the eventual attainment of peace and cooperative behavior among all states.

Thus, by their very nature, alliance structures tend to have stronger bonds of commitment, at least over the short term, than universal structures where the commitment tends to be weak but persists over longer periods of time. Furthermore, though states argue otherwise, the sets of values of these two levels of organization may not be compatible. In crisis situations, states usually give highest priority to their own perceived national interests, next to the objectives of alliances to which they adhere, and lastly to the values of regional or universal organizations, unless the three are largely consistent. When they are not, states try to convince themselves and others that there is no incompatibility between their national interests, alliance objectives, and the values of regional or universal organizations. Failing this, they defend their position by asserting that the values of international peace and cooperation among states must be postponed until the crisis at home is satisfactorily resolved. (This type of self-justification is similar to the argument that the only way to achieve disarmament is to arm and therefore negotiate from strength.)

Despite this frequent incompatibility of policy objectives, peacekeeping has evolved as a function of the "universal" values inherent within regional and/or international organizations, which are thereby meant to take precedence over national or alliance ideological, political, economic, or strategic interests. When peacekeeping operations are proposed, the compatibility of these two sets of values is thereby put to a severe test. It is at moments such as these when states in conflict are called upon to consent to the interposition of politically neutral and impartial peacekeeping forces. Thereby, in relative terms, they are required to moderate or defer their immediate objectives engaged in the conflict and to submit to a cessation of hostilities in the broader interests of international peace and security unless they deem that a cease-fire is also in their immediate best interests, thereby avoiding the necessity of choice. As well those states which are party to the decision making process of whether or not to launch a peacekeeping operation face a similar question of the choice of interests. How these states choose is then reflected in whether they support, accommodate, abstain, or oppose the resolution to implement the peacekeeping operation.

From the deliberations on the legal and practical guidelines for peacekeeping operations in the Committee of 33, it is clear that states must make a similar choice of values. Any decision to opt for the "universal" level of values carries with it not only the rhetorical commitment to these values, to which all states, at least nobly and vocally, declare their espousal, but also the willingness to grant the requisite authority and discretion to the respective international organization to operationalize these values, as and when required.

All this is predicated on the view that the concept of peacekeeping is based on a universal set of values of peace and cooperation among states and that it functions as a politically neutral third party in an impartial manner. The development of peacekeeping to the level of legitimacy gained by the 1980s has been largely dependent on the growing recognition of these third party principles. These are the principles which have made it possible for the USSR and the United States to utilize the instrumentality of peacekeeping during periods of cold war antagonism as well as emerging detente; that enable parties in conflict to consent to the interposition of international forces; that Third World countries regard as essential to contain and insulate conflicts from being exacerbated by superpower intervention; and that have made it possible for peacekeeping to be applied to diverse types of conflict generally representative of the nature of conflict in the international system. And, because these third party principles have so successfully proven their value in numerous applications, even under the most difficult of circumstances, peacekeeping operations are now being proposed for numerous seemingly intractable conflicts, and why there are so many recommendations and political initiatives to improve and to strengthen the practice of UN and regional peacekeeping.

CONCLUSIONS

At the outset of this chapter, I argued that peacekeeping has, since its inception in the early years of the UN, been extended in use and expanded in function, complexity, and utility. The historical record, as analyzed herein, corroborates this assertion. I also argued that peacekeeping is a uniquely appropriate and viable mechanism for the containment of conflict in the present international system. Again, I believe that the evidence corroborates this view, though it must also be acknowledged that peacekeeping has been applied to only a small, though significant, proportion of conflicts in the international system since 1946. Most conflicts have been unreceptive to third party intervention and have persisted without resolution or concluded by exhaustion or defeat of one or another of the parties.

Though the positive aspects of peacekeeping have been emphasized, there are many practices and procedures that require change and improvement; the most important being the matters of financing, improved logistics and supply, greater coordination and understanding between UN headquarters in New York and the commander in the field, adequate preplanning and coordinated training, and standby arrangements. Many of these matters are discussed in the chapters herein by

Beattie, Murray, and Urquhart and are issues before the Committee of 33. Many of these problems could be overcome with greater resources, others require policy decisions which have yet to be made. If, however, persistent pressure as discussed above is maintained, a political climate conducive to improving the practice and procedures of peacekeeping by regional organizations as well as the UN could be achieved, even to the point of establishing cooperative measures for the joint administration of peacekeeping operations.

There is sufficient momentum to assure that this will occur on an incremental basis. But any agreement on legal and structural matters which are issues of principle is not likely to be achieved in the present international political climate. Nonetheless, as discussed, the pattern of historical practice demonstrates a great capacity for innovation and flexibility so that delay in agreement on legal and structural questions should not inhibit continued growth and development. Agreement on the basic issues of principle will come only when states are willing to reify the universal values of peace and cooperation among states in a firm third party structure with a degree of independent authority and capacity to act greater than that now possessed by the secretary-general as the symbolic head and chief administrative officer of the UN.

Any significant movement in that direction would denote a qualitative and, from the point of view expressed herein, a progressive change in the international system. Though this is not to be expected in the near future, it is more likely to happen than a realization of a more radical transformation of the international system, much as that may be desired. Peacekeeping is an established international modality following a path of growth and development within the present international system. Extrapolation from historical and contemporary evidence also indicates that that process will continue into the future. As it does so, and as the underlying third party principles gain greater and wider recognition and confirmed legitimacy, then the structures of peacekeeping could become the foundation stones for a more radical transformation of the international system. Whether or not that does occur, peacekeeping will continue to evolve and serve as a very important, even primary, modality for the management of conflict in the imperfect world in which we live.

NOTES

1. See Peace and World Order Studies, Transnational Academic Program, Institute of World Order, New York, 1981.

2. For an excellent discussion of these and related questions see Richard A. Falk, "Contending Approaches to World Order," Journal of International Affairs 31 (2 Fall/Winter 1977), or in Peace and World Order Studies.

3. See James Jonah, "Peacekeeping in the Middle East," International Journal XXXI (Winter 1975-6).

4. UN doc. A/34/592, 19 October 1979.

5. UN doc. A/AC.121/L.18, 23, 1973.

6. Ibid.

7. Ibid.

8. UN doc. A/7742, appendix.

9. UN doc. A/AC.121/L.18, 25 Jan. 1973.

10. See H. Wiseman and A.M. Taylor, From Rhodesia to Zimbabwe: The Politics of Transition (New York: Pergamon Press, 1981).

11. Much of this material is located in the regular reports of the secretaries-general on peacekeeping operations and as systematically presented in the Working Files of the Special Committee on Peacekeeping Operations, Nos. 1, Parts I & II, 15 April 1969; 2, 11 April 1977; 3, 11 July 1979; and 4, 21 August 1980.

12. SC res. 339, 19 Dec. 1946.

13. SC res. 525, 25 Aug. 1947.

14. SC res. 50 (Doc. 801) 29 May 1948.

15. SC res. 47 (Doc. 651), and doc. 726, 21 Apr. 1948.

16. GA res. 1000 (ES-1), 5 Nov. 1956.

17. SC res. 128 (Doc. 4022) 11 Jan. 1958.

18. SC res. 143 (Doc. 4387) 14 July, 1960.

19. GA res. 1474, Rev. 1 (ES-IV), 20 Sept. 1960.

20. SC res. 161 (Doc. 4722) 21 Feb. 1961.

21. CL res. 169 (Doc. 5002) 24 Nov. 1961.

22. United Nations Forces, (New York: Praeger, 1966), p. 171.

23. SC res. 353, 20 July 1974.

24. See Wiseman, "United Nations Peacekeeping: An Historical Overview," chap. 2 in this volume.

25. SC res. 186 (Doc. 5575), 4 March 1964 (emphasis added).

26. SC res. 211, 20 Sept. 1965.

27. SC res. 340, 25 Oct. 1973.

28. UN doc. S/11052, Rev. 1, 26 Oct. 1973.

29. SC res. 425, 19 March 1978.

30. For a graphic account of the many and diverse functions performed in the field of operations in Cyprus, see Michael Harbottle, The Impartial Soldier: A Study of the UN Operation in Cyprus (London: Oxford University Press, 1970).

31. "From Rhodesia to Zimbabwe," International Affairs 56 (Summer 1980): 413.

32. See Wiseman and Taylor, From Rhodesia to Zimbabwe.

33. Uganda Election, December 1980 - The Report of the Commonwealth Group, The Secretariat, Malborough House, London, 1981.

34. Ibid.

35. See chapter 10 by Paz-Barnica; and also John Child, "Peacekeeping and the Interamerican System," Military Review LX (Oct. 1980).

36. See Pelcovits, chapter 12 this volume.

37. OAU res. S/14378, Annex II, p. 1.

38. Ibid., annex III, pp. 1-3.

39. OAU doc. AGH/IMP.C/WS/Dec. 1 (1).

40. OAU doc. CM/Res. 789 (XXLV).

41. For a discussion of these matters see Report No. 12 of the "Off-the-Record Workshop of the International Peace Academy," New York, Nov. 1981.

42. The New York Times, 24 Sept. 1980.

43. The Economist, 14 March 1981 and The New York Times, 3 April 1981.

44. The Globe and Mail, 19 June 1981.

45. The Globe and Mail, 20 June 1981. See also "Canada, Notes for an Address by the Secretary of State for Foreign Affairs to the 36th Regular Session of the United Nations General Assembly," 21 Sept. 1981.

46. North-South, A Program for Survival (Cambridge, Mass.: The MIT Press, 1980), p. 125.

47. Unpublished document.

48. Unpublished document. See reference "Nine Call for More UN Peacekeeping Help," Der Taggesspiegel, 15 Sept. 1981.

49. GA res. 33/114, 18 Dec. 1978.

15
United Nations Peacekeeping and the Future of World Order
K. Venkata Raman

INTRODUCTION

A major task involved in preserving world order is keeping the
peace in the sense of both preventing serious armed conflicts
threatening the status quo and facilitating desired changes by
peaceful means.   Through successive efforts dating back to
the Kellogg-Briand Pact and the experience of two disastrous
world wars, the international community has finally come to
recognize in principle the concept of "collective security" and
its attendant notions of "common responsibility" for the
maintenance of international peace and security.(1)   It is to
the triumph of this important achievement, as reflected in the
Charter of the United Nations at San Francisco in 1945, that
the most important and epoch-making political evolution of
recent centuries - decolonization - owes its achievement within,
relatively speaking, peaceful and orderly circumstances.   The
idea that preservation of international peace is a vital common
interest of every sovereign state eventually led to the adoption
of a fairly elaborate "system" for that purpose, as reflected in
Chapters VI and VII of the Charter of the United Nations.   It
is a two-phased system designed to function initially under a
strong consensual regime as envisaged in Chapter VI where
the organization's role is to encourage, assist, or otherwise
achieve through diplomacy peaceful solutions to international
conflicts.   Threats to international peace and security
including allegations of aggression fall within a second phase
and are the primary concern of the Security Council where, if
necessary, the use of sanctions or other enforcement measures
as envisaged in Chapter VII of the Charter are available.   The
fact that in the real world it is difficult to classify
international conflicts in such neat compartments is amply

demonstrated by the practice of the Security Council. The use of UN forces for containing conflict can arise in both phases although the Charter basis in each may differ in some substantive manner. The obligation to preserve peace and promote peaceful resolution of conflicts, as envisaged in article 25 of the Charter is common to both phases and it is this "collective responsibility" that is commonly invoked in support of peacekeeping obligations in general. However, neither in theory nor in subsequent practice has this initial premise of a common and collective responsibility to preserve international peace and security been achieved, and the reasons for its failure are quite well known. In a recent report to the General Assembly, the secretary-general observed:

> A reliable system of international peace and security
> - the central theme of the Charter of the U.N. - has
> developed little further in practice than haphazard
> and last minute resorts to the United Nations.(2)

UN peacekeeping has remained part of those haphazard, last minute efforts; it is an uncertain, unpredictable, and unregulated international operation. Its primary concern is to maintain international peace but, because of its ad hoc nature, it has been able to play that role only within a limited range of circumstances.(3)

The purpose of this chapter is not to offer a systematic survey of UN peacekeeping activities, much less to undertake an analysis of its probable future given the slow and halting progress of the Committee of 33, mandated by the United Nations to clarify the structure and functions of peace-keeping.(4) Such a task needs to be undertaken within the larger context of the changing dimensions of international relations in which the UN system has to operate. Concern here is, rather, with a general philosophical issue. The United Nations as it now stands serves as a channel of communication for wideranging demands for political reorganization, global economic equity and redistribution, social justice, and human rights; it is not even remotely similar to the entity that the founding members had originally envisaged in 1945 at San Francisco. What role should this contemporary organization play to promote the common collective vital interests of the majority of its members in the area of their security needs? There is a sense of urgency to this problem among the developing countries; there is also a sense of helplessness among most developed countries as well, including generally, even the five veto-wielding states, about the irrelevance of the UN-based security system in the context of prevailing trends in international relations. The issue can be framed by asking what role the great majority of UN members, including the newly independent members of the United Nations

for whom the preservation and promotion of international peace
and security has a new and all-pervasive connotation, would
be willing to accord for international peacekeeping in the
context of this newly expanded Charter of the United Nations?(5) Even in a brief general discussion, it is obvious
that the general theme of peacekeeping appears to relate itself
directly or indirectly to a number of other issues. While it is
not possible to elaborate in detail each of those subthemes, it
is, nevertheless, useful to point out in any consideration of
the future of peacekeeping what are its prospects and real
constraints, and why it is still important for the maintenance
of world order that the central theme be taken seriously and
with conviction.

Tremendous changes in perspective have been brought
about in part by the very presence of the United Nations and
the impetus it has given to many global developments. Apart
from decolonization as a legal entitlement for political
independence, these developments include efforts at the Law of
the Sea Conference to recognize the concept of a "common
heritage of mankind"; in UNCTAD to ensure international
equity and economic justice; within the agencies of ECOSOC to
promote basic fundamental human rights; and in the political
organs of the United Nations to prevent, through the same
collective action, private aggression and terrorism in
international relations. Viewed in the context of these
evolving common concerns, what is the place for UN peacekeeping?(6) Given the enormous rise in recent times in global
spending on conventional armaments in which, unfortunately,
the developing countries have also an ever increasing share, is
it not in the vital national interest of these states to
reconsider an effective and responsive role for United Nations
peacekeeping as part of the international community's shared
collective obligation to preserve and promote international
peace and security?(7) Is the time auspicious for the Group
of 77 to invite the others to join their demand for establishment of a New International Security Order to complement a
New International Economic Order?

THE FAILURE OF THE CHARTER-BASED COLLECTIVE
SECURITY SYSTEM

The basic premises of the UN collective security system -
reflected generally in articles 2, 51, and 99 and in a schematic
manner throughout in Chapters VI and VII of the Charter -
are that the victorious allied powers' coalition prevailing
during the concluding phase of World War II would remain, and
that it would be adequate to respond to threats to international
peace and security anywhere in the world.(8) The key func-

tions thus entrusted to the Security Council quickly became victims of the "cold war." Several factors accounted for this failure. First, the Charter system came into being before the world community became aware that atomic power, as an effective instrument of national security policies of the major powers, would be a reality. Second, there was inadequate appreciation of the intensity of the demands of the colonies for independence and the new challenge that this would bring about for the United Nations to cope with internal conflicts calling for international action of one kind or other.(9)   Even without the Korean experience and the so-called "Uniting-for-Peace" arrangement, there would have been a slow and inevitable drift toward the General Assembly for a major policy decision and direction to guide United Nations management of outbreaks of armed conflicts. Third, the very conceptual matrix of the Charter limiting the formal involvement of the organization to only conflicts of an international character has proven in practice to be unworkable.(10)   But the great majority of disputes involving armed conflict that have come before the United Nations, especially those from Asia and Africa, have been predominantly "domestic conflicts" which invited precisely the same kind of international attention and United Nations assistance. Fourth, the initial assumption, that those states which have the capability to enforce international peace through military action must therefore be endowed with a special voting prerogative, has characterized the structure and functions of the Security Council. In effect, this has meant that without the agreement, or at least some tacit understanding, of the two superpowers the Security Council cannot play an effective role. Fifth, and perhaps most important, the Charter did not envisage the use of internationally recruited military personnel for peacekeeping purposes. Its conception of "enforcement action" under Chapter VII was designed to operate against sovereign states, is decidedly coercive in spirit and direction, and lacks possibilities of its employment for any meaningful role as an element for peaceful settlement of international conflicts or domestic conflicts where a discredited government is challenged by a substantial majority of the population.(11)

THE AD HOC NATURE OF UN PEACEKEEPING

The peacekeeping role of the United Nations, like the "good offices" functions of its secretary-general, has evolved in the practice of the organization more out of functional necessity than from any express direction in the Charter. It was originally intended that the Security Council, in pursuance of its primary responsibility for the maintenance of international peace and security, would receive the assistance of a military staff committee in respect of all its military (meaning enforcement as well as peacekeeping) requirements. That original plan failed to materialize, and the functions of peacekeeping as we now know them have evolved as elements in the organization's peacemaking process. In all its rich variations, the peacekeeping functions - ranging from the patrol of a border, provisions of a buffer between two feuding armies, supervision of a truce, disengagement of armed bands, and peace observation to actual administration and control of a territory - today constitute an indispensable component of what is still a fragile and voluntary process of United Nations assistance. The concept of UN peacekeeping has never been formally defined in UN practice. But, the wide variety of functions to which it refers encompasses activities generally regarded as falling within both domestic and international concerns of states.(12)

Whether it is of the nature of an enforcement action - as in the case of UN action in Korea in 1950 - or the more usual type of international military observation or supervision of troop withdrawals or policing which depends upon the consent of the host country, clear policy guidelines and administrative procedures for this activity are required to ensure its fair and proper implementation.(13) As a matter of fact, the so-called UN action in Korea is an anomaly unlikely to be repeated again. This is not to suggest that the United Nations, through a consensus in the Security Council, cannot undertake military action to enforce peace. Notwithstanding the failure of the Security Council to enter into international military agreements with member states under article 43 of the Charter, the prevailing system of voluntary participation can still serve to constitutionally permit the Council to undertake "enforcement" functions.(14)

However, the more important and widely resorted to role of the United Nations has been in respect to the use of UN forces for nonenforcement purposes. The techniques and approaches to peaceful settlement of disputes provided in Chapter VI and the peacekeeping obligations of the UN under Chapter VII of the Charter are not, and have never been considered to be, mutually exclusive. Formal determinations under article 39 of the Charter involve making major policy decisions, and where consensus for such a finding is not forthcoming, a formal finding to that effect is usually avoided.(15) In other words, it became functionally necessary not to reach any formal decision as to who is an aggressor under article 39 of the Charter. Peacekeeping has been resorted to as a temporary expedient to contain conflict and prevent further violence and to create a favorable climate conducive to peacemaking. That also explains the fact that military peacekeeping by itself is not at all a strategy for resolving international conflicts. There is, consequently, little justification in blaming peacekeeping for the failure to reach a solution in a conflict. It is true that in some situations, notably Cyprus, the indefinitely extended peacekeeping operations have not served to produce a settlement. But the absence of peacekeeping would have aggravated the situation much further.(16)

It has been previously noted that the Charter did not specifically envisage the use of the kind of military peace-keeping which has in fact developed over the years. On the other hand, it is also true that various types of peacemaking functions envisaged under the Charter failed to materialize in practice and, consequently, no institutional development has occurred in that respect. The philosophy of Chapter VII and its underlying assumptions were too formalistic and rigid, just as the underlying assumptions of Chapter VI were too passive and noncommittal.

There are two aspects of UN peacekeeping which have attracted some further consideration. The operational part of the use of UN-sponsored military personnel, including the question of composition, command, and scope of their opera-tions, is the subject of discussion within the Committee of 33 at the United Nations. A political consensus within the committee will certainly strengthen the role of UN peacekeeping and also offer some useful guidelines for the secretary-general to follow. The second, and by far the most important develo-pment in recent practice, has been the consensual aspect of UN peacekeeping. Efforts to strengthen this evolving practice of the organization are likely to be productive if appropriate clarification of the policies relevant thereunder and institutions responsive to them are envisaged and put in place. When, how, and for what purposes can or might a UN peace force be used to assist peaceful resolution of disputes? This question can be reformulated in a more outrageous manner: Is there a legal entitlement for any member state of the United Nations to demand UN peacekeeping assistance when it perceives (or is actually confronted by) serious military threats to its territorial integrity or political independence?

THE NATURE AND SCOPE OF UN PEACEKEEPING

The stated purpose of UN peacekeeping activities is to assist member states in preserving international peace, promoting security, and facilitating peaceful resolution of conflicts. UN peacekeeping has, therefore, been evolved to meet the needs of a special situation where an "outside military force" sup-ported by voluntary pledges could help to improve the chances for eventual resolution of a dispute without engaging in any

coercive action against a state, except for self-defense, and
where the involvement of such a force is based upon the
consent of the host country and supported by a general consensus of the Security Council or the General Assembly.   This
is a somewhat convoluted statement, but it describes accurately
the present state of the art.   It implies the following: UN
peacekeeping is a kind of executive action mounted by the
United Nations and based upon the consent of the host country.   The context for obtaining such consent must be seen
favorably by the Security Council or, if the Council is unable
to act, by a substantial majority of the Assembly.   Moreover,
the overall general criteria for placing UN authority or
"presence" in a conflict situation must clearly be located in the
principles and norms of the Charter of the United Nations.
Not only is the consent of the states involved in conflict
necessary, but a general consensus among the major or influ-
ential member states of the United Nations in support of an
operation is also essential; and, of course, the recruiting and
financing aspects of such peacekeeping operations must also be
clearly feasible in order for the secretary-general to implement
the consensus.
     Each of these issues, and a host of other attendant
problems, deserves a detailed analysis which is beyond the
scope of this chapter.   There is a rich heritage of accumulated
experience within the organization itself on these issues.(17)
On   matters   of   constitutional   principle   and   legitimizing
authority, the practice, since the advisory opinion of the
International Court of Justice in the matter of Certain Expenses, clearly establishes what is feasible under prevailing
conditions.(18)   The uncertainty of a mandate, the ad hoc
nature of the operations, the voluntary character of the troops
and other contingents made available to the secretary-general,
and the precariousness of the financial situation of peacekeeping have all contributed to making the effort that much
less effective.   But the fact remains that, notwithstanding the
earlier opposition of the Soviet Union, France, and several
other countries, they have not opposed UN action when their
own interests appeared to be served by the presence of UN
forces in troubled areas of the world.   Indeed, there is a
certain psychological receptivity to the idea that UN presence
is an acceptable, even if ineffective, alternative to unilateral
superpower intervention.   Nevertheless, within the superpowers' own "spheres of interest" the UN has been excluded from
playing any such role, practically consistently, not only in
disputes in the Western hemisphere but also in conflicts arising
within socialist states.
     Yet, no one seriously questions today the view that the
United Nations is entitled to engage in peacekeeping where the
necessary consensus is present, the parties involved are
generally willing to utilize such assistance, and the financial

and logistical support are predictable and forthcoming. If peacekeeping is more likely to be based on the request of the host state than upon the original idea of enforcing the peace, thereby avoiding the necessity of making a determination under article 39 of the Charter, it will then be necessary to define, clarify, and state in advance of a conflict when such an assistance can be expected as a matter of right, when it can be made available after some explanation and arm-twisting, and when it is illegal or immoral to give any such assistance. These issues are fundamentally different from those argued in connection with the ONUC and UNEF operations before the International Court of Justice. The Court took the view that peacekeeping by consent, as long as it is not contrary to the principles and purposes of the Charter, is within the purview of the UN's legitimate concern.

While such an expansive view of the Charter may have been found necessary to bring the costs of UNEF operations within the meaning of the term "expenses of the organization," it has also raised interesting questions of competence and authority of the decision-making organs. Briefly, it raised questions about the authority of the General Assembly and the competence of the secretary-general, but it did not resolve either these or other underlying issues. For example, the domestic jurisdiction limitations of article 2(7) of the Charter presumably applies with equal vigor to any efforts at putting some UN presence in a dispute of domestic revolt in which a foreign state has not yet intervened militarily; thus qualifying the situation as one purely of a domestic nature, notwithstanding a formal governmental request for assistance from the UN.(19) Recall the last-minute request of Pakistan for UN presence during the East Pakistan (Bangladesh) crisis, or the formal request to the secretary-general of the United Nations by Idi Amin facing ouster from power in Uganda in 1979. The situation is seldom sufficiently clear-cut for outsiders to make rational decisions. There is, consequently, a need for fairly well understood working guidelines.(20) The matter is made relatively easy in the case of Uganda or other situations in Africa where the voice and concerns of the Organization of African Unity are available to provide useful guidance. But in other areas (e.g., South East Asia) where a regional consensus is hard to find, by what criteria should the General Assembly (after a deadlock in the Security Council) decide such requests?

Rarely in the debates on the establishment of UN operations does one find any explicit reference to any Charter provisions to indicate the constitutional basis. Neither the Security Council resolutions nor the reports of the secretary-general formulating specific guidelines for peacekeeping forces contain any reference to specific Charter principles as a basis for its peacekeeping activities. The attitude of individual states toward UN peacekeeping has been, with the possible exception of China, generally favorable; holding the view that it is an essential function of the organization to assist the parties in conflict when they are willing to utilize such assistance. China has objected to the "so-called UN peace-keeping" on the ground that "such a practice can only pave the way for further international intervention and control with the superpowers as the behind-the-scenes boss," and consistently refused to participate in the council debates on those matters.(21)

Even when a member, whether permanent or nonpermanent, found occasion to disagree with some aspect or other of a resolution seeking the establishment of a peacekeeping operation, some states have chosen to abstain, rather than veto or vote against such a proposal. For example, that has been the attitude taken by the Soviet Union and Czechoslovakia in the Middle East peacekeeping operations of UNDOF and UNIFIL.(22) Although this practice of allowing the United Nations to establish peacekeeping operations has been the case particularly (as in UNIFIL) when it is in response to the host country's own request, it remains true that, without the consent or tacit approval of the permanent members of the Security-Council, no peacekeeping operation can be put in place, or extended by renewal of its mandate. The failure of the Council to renew UNEF's mandate in 1979, for example, arose from the close dependence of the UNEF's mandate on the changed circumstances in the Middle East situation,(23) and the substantial opposition from several states to the peace treaty between Egypt and Israel (which came into force on April 25, 1979). Commenting on the issue of general consent to peacekeeping operations and the attitude taken by the Soviet Union and France, Professor Rosalyn Higgins stated:

> Neither we [the United Kingdom] nor the Soviet Union really want U.N. forces to be mounted in the General Assembly. We virtually accept the Soviet view that future peacekeeping should be authorized by the Security Council where the veto obtains. . . .(24)

It is true in a sense that, although an article 43-type of major power involvement in UN peacekeeping has fortunately not been realized in practice, major power agreement - in reality, consensus among the two superpowers - is necessary for mounting a UN peace force. This tacit practice between the two superpowers has the virtue of preserving their veto power under the guise of protecting the integrity of the Security Council's primary responsibility for promoting international peace and security.

But recent indications, as in the thirty-third session of the General Assembly in 1978 when Resolution 33/114 (outlining in some measure general principles of UN peacekeeping) was discussed, suggest the obvious interest of the majority of UN members in the General Assembly playing a prominent role in this regard.(25)   The European Economic Community pioneered this resolution and the Non-Aligned Group gave considerable support to it.   The Soviet Union and a number of socialist bloc states vehemently opposed the resolution, characterizing some of the principles there expounded as "illegal, null and void."(26)   In a number of UN peacekeeping activities (peace-keeping understood in its broadest sense as I have defined earlier), commencing with the UNSCOB in the Balkans to the proposed UNTAG (UN Transition Assistance Group) for Namibia, the General Assembly has played a vital role which is largely responsible for generating confidence in UN peace-keeping activities.(27)   The Group of 77 - without a veto in the Security Council - is increasingly interested in utilizing the forum of the General Assembly for peacekeeping assistance.   But, so far, no formal steps have been taken in this regard.

It is possible to envisage a more expanded peacekeeping role for the organization in view of the broad range of global concerns indicated earlier, which may involve newer forms of cooperation transcending the narrow rivalries about jurisdiction.   For instance, cooperation between a regional organization such as the OAU and the General Assembly or the Security Council on disputes pertaining to Africa, as in the case of Chad, may present the question of major power consent in an entirely different context.   Although it is true that such regional organizations may develop their own peacekeeping mechanisms, linkage with the United Nations may be sought to gain legitimacy for the causes reinforced by such peacekeeping operations.

THE RIGHT TO UN PEACEKEEPING ASSISTANCE

Is there an objectively determinable general right to UN peacekeeping assistance?   It is becoming increasingly evident that there is a real need to explore the possibility of extending UN peacekeeping assistance independently of the consent of the major veto-wielding powers of the United Nations.   Such a need is all the greater when one realizes that there is a close correlation between the massive trade in conventional armaments and the outbreaks of conflict which make use of those armaments.   Finally, the interdependence between economic development and trade in armaments is a fact affecting the poor underdeveloped as well as the rich industrialized economies of the world; although its impact is obviously different in the two types of societies.

An effective preliminary role for a multinational peacekeeping function (as a strategy for avoidance of armed conflict) is in the interests of all the developing countries, especially because of the necessity for them to seek the avoidance of protracted and costly wars. At the present time, the worldwide resort to nuclear technology for energy has also created some other wider risks. And even in regard to conventional weapons, the developing countries' share in that trade has now reached alarming proportions. The arms race, especially in the sophisticated high technology conventional weapons, cannot bring the reward of security but drags them into a senseless game of numbers designed to boost their ego only temporarily at the risk of compromising their much needed developmental priorities and more productive purposes.(28) The greatest possible threat to international peace and security in the coming decades will come from regions where localized arms races are rampant. Effective preventive strategies are urgently needed.

The development of an appropriate peacekeeping mechanism adequate to offer the necessary security in potentially volatile conflict situations is one viable alternative that should be seriously considered. It would be necessary in such a scheme to develop international peacekeeping as a "positive-sum function" to serve to reinforce national or regional security mechanisms; it must have preventative functions in contrast to the normal and limited post hoc response with reduced effectiveness once hostilities have broken out.(29) It is perhaps far easier to put together an impressive list of all-inclusive "principles" in a convention prohibiting international peddling of soft or hard military hardware and get a numerical majority in the General Assembly to vote in favor of it, than to achieve meaningful consensus on the use of peacekeeping for preventative purposes. But it is worth the attempt.

Even if its outcome is uncertain, the initiation of such a process will, at least, serve to dispel some of the psychological inhibitions preventing sovereign states from exploring this alternative. One possible outcome may be that the seeking of peacekeeping assistance by a state would not be regarded as an "unfriendly act" by its adversary. A second outcome can be a formal reiteration of the post-Charter principle, now well established by customary practice, that any political advantages (not limited to territorial changes) secured by the use of armed force will not receive international recognition. Consequently, it would serve no useful purpose to plan for military options as a way of resolving problems even when such problems involve vital national interests. If, on the other hand, attempts to protect such vital national interests receive the support of the international community through its peacekeeping operations, the initial issue of their legitimacy would have been resolved in their favor. A third outcome in the consideration of the use of peacekeeping for preventive purposes can be the exploration of ways of using this institution for assisting the parties to explore peaceful solutions to their difficulties.(30)

Peacekeeping sometimes has been criticized for not performing the functions of peacemaking. These possibilities may not be available unless some antecedent crucial policy issues are resolved: who decides on when and where such preventative measures can or should be introduced and by what procedures those decisions are made. Should the response be limited to requests from sovereign governments even when an underlying conflict is about a popular revolt against that government?(31)

It has been noted that, in UN practice, peacekeeping has developed essentially as a voluntary operation limited to assisting parties in dispute to achieve a variety of agreed outcomes. These include agreement on cessation of hostilities, observation of cease-fire arrangements, supervision of force withdrawals, and similar other functions. Even when these tasks are imposed on the parties as a result of a decision of the Security Council, the parties' consent will still be necessary for their implementation. In that sense, peacekeeping functions are not "enforcement functions"; they are not "sanctions" imposed by the organization of the kind contemplated under Chapter VII of the Charter. It is true in respect to Rhodesia the council decided upon certain sanctions.(32) Similar unsuccessful efforts were made in the recent attempts to secure a Council decision in respect to South Africa concerning its stand in Namibia.(33) However, in those instances, obvious peacekeeping responsibilities which could have been entrusted to a UN agency were not considered at all. Their implementation was left to the workings of individual members. Had the Council decided to entrust specific tasks of verification, supervision, search and seizure, and arrest and detention in respect to illegal traffic in arms in contravention of the Security Council sanctions, then there would have evolved peacekeeping functions aimed at enforcing the policies of the Council. Such a role for peacekeeping can nevertheless arise albeit marginally, even in respect to situations where the UN presence is voluntarily agreed upon by the parties. Such occasions have arisen in respect to ONUC operations in the Congo.(34) But they were justified either on grounds of self-defense or as necessarily arising out of the tasks voluntarily entrusted to the organization. Whatever may have been the proper basis for such actions, they cannot but have important consequences for one or both sides in the conflict. The fact remains that, in most cases, the

introduction of peacekeeping functions, usually after the
outbreak of armed hostilities, required a high degree of
cooperation on the part of the host state. As the experience
with UNEF clearly indicates, this cooperation on the part of a
host state may take the form of its clear acceptance of such
assistance. We need only recall here the debate over
Secretary-General U Thant's interpretation of the contractual
nature of UN peacekeeping in the UNEF-I situation and the
circumstances for its termination.(35) It is worth contrasting
that experience with the termination of the UNEF-II mandate in
1979. In the latter type of instance, an interesting question
for consideration will be whether UN peacekeeping should be
made available when parties directly involved in conflict agree
upon its use even though there is substantial opposition to
granting them such assistance in the Council or the Assembly
as a whole. Here, consent to the use of peacekeeping is still
relevant, but it is somewhat different from saying that this
consent must also include the consent of all the permanent
members of the Security Council.(36)

The emphasis on consent in the foregoing discussion
necessarily raises other questions such as what is a "valid"
decision of the organization and what are the "obligations"
following such a decision vis-a-vis the members of the organization in general. It is generally assumed - although such
assumptions have not gone unchallenged - that obligations
arising in respect to decisions falling clearly within Chapter
VII of the Charter are not dependent upon the consent of any
state. A valid decision of the Security Council under Chapter
VII or, as has been the case, a recommendation by the Security Council outlining measures that may be taken in respect to
a situation, without mentioning articles 39, 40, or 41, can give
rise, it is generally assumed, to legal obligations for all
member states as envisaged under articles 25, 48, and 49 of
the Charter. It must be assumed that the obligation to extend
assistance under article 49 is in essence a reiteration of the
general obligation of all members assumed under articles 2(5)
and more clearly in article 25 of the Charter.(37) It may even
be suggested that the general obligation of member states to
give assistance, in the application of collective measures,
remains the same whether such measures are recommended by
the Security Council under articles 43 and 49 or by the
General Assembly under article 14.

These Charter-based principles which define the nature
and scope of the obligations of members toward the maintenance of international peace and security are no doubt stated
in broad general terms. In The Expenses(38) and Namibia(39)
opinions, the International Court of Justice dwelt at length on
the consequences for members arising from validly adopted
decisions of the organization in pursuit of its major objectives
and goals. Given the present demands on the organization to

ensure the protection of the common interests of the vast majority of the developing countries in the economic, social, and scientific spheres of human activity, the potential for future peacekeeping mechanisms is indeed vastly expanded. It calls for innovative and newer types of observation, supervision, fact-finding, monitoring, policing, and other functions.

If the organization is to be prepared to meet those intense demands of its members, it will be necessary to explore the ways and means. The role and special expertise of the various specialized agencies of the United Nations can be important in this regard.(40) This has already become obvious during the current negotiations in the Third United Nations Conference on the Law of the Sea. Not only agreement on specific procedures is needed but, perhaps more importantly, agreement on principles and policies clarifying the Charter obligations mentioned above in those newer areas of international activity must receive urgent consideration. Beyond the question of the political feasibility, the matter of "authority," including legal competence derived from the principles and policies of the Charter, will shape and influence the final outcome of the efforts to initiate a UN peacekeeping operation. As Oscar Schachter pointed out: " . . . in most of the U.N. peacekeeping operations the presence of a legal foundation for the necessary activities has been found to be essential to effective performance."(41) Even in situations where the Charter principles and a substantial general consensus support putting in place a UN peacekeeping presence, in actual practice, the states directly affected must also be willing to utilize such assistance. Their perceptions of the usefulness of that assistance may be colored by their view of their conflict and fears of "internationalizing" the issues in conflict. In the absence of clear consent from the host state, the principles of territorial sovereignty and political independence prevail over any decision, no matter how strongly it is supported by the General Assembly. The UN system has not been effective in responding to crises prompted by external aggression when the territorial sovereign itself is the target of external action. That is why ONUC remains a unique and important experience for the United Nations. The ad hoc peacekeeping operations made possible on the purely voluntary basis of financing and consent of the parties, as in Yemen (UNYOM), Cyprus (UNFICYP), and Lebanon (UNOGIL), have in fact set in motion a trend likely to influence the future UN peacekeeping.(42) If in fact such peacekeeping operations prove economical and effective and are seen as a viable alternative to any other options open to states to reinforce their security needs, then the basis for the future peacekeeping process cannot remain on such a fragile foundation.

It follows logically from the absolute prohibition against the use of force in article 2(4) of the Charter, that, when a member state is clearly in need of external protection, it should be able to have recourse to either of the two options recognized in the Charter. First, it may invoke the regional or bilateral options made possible by article 51 under which any individual or collective self-defense arrangement, either already in place or which can be arranged and made available within the context of the multipolar nature of the international power system. Past experience with bilateral "interventions by invitation," whether in the Soviet or the American spheres of action, has made it abundantly clear that such requests can be made at one's own peril and that their long-term consequences easily outweigh any plausible short-term advantages. From a policy perspective, there is nothing wrong with including such possibilities within article 51. They may be justified as coming within the structure of collective security as envisaged in the Charter of the United Nations. What is wrong is the omission of any criteria or principles to govern the possible use to which article 51 arrangements can be put to. Presumably, the restraints of article 2(7) apply to any such "organization" or "arrangement" from agreements made under article 51 of the Charter. The Soviet action in Afghanistan (1980) and the United States intervention in Vietnam amply demonstrate the dangers inherent in assuming that those constraints do in fact restrain external interventions.

A second alternative to states requiring the support of externally arranged military assistance is to seek major UN peacekeeping support within the guidelines established under the Charter. Here, unlike the system of regional arrangements envisaged by the Charter and mentioned above, one can take advantage of the scheme presented for "United Nations concern" in the various provisions of Chapter VI and VII of the Charter.(43) Certainly, under Chapter VI itself, the Security Council can consider lending UN peacekeeping support as a "measure" to facilitate and promote a peaceful resolution of a dispute. But the fact remains that, notwithstanding the experience of the organization in the ONUC and UNEF-I and II operations, its peacekeeping mandate is generally perceived to be fundamentally neocolonialist, merely serving the status quo or available only to established governments. There is also the fundamental constitutional impediment of article 2(7), which makes UN peacekeeping legitimate only when there is actual armed conflict involving more than one sovereign state, unless such a measure is seen coming within the terms of Chapter VII.(44)

It is useful to consider the implications of denying altogether any role for the United Nations to respond favorably to appeals for assistance when requested by only one side to the conflict. The effect of this would be to encourage certain

major powers to respond to such requests, with all its attendant consequences. It may be that regional organizations,
where present, could fill the gap. For example, in the Middle
Eastern dispute, the basic agreement of the two superpowers
as well as of all the parties to the general guidelines set in
Resolution 242 enabled the two superpowers to "police" the
1970 "standstill agreement" using satellite and high reconnaissance techniques.(45) When this consensus ceased to
exist, as on the Camp David agreements, the support for a
broad-based peacekeeping role fell through. The nonrenewal
by the Security Council of the UNEF-II mandate clearly attests
to the importance of the underlying basic policies upon which
the implementation of peacekeeping can be made available.(46)

FACTORS CONDITIONING UN PEACEKEEPING OPERATIONS

There are important reasons why UN peacekeeping must be
reappraised now and developed further. The entry into the
United Nations of a vast number of small states has, contrary
to certain misgivings in some quarters, brought into that body
a new and refreshing perspective to bear on old controversies
and issues. The contributions of the smaller powers in
support of the UN peacekeeping operations have been more
constructive than the vituperative cold-war rhetoric that
usually emanates from the Security Council. These medium
and small states have a vital stake in a strong UN-based
security system. They may be expected to use their collective
authority to promote their vital interests since they are the
states which, when confronted by a real emergency threatening
international peace and security, are most likely to place
greater reliance on the United Nations in preference to other
alternatives, and to show some willingness to accept limitations
on their unfettered sovereign rights. Finally, they are also
the states upon which, as a rule, the organization draws for
participating troops when the need for mounting a peacekeeping force arises.

The major political and financial problems which have
conditioned the effectiveness of UN peacekeeping operations
cannot be satisfactorily resolved unless the basic policies
governing the availability and invocation of peacekeeping are
sufficiently appreciated and clearly accepted by member states.
This, in turn, will raise at least three fundamental issues:

1.   The need for mutual consent where the peacekeeping
      operations are to be located within the territory of only
      one of the parties (as in UNEF-I) usually based upon the
      host state's consent;

2.   In a functionally expanded system of UN peacekeeping, the option under special conditions for either the Security Council or General Assembly to establish peacekeeping operation; and

3.   The criteria, legal principles, and Charter policies upon which the decisions with respect to UN peacekeeping must be made.

These fundamental issues are briefly examined below (within the limitation of this exposition) to the extent necessary to emphasize the need to consider further expanding the potentialities of UN (or any other multinational) peacekeeping mechanisms as strategies in the management of international conflicts.

The Scope of Mutual Consent

Except in enforcement actions involving military sanctions, it is recognized that the consent of the parties involved in dispute is essential for mounting a peacekeeping operation. However, within the parameters of such initial consent, the authority of the UN must be presumed to extend to all aspects of its operations, including the composition, command, and authority to use force in self-defense or, where necessary, in order to safeguard the interests for which the peacekeeping force was invited and agreed to be established. The difficulty as to where the dividing line between consent and implicit authority must be drawn cannot be easily resolved as the experience of ONUC has shown.

The Option of Security Council or General Assembly to Establish Peacekeeping Operations

When a peacekeeping operation, other than an enforcement or a formal sanction, is envisaged for purposes of preventing an armed conflict or serious domestic violence within a state, either pursuant to a decision of the Security Council or a recommendation of the General Assembly, the requirements of formal consent may appear to run counter to the objectives and principles of the Charter. In law, the Security Council can make decisions binding on all member states (article 25). Where there is a serious breakdown in law and order and the domestic governmental authority is clearly incapable of exercising its control, and massive internal violence is in evidence, either the Security Council under Chapter VI or VII or the General Assembly under Article 14, recognizing that its operational scope and implications may be in dispute, should be able to adopt measures including UN peacekeeping assistance to

preserve peace and security. In such situations insistence
upon prior consent is likely to be counterproductive, although
it is true that in practice a peacekeeping force requires the
cooperation of the domestic elements within that state in order
to be able to perform its functions effectively.(47) Finally, in
respect to UN actions which are not an enforcement or a
sanction, notwithstanding the primary interest of the UN in
containing serious threats to international peace and security,
the actual consent of the parties in conflict is undoubtedly
necessary. This became clear, for example, during the Council discussions in 1965 in the India-Pakistan dispute concerning
the establishment of UNIPOM.

In the early 1960s, even before the "financial crisis" of
1962, the question came up for consideration as to whether a
specific request of the state or states in question is adequate
as such to initiate a peacekeeping operation. In the Yemen
situation, in which Egypt and Saudi Arabia were involved in
an internal war in that country, all three agreed to request
the secretary-general to provide a UN military observer group
to supervise the cease-fire and withdrawal of all foreign
troops. They agreed to pay voluntarily the expenses for the
entire UN operation. Nevertheless, the decision to establish
such an operation was seen to require the approval of the
Security Council.(48) Why? When assistance involving certain
peacekeeping functions is requested by the parties to a
dispute and they agree to pay for said assistance, what
provisions of the Charter require that that request must first
be approved by the Security Council before it can be acted
upon by the secretary-general on behalf of the organization?
In other words, how could a permanent member veto an agreement of the parties in a conflict to utilize the peacekeeping
assistance of the United Nations? For, surely such a program
can be described as a "measure" to assist the parties in
conflict under article 14 of the Charter, provided there is no
substantial consensus against giving such assistance in the
General Assembly. What has happened is that when a major
power or powers consider that such a move is likely to
compromise their interests, they are likely to prevent the
organization from undertaking such a function.

Precisely because this problem has been treated as a
question of competence between the Security Council versus
the secretary-general, it has not received the kind of attention
it deserves, viewed especially from the perspective of the
majority of the developing or smaller countries. In the future,
we must assume that the occasions for such peacekeeping
functions may arise more frequently with considerable variable
innovation in the nature and scope of the peacekeeping
functions. It will then be necessary for the organization to
redefine more comprehensively its role and that of its individual organs and agencies.

The Criteria and Principles of the Charter for an
Expanded Peacekeeping Role

The foregoing discussion of the institutional capabilities of the organization naturally raises the issue of Charter principles and legal criteria for UN peacekeeping assistance. As noted earlier, neither in Chapter VI nor in Chapter VII is there any guidance or a statement of principles governing the peaceful uses of UN forces when the consent of the parties is available or when a host country requests them. Indeed, since the Security Council is the only permanent organ of the United Nations that is expected to remain continuously in session, it must have at its disposal procedures for monitoring potential threats to international peace and security before such situations escalate and result in serious armed conflicts. The need for a built-in early warning system in the United Nations to monitor political and social trends and to provide an informal and advisory assessment on such situations has been recognized, although no attempt has been made to establish such a mechanism.(49) The revival of the "little Assembly" concept as a procedure under article 14 of the Charter (independent of its prior association with the Korean experience) may serve to accomplish such an objective.

The criteria for taking any action or suggesting any measures to parties in a conflict must at all times be related to the basic premises, objectives, and goals of the Charter of the United Nations. An important consideration which cannot be overlooked is the constitutional competence of the organization and its authority to undertake certain types of activities. A second order of principles concerns the composition, role, and administration of the United Nations operations. The norms in these categories are interlinked and can have an influence on the outcome. Oscar Schachter has suggested some normative considerations used as having provided a basis for the UNEF situation which are no doubt relevant in this regard:

1. The United Nations operation should not prejudge the solution of controversial questions;
2. the U.N. action should not change the political balance affecting efforts to settle the conflict; and
3. the action should not modify the prior status juris.

> The conservatory and self-limiting rules followed in these peace-keeping operations may be said to have been a consequence of the fragility of the Organization's authority and its inability to bring about an imposed solution without obtaining the consent of all the States concerned. At the same time they re-

flected the general consensus that, under present
conditions, priority must be given to the prevention
of international violence even if neither party to a
dispute considers that the status quo satisfies justice
and equity.(50)

I believe this basic philosophy of the organization has not been
seriously challenged by the practice in the decades following
this observation. Additional criteria which could very easily
be deduced from previous practice, include the following: (1)
the need to take steps to localize the conflict and prevent
outside powers from intervening in the conflict; (2) in respect
to conflicts predominantly of an internal character, it may be
reasonable to insist upon the need to secure from all elements
within the state an obligation to respect the minimum or basic
fundamental human rights such as avoidance of torture, mass
killings, or any other forms of gross violation of human
rights; and (3) it may not be possible for the organization to
strictly observe the principle of nonintervention in internal
matters when it is entrusted with responsibilities for
maintaining law and order.

The present and likely future contexts calling for external recognition and UN assistance - whether originating
within the UN framework or independently of it - are likely to
be limited to those conventional areas of military peacekeeping.
Policing the environment, monitoring the exploitation of seabed resources, supervising the processes of self-determination,
safeguarding the privacy of nation-states from interventions
from space - to name only a few possibilities - may entail quite
different types of peacekeeping functions. The general
principles of the Charter may take precedence over the consent of the parties to invoke UN assistance to legitimize their
actions when such actions appear to a substantial majority of
states to counter those general principles. For example, in
the Western Sahara situation, the secretary-general was reluctant to extend the support of the organization to certain
measures proposed by some of the parties involved, when
these measures appeared to him incompatible with the concept
of self-determination.(51)

Overall, the criteria for providing preventive military
assistance have thus been fairly well established in the
practice of the Security Council, although explicit Charter
provisions are seldom, if ever, cited each time the Council
makes arrangements for mounting a peacekeeping operation.
Nonetheless, the "contractual character" of UN assistance is
not disputed; the justification for extending such assistance
and the responsibility of member states to cooperate toward
that end are clearly recognized in the Charter.

What, then, appears to prevent an effective and timely
UN involvement in armed conflict situations are the perceptions

of the parties of the consequences of precisely those basic principles. These perceptions include their apprehension that any UN involvement is likely to alter the nature of the dispute; accord advantages to one side or the other that would not otherwise be forthcoming; tend to prolong the dispute indefinitely; or otherwise assume that resort to force can somehow offer a permanent solution in that context.

After nearly a half-century of debate, the United Nations was able to adopt an innocuous "definition of aggression." Nevertheless, it is now a well established principle that any territorial advantages gained by a state through resort to force cannot secure a valid legal title. Yet, this is not by itself sufficient to deter states from resorting to the use of armed force. Comparable norms of "international recognition" also operate in regard to domestic changes brought about by the use of force. It will be useful for the United Nations to reiterate these normative developments, if necessary in a formal convention or declaration, in order to complement Charter prescriptions governing the competence of the General Assembly as well as the Security Council for extending peacekeeping assistance whenever there are situations likely to threaten international peace and security.(52)

CONCLUSIONS

Though these observations are perhaps sketchy and impressionistic, requiring further elaboration, they point to the need for a new perspective designed to strengthen the role of the United Nations in the matter of promoting international peace and security goals. A new perspective is necessary because of the radically altered nature of the international system within which those goals have to be pursued. The Group of 77 has brought into global negotiations an Afro-Asian perspective and has redefined the purposes and goals of the United Nations as well as of the associated agencies, thus setting up a new image for the organization. No other earlier factors were able to influence world order goals to the same extent. Political independence, global equity and justice, as well as international security are today highly loaded concepts which carry special connotations. While there has been considerable success on the first and extensive debate to achieve progress on the second, virtually no attention has been given to the last item, namely, new approaches within the United Nations to promote international peace and security. The process of detente culminating in the Helsinki Accord occurred largely outside the United Nations. Moreover, it has only a regional appeal, in the sense of being primarily concerned with facilitating greater communication and understanding among the European states.

The urgency of the problem for the developing countries arises in part from escalating national investments in conventional armaments. The availability of effective, dependable, and responsive UN peacekeeping assistance is likely to be in the larger interests of these developing countries. The importance of UN peacekeeping assistance in contrast to imported armaments for improving national security goals requires further and more careful consideration.

Finally, there is need for norm-setting, or further policy clarification, to enable the General Assembly to play a useful role in respect to conflicts that are barred by the restrictions of article 2(7) or by benign indifference dictated in part by the political constraints of the time and place of conflict.

Once these major tasks are accomplished the political problem of achieving consensus in the Committee of 33 is likely to become that much easier. Lastly, despite its uncertainty and the voluntary character of funding, a peacekeeping operation mounted by the United Nations and supported by a wide spectrum of the General Assembly is most unlikely to suffer from lack of sufficient financial support.

I have ventured to indicate a probable future development for UN peacekeeping. In the multipolar power structure prevailing in present day international relations, naive as it might sound, the UN system is the only plausible alternative we now have to work with. Surely it is imperfect; it needs further strengthening; it must be supported by some independent source of finance; but it can be improved by providing UN-sponsored specialized training instruction to specially recruited national contingents; it can be operated on the basis of principles resting upon a widely shared consensus; and it can still remain not as a "permanent military force" but as an ad hoc mechanism capable of being pressed into service at shortest possible notice. All these and other related problems, so well canvassed by experts and documented in official publications, will be relevant only when the requisite consensus and agreement of the membership at large is sufficient enough to convince - not coerce - the potential disputants in a conflict situation that the introduction of a UN presence is beneficial to both and will not result in a situation compromising their respective rights and advantages.

The process of "convincing" to which I have alluded above can be a long and arduous one. There are very few areas of vital, nonnegotiable, national interests for any state today which do not, at the same time, involve elements possessing a crucial "international" dimension. The international features of such problems need not necessarily be seen to operate in a negative manner, foreclosing or compromising the vital national interests of the parties in conflict. The introduction of mutually advantageous joint or integrated approaches toward the organization, management, administration, or control of such situations, in ways that are likely to yield more net aggregate benefits to all parties involved in a dispute, will present them with conceptions of their problems and opportunities in a radically different perspective. I have mentioned elsewhere the example of the role of the World Bank in the Indus Waters Dispute between India and Pakistan.(53) Surely, in hindsight, it is possible to view this example as either exaggerating the potential for transnational cooperation (since the parties themselves are preeminently capable of working out such arrangements for themselves), or making it appear that this is in fact a success story. I am not disturbed even if these doubts are well placed. In fact, even if the Indus scheme has not become a workable proposition, I would still applaud the far-sightedness of the parties in devising such a scheme and the World Bank for the novel mediatory role it played. Another example suggested in this respect is the terms of settlement worked out in the Trieste situation.(54) Some such approaches were also known to have been envisaged in the peacemaking attempts or schemes actually suggested by the mediators in the Middle Eastern and other disputes.

The point I wish to emphasize here is that an effective peacekeeping role of the United Nations must generate renewed opportunities for mounting effective peacemaking attempts. The very fact that we put in place procedures to ensure the conflicting parties that UN peacekeeping is unlikely to favor one side at the expense of compromising the vital interests of the other will, in the long run, strengthen the attitude of warring nations toward seeking UN peacekeeping assistance.

NOTES

1. On the concept of collective responsibility, it is worthwhile to recall the interpretations of Charter principles offered by jurists. See McDougal and Feliciano, Law and Minimum World Public Order, Ch. 3, (1961); Julius Stone, Aggression and World Order, Ch. 9 (1958); Schwebel, "Aggression, Intervention and Self-Defense in Modern International Law," Recueil des Cours II (1972); Moore, "The Role of Law in the Management of Conflict" in Law and the Indo-China War (1972) pp. 8-46; contrast these perspectives with Falk, The Status of Law in International Society (1970) pp. 654-59; McDougal, "International Law and the Future," Mississippi Law Journal 50 (1979): 259-334 offers a comprehensive and systematic critique of some of the approaches cited above.

2. Introduction to the "Report of the Secretary-General on the Work of the Organization," DPI 41250, OPI 4/250, Sept. 1980.

3. A major study on the role of UN peacekeeping by Rikhye, Harbottle, and Egge, The Thin Blue Line: International Peacekeeping and its Future (New Haven: Yale University Press, 1974). For a comprehensive documentation on UN peacekeeping practice see Rosalyn Higgins, U.N. Peace-keeping vol. 3 (London: Oxford Press), The International Peace Academy's publication entitled Peacekeeper's Handbook (1978) offers the most succinct guidelines of a practical character (IPA, N.Y., 1978).

4. The Special Committee on Peacekeeping Operations (the Committee of 33) was established in 1965 for the purpose of a comprehensive review of "the whole question of peacekeeping operations." For a review of the activities of this committee see A. Cassese, "Recent Trends in the Attitude of the Super Powers Towards Peace-Keeping" in United Nations Peace Keeping: Legal Essays, ed. by A. Cassese, (1978) pp. 223–44; Raymond Sommereyns, "United Nations Peace-Keeping Forces in the Middle East," Brooklyn Journal of International Law 6 (Spring 1980): 1–54.

5. A widely shared assessment of the present role of the organization, recently echoed by Secretary-General Waldheim, has been that "The present range of activity of the Organization, encompassing great economic and social aims, humanitarian programmes, human rights concerns and global problems of universal interest is far wider and more comprehensive than anything envisaged at San Francisco." Introduction to the "Report of the Secretary-General on the Work of the Organization," SPI 4/250, September 1980.

6. The need to establish working mechanisms to monitor trends in the use of jointly shared resources whether on land, on sea areas, or outerspace at once reveals the possibilities for newer types of peacekeeping mechanisms to serve to preempt the occurrence of major conflicts. See in this respect Falk, "Settling Ocean Fishing Conflicts: The Limits of Law Reform in a Horizontal Legal Order," in Status of Law in International Society 3 (1970): 541; Carroz and Roche: "The International Policing of High Sea Fisheries," Canadian Y.B.I.L. 6 (1968) on pollution and boundary resources issues. See discussion in vol. 1 Canada-U.S. Law Journal pages 36–98 and 154–161 (1978). See also "Convention on the Prohibition of Military or Any Other Hostile Use of Environmental Weather Modification Techniques," Int'l Leg. Mat. 6 (18 May 1977) :589–94; Bourne, "Procedure and Mechanisms for Settlement of Disputes in the Development of International Drainage Basins," Canadian Y.B.I.L. (1972) pp. 212–34; Osgood and Hollick, New Era of Ocean Politics (1974).

7. Based on SIPRI statistics. Dr. Mark MacGuigan, the Canadian secretary of state for external affairs recently noted:

> Annual global military expenditures are now estimated
> to be $500 billion. This is equal to more than one
> billion dollars a day or, if you wish, almost a million
> dollars a minute. . . . As for developing coun-
> tries, they have about 50 percent of the world's
> population and account for only about 14 percent of
> the world's military expenditures, with China
> accounting for more than two-thirds of this. But
> while they appear small in the global context, the
> arms budgets of the developing countries loom much
> larger when compared to their limited resources and
> their urgent social and economic needs. Unfortun-
> ately the growth rate of these expenditures is
> running ahead of average world rates, and their
> share has risen from six percent ten years ago to
> fourteen percent today."

MacGuigan, "Disarmament and Development," Address to Parlia-
mentarians for World Order, 23 Sept. 1980.

8. See Ruth Russell and Jeanette E. Muther, A History of
the United Nations Charter. (Washington, D.C.: Brookings,
1958.)

9. Oscar Schachter, "The United Nations and Internal Conflict," in Dispute Settlement through the United Nations,
edited by K.V. Raman (1977) pp. 301-64; Falk (ed.), The
International Law of Civil War (1971).

10. This does not mean that the organization has not involved
itself in domestic conflicts. Obviously it does. But, its
ability to be seized of a situation is thwarted by this procedural impediment often reflected in the inability of the
secretary-general or of the Security Council to initiate consideration of a conflict. See Raman, Dispute Settlement
Through the United Nations (Oceana, 1977), pp. 384-97.

11. See Bowett, "United Nations Peace-Keeping," in The
Evolving United Nations, edited by Twitchett (1971), pp.
71-83. See also Miller, "Legal Aspects of the United Nations
Action in the Congo," Am. J.I.L. 55 (1961): 1-15.

12. Rosalyn Higgins described UN peacekeeping in formal
terms thus: "U.N. peacekeeping generally refers to operations
in which personnel owing allegiance to the United Nations are
engaged in military or para-military duties, and/or carrying
weapons for their own defence in the pursuit of duties
designated by the U.N. as necessary for the maintenance or
restoration of peace." Higgins, "United Nations Peacekeeping:
Past Lessons and Future Prospects," Lecture, Royal Institute
of International Affairs, London, 1977.

The objective of UN peacekeeping has been defined as: "the
prevention, containment, moderation and termination of hostil-

ities between or within States, through the medium of a peaceful third party intervention organized and directed internationally, using multinational forces of soldiers, police and civilians to restore and maintain peace," Peacekeeper's Handbook, s. 2 (1978).

13. Generally, the Status of Forces Agreements between the United Nations and the host countries spell out the detailed principles concerning the scope of the peacekeeping operations. See Dewast, "Quelques Aspects du Statut des 'Casques Bleus'," Revue Generale de Droit International Public 81 (1977): 1007-46. In reference to the establishment of UNEF operations, the secretary-general, drawing upon the consensus in the Committee of 33, outlined some general principles. See 29 U.N. GAOR, U.N. Doc. A/AC. 121/SR.63 (1974). See also James, "Recent Development in United Nations Peacekeeping," Year Book of World Affairs, 1977, pp. 87-88.

14. See generally Reisman, "Sanctions and Enforcement," in The Future of International Legal Order,, Vol. 3, (1971) pp. 273-335. On the scope of these sanctions at the domestic level see Note, "Namibia, South Africa and the Walvis Bay Dispute," Yale Law Journal 89 (1980): 903-22. See also Boggs and Paxman (eds.), United Nations: A Reassessment: Sanctions, Peacekeeping and Humanitarian Assistance, (1973).

15. See Repertory of Practice of United Nations Organs. Vol. 2, Suppl. No. 3, (1959-1966) pp. 224-35 (1971).

16. The developments concerning the operations of Cyprus peacekeeping forces (UNFICYP) are treated in Cassese, "Recent Trends in the Attitude of the Superpowers Towards Peacekeeping," pp. 223-44. See also J. Stegenga, The United Nations Force in Cyprus (1968).

17. L. Bloomfield, International Military Forces (1964); Burns and Heathcote, Peacekeeping by U.N. Forces: From Suez to Congo (1963); D.W. Bowett, "United Nations Peacekeeping."

18. I.C.J. Reports, 163 (1962). For a critque see Gross, "Expenses of the United Nations for Peacekeeping Operations" 1963, Int'l Org. 1 - 35. See also R. Simmonds, Legal Problems Arising From the United Nations Military Operations in the Congo (The Hague: 1968), pp. 96-130.

19. In the introduction to his annual report to the 27th session of the General Assembly, Secretary-General Waldheim observed:

The Secretary-General faces recurring dilemma whenever and wherever large-scale military conflict or civil strife within a State results in massive killings of innocent civilians. In the latter case, the Secretary-General has to reconcile Article 2, Paragraph 7 of the Charter with the moral principles, especially those concerning the sacredness of human life, which the Charter embodies. . . . [GAOR, 27th Session, Suppl. 1A (1973)].

If read with the attributed policy of the organization not to support "secession," this can create a bar for potentially dangerous domestic conflicts from ever coming before the UN organs for peaceful resolution. That "policy" has been attributed to a remark made by U Thant:

So, as far as the question of secession of a particular section of a Member State is concerned, the United Nations' attitude is unequivocal. As an international organization, the United Nations has never accepted and does not accept and I do not believe it will ever accept the principle of secession of a part of its (sic) Member State. [Secretary General U Thant's Press Conference, 7 U.N. Monthly Chronicle 36 (1970)].

20. By "guidelines" what is meant here is clarification of policies relevant to the initiation of international concern, exploration of fact-contingencies appropriate for invoking such concern, and the whole sequence of operations pertaining to the application of such policies in specific fact situations. For a useful earlier account of these aspects see Schachter, "The Relation of Law, Politics and Action in the United Nations," Hague Recueil 109 (1963).

21. 28 U.N. SCOR (1750th Meeting) U.N. Doc S/PV.1750 (1973) as quoted by Sommereyns, "United Nations Peacekeeping Forces in the Middle East," 18. See in this regard Kim, "The People's Republic of China and the Charter-Based International Legal Order," Am. Journal of Int'l Law 72 (1978): 334-35.

22. 33 U.N. SCOR, 3-4 and 3-11 (1978) U.N. Doc. S/PV.2091 and U.N. Doc. S/PV. 2074 at 12-13 and 18 (1978).

23. The role of consent of the parties and the supporting consensus of the major powers is well illustrated by the practice of UNEF-I and UNEF-II operations. For the 1979 discontinuance of UNEF-II operations see Sommereyns, "United Nations Peace Keeping Forces in the Middle East," pp. 47-53; on the previous UNEF-I withdrawal, see the secretary-general's report on the reasons for UNEF's withdrawal, S/9906 of 26 May 1967 and A/6730/Add. 3 of 26 June 1967.

24. Rosalyn Higgins, "United Nations Peacekeeping: Past Lessons and Future Prospects," The David Davies Memorial Lecture (London) 1971, page 6.

25. General Assembly Resolution 33/114 entitled "Comprehensive Review of the Whole Question of Peacekeeping Operations
in all Their Aspects" was adopted on 18 December 1978 by
106-19-11. See 33 U.N. GAOR, Suppl. (No. 45) 72. For the
Soviet and East European objections to certain of the principles
contained in the resolution, see U.N. Doc. A/33/PV. 87 at 89
(1978) and A/SPC/33/SR. 37 at 9-10 (1978).

26. Ibid., U.N. Doc A/33/PV.87 at 90 (1978).

27. On the role of the Assembly in these matters see Bowett,
"United Nations Peacekeeping"; Higgins, U.N. Peacekeeping;
and the IPA monograph on Namibia, IPA Reports (1978).

28. See in this regard Richard Barnett, "The Search for
National Security," New Yorker (April 27, 1981), p. 77.

> Once the purpose of military spending has become
> the creation of "perceptions" with weapons being
> bought primarily as symbols, there can never be
> enough of them. Once statesmen have been enticed
> into the hermetic world of war games, they lose
> touch with reality.

29. This kind of peacekeeping role is successfully used in the
supervision of jointly shared international river basin resources. See UN, "A Survey of Treaty Provisions for the
Pacific Settlement of International Disputes, 1949-1962," (New
York, U.N. sales No.: 66.V.5, 1962). Documentation of the
UN Water Conference of 1977 also contains useful information.
See for example, Judge Manner's Report from Finland (E/Conf.
70/TP 53 (1977) entitled "Experiences in Joint Administration
of Border Water Courses"; the Ganzes Waters Treaty
(Bangladesh-India) of 1977, in 17 International Legal Materials
103 (1978). See also Tariq Hasan, "Recent Developments," 19
Harvard Int'l L. Journal 708 (1978). In many instances,
these "mechanisms" or "procedures" are designed to serve the
functions of inquiry and fact-finding and offer advisory
assistance. In that capacity, agreement upon their establishment automatically helps to make those procedures
mandatory. In the political-security area, if there is sufficient
consensus on "the right to UN peacekeeping assistance," then
its use can be made conditional on the parties' willingness to
agree upon a binding peaceful method for resolution of their
differences in an expeditious manner.

30. See Raman, "The Ways of the Peace-Maker," UNITAR,
1975, Ch. 2, pp. 25-28.

31. Falk, The International Law of Civil War. Also on "The
Threat of War and U.S. Posturing" see his address to the 1981
session of the Canadian Council on International Law; Falk,

"Contending Approaches to World Order," Journal of Int'l Affairs 31 (1977).

32. See Margaret P. Doxey, Economic Sanctions and International Enforcement, (London, 1971); Galtung, J., "On the Effects of International Economic Sanctions, with Examples from the Case of Rhodesia," World Politics 19 (April 1967).

33. See "Negotiating the End of Conflicts: Namibia and Zimbabwe," I.P.A. Reports (1978). The debate in the Security Council during April 1981 on the subject of mandatory sanctions against South Africa highlights the sharp differences of opinion between the Western powers who vetoed the sanctions resolution and the African bloc which considered such a blanket approach to sanctions feasible in the ongoing dispute over Namibia.

34. For a useful discussion of the crucial legal problems which have arisen in connection with ONUC operations, see Simmonds, Legal Problems Arising from the United Nations Military Operations in the Congo.

35. See in this regard Higgins, "United Nations Peacekeeping 1946-1967," Documents and Commentary, Vol. 1, pp. 524-26.

36. See the useful analysis of James Jonah, "Peacekeeping in the Middle East," Int'l.J. 31 (1975-76); Sommereyns, "United Nations Peacekeeping Forces in the Middle East." Subsequent to the termination of the UNEF-II mandate, the parties to the Camp David Accords are reported to have agreed upon a joint United States, Israel, and Egypt peacekeeping mechanism to police the Israeli withdrawal from occupied territories and perform certain observational functions for some years after the withdrawal in those territories. See New York Times, October 8, 1979. Although such a system partakes some of the functions of UN peacekeeping, its status, terms of operation, functions, and scope of the authority of the peacekeepers on the spot may very well differ in considerable manner. The External Affairs Minister of Canada, for example, is reported to have experienced some misgivings concerning the participation of Canada, one of the most experienced countries in UN peacekeeping, on the ground that "we would be becoming involved in a process over which we would have no control and which may not be going anywhere," The Globe and Mail, June 9, 1981, p. 10. There are, however, indications of substantial European involvement in this US-Israel-Egypt venture. France, Italy, and other European powers are reported to have agreed to participate in it. See also Richard W. Nelson "Peacekeeping Aspects of the Egyptian-Israeli Peace Treaty and Consequences for United Nations Peacekeeping," Denver J.I.L. & Pol. 10 (1980): 113-53.

37. See Rosalyn Higgins, "The Advisory Opinion on Namibia: Which U.N. Resolutions Are Binding Under Article 25 of the Charter?" Int'l Comp. Law Quarterly 21 (1972): 270-86.

38. "Certain Expenses of the United Nations," I.C.J. Reports (1962): 151-80; see also Sohn, Cases on United Nations Law (1967) pp. 763-98 for detailed reports of the discussions within the various organs of the United Nations.

39. "Legal Consequences For States of the Continued Presence of South Africa in Namibia (South West Africa). Notwithstanding Security Council Resolution 276 (1970)." Advisory opinion, I.C.J Reports (1971), p. 16.

40. Sohn, "Conflict Management under the Law of the Sea Convention," unpublished paper prepared for the International Peace Academy's seminar on Peacekeeping in the Oceans, April 1977; and Oscar Schachter, "The Uses of Law in International Peacekeeping," Virginia Law Review 50 (1964): 1096-114.

41. Schachter, ibid.

42. On the establishment and functioning of UNIFIL in Lebanon see Henry Wiseman, "Lebanon The Latest Example of U.N. Peacekeeping Action," in International Perspectives (Ottawa, Canada) January 1979.

43. These include procedures for early warning of potentially explosive situations (e.g., the 1969-1970 World Bank predictions of impending social unrest in the then East Pakistan), global monitoring systems, confidence building procedures (as in the disarmament conventions), informal conciliation mechanisms (as envisaged in the Law of the Sea Draft Convention), and similar other devices. On Namibia, see "Negotiating the End of Conflicts," Report of the International Peace Academy [B. Rikhye ed.] (I.P.A., N.Y. 1980).

44. See Raman, "The Ways of the Peacemaker," p. 23; also M.S. Rajan, The United Nations and Domestic Jurisdiction, (1958). On the UN practice concerning article 2(7), see U.N. Repertory of Practice of U.N. Organs, Vol. 1, pp. 55-159.

45. See "Weapons of Peace: How New Technology Can Revitalize Peacekeeping," Report No. 8, International Peace Academy (N.Y.), (1980).

46. See Sommereyns, "United Nations Peacekeeping Forces in the Middle East," pp. 47-52.

47. See Bowett, "United Nations Peacekeeping."

48. 1962 Yemen situation is cited by Higgins, "United Nations Peacekeeping: Past and Future," p. 7; on the matter of the establishment and operation of UN Yemen Observer Mission (UNYOM) see Higgins, U.N. Peacekeeping, Vol. 1, pp. 609-69.

49. There are no dependable objective and authoritative mechanisms to alert public opinion to impending threats to global public order before they actually erupt in violence and loss of human life. At a very nascent level, such a role can usefully be performed by the secretary-general, for example, through his annual introduction to his report to the General Assembly on the "State of the UN" as it were. As it stands, neither the format nor the effort that goes into its preparation are adequate to meet those needs. See in this respect Lasswell, Snyder, and Hermann, "A Global Monitoring System: Appraising the Effects of Government on Human Dignity," Am. Pol. Science Review, 1975.

50. See Schachter, "The Uses of Law in International Peacekeeping," p. 1105.

51. On the Western Sahara situation, see SA/SM/2308 and its treatment in Raman, Dispute Settlement, pp. 91-92.

52. At various times, the General Assembly has directed its attention to improving the procedures of the Charter for peaceful resolution of disputes although nothing concrete has emerged by way of institutional or structural development. See, for example, the various proposals outlined in the "Report of the Special Committee on the Charter of the United Nations and on the Strengthening of the Role of the Organization," GAOR, 33rd session, Suppl. No. 33, (A/33/33) pages 63-74 (1978).

53. Eugene R. Black, "The Indus: A Moral for Nations," N.Y. Times Magazine, 11 December 1960. See also Wilkes "New Emphasis and Techniques for International Law - The Case of the Boundary Dispute," Western-Reserve Law Rev. 15 (1964): 623-40.

54. See John C. Campbell, "The Trieste Negotiations of 1954: An Example of Successful Negotiation," (1973).

16
Peacekeeping: A Component of World Order
Alastair M. Taylor

The stark and inescapable fact is that today we cannot defend our society by war, since total war is total destruction, and if war is used as an instrument of policy, eventually we will have total war. Therefore, the best defence of peace is not power, but the removal of the causes of war, and international agreements which will put peace on a stronger foundation than the terror of destruction. . . . The grim fact, however, is that we prepare for war like precocious giants and for peace like retarded pygmies. . . .

Lester B. Pearson (Acceptance of the Nobel Prize for Peace, 1957)

OUR ANARCHICAL INTERNATIONAL SOCIETY

Let us suppose that you have been offered a new job in another community and, in order to help come to a decision, you check on its size and vital statistics. You find that of its some 450,000 inhabitants, more than 25,000 children have no schools; 57,000 persons are undernourished and hungry; 80,000 adults are illiterate; 103,000 inhabitants live in substandard housing (with a high proportion having neither clean drinking water nor sewerage); 130,000 receive less than $90 annual income; 150,000 have no access to adequate medical care; and 170,000 can expect to die before the age of 60. Meanwhile, however, the city is spending $50,000,000 annually on purchasing weapons and maintaining its police force.(1) Question: are you likely to accept the new job?

402

Actually, the question is irrelevant, because you live already in such a community, albeit one 10,000 times the size of our example since it is of global dimensions. Given these statistics, coupled with the still increasing gap between the rich industrial countries of the "North" and the poor nations of the "South" and the latter's demand for a New International Economic Order, as well as the mounting political tensions resulting from the energy crisis and competition for other resources unevenly distributed on our planet, the prospects for a quiet passage to the end of the century appear to be minimal. Moreover, at a time when the winds of change blowing across the Third World threaten to increase to gale proportions, the First and Second Worlds are engaged in the most expensive and lethal arms race in history. In June 1980, the United Nations secretary-general quantified his warning of the perils of this accelerating competition by pointing out that the sovereign states of the world were spending a million dollars a minute on armaments and "defense" - which works out at more than $500 billion annually.

This is our world in 1980. Upwards of 40 percent of its scientific and technological manpower is working on military and related projects which, given the open-ended dynamics of science, fail to provide us with some fail-safe guarantee of either national or collective security. Instead, our political decision makers and defense strategists play the role of acrobats on a high-wire act called the "balance of terror."

What has been happening to out nation-state system? Has it remained basically unaltered in structure and behavior over the centuries, or has it undergone an evolutionary transformation? If, to use Hedley Bull's term, we continue to line in an "anarchical society," to what extent is such a society capable of transforming its political institutions so as to be able to cope with an accelerating change in the nature and conduct of warfare? Our inquiry begins by putting these questions in an historical context.

THE INTERNATIONAL POLITICAL ENVIRONMENT: TRADITIONS AND PARADIGMS

In 1648, when European princes and diplomats gathered at Westphalia to sign a peace treaty ending the Thirty Years' War, they declared that the Holy Roman Empire could no longer extend its dominion into the territories of princes, and that the latter were in no way obliged to respond to the emperor's directives. "This act symbolized the emergence of the modern European nation-state system, replacing the feudal political order, which . . . had at least theoretically placed an emperor as head, with power radiating down through such lesser political entities as free cities, duchies, and developing dynastic territories."(2)   Consequently, for more than three centuries, "sovereign states have been the important political organizations in the global system. . . .   Their pre-eminence has not gone unchallenged, and there are good reasons to believe that this particular kind of organization is outmoded, that it will not allow mankind to deal with problems that become more serious as the twenty-first century approaches."(3) Nevertheless, because of this preeminence of sovereign polities today, we may find it useful to trace briefly the evolution of the nation-state system to understand its significance today.

The "Logic of Westphalia"

The nation-state system is based on what has been described as the "logic of Westphalia."(4)   Gone is the medieval metaphysical assumption of a superordinate authority possessing ultimate sovereignty derived presumably from God.   The new metaphysical construct ascribes to all states equality of juridical authority, i.e., each possesses illimitable sovereignty. Hence, all states are equal in status, if not in stature.   (To paraphrase Orwell's Animal Farm, while all states are equal, some are more equal than others - as the permanent members of the Security Council can attest.)   In addition to sovereignty, all nation-states share the following essential elements: a defined territory; a permanent population; an organized government; and recognition by other nation-states (and hence a capability to engage in foreign relations).

This juridical equality is shared by a behavioral one-to-one correspondence (isomorphism).   Thus, all sovereign states claim the right to conduct both their domestic affairs and their relations with other governments free from external interference - so that we see the claim of unfettered domestic jurisdiction enshrined as article 2(7) in the United Nations Charter.   Another behavioral isomorphism is the penchant to seek to resolve problems unilaterally wherever self-described "vital interests" are concerned - and, if necessary, to resort to the ultima ratio, i.e., the threat or actual use of physical force.

But, despite these one-to-one juridical and behavioral correspondences, the logic of Westphalia provides no parallel correspondence among nation-states as regards their physical dimensions and capabilities.   While China has a population of some 900 million or more, that of Sao Tome and Principe - admitted to United Nations membership in 1975 - is around 70,000.   And though the Soviet Union and Lebanon both qualify as sovereign states, the former's political space amounts to 8.6 million square miles, while the latter has to be content with only 3,400 square miles.   Demographic and spatial dissimilarities are matched by vast disparities in economic resources, levels of technological advancement, gross national product, popular education and literacy, location in earth-space, and climatic advantages or constraints - in short, all the variables that can make factual absurdity out of juridical equality. Because the metaphysical assumptions underlying the nation-state system fail to draw any correspondence between status and stature, the "logic of Westphalia" runs afoul of reality - the reality of the international political environment perceived as a global extension of Orwell's Animal Farm.

Three Traditions in Political Philosophy

According to Martin Wight and Hedley Bull, three traditions of thought have competed throughout the history of the nation-state system.(5) From the work of the English philosopher Thomas Hobbes we derive the realist tradition. Here, international society is regarded as one of anarchy without any overarching set of rules. In the Hobbesian view, since conflict is natural to the human condition, conduct among nations is based in turn upon continuous competition and conflict. War is the most typical international activity, and peace represents a period of recuperation from the previous conflict and preparation for the next. Each state's interests exclude those of all other states, and war is perceived (in game theory) as zero-sum: one side wins, the other loses. In this view of political reality - held by Kantilya in ancient India, by Machiavelli in Renaissance Italy, and by Hobbes and his "realist" successors since early modern times - while ideas of morality and law are valid in the domestic sphere of a state, they do not apply outside its boundaries. The only rules which should circumscribe the behavior of states with one another are those of prudence or expediency - which determine, in turn, whether agreements are to be kept or broken.

The second - or internationalist - tradition derives from the writings of natural-law thinkers such as Hugo Grotius. While regarding sovereign states as the principal reality - and actors - in international politics, "the Grotians contend that states are not engaged in simple struggle, like gladiators in an arena, but are limited in their conflicts with one another by common rules and institutions. . . . The particular international activity which . . . best typifies international activity as a whole is neither war between states, nor horizontal conflict cutting across the boundaries of states, but trade or, more generally, economic and social intercourse between one country and another."(6) In the Grotian tradition, states in their dealings with one another are bound by the rules and institutions of the international society which they form, as

"LOGIC OF WESTPHALIA"

(HEDLEY BULL)   (TAYLOR)

Three Traditions of   Three Geopolitical
Political Thought   Paradigms

1 HOBBES ←——→ PTOLEMAIC (16th-17th Century)

2 GROTIUS ←—→ COPERNICAN (18th-19th Century)

3 KANT ←————→ FORCE FIELD (20th-21st Century?)

[1st & 2nd Paradigms: Two-Valued Logic-"Either/or";
Game Theory: zero-sum

3rd Paradigm: Multi-Relational Logic-"Both-and";
Game Theory: non-zero-sum]

Fig. 16.1   Logic of Westphalia

well as by the rules of prudence or expediency. The imperatives of morality and law call for "acceptance of the
requirements of coexistence and cooperation in a society of
states."(7)

Farthest from the Hobbesian tradition is the universalist
view propounded by Immanuel Kant and his modern successors.
Here, the "central reality" in international politics is not the
system of states but, rather, "community of mankind," sus-
tained by moral imperatives. These call for the limiting of
actions by nations and the introduction of a truly cosmopolitan
society. To this end, the higher morality requires subordina-
tion of the pretensions and interests of states, including their
claims to sovereignty and right of independent action and
implementation of self-avowed national objectives. The Kantian
tradition, then, enjoins not simply coexistence and cooperation
among states but the progressive replacement of the state
system by a global society. In this new society, the
war/peace equation is perceived in non-zero-sum terms: in war
everyone loses whereas peaceful enterprise enables all peoples
to profit.

Three Geopolitical Paradigms (Models)

As the logic of Westphalia attests, the surface of our planet is
divided into segments of politically organized space. In effect,
the earth's habitat has been fragmented into political and
economic property containers. Because the human family is

separated into exclusive political communities, each possesses its particular body of loyalties and prejudices, together with a predilection to view its values and objectives as superior to others. The logic of Westphalia recognizes states as being the only subjects in international law. Also, it has the effect of supporting (or, again, opposing) pretensions to sovereignty and independence by recourse to coercion by means of physical force, a course of action with broad implications for the geopolitical environment.

In seeking to explain the evolution of the nation-state system within earth-space, it may not be amiss for us to provide a series of paradigms (or conceptual models) that are roughly analogous to the models which scientists have advanced to explain the behavior of stellar planetary bodies in the space that envelops our solar system. Whether we are regarding the nation-state system as it operates in our planet's space, or the solar system functioning in outer space, the models which human minds construct in all cases reflect a specific perspective. Moreover, as with science, we have to shift from one paradigm to another as our knowledge of the evidence increases and our understanding improves. In other words, when the given "system" is shown to be more complex than we had originally understood, we have to employ new criteria and assume a different perspective in order to reinterpret the system's behavior. This is especially true in the case of the nation-state system which is dynamic and continually undergoing complexification and societal transformation.

The Ptolemaic Paradigm

As anyone familiar with even a brief introduction to the history of science knows, Ptolemy is associated with the geocentric theory of celestial mechanics, namely, that the earth is the center of the universe with all other bodies revolving around it. In our first geopolitical paradigm, the individual nation-state is perceived as the primary actor, one that emphasizes ethnocentrism in culture, politics, economics (such as mercantilism and other forms of autarchy), and positivist international law, the doctrine which "teaches that international law is the sum of the rules by which states have consented to be bound, and that nothing can be law to which they have not consented."(8) In other words, by this paradigm - which most closely approximates the logic of Westphalia - each nation-state regards itself not only as completely independent but as acting in an essentially hostile geopolitical environment. Moreover, it regards itself as the center of the political environment, surrounded by other states which it assesses from the standpoint of its claim to unfettered sovereignty, priorities of vital interests, and power capability.

We are dealing here with the tradition of Machiavelli and, especially, Hobbes who viewed polities as akin to discrete political atoms inevitably bound on collision courses. In this paradigm, power is amassed to gain unilaterally defined objectives, and subordinate other states (ideally, from the standpoint of this paradigm, to make them "satellites"). The geopolitical strategy calls for extending spatial perimeters and acquiring materials and human resources, such as through territorial annexation and overseas dependencies.

While our three geopolitical models should not be regarded as existing in watertight chronological compartments, the Ptolemaic paradigm prevailed during the genesis and early development of the nation-state system. State power was gradually strengthened and centralized among the members of the system, the dominant type of state structure being absolute monarchy, so that foreign relations were conducted largely by sovereigns themselves, often because of personal or dynastic rivalries. The main features of the nation-state system at this time have been described as "dispersed territorial competition among emergent state structures," the existence of "variable frontiers," and the fact that there "were no truly international institutions," so that "the only regulating factor in the system was the resistance of other states to the dominance of the most powerful, first Spain and then France."(9)

The Copernican Paradigm

As we know, the Ptolemaic geocentric model of celestial mechanics was superseded by Copernicus's heliocentric model which placed the sun at the center and relegated our planet to the perimeter. Still more importantly, it conceived of the relationships and behavior of the sun and its planets as a "system" (which may be defined as "a whole functioning as such by virtue of the relations of its parts"). In this system, as Newton in turn demonstrated, gravitational forces acted upon all the comprising parts so as to create specific relationships among them. In our second geopolitical paradigm, the concept of a "system" - nascent in its predecessor - becomes fully established. The nation-states remain primary actors with relative automony, but now they have also to exist as sovereign polities consciously interconnected and interacting with other such polities so as to maintain an overall equilibrium within the global political system. Not only must there be the progressive recognition of other nation-states but a greater willingness to find accommodations for mutual benefit.

The Copernican geopolitical model became fully established and operative during the eighteenth and nineteenth centuries. Prior to the Congress of Vienna, some ten major units - France, Great Britain, Austria, Prussia, Russia, Sweden,

Spain, Portugal, Poland, and Turkey - dominated the system, marked by "the relatively even distribution of diplomatic influence and military capabilities."(10)   As these political units became more organized and contacts (of a peaceful and warlike character alike) between them were more firmly established, the system itself became increasingly institutionalized. This is apparent, for example, in the sphere of diplomacy. Previously, the affairs of one state impinged only infrequently on the interests of another, so that diplomatic procedures comprised a disjointed code that resulted in confusion with respect to precedence and protocol.   But the eighteenth and nineteenth centuries saw the growth of multilateral diplomacy and ad hoc multilateral conferences, as well as the classification of diplomatic agents and the formalization of their functions.   The Copernican paradigm further institutionalized foreign policy procedures and activities, as well as developed the norms of international commerce.   And, because of its concern in maintaining an overall geopolitical equilibrium, it activated the concept of "balance of power" - which by means of alliances sought to prevent any one state or congeries of state from dominating the international environment.

That the advent of major alliances in the latter part of the last century failed to prevent - but instead contributed to - the outbreak of World War I can be largely attributed to certain developments which altered fundamentally the structure and processes of international politics.   One was the rise of nationalism.   This was seen in numerous movements for national independence, and the use by governments of mass public involvement to increase diplomatic and military bargaining capabilities such as by instituting conscription.   Another nineteenth century development was the rise of ideological principles as a major factor in foreign policy behavior. "Thus, many of the conflicts within Europe during the nineteenth century were fought in a context of the incompatible values represented by French revolutionary republicanism and royal legitimacy and conservatism.   In this century, different and incompatible images of a world order have derived from the doctrines of nazism, communism, and liberal democracy."(11)   A third development was the application of science and technology to warfare, exponentially increasing both the mobilization and destruction of human and physical resources (as is demonstrated below by Quincy Wright).   Like the Ptolemaic paradigm, the Copernican model was based upon the principle of zero-sum - in this case, by permitting individual national actors to win or lose while maintaining an overall geopolitical equilibrium - but the dynamics of mass mobilization and behavior coupled with nuclear science were to vitiate this hope.

The Copernican paradigm is not only compatible with, but the exemplification of, the Grotian political tradition.   As

Hedley Bull points out, "the Grotian idea of international society has always been present in thought about the states system" - although it has undergone "metamorphoses" as a result of the transformation from "Christian international society" in the fifteenth-seventeenth centuries into a "European international society" in the eighteenth-nineteenth centuries, and now into a "World international society" in our own century.(12)

The Force Field Paradigm

Our third geopolitical paradigm is strongly analogous to a major development in modern scientific theory. The Copernican model of celestial mechanics culminated in the Newtonian synthesis, in which space, time, and matter each existed separately. Space by itself was independent and empty; time was also independent and absolute; while matter inhabited these two forms of extension but did not affect them. In short, the world was envisaged as composed of particles poised in a void. However, attempts in the last century to understand electromagnetism in terms of the classic notions of forces acting between particles gave rise to a new concept - that of the "field." (Clerk Maxwell worked out the equations determining the structure of the electromagnetic field.) As field physics developed, attention shifted from the particles per se to a concentration upon the field filling the space between them. "In the new field language," we learn from Einstein and Infeld, "it is the description of the field between the two charges, and not the charges themselves, which is essential for an understanding of their action."(13) In time, the distinction between particles (or waves) and field was to disappear altogether.(14) In the field model, space is not a void but a plenum, and no part of the physical universe remains unaffected by the field. The concept gives rise to a more unified picture of the material world, in which every particle "becomes involved with every other in a complex of overlapping fields." In short, every particle "is the center" of gravitational and other fields, whose limits cannot be sharply drawn, and which "modify the physical environment of every other particle."(15)

Twentieth century science and technology are thus chiefly responsible for our Force Field geopolitical paradigm. While quantum mechanics and relativity theory revolutionized our concepts of the basic nature of space, time, and matter, technology effects no less a revolution in transportation and communications. Networks have been created which are global in scope and operate within a sociospatial plenum - a planetary sociocultural force field in which societal "particles" everywhere are being acted upon and modified by whatever is transpiring elsewhere. In addition to transportation and

communications, two other advancements have revolutionized
our geopolitical environment. Whereas in the Ptolemaic and
Copernican paradigms, sovereignty was conceptualized and
juridically formalized in terms of a two-dimensional environment
- that of "flat earth" - the exploits of the Wright brothers and
their successors have given us a three-dimensional environmental control capability. What does the extensibility into the
inner space of our ocean beds and outer space of Mariner
taking photographs of Saturn and Neptune do to the traditional
encapsulation of sovereignty in national space containers?
Similarly, military technology has taken a quantum leap in its
destructive capability because of the advent of the nuclear
age. In effect, this development has radically altered - and
even rendered paradoxical - the concept of power as deployed
and justified in the Ptolemaic and Copernican paradigms.

Even as every physical particle is the center of a gravitational or electromagnetic field, so every societal entity
comprises a center in the geopolitical force field. This is
illustrated by contrasting traditional with contemporary
cartographical projections. In the Copernican paradigm,
coexisting with the period of European hegemony, the Mercator
projection (the presentation par excellence of two-dimensional
"flat space") placed Europe in the center of the map, so that
Europeans regarded easterly-lying regions as the "Near East,"
"Middle East," and "Far East." But in today's world, such
ethnocentric terms become progressively anachronistic: there
can be no single fixed, or central, position. Furthermore,
given the need in our air age to take account of the earth's
curvature, the Mercator projection has been superseded by
more appropriate projections, such as the polar azimuthal
equidistant (incidentally, the projection employed in the United
Nations' official symbol).(16)

Moreover, in keeping with force field actualities wherein
every particle comprises the center, so that it modifies and is
in turn modified by every other particle in the field, our new
political paradigm has to take account of all phenomena interacting in the global environment. This is a crucial innovation
because it is no longer possible to regard nation-states as the
only actors in the geopolitical environment, nor can they claim
to be the only subjects in international law. A host of new
actors has entered upon the international stage. Our century
has been notable for both the globalization of the nation-state
system - so that the original United Nations membership has
tripled since 1945, primarily as a consequence of decolonization
in the Third World - and the advent of a transnational network
of intergovernmental and nongovernmental organizations.
The proliferation of IGOs and NGOs is a phenomenon of the
last hundred years, and markedly since World War II. As of
1981, 337 IGOs were in existence; of the global organizations,
the most important consisted of the United Nations and Spe-

cialized Agencies, while the European Community headed the
regional intergovernmental groupings. Meanwhile, the NGOs
outnumber the IGOs by a ratio of some 12.7:1 and serve the
purpose of creating transnational networks in literally all fields
of human endeavor.(17). And, whereas in the Copernican
paradigm, multilateral conferences were of an ad hoc character
(primarily for dealing with terms of peace after major wars),
today we have the concept of permanent multilateral conference
diplomacy institutionalized in the UN and its Specialized
Agencies – while multilateral diplomacy also occurs constantly
in thousands of ad hoc conferences and less formal international gatherings. ("During the nineteenth century, for
example, the American government sent diplomatic representatives to 100 conferences, or an average of one per year; in
the period 1956-1958, American diplomats, specialists, and
politicians attended 1,027 international conferences, an average
of one conference per day."(18))

Meanwhile, yet another type of actor has come to occupy
the international geopolitical and geoeconomic stage: the
multinational corporation. It may be incorporated in the state
of Delaware, but its activities cut across national boundaries,
and its perceptions and loyalties are scarcely constrained by
the logic of Westphalia. That this is a phenomenon of our
century is illustrated by the increase of foreign manufacturing
subsidiaries of 187 U.S. controlled multinational enterprises:
from 46 in 1901 to 618 in 1929, and to 2,831 in 1967.(19) By
1979, there were 4,300 American corporations that controlled
more than 16,500 foreign business enterprises.(20) When the
gross annual sales of corporations are compared with the GNPs
of nation-states, we find that many of the largest economic
units in the world are not states but corporations.(21) ("In
these terms, General Motors is larger than Argentina, the Ford
Motor Company out-classes Hungary, and Royal Dutch Shell is
more important than Turkey."(22)) Nor is there much doubt
that the MNCs are progressively influencing the global political
as well as economic order – as in the efforts by one of them to
overthrow the Allende government in Chile, and their continuing impacts upon developing countries. The latter in turn are
calling for the regulation and supervision of MNC activities as
part of their own strategy for creating a New International
Economic Order – a concept which is much more in keeping
with the Force Field than the Copernican paradigm.(23)

From what has been already suggested, the Force Field
geopolitical paradigm can be correlated with the third
philosophical tradition in political theory: the Kantian or
universalist. To Kant, because rational nature exists as an
end in itself, it follows as a "categorical imperative" that every
human being must never be treated as a means to be arbitra-
rily used but as an end in himself.(24) This can be
interpreted that all men should count equally in determining

actions by which many are affected. And in <u>Perpetual Peace</u> (1795), he argued that reason utterly condemns war, which only an international government can prevent. In effect, every person is a subject with his or her own "center," and the concept of a global human society must supersede the tradition of disparate warring states.

But, at this point, we must recognize that the nation-state system has embraced the Hobbesian and Grotian philosophical traditions - not as yet the Kantian. And which of our three geopolitical paradigms most closely matches the realities of our contemporary sociocultural environment? We have shown that science and technology have created a sociocultural field that is global in its dimensions and which affects every aspect of our lives. Also, that within this field new actors - such as IGOs and MNCs - have to be taken account of increasingly by the traditional nation-state actors. But the Force Field geopolitical paradigm has not been recognized formally, that is, in terms of the creation of new political institutions and juridical norms such as would be required to supersede the traditional nation-state system. Instead, we are still wedded to the Grotian tradition and the Copernican paradigm - which are not "international" in the sense of reflecting an emerging global society, but more precisely are "inter-national" (inter-state) in their structure and modes of behavior. In effect, the last half of the twentieth century finds us in a state of profound <u>culture lag</u> in which science and technology are propelling us acceleratively to function within a planetary environment, but to try to do so with political and juridical institutions which evolved within a geopolitical environment that was two-dimensional in space, prenuclear in power, and prerelativistic in its worldview. Because of this culture lag, we must designate our present era as a transitional stage between two paradigms. And it is this transitional stage which, inter alia, accounts for both the emergence of peace-keeping as an ad hoc instrument in the war/peace equation, and its current institutional and behavioral shortcomings.

THE COPERNICAN PARADIGM AND THE WAR/PEACE EQUATION

In his study of warfare, Quincy Wright found that, since the Renaissance, (1) it is the fighting propensity of the great states which has primarily increased; (2) the size of armed forces has grown both absolutely and in proportion to the population; (3) there has been an increase in the length of conflicts, the number of battles in a war year, and in the total number of battles during a century - with the intensity of warfare reaching unprecedented proportions in the twentieth century; (4) there has been an increase in the number of belligerents in a war, in the rapidity with which a war spreads, and in the area covered by a war - World Wars I and II involved all sections of Europe, the Near East, the Far East, Africa, and the waters of the Atlantic and the Pacific; and (5) the human and economic costs of war have been soaring, both absolutely and relative to the population. The total deaths from military action and war-related disease attributable to World War I have been estimated as over 40 million, a figure which increased to more than 60 million in World War II. Moreover, a consensus exists that a third world war fought with nuclear weapons would introduce a new magnitude of destruction and cost in warfare.

> These trends of war have been related to the ideological, economic, social, and political trends of modern civilization. The acceleration of technological and social change in the modern world, the more rapid geographical diffusion of ideas and methods, the increasing economic and political interdependence of separated areas, the growth of population and standards of living, the rise of public opinion and popular initiative in politics, have together tended to concentrate military activity in time and to extend it in space; to make it less easy to begin, to localise, and to end; to make it appear psychologically more catastrophic and less rational; to make it more difficult for any state to isolate itself from militarization in time of peace and from hostilities in time of war once the controls of international law and organization have been successfully defied.(25)

As we noted in the Hobbesian and Grotian traditions, the nation-state system is based upon the correlative attributes of "sovereignty" and "power." Only states can be sovereign, and they possess the right to define unilaterally their self-prescribed vital interests and to pursue them by peaceful or warlike means. In the Copernican paradigm, we saw the institutionalization of diplomatic behavior and procedures, the employment of balance-of-power techniques, and the aggregation of power by means of alliances. Both the aggregation of power and use of alliances are designed to win wars, i.e., the war/peace equation is conceived and justified in terms of "zero-sum," so that, while there is a winner and a loser, their respective gains and losses permit the international system to retain an overall equilibrium. But, since the concepts of sovereignty and power were formulated to function both physically and politically within an environment of boundaried two-dimensional space, the attempted application of these concepts to an open-ended three-dimensional environment

encounters understandable difficulties, indeed logical con-
tradictions.

Although the United Nations qua IGO is one of the new
transnational actors - and as such could be regarded as an
institutional forerunner of an emerging supranational system -
it is both the product and mechanism of the Copernican
paradigm. Interestingly, the preamble of the Charter
proclaims the Kantian vision, but the substantive articles make
abundantly clear that the purpose of the organization is to
operate within the Grotian philosophy (and with the Charter
also recognizing the tendencies of states to indulge in
Hobbesian proclivities). And though, despite the Copernican
emphasis upon positivist international law, IGOs have had to
be accorded a juridical personality, the United Nations was of
course accorded neither of the attributes central to the
Copernican paradigm. The refusal to grant it either sovereignty or coercive powers of its own can scarely be ascribed
to a belief in 1945 that such powers would be superfluous. As
one diplomat remarked during a debate in the organization's
early days, the United Nations was not founded as a "gentle-
men's club" but as a "reformatory." In fact, from its genesis,
the United Nations has been the forum of three interrelated
types of conflicts:

- Ideological (East-West rivalry)
- Colonial (struggle for political independence)
- Haves verses Have-nots (the North-South
  economic struggle)

Meanwhile, this century's sanguinary history makes abundantly
clear that, while the Hobbesian-Ptolemaic world view unabash-
edly embraced the dual primacy of the individual state and
recourse to war, the Grotian-Copernican interpretation of the
logic of Westphalia - as embodied in Bull's phrase "anarchical
society" - has been no more successful in tipping the societal
scales in the direction of peace. Here, we need only briefly
update Quincy Wright's study to prove our argument. Nations
now spend annually on arms an amount exceeding the value of
the world's entire output in 1900 (measured in constant
dollars); this equals the present value of the GNP of all Latin
American and African countries combined. As President Carter
told the United Nations in 1976, "the nations of the world
spent more than 60 times as much equipping each soldier as we
did educating each child." While six countries account for
about 75 percent of world military spending, for nations with
the poorest 20 percent of the world population, the military
share of GNP rose from 1.9 percent in 1960 to 3.2 percent in
1976, a burden out of all proportion for peoples with yearly
incomes averaging $124 and the slowest growth rate in the
world.

Between 1960 and 1980...the annual per capita
income of the poorest fifth of the (world) population
advanced about $54; for the richest fifth, the gain
averaged $4,224." (By contrast), "at 1980 levels of
per capita income, military outlays represented 143
million man-years of income in developing countries
and 50 million in developed.(26)

When the SALT talks began in 1969, the United States
and U.S.S.R. possessed, in all, fewer than 3,000 strategic
nuclear-missile warheads; by 1982 they had some 51,000 deliv-
erable strategic-missile warheads. An estimated 40 percent of
all research and development spending is now devoted to
military purposes. According to one expert, if all arms-
control negotiations held under SALT, the General Disarmament
Conference, and the mutual force reduction talks at Vienna
were to succeed in their objectives, it would not result in
significantly slowing down the arms race. "The slow pace of
disarmament negotiations lags far behind the speed of
advancing technology. The world is on the verge of a new
technology explosion in both nuclear and conventional
weaponry, and nuclear proliferation and possible nuclear
terrorism loom as increasing threats."(27) One example of this
"new technological explosion" was disclosed in August 1980 by
the United States Defense Department: its "stealth technology"
is expected to enable bombers, fighters, and cruise missiles to
penetrate any present or future air defenses, thereby inau-
gurating a new phase of military escalation.

Given the open-ended dynamics of science coupled with a
paranoia generated by the Hobbesian predilection to abort
periodic attempts at detente, the system's efforts to ensure
security creates its opposite. As Waldheim has pointed out,
the arms race not only reflects world tension but aggravates
that tension in turn. The paradox is compounded by SALT
and other arms agreements because they serve to legitimize the
proliferation of weapons, since the ceilings are set higher than
the actual number of arms existing at the time. As regards
the counterproductivity of the current arms race, we are
content to abide by the summation from General Eisenhower:

Every gun that is made, every warship launched,
every rocket fired signifies, in the final sense, a
theft from those who hunger and are not fed, those
who are cold and are not clothed. This world in
arms is not spending money alone. It is spending
the sweat of its laborers, the genuis of its scientists, the hopes of its children.(28)

Actually, in this century, the Copernican geopolitical construct
has been on the defensive.

On the one hand, the Hobbesian or realist interpretation of international politics has been fed by
the two World Wars, and by the expansion of
international society beyond its originally European
confines. On the other hand, Kantian or universalist interpretations have been fed by a striving to
transcend the states system so as to escape the
conflict and disorder that have accompanied it in this
century, and by the Russian and Chinese revolu-
tions, which have given a new currency to doctrines
of global transnational solidarity, both communist and
anti-communist. Ideas of international society in the
twentieth century may be said to be closer to those
that were entertained in the early centuries of the
states system than to those that prevailed in the
eighteenth and nineteenth centuries.(29)

THE FORCE FIELD PARADIGM AND THE
WAR/PEACE EQUATION

Unlike the Copernican geopolitical paradigm, the Force Field
model relates (as we have seen) to three-dimensional global
space in which many actors in addition to nation-states are
assuming progressively significant roles. These cut across
compartmentalized national territory, so that all this unprecedented interaction, coupled with a quantum leap in military
destructive potency, means that any major conflict must have
non-zero-sum results for belligerents and non-belligerents alike
in a biosphere which could be radioactively contaminated. For
our part, we maintain that the logic of Westphalia has become
in our century the illogic of Westphalia. The Copernican
geopolitical paradigm must be progressively superseded by its
Force Field successor. To make this possible, the nation-state
system itself will have to undergo a profound attitudinal and
institutional transformation.
        To be specific, why? Because the agendas of the United
Nations organs and the Specialized Agencies provide irrefutable
proof that the critical problems confronting the human family,
and the continuing viability of the planet's biosphere, are
transnational in their dimensions and impact, and therefore
must be addressed in the context of a global system of
interacting human and material factors. These problems - con-
flictual in their implications - are inscribed on IGO agendas
precisely because, in the first place, they cannot be solved in
terms of the Ptolemaic paradigm, i.e., by unilateral national
action. And so far, they have eluded solution in terms of the
Copernican paradigm, i.e., by any one group of states acting
transnationally so as to try to reach mutual accommodations -

but within the constraints imposed by Westphalian logic which places national sovereignty and power interests first. The problems listed below defy such piecemeal, state-serving attempts precisely because they cut across national boundaries, and have their bases in the socioeconomic needs of all human societies rather than the political interests of disparate states – they invoke Kant's moral imperative. And there is a further overriding factor: these problems are by their nature system-ic: they are interrelated and interacting, and must therefore be addressed, and solved, as a planetary societal totality.

Population and its global, but unevenly distributed, pressures

Perhaps the most critical single issue in the decades ahead, the world's population will approximate 6 billion by the end of the century and, because of "demographic inertia," i.e., the impetus caused by sheer mass of numbers, the planet's popu-lation cannot be expected to reach steady-state at least until the middle of the next century. True, the industrial countries are now as a group approaching no-growth, but population continues to advance in the Third World, especially in Latin America, sub-Sahara Africa, and South and Southeast Asia. In effect, the regions with the least developed agricultural and industrial technologies will have the greatest pressures to contend with in the people/food equation. Their problems are compounded by the worldwide urban explosion, which during the second half of this century is expected to increase six-fold in the developing regions – attendant by the physical problems of obtaining sewage systems and clean drinking water, to say nothing of the fulfillment or frustration of all the drives and demands of aspiring modernity.

Space and Resources: The End of the "Infinite Earth" Image

The Copernican paradigm was associated historically with European overseas discoveries and geopolitical annexation. There was always terra incognita, a frontier to be pushed back and new lands to settle, and this perception was comple-mented by an image of well-nigh infinite resources. But, in our century, the north and south poles were reached and Everest scaled so that all terra has now become cognita. Spatial boundaries are being matched by global limits to nonrenewable resources, by concerns about food-growing capability and population-carrying capacity, and by the earth's ability to support unchecked demographic and industrial growth.

The Demand for "Fair Shares" of Planetary Resources

The nation-state system has always maximized individualism: juridically, it assumes the metaphysics of sovereignty; politically, the freedom of a state to define and advance its "vital interests" unilaterally; and economically, to institutionalize the doctrine of free enterprise (which has assumed such guises as mercantilism and state autarchy, laissez faire, and corporate and state capitalism). Possessing naval and military superiority, Europe's nation-states carved out great empires, either overseas or over their continental hinterlands, and then employed their industrial technology to exploit indigenous human and physical resources. The geopolitical and geoeconomic consequences have been remarkable. Thus, the United States and Canada, together with less than 7 percent of the world's population, consume 40 percent of its resources - while the First and Second Worlds, with some 20 percent of the world's peoples, consume over 80 percent of global resources. The contemporary North-South confrontation and the demand on the part of Third World peoples for a New International Economic Order calls for remedial action in terms of a global system in which a reallocation of resources, the transfer of technology, and new priorities and patterns of aid and trade cannot be left to bilateral negotiations but require supranational, i.e., regional and global, strategies.

Protection of the Biosphere

The systemic character of the foregoing crises is also seen in the accelerating degradation of our planetary habitat: its land, waters, and atmosphere. We are all painfully aware of this pollution - described as the "rich countries' disease" at the Stockholm Conference in 1972 but which is fast enveloping Third World countries as the pace of industrialization and urbanization quickens there. Nor can biospheric degradation be nationally compartmentalized - as is graphically illustrated by the atmospheric pollution generated in the United States falling as acid rain on Canadian lakes, and from Ontario on New England, while the source of the same phenomenon in Scandinavia is to be found in the United Kingdom. Obviously, neighbors should not dump their garbage in each other's backyard, but the problem of protecting the biosphere has become global in its dimensions and calls for stringent remedies ultimately of an enforceable nature. A logic other than that of Westphalia would argue that the planet's life-sustaining biosphere must be given a higher priority than the sovereignty of an individual state.

The crucial character of these problems raises in turn the factor of <u>conflict</u> - a conflict of attitudes toward the ownership, use, and management of global resources for global congeries of societies. The still-increasing disparity in the use of resources and in living standards results in the rich nations getting richer and the poor nations getting children. To the world's disadvantaged and economically disenfranchised, this is an intolerable situation, whether judged on moral, economic, or political grounds. But the Third World has no intention of continuing to be acquiescent. Demographically their majority in the world is increasing, and this is reflected in the permanence of their political majority in the U.N. General Assembly. Meanwhile, in the economic sphere, they are learning to aggregate their strength. The energy crisis demonstrated the vulnerability of the developed world's industrial economies and, conversely, the economic and political power of OPEC. But the United States and other Western states are vulnerably deficient as well in various mineral resources critical to their industries - including armaments. Hence, the formation of additional Third World cartels can be easily envisaged.

Secretary-General Waldheim warned the special General Assembly session on the world economy (held in August-September 1980) that unless a realistic process for restructuring the world economy were initiated, "we will have failed in our duty to the coming generations." But he did so at a time when the rich countries were suffering serious recession and in no mood to respond affirmatively to the call by India - as a leader of the Group of 77 - for a "massive transfer of resources" to the deficit-ridden poor states.(30) Meanwhile, a United States government report predicted in July 1980 that civilization had perhaps 20 years to head off a worldwide disaster. This would result from food shortages and malnutrition, steady loss of croplands, forests, plant and animal species, fisheries, degradation of the earth's water and atmosphere, and the widening of the gap between rich and poor peoples. The report's findings pointed to increasing stress on international financial arrangements and "increasing potential for international conflict."(31) Still another area of potential conflict, we would point out, are the competing national attitudes toward the ownership and use of resources not currently in the domain of any sovereign state. These include the right of unilateral claims by nations possessing the technological sophistication to exploit the resources of the seabed, the Arctic and Antarctic, and of outer space, as opposed to the demand voiced especially by various Third World countries that such resources must be viewed as the "heritage of mankind" in their allocation, consumption, and conservation.

These areas of current competition and potential conflict underscore the dynamic changes that have been occurring in the war/peace equation. Traditionally, as the Ptolemaic and Copernican paradigms attest, competition and wars were largely due to interstate political and territorial rivalries. But in today's world, rivalries and the potential for conflict have become progressively economic and ideological which, as we have noted, are essentially transnational in nature. Again, for some three decades after World War II, actual hostilities occurred to a large extent as a concomitant of the historical process of decolonization, so that, from a juridical standpoint, these colonial wars and their aftermath of domestic upheaval and reorganization were intranational. It was in this sphere that peacekeeping as a conflict-management technique has played a major role. But, today, the process of political decolonization is all but completed. What we can now envisage is the next stage: the need for interstate conflict management, especially among former colonies which, in many cases, appear to be politically unstable and of questionable economic viability. Here we must expect not only continued domestic and interstate political friction but economic competition for resources whose costs rise in proportion to their scarcity.

Still another area of concern stems from the historical evolution and asymmetry of the nation-state system itself. Emerging from their medieval antecedents of religious and political dependence to the suzerainty of the Church and Holy Roman Empire, Western European nation-states fiercely embraced the concept of national independence, but have now further evolved to the stage of interdependence, as manifested in the European Community. But, in the Third World, scores of countries have just emerged from dependence and are jealously protecting their hard-won independence – and with it the perceptions and ambitions of the Ptolemaic paradigm. Within this historical asymmetry can be profound psychological misperceptions, fears of economic neocolonialism, ideological tensions – in short, the North-South confrontation and its grave potential for physical conflict, and even a resurgence of racism, unless all the regions of the world accept and implement the concept of interdependence – the operative term in the Force Field paradigm.

PEACEKEEPING AND PEACEMAKING AS COMPONENTS OF WORLD ORDER

Conflict has been part of the human condition since Paleolithic times. All societies, past and present, have employed the major segments of their respective cultures - social, economic, technological, political, legal, and even aesthetic and religious

- either to control or to promote violence. Often a dual approach has been adopted: to control conflict within the given society while fostering it outside the societal boundaries (the Hobbesian tradition). The Copernican paradigm has attempted to lay ground rules to minimize, but not eradicate, interstate conflict. Yet, its record has not been auspicious in a century marked by an almost incessant sequence of conflicts. Consequently, we have to expect the high probability of conflict continuing in the years ahead.

Let us now relate this probability factor to our three paradigms. We have argued that each of them has its counterpart in a philosophical tradition: Ptolemaic-Hobbesian; Copernican-Grotian; and Force Field-Kantian. The Hobbesian proclivity for violence could dominate the few actors in the Ptolemaic paradigm and still permit the political environment to maintain its balance. But given the systemic character and multinational dimensions of the Copernican paradigm, coupled with the accelerating destructive power of military technology, the Grotian approach has become demonstrably ineffective in containing conflict. The critical question is whether it can now be amended to cope with the dynamics for war and peace alike of the Force Field paradigm? Two world wars attest to its failure thus far to manage conflict in the emerging stage of this new environmental stage.

The problem is compounded by the fact that, at the Force Field level of societal organization, everything tends to globalize: science/technology; economic activities; ideologies; and the movement of goods, service, and people (technologists, scholars, and tourists alike). Hence, the difficulty to compartmentalize or localize conflict situations has increased. This challenges any attempt at keeping the peace - unless the non-zero-sum character of all conflicts in a Force Field environment is universally understood and acted upon by the creation of new conflict-management methods. Similarly, peacemaking must be recognized as also possessing universal ramifications.

We cannot know at this time to what extent, if at all, the Kantian tradition will ultimately prevail, or what new socio-political agencies will evolve in consonance with the needs and opportunities of the fully formed Force Field paradigm. Will this involve transformation - but not the supersession - of the nation-state system; or alternatively, a group of regional communities (based on the European Community model), world government, globalism based on ideological uniformity, or globalism a la the scenarios of the Trilateral Commission? There are numerous other preferred world models.(32) Here, we are concerned only with making the point that the world has to contend with the difficult, if not impossible, task of trying to make the Grotian tradition function sufficiently well to enable humanity to effect a viable transition to a superseding Force Field paradigm. And that transitional process calls for new methods in both conflict management and peace-making.

We have to recognize the paradoxical nature of our quest. We are trying to reform the dangerous situation created in today's world by the illogic of Westphalia, yet are constrained to employ modalities based upon Westphalian concepts, i.e., which derive their authority and acceptance from Grotian-Copernican sources. This is the paradox in which the United Nations finds itself - and logically extends to United Nations peacekeeping and peacemaking. The problems and prospects of peacekeeping have been appraised earlier in this book, and it is not our intention to add to those critiques. Rather, we want to stress that peacekeeping cannot hope to maintain the Copernican paradigm per se but must be employed in a transitional period of societal reorganization so as to dampen down the chances of recourse to Hobbesian violence - which must tend in turn to globalize in our interdependent world. And, as a corollary, we would further emphasize that, just as a truce to hostilities is only a stop-gap pending a political conclusion of some kind, so peacekeeping can be but the first step in a three-fold sequence: peacekeeping, peacebuilding, and peacemaking.

We can illustrate our argument by drawing a parallel from allied postwar planning. During World War II, three stages in the shift from war to peace were envisaged: (1) to obtain cessation of hostilities; (2) in the wake of the destruction caused by warfare, to introduce relief and rehabilitation supplies and services to bind up human wounds and get war-shattered agriculture and industry functioning again; and (3) to help create a more permanent peace by means of long-term programs of reconstruction and development. (Note that the United Nations Relief and Rehabilitation Administration - a temporary UN agency - was set up in connection with the second stage, while the International Bank for Reconstruction and Development was created, together with the International Monetary Fund and other agencies, to foster the third stage.) In the context of this book, peacekeeping comprises stage (1). But, despite the emplacement of blue berets so as to separate physically the protagonists, the conflict situation has not ceased but simply changed in its character. The original problem which led to the violence has been exacerbated by fighting which, in its wake, has left a legacy of physical and psychological suffering. As Michael Harbottle has pointed out, the UN initiative, if it is to maintain a progressive effectiveness, has to adjust to these changes, in effect by shifting to stage (2), that of peacebuilding. The circumstances now call for a civilian rather than a military-type operation (as occurred with the creation of UNRRA in 1943). Peacebuilding envisages the mending of fences by recreating confidence and

trust between warring communities, assistance, and by laying
the foundations for a new social and economic relationship that
could encourage improved intercommunal cooperation and peaceful existence. Successful implementation of stage (2) would
logically lead in turn to long-term peacemaking strategies,
such as by providing international assistance to reconstruct
war-shattered economic activities to their prewar conflict
levels, and by utilizing regional and/or global machinery both
to raise living standards to still higher levels, and in other
ways help to remove the original causes of conflict.

Peacekeeping is often criticized for its essential
untidiness: its operations have beginnings but all too often no
conclusion (as in Kashmir or Cyprus). In other words, if
peacekeeping cannot bring about the pacific resolution of a
dispute, then we have to settle for a much less satisfactory,
and very expensive, alternative: the dispute's pacific perpetuation. This is a seemingly valid criticism which we would
attempt to answer in three ways: (1) As Whitehead said about
nature, unfortunately she is not as simple as we would like to
believe. Similarly, our Force Field geopolitical environment
cannot be compartmentalized in terms of simply either war or
peace in a given locality. As we suggested earlier, everything
seems to be linked to everything else. Hopefully, peacekeeping can quarantine an area until the infection is removed. If
the latter does not occur, the next logical step is to contain it
from becoming virulent throughout all of the system. It may
well be the cheapest remedy in the long run. (2) On this
matter of the relative merits of resolution/perpetuation, why
should the critics of peacekeeping be permitted to employ a
double standard? Alliances such as NATO, NORAD, and the
Warsaw Pact have been in existence for decades, but we have
never heard it suggested that their inability to resolve
pacifically the issues which created them in the first place
must lead to the conclusion that they should be liquidated.
On the contrary, the proponents of NATO, for example, will
argue that the alliance's worth is proved precisely by its value
in pacifically perpetuating the interests of the Western world
rather than subjecting them to a violent conclusion. We agree
with Hedley Bull that "war is endemic in the system of
states."(33) So let us blame the logic of Westphalia, not that
of the peacekeeper attempting to control violence in an anarchical international environment. (3) Given the interaction of
all components in a geopolitical Force Field, the failure of
"pacific resolution" calls not for liquidating peacekeeping but
recognizing that it has been assigned thus far a truncated
role. As we argued above, peacekeeping should be regarded
as an indispensable, not nevertheless only initial, step in
managing and resolving conflict: it must be linked in turn to
peacebuilding and peacemaking - which, inter alia, can bring
into play the full apparatus of the United Nations and appropriate Specialized Agencies.

The need to establish a nexus between peacekeeping and peacemaking becomes apparent when we examine the two terms. Peacekeeping has been associated with collective security, under the aegis in the first place of the Security Council. In this regard it has a strong affinity with the maintenance of geopolitical equilibrium. Consequently, it functions as part of a machinery which assesses any incremental change in almost exclusively political-military terms so that the overall status quo is not upset. But the United Nations has other major organs – such as the Economic and Social Council – which are basically counter-status quo in their purposes: they were created to alter drastically the economic and social standards of billions of people. Here, we encounter peacemaking – such as is being currently sought in the increasingly vocal demands for a New International Economic Order. Peacekeeping has a natural affinity with the concept of "order"; peacemaking with the concept of "justice." Unless justice in the economic and social spheres (which includes the eradication of all forms of racism in southern Africa) is implemented, no amount of tommy-guns or tanks will be able to maintain "order."

Applying the constant of change to the turbulent decades ahead, we shall need to recognize peacekeeping and peace-making as related and integral components of a new world order. One way might be to have this nexus assume the form of a dual "strategy." At the UN Special Session on Disarmament, Prime Minister Trudeau of Canada called for a new "strategy of suffocation . . . to halt the arms race in the laboratory." (He envisaged impeding the further development of new strategic weapons systems by freezing the available amount of fissionable material; by preventing any technology that may be developed in the laboratory from being tested; and by reducing the funds devoted to military expenditure.) We must either suffocate the arms race and its baleful promise of Mutual Assured Destruction (MAD) or it must assuredly suffocate our national economies and international resources. Any such reversal of the arms race can not only logically call for a strengthening of international machinery for conflict management (peacekeeping) but in turn make available financial, scientific, and technological resources for a "strategy of vitalization" to assist the Third World. Only by living up to their collective promises to make available for developmental purposes to the United Nations the latter's target for 0.7 percent of their GNPs can the industrialized countries of the North engage in the kind of peacemaking that will satisfy the South's demand for justice in a new world order.

We began with the words of a Nobel laureate; we might conclude with the admonition of another, Albert Einstein:

Through the release of atomic energy, our generation has brought into the world the most revolu-

tionary force since prehistoric man's discovery of fire. This basic power of the universe cannot be fitted into the outmoded concept of narrow nationalisms. For there is no secret and there is no defense; there is no possibility of control of atomic energy except through the aroused understanding and insistence of the peoples of the world.

NOTES

1. These statistics are based upon estimates for world conditions as of 1976, prepared by Sam Nilsson, Director of the International Federation of Institutes for Advanced Study, Stockholm, 1979.

2. K.J. Holsti, International Politics: A Framework for Analysis, 2nd ed. (Englewood Cliffs, N.J.: Prentice-Hall, 1973), p. 4.

3. James Lee Ray, Global Politics (New York: Houghton Mifflin, 1979), p. 90.

4. We associate this term with the thinking and writings of a distinguished American scholar in international law, Richard A. Falk.

5. See Martin Wight, "Western Values in International Relations," in Diplomatic Investigations, edited by Herbert Butterfield and Martin Wight (London: George Allen and Unwin, 1967); Hedley Bull, "Martin Wight and the Theory of International Relations. The Second Martin Wight Memorial Lecture," British Journal of International Studies II (1976). We have drawn, especially for this discussion of the three traditions of political thought, upon Bull's The Anarchical Society: A Study of Order in World Politics (New York: Columbia University Press, 1977).

6. Bull, The Anarchical Society, pp. 26-27.

7. Ibid, p. 27.

8. J.L. Brierly, The Law of Nations (London: Oxford University Press, 1976), p. 51.

9. Evan Luard, Conflict and Peace in the Modern International System (Boston: Little, Brown, 1968), pp. 8-9.

10. Holsti, International Politics, p. 64.

11. Ibid., p. 69.

12. Bull, The Anarchical Society, pp. 27-40.

13. Albert Einstein and L. Infeld, The Evolution of Physics (New York: Simon and Schuster, 1954), chapter 3; Albert Einstein, Relatively, The Special and General Theory (London, 1954), pp. 146 ff.

14. Errol E. Harris, The Foundations of Metaphysics in Science (London: George Allen and Unwin, 1965); see chap. VI, pp. 112, 126-131, 140 ff.

15. Ibid., pp. 52-53.

16. For an example of global-oriented, relativistic carto-graphical projections, see Richard E. Harrison, Look at the World: The Fortune Atlas for World Strategy (New York: Alfred A. Knopf, 1944).

17. Developments in the establishment of IGOs and NGOs and their activities are found in the Yearbook of International Organizations and other publications of the Union of International Associations, Brussels.

18. Holsti, International Politics, p. 177.

19. J.W. Vaupel and J.P. Curhan, The Making of Multinational Enterprise (Cambridge, Mass.: Harvard University Press, 1969), chap. 3.

20. Directory of American Firms Operating in Foreign Countries. Vol. 3. (New York, Uniworld Business Publications, 1979).

21. See Marshall R. Singer, "The Foreign Policies of Small Developing States," in World Politics edited by James N. Rosenau, Kenneth W. Thompson, and Gavin Boyd (New York: Free Press, 1976), pp. 265-69.

22. Ray, Global Politics, p. 223.

23. See The Objectives of the New International Economic Order, Ervin Laszlo, Robert Baker, Jr., Elliott Eisenbert, and Venkata Raman, eds., published for UNITAR (New York: Pergamon Press, 1978).

24. Immanuel Kant, Fundamental Principles of the Metaphysics of Morals (New York: Appleton-Century-Crofts, 1938).

25. Quincy Wright, A Study of War, abridged edition (Chicago, Ill.: University of Chicago Press, 1964), p. 63.

26. Ruth Leger Siuard, World Military And Social Expenditures 1982, Virginia, World Priorities.

27. William Epstein, "Canada's Disarmament Initiatives Mark Return to Active Role," International Perspectives, Department of External Affairs, Ottawa, March/April 1979, p. 3.

28. Quoted in Harold and Margaret Sprout, The Context of Environmental Politics: Unfinished Business for America's Third

Century (Lexington: University Press of Kentucky, 1978), p. 142.

29.   Bull, The Anarchical Society, p. 38.

30.   The Whig-Standard (Kingston, Ontario), 26 August 1980.

31.   Associated Press, published in The Whig-Standard (Kingston, Ontario), 24 July 1980.

32.   See, for example, the work of the World Order Models Project (WOMP), which addresses itself to the delineation of preferred worlds for the 1990s, described in a series of books by scholars from various parts of the world. Associated with WOMP's creation and direction are Saul Mendlovitz and Richard A. Falk.

33.   Bull, The Anarchical Society., p. 283.

Appendix

UNITED NATIONS PEACEKEEPING OPERATIONS
(PEACEKEEPING FORCES AND OBSERVER MISSIONS)*

BASIC DATA AND DOCUMENTARY REFERENCES**

OPERATION	DATE OF INITIAL AUTHORIZATION
United Nations Military Observer Group in India and Pakistan (UNMOGIP)	21 April 1948
United Nations Truce Supervision Organization in Palestine (UNTSO)	29 May 1948
United Nations Emergency Force (UNEF I)	4 Nov. 1956
United Nations Observer Group in Lebanon (UNOGIL)	11 June 1958
United Nations Operation in the Congo (ONUC)	14 July 1960
United Nations Security Force in West New Guinea (West Irian)	21 Sept. 1962
United Nations Yemen Observer Mission (UNYOM)	11 June 1963
United Nations Peacekeeping Force in Cyprus (UNFICYP)	4 March 1964
Mission of the Representative of the Secretary-General in the Dominican Republic (DOMREP)	14 May 1965
United Nations India-Pakistan Observer Mission (UNIPOM)	20 Sept. 1965
United Nations Emergency Force II (UNEF II)	25 Oct. 1973
United Nations Disengagement Oberver Force (UNDOF)	31 May 1974
United Nations Interim Force in Lebanon (UNIFIL)	19 March 1978

*Presented in chronological order of date of initial authorization, and collated to 1 July 1982. Data for the United Nations Special Committee on the Balkans and for the operation in Indonesia are not officially collated so are not included.

**Financial expenditures for operations ongoing as of July 1982 include appropriations for the fiscal period 1981/82 and may differ from actual expenditures.

UNITED NATIONS MILITARY OBSERVER GROUP IN INDIA AND PAKISTAN - UNMOGIP

Resolutions: S/RES/47 (1948) - 21 April 1948
                                    91 (1951) - 30 March 1951
                                   210 (1965) - 6 September 1965 (to strengthen UNMOGIP)*

Mandated Functions: To supervise, in the State of Jammu and Kashmir, the ceasefire between
                            India and Pakistan.

Location: The State of Jammu and Kashmir and the Border between that state and
                             Pakistan.

Headquarters: Rawalpindi (November–April)
                             Srinagar (May–November)

Duration: 24 January 1949 to date

Maximum strength: 102 (October 1965)

Strength as of
1 July 1982:   37 military observers

Fatalities: 5, with 4 killed in action and various accidents and 1 from other causes.

Financial Costs: From inception of mission to 31 December 1979: $31,995,819.

Contributing Countries:		Duration	Contribution Military observers	
	Australia	1952 to date		
	Belgium	Jan. 1949 to date	"	"
	Canada	Jan. 1949 - Jan. 1979	"	"
	Chile	1950 to date	"	"
	Denmark	1950 to date	"	"
	Ecuador	1952 - 1952	"	"
	Finland	1963 to date	"	"
	Italy	1961 to date	"	"
	Mexico	Jan. 1949 - 1949	"	"
	New Zealand	1952 to date	"	"
	Norway	Jan. 1949 - 1952; 1957 to date	"	"
	Sweden	1950 to date	"	"
	Uruguay	1952 to date	"	"
	United States	Jan. 1949 to date	"	"

Other Contributions (free of all costs to the UN):

	United States	1949 - 1954	Aircraft
	Italy	1957 - 1963	Aircraft
	Canada	15 June 1964 - 31 Mar. 1975	Aircraft
	Australia	1 Apr. 1975 - 31 Dec. 1978	Aircraft

*other resolutions and related actions

Chief Military
Observers: Col. Siegfried Pl. Coblentz (United States) (Acting)   1 Nov. 1949-27 Oct. 1950
                  Lt. Gen. R.H. Nimmo (Australia)   28 Oct. 1950-3 Jan. 1966
                  Col. J.H.J. Gauthier (Canada) (Acting)   4 Jan.-7 July 1966
                  Lt. Gen. Luis Tassara-Gonzalez (Chile)   8 July 1966-18 June 1977
                  Lt. Col. P. Bergevin (Canada) (Acting)   19 June 1977-8 April 1978
                  Col. Pospisil (Canada) (Acting)   9 April-3 June 1978
                  Brig. Gen. Stig Waldenstrom (Sweden) (Acting)   4 June 1978-31 May 1979
                  Brig. Gen. Stig Waldenstrom (Sweden)   1 June 1979-June 1982
                  Brig. Gen. Thor Johnsen (Norway)   June 1982 to date

20 January	1948 S/RES/39 (1948)	Security Council established United Nations Commission for India and Pakistan (UNCIP).
21 April	1948 S/RES/47 (1948)	Security Council authorized UNCIP to establish observers in Jammu and Kashmir.
20 July	1948	UNCIP asked secretary-general to appoint military adviser and observers to UNCIP (S/1100, annex 25).
22 July	1948	UNCIP sent military mission to area (S/1100, para. 54).
13 August	1948	Part I of UNCIP resolution provided for the appointment by the Commission of "military observers who under the authority of the Commission and with the cooperation of both Commands will supervise the observance of the cease-fire order" (S/995, sect. I).
2 January	1949	Arrival in area of Belgian general appointed military adviser to UNCIP secretariat by secretary-general.
September	1949	UNCIP left subcontinent - military adviser and observers remained.
1 November	1949	UNCIP military adviser left area - chief military observer assumed command.
14 March	1950 S/RES/80 (1950)	Security Council decided to appoint a UN representative for India and Pakistan. Council terminated UNCIP.
12 April	1950	Security Council appointed Sir Owen Dixon UN representative for India and Pakistan (UNRIP).
30 March	1951 S/RES/91 (1951)	Security Council accepted Sir Owen Dixon's resignation. Council decided "that the military observer group shall continue to supervise the cease-fire in the state."
30 April	1951	Security Council appointed Mr. Frank P. Graham UNRIP.
21 February	1957 S/RES/123 (1957)	Security Council requested President of Council (Mr. Gunnar Jarring of Sweden) to undertake fact-finding mission to area.
		No UNRIP has been appointed to replace Mr. Graham who died in February 1972.

UNITED NATIONS TRUCE SUPERVISION ORGANIZATION IN PALESTINE - UNTSO

Resolutions:	S/RES/50 (1948) - 29 May 1948 54 (1948) - 15 July 1948 59 (1948) - 19 October 1948 73 (1949) - 11 August 1949 101 (1953) - 24 November 1953 (to strengthen UNTSO) 114 (1956) - 4 June 1956 236 (1967) - 11 June 1967 S/8047 Consensus - 9/10 July 1967 (Suez Canal) S/8289 Decision - 8 December 1967 (additional UNMOs for Suez Canal) S/10611 Consensus - 19 April 1972 (additional observers for Lebanon) S/RES/339 (1973) - 23 October 1973 (Sinai)
Mandated Functions:	UNTSO was established in June 1948 to assist the mediator and the truce commission in supervising the observance of the truce in Palestine called for by the Security Council. Since then, UNTSO has performed various tasks entrusted to it by the Security Council, including the supervision of the General Armistice Agreements of 1949 and the observation of the cease-fire in the Suez Canal area and the Golan Heights following the Arab-Israeli war of June 1967. As of July 1982, UNTSO assists and cooperates with UNDOF and UNIFIL in the performance of their tasks; an observer group is stationed in Egypt; UNTSO also maintains offices in Lebanon, Syria, and Jordan within the framework of the General Armistice Agreements.
Headquarters:	Government House, Jerusalem
Duration:	11 June 1948 to date
Maximum strength:	572 (1948)
Strength as of 1 July 1982:	295
Fatalities:	21, as of 1 July 1982 - of these, 18 were killed in action and various accidents and 3 from other causes.
Financial costs:	From inception of mission to 31 December 1979: $130,851,866.

Mediators:		
	Count Folke Bernadotte (Sweden)	May-Sept. 1948
	Ralph J. Bunche (United States) (Acting)	Sept. 1948 - Aug. 1949

Chiefs of Staff:		
		Duration
	Lt. Gen. Count Thord Bonde (Sweden)	June - July 1948
	Gen. Aage Lundstrom (Sweden)	July - Sept. 1948
	Lt. Gen. William E. Riley (United States)	Sept. 1948 - June 1953
	Maj. Gen. Vagn Bennike (Denmark)	June 1953 - Aug. 1954

Chiefs of Staff (cont.):   Duration

Lt. Gen. E.L.M. Burns (Canada)   Aug. 1954 - Nov. 1956
Col. Byron V. Leary (United States)
(Acting)   Nov. 1956 - Mar. 1958
Lt. Gen. Carl C. von Horn (Sweden)   Mar. 1958 - July 1960
                                          Jan. 1961 - May 1963

Col. R.W. Richert (United States)
(Acting)   July 1960 - Dec. 1960
Lt. Gen. Odd Bull (Norway)   June 1963 - July 1970
Maj. Gen. Ensio Siilasvuo (Finland)   Aug. 1970 - Oct. 1973
Col. Richard W. Bunworth (Ireland)
(Acting)   Nov. 1973 - Mar. 1974
Maj. Gen. Bengt Liljestrand (Sweden)   Apr. 1974 - Aug. 1975
Col. K.D. Howard (Australia) (Acting)   August - December 1975
Maj. Gen. Emmanuel A. Erskine (Ghana)   Jan. 1976 - Apr. 1978
Col. William Callaghan (Ireland)
(Acting)   Apr. 1978 - June 1979
Col. O. Forsgren (Sweden) (Officer-in-
Charge)   June 1979 - Jan. 1980
Maj. Gen. Erkri R. Kaira (Finland)   Feb. 1980 - Feb. 1981
Maj. Gen. Emmanuel A. Erskine (Ghana)   Feb. 1981 to date

Contributing
countries: Duration   Contribution

Argentina	1967 -	Military observers	
Australia	1956 -	"	"
Austria	1967 -	"	"
Belgium	June 1948 -	"	"
Burma	1967 - 1969	"	"
Canada	1954 -	"	"
Chile	1967 -	"	"
Denmark	1954 -	"	"
Finland	1967 -	"	"
France	June 1948 -	"	"
Ireland	1958 -	"	"
Italy	1958 -	"	"
Netherlands	1956 -	"	"
New Zealands	1954 -	"	"
Norway	1956 -	"	"
Sweden	June 1948 -	"	"
USSR	1973 -	"	"
United States	June 1948 -	"	"

Other contributions (free of all costs to the UN)

United States	1949 - June 1967	Aircraft
Netherlands	June 1967 - Nov. 1967	Aircraft
Switzerland	Nov. 1967 - to date	Chartered commercial aircraft and crew; cost borne by Swiss government.

UNITED NATIONS EMERGENCY FORCE I - UNEF I

Resolutions:	GA RES 998 (ES-I) - 4 November 1956 1000 (ES-I) - 5 November 1956 1001 (ES-I) - 7 November 1956 1125 (XI) - 2 February 1957
Mandated Functions:	To secure and to supervise the cessation of hostilities, including the withdrawal of the armed forces of France, Israel, and the UK from Egyptian territory, and after the withdrawal to serve as a buffer between the Egyptian and Israeli forces.
Location:	Along the ADL in the Gaza area, and on the Egyptian side of the international frontier in the Sinai Peninsula.
Headquarters:	Gaza
Duration:	12 November 1956 - June 1967
Maximum strength:	6,073 (February 1957)
Strength at withdrawal:	3,378 (June 1967)
Fatalities:	90, of these 64 were killed in action or various accidents and 26 through other causes.
Financial costs:	From inception to end of mission: $220,124,012. The financial cost of UNEF I was considerably reduced by the absorption of varying amounts of the expenses involved by the countries providing contingents.

Commanders:		
	Lt. Gen. E.L.M. Burns (Canada)	Nov. 1956 - Dec. 1959
	Lt. Gen. P.S. Gyani (India)	Dec. 1959 - Jan. 1964
	Major-Gen. Carlos F. Paiva Chaves (Brazil)	Jan. 1964 - Aug. 1964
	Col. Lazar Musicki (Yugoslavia) (Acting)	Aug. 1964 - Jan. 1965
	Major-Gen. Syseno Sarmento (Brazil)	Jan. 1965 - Jan. 1966
	Major-Gen. Indar Jit Rikhye (India)	Jan. 1966 - June 1967

Troop contributors:	Duration	
Brazil	20 Jan. 1957 - 13 June 1967	Infantry
Canada	24 Nov. 1956 - 28 Feb. 1959	Medical unit
	24 Nov. 1956 - 31 May 1967	Signal, engineer, air transport, maintenance and movement control units.
Colombia	16 Nov. 1956 - 28 Oct. 1958	Infantry
Denmark	15 Nov. 1956 - 9 June 1967	Infantry
Finland	11 Dec. 1956 - 5 Dec. 1957	Infantry
India	20 Nov. 1956 - 13 June 1967	Infantry. Supply, transport & signal units.
Indonesia	5 Jan. 1957 - 12 Sept. 1957	Infantry
Norway	15 Nov. 1956 - 9 June 1967; 1 Mar. 1959 - 9 June 1967	Infantry Medical unit
Sweden	21 Nov. 1956 - 9 June 1967	Infantry
Yugoslavia	17 Nov. 1956 - 11 June 1967	Infantry
UNTSO	12 Nov. 1956 - June 1967	Military observers

Duration

Other contributions - free of all costs to UN

	Duration	
Italy	Nov. 1956	Airlift, logistics support
Switzerland	Nov. 1956	Airlift
United States	Nov. 1956	Airlift
RCAF (Canada)		Airlift
SCANAP		Airlift

UNITED NATIONS OBSERVATION GROUP IN LEBANON - UNOGIL

Resolution: S/RES/128 (1958) - 11 June 1958

Mandated Functions: To ensure that there was no illegal infiltration of personnel or supply of arms or other material across the Lebanese borders.

Location: Lebanese border areas and vicinity of zones held by opposing forces.

Headquarters: Beirut

Duration: 12 June - 9 December 1958

Maximum strength: 591 military observers (November 1958)

Strength at
withdrawal: 375 military observers

Fatalities: None

Financial Costs: From inception to end of mission: $3,697,742.

Members of
Observation Group: Mr. Galo Plaza (Ecuador)   -   Chairman
                    Mr. Rajeshwar Dayal (India)   -   Member
                    Major-Gen. Odd Bull (Norway)   -   Executive member in
                                                        charge of military
                                                        observers

Contributing
Countries: Afghanistan   Military observers

                    Argentina   "   "
                    Burma   "   "
                    Canada   "   "
                    Ceylon (Sri Lanka)   "   "
                    Chile   "   "
                    Denmark   "   "
                    Ecuador   "   "
                    Finland   "   "
                    India   "   "
                    Indonesia   "   "
                    Ireland   "   "
                    Italy   "   "
                    Nepal   "   "
                    Netherlands   "   "
                    New Zealand   "   "
                    Norway   "   "
                    Peru   "   "
                    Portugal   "   "
                    Sweden - provision of aircraft   "   "
                    Thailand   "   "

UNTSO military observers were seconded at the initial stage to assist in the mission.

UNITED NATIONS OPERATIONS IN THE CONGO - ONUC

Resolutions:	S/RES/143 (1960) - 14 July 1960 145 (1960) - 22 July 1960 GA RES 1474 (ES-IV) - 20 Sept. 1960 146 (1960) - 9 Aug. 1960 161 (1961) - 21 Feb. 1961 GA RES 1600 (XV) - 15 April 1961 169 (1961) - 24 Nov. 1961
Mandated Functions:	Initially, to ensure withdrawal of Belgian forces, to assist the government in the maintenance of law and order, and to provide technical assistance. The function of ONUC was subsequently modified to include maintaining the territorial integrity and the political independence of the Republic of the Congo, preventing the occurrence of civil war, and securing the removal from the Congo of all foreign military, paramilitary, and advisory personnel not under the United Nations command, and all mercenaries.
Location:	Republic of the Congo (now Zaire)
Headquarters:	Leopoldville (now Kinshasa)
Duration:	15 July 1960 - 30 June 1964
Maximum strength:	19,825 (July 1961)
Strength at withdrawal:	5,871 (30 December 1963)
Fatalities:	237, of which 195 were killed in action or various accidents and 39 from other causes.
Financial Costs:	From inception to end of mission: $400,130,793.

Special Representatives:	Ralph J. Bunche (United States)	July-August 1960
	Andrew W. Cordier (United States)	August-September 1960
	Rajeshwar Dayal (India)	Sept. 1960 - May 1961
	Mekki Abbas (Sudan) (Acting)	March-May 1961
Officers-in-Charge:	Sture Linner (Sweden)	May 1961 - Jan. 1962
	Robert K. A. Gardiner (Ghana)	Feb. 1962 - May 1963
	Max H. Dorsinville (Haiti)	May 1963 - Apr. 1964
	B.F. Osorio-Tafall (Mexico) (Acting)	April - June 1964
Commanders:	Ralph J. Bunche (United States)	15 - 17 July 1960
	Lt. Gen. Carl C. von Horn (Sweden)	18 July - December 1960
	Lt. Gen. Sean MacEoin (Ireland)	Jan. 1961 - Mar. 1962
	Lt. Gen. Kebbede Guebre (Ethiopia)	Apr. 1962 - July 1963
	Major-Gen. Christian Kaldager (Norway)	August-December 1963
	Major-Gen. Aguiyu Ironsi (Nigeria)	January - June 1964

Troop contributors:	Duration	Contribution
Argentina	July 1960 - Feb. 1963	Aircraft personnel (air and ground)
Austria	14 Dec. 1960 - Aug. 1963	Aircraft personnel (air and ground), field hospital and personnel, staff personnel

Troop contributors: (cont.)	Duration	Contribution
Brazil	July 1960 - June 1964	Aircraft personnel (air and ground), staff personnel
Burma	Aug. 1960 -	Staff personnel
Canada	July 1960 - June 1964	Aircraft personnel (air and ground), staff personnel, signals
Ceylon (Sri Lanka)	Aug. 1960 - Apr. 1962	Staff personnel
Denmark	Aug. 1960 - June 1964	Aircraft personnel (air and ground), staff personnel, workshop control, transport company
Ethiopia	15 July 1960 - 16 June 1964	Infantry, aircraft personnel (air and ground), staff personnel
Ghana	15 July 1960 - 25 Sept. 1963	Infantry, 2 medical units, staff personnel, police companies
Guinea	25 July 1960 - Jan. 1961	Infantry
India	July 1960 - June 1964	Infantry, aircraft personnel (air and ground), field hospital and personnel, staff personnel, supply unit, signal company, air despatch team, postal unit
Indonesia	4 Oct. 1960 - Apr. 1964	Infantry
Iran	Dec. 1962 - July 1963	Aircraft and air and ground personnel
Ireland	28 July 1960 - 11 May 1964	Infantry, staff personnel
Italy	Oct. 1960 - June 1964	Aircraft personnel (air and ground), field hospital, staff personnel
Liberia	25 July 1960 - May 1963	Infantry, movement control, staff personnel
Malaya	30 Oct. 1960 - Apr. 1963	Infantry, staff personnel
Mali	1 Aug. 1960 - Nov. 1960	Infantry
Morocco	15 July 1960 - 31 Jan. 1961	Infantry, parachute company
Netherlands	Aug. 1960 - Oct. 1963	Hygiene teams, staff personnel
Nigeria	10 Nov. 1960 - 30 June 1964	Infantry, police unit, staff personnel
Norway	July 1960 - Mar. 1964	Aircraft personnel (air and ground), staff personnel, workshop control
Pakistan	31 Aug. 1960 - May 1964	Ordnance and transport units, staff personnel
Philippines	Feb. 1963 - June 1963	Aircraft personnel (air and ground), staff personnel
Sierra Leone	Jan. 1962 - Mar. 1963	Infantry
Sudan	Aug. 1960 -Apr.- Dec. 1961	Infantry

Troop contributors: (cont.)	Duration	Contribution
Sweden	20 July 1960 - 15 May 1964	Infantry, aircraft personnel (air and ground), movement control, engineering personnel, workshop unit, signal detachment, staff personnel
Tunisia	15 July 1960 - May 1963	Infantry
United Arab Republic	20 Aug. 1960 - 1 Feb. 1961	Infantry, parachute battalion
Yugoslavia	July 1960 - Dec. 1960	Aircraft personnel (air and ground)
UNTSO and UNEF	July 1960 - 1964	Military observers

From February 1963 to the end of UN operations in the Congo, elements of the Congolese National Army (ANC) in south Katanga were under the operational control of the ONUC Force Commander.

Other contributions (free of all costs to UN)

Canada	Beginning of operation	Airlift of food
Switzerland	" " "	" " " and other supplies
UK	" " "	" " " and Ghanaian troops
USSR	" " "	" " "
United States	" " "	" " " supplies and equipment
United States	" " "	Aircraft, airlift of Tunisian, Moroccan, Ghanaian, Swedish, and Guinean troops, and sealift of Malayan troops
Some member states		Troop carrying trucks, aircraft (DC-3 type), small reconnaissance aircraft and helicopters (as part of the equipment of the Force).

UNITED NATIONS SECURITY FORCE IN WEST NEW GUINEA (WEST IRIAN)

Resolution: GA resolution 1752 (XVII) - 21 September 1962

Mandated Functions: To maintain peace and security in the territory under the United
                         Nations Temporary Executive Authority (UNTEA) established by
                         agreement between Indonesia and the Netherlands.

Location: West New Guinea (West Irian)

Headquarters: Hollandia

Duration: 3 October 1962 to 30 April 1963.

Maximum strength: 1,500 infantry personnel and 76 aircraft personnel

Strength at
withdrawal: 1,500 infantry personnel and 76 aircraft personnel

Fatalities: None

Financial costs: The governments of Indonesia and the Netherlands paid full costs in
                         equal amounts.

Commander: Major-General Said Uddin Khan (Pakistan)

Contributors: Duration   Contribution

                     Pakistan   3 Oct. 1962 - 30 April 1963   Infantry

                     Canada   3 Oct. 1962 - 30 April 1963   Supporting aircraft
                                                                  and crews

                     United States 3 Oct. 1962 - 30 April 1963   Supporting aircraft
                                                                  and crews

*From 18 August to 21 September 1962, the secretary-general's military adviser, Brig.
Gen. Indar Jit Rikhye (India), and a group of 21 military observers assisted in the
implementation of the Agreement of 15 August 1962 between Indonesia and the Netherlands on cessation of hostilities.   The military observers were provided by Brazil,
Ceylon, India, Ireland, Nigeria, and Sweden.

UNITED NATIONS YEMEN OBSERVATION MISSION - UNYOM

Resolution:	S/RES/179 (1963) - 11 June 1963
Mandated Functions:	To observe and certify the implementation of the disengagement agreement between Saudia Arabia and the United Arab Republic.
Location:	Yemen
Headquarters:	Sana
Duration:	4 July 1963 - 4 September 1964

Maximum strength: 25 military observers
114 officers and other ranks of reconnaissance unit (Yugoslavia)
 50 officers and other ranks of air unit (Canada)
<u>189</u>

Stength at withdrawal:	25 military observers and supporting air unit (Canada)
Fatalities:	None

Financial Costs: From inception to end of mission: $1,840,450.
Contributions from Saudi Arabia and UAR: 800,000 each

Commanders: Major-Gen. Carl C. von Horn (Sweden)   4 July 1963 - 25 Aug. 1963

Col. Branko Pavlovic (Yugoslavia)
(Acting)   26 Aug. 1963 - 11 Sept. 1963

Lt. Gen. P. S. Gyani (India)   12 Sept. 1963 - 7 Nov. 1963

Special Representative
of the Secretary-General
and Head of Mission:
   Mr. P. P. Spinelli (Italy)   8 Nov. 1963 - 4 Sept. 1964

Chiefs-of-Staff: Col. Branko Pavlovic (Yugoslavia)   8 Nov. - 25 Nov. 1963
Col. S. C. Sabharwal (India)   26 Nov. 1963 - 4 Sept. 1964

Troop contributors:

	Duration	Contribution
Australia	July 1963 - Nov. 1963	Military observers
Canada	July 1963 - Sept. 1964	Air unit (aricraft and helicopters)
Denmark	July 1963-Sept. 1964	Military observers
Ghana	July 1963-Sept. 1964	" "
India	Jan. 1964-Sept. 1964	" "
Italy	Jan. 1964-Sept. 1964	" "
Netherlands	Jan. 1964-Sept. 1964	" "
Norway	July 1963-Sept. 1964	" "
Pakistan	Jan. 1964-Sept. 1964	" "
Sweden	July 1963-Sept. 1964	" "
Yugoslavia	July 1963-26 Nov. 1963; July 1963 - Sept. 1964	Reconnaissance unit Military observers
UNTSO	At initial stage of mission	" "

UNITED NATIONS PEACEKEEPING FORCE IN CYPRUS - UNFICYP

Resolution: S/RES/186 (1964) - 4 March 1964

Annex

S/RES/186 (1964) - 4 March 1964	305 (1971) - 13 Dec. 1971
187 (1964) - 13 March 1964	315 (1972) - 15 June 1972
192 (1964) - 20 June 1964	324 (1972) - 12 Dec. 1972
Consensus - 11 Aug. 1964	334 (1973) - 15 June 1973
194 (1964) - 25 Sept. 1964	343 (1973) - 14 Dec. 1973
198 (1964) - 18 Dec. 1964	349 (1974) - 29 May 1974
201 (1965) - 19 March 1965	364 (1974) - 13 Dec. 1974
206 (1965) - 16 June 1965	370 (1975) - 13 June 1975
219 (1965) - 17 Dec. 1965	383 (1975) - 13 Dec. 1975
220 (1966) - 16 March 1966	391 (1976) - 15 June 1976
222 (1966) - 16 June 1966	401 (1976) - 14 Dec. 1976
231 (1966) - 15 Dec. 1966	410 (1977) - 15 Dec. 1977
238 (1967) - 19 June 1967	422 (1978) - 16 June 1978
244 (1967) - 22 Dec. 1967	430 (1978) - 16 June 1978
247 (1968) - 18 March 1968	443 (1978) - 14 Dec. 1978
254 (1968) - 18 June 1968	451 (1979) - 15 June 1979
261 (1968) - 10 Dec. 1968	458 (1979) - 14 Dec. 1979
266 (1969) - 10 June 1969	472 (1980) - 13 June 1980
274 (1969) - 11 Dec. 1969	482 (1980) - 11 Dec. 1980
281 (1970) - 9 June 1970	486 (1981) - 4 June 1981
291 (1970) - 19 Dec. 1970	495 (1981) - 14 Dec. 1981
293 (1971) - 26 May 1971	510 (1982) - 15 June 1982

Mandated Functions: In the interest of international peace and security, to use its best efforts to prevent the recurrence of fighting; to supervise the cease-fire, including maintenance of the status quo in the buffer zone between the cease-fire lines of the Cyprus National Guard and the Turkish forces; to contribute to the maintenance and restoration of law and order and the return to normal conditions; to discharge humanitarian functions.

Location: Cyprus

Headquarters: Nicosia

Duration: 27 March 1964 to date

Maximum strength: 6,411 (June 1964)

Stengths as of
1 July 1982:   2,348

Fatalities: 124, of which 74 were killed in action or various accidents and 50 from other causes.

Financial Costs: From inception of mission to 1 June 1982: $398.5 million
                      UNFICYP is financed entirely by means of voluntary contributions and by troop contributing countries - Australia, Austria, Canada, Denmark, New Zealand, Sweden, and the United Kingdon - which pay for direct salaries and related costs and some for supplies and a variety of other direct costs. Finland and Ireland assured personnel costs to 1965. In addition, the United States, United King-

dom, and Italy provided some air transport services (see S/6954-19 Nov. 1965 annex III).

| Mediators: | Sakari S. Tuomioja (Finland) | March-Sept. 1964 |
| | Galo Plaza Lasso (Ecuador) | Sept. 1964 - Dec. 1965 |

Special Representatives:	Galo Plaza Lasso (Ecuador)	May-September 1964
	Carlos A. Bernardes (Brazil)	Sept. 1964-Jan. 1967
	P. P. Spinelli (Italy) (Acting)	January-February 1967
	B.F. Osorio-Tafall (Mexico)	Feb. 1967 - June 1974
	Luis Weckmann-Munoz (Mexico)	July 1974 - Oct. 1975
	Javier Perez de Cuellar (Peru)	Oct. 1975 - Dec. 1977
	Remy Gorge (Switzerland) (Acting)	Dec. 1977 - Apr. 1978
	Reynaldo Galindo-Pohl (El Salvador)	May 1978 - April 1980
	Hugo Juan Gobbi (Argentina)	May 1980 to date

Commanders:	Lt. Gen. P. S. Gyani (India)	March - June 1964
	Gen. K. S. Thimayya (India)	June 1964 - Dec. 1965
	Brig. A. J. Wilson (UK) (Acting)	Dec. 1965 - May 1966
	Lt. Gen. I.A.E. Martola (Finland)	May 1966 - Dec. 1969
	Lt. Gen. D. Prem Chand (India)	Dec. 1969 - Dec. 1976
	Major-Gen. J. J. Quinn (Ireland)	Dec. 1976 - March 1981
	Major-Gen. G. Greindl (Austria)	March 1981 - to date

Troop contributors:

		Duration	Contribution
	Australia	25 May 1964 to date	Civilian police
	Austria	14 Apr. 1964-27 July 1977	Civilian police
		17 May 1964-Oct. 1973	Field hospital, personnel
		Oct. 1973 - Apr. 1976	Medical center
		25 Apr. 1972 to date	Infantry, staff officers
	Canada	27 Mar. 1964 to date	Infantry, staff officers
		Apr. 1976 to date	Medical center
	Denmark	22 Mar. 1964 to date	Infantry, staff officers
		25 May 1964-4 June 1975	Civilian police
	Finland	28 Mar. 1964-13 Oct. 1977	Infantry
		31 Oct. 1977 to date	Staff officers, military police
	Ireland	19 Apr. 1964-31 Oct. 1973	Infantry
		31 Oct. 1973 to date	Staff officers
	New Zealand	22 May 1964-28 June 1967	Civilian police
	Sweden	28 Mar. 1964 to date	Infantry, staff officers
		5 May 1964 to date	Civilian police
	UK	27 Mar. 1964 to date	Infantry, staff officers, logistics, air-unit
		Apr. 1976 to date	Medical Center

Other contributions (free of all costs to UN)

Italy		Airlift
UK		Airlift
United States		Airlift

MISSION OF THE REPRESENTATIVE OF THE SECRETARY-GENERAL IN THE DOMINICAN REPUBLIC

DOMREP

Resolutions:	S/RES/203 (1965) - 14 May 1965 S/RES/205 (1965) - 22 May 1965
Mandated Functions:	To observe the situation and to report on breaches of the cease-fire between the two de facto authorities.
Location:	Dominican Republic
Headquarters:	Santo Domingo
Duration:	15 May 1965 - 22 October 1966
Maximum strength:	2 military observers
Strength at withdrawal:	1 military observer
Fatalities:	None
Expenditures:	From inception to end of mission: $275,831.
Representative of the Secretary-General:	Mr. Jose Antonio Mayobre (Venezuela)
Military Adviser:	Major-General Indar Jit Rikhye (India)

(The Military Adviser was provided with a staff of two military observers at any one time. These observers were provided, one each, by Brazil, Canada, and Ecuador.)

UNITED NATIONS INDIA-PAKISTAN OBSERVATION MISSION - UNIPOM

Resolutions: (1) S/RES/211 (1965) - 20 September 1965
(2) S/RES 215(1965) - 5 November 1965

Mandated Functions: Under (1):   To supervise the cease-fire along the India/Pakistan border except the states of Jammu and Kashmir where UNMOGIP operated, and the withdrawal of all armed personnel to the positions held by them before 5 Aug. 1965.

     Under (2):   Secretary-general's representative to meet with representatives of India and Pakistan for the purpose of formulating an agreed plan and schedule for the withdrawal by both parties.

Location: Along the India/Pakistan border between Kashmir and the Arabian Sea.

Headquarters: Lahore (Pakistan)/Amritsar (India)

Duration: (1) 23 September 1965 - 22 March 1966
(2) 6 December 1965 - 28 Feb. 1966

Maximum strength: 96 military observers (October 1965)

Strength at
withdrawal: 78 military observers

Fatalities: None

Financial costs: From inception to end of mission: (1) $1,713,280.
(2) $ 33,500. (approx.)

Chief Officer: Major-Gen. B. F. MacDonald (Canada) 28 Sept. 1965-22 Mar. 1966 (UNIPOM was under the direction of Lt. Gen. R. H. Nimmo (Australia), Chief Military Observer (UNMOGIP) from 23 Sept. 1965-27 Sept. 1965)

Secretary General's
Representative: Brig. Gen. Tulio Marambio (Chile)   6 Dec. 1965 - 28 Feb. 1966

Contributing
countries: In its initial state   From 28 Sept. 1965 - 22 Mar. 1966
from UNTSO and UNMOGIP

In its initial state from UNTSO and UNMOGIP	From 28 Sept. 1965 - 22 Mar. 1966
Australia	Brazil
Belgium	Burma
Canada	Canada
Chile	Ceylon (Sri Lanka)
Denmark	Ethiopia
Finland	Ireland
Ireland	Nepal
Italy	The Netherlands
The Netherlands	Nigeria
New Zealand	Venezuela
Norway	
Sweden	Canada, air unit from Oct. 1965 to March 1966.

UNITED NATIONS EMERGENCY FORCE II - UNEF II

Resolutions: S/RES/340 (1973) - 25 October 1973
                            341 (1973) - 27 October 1973
                            346 (1974) - 8 April 1974
                            362 (1974) - 23 October 1974
                            368 (1975) - 17 April 1975
                            371 (1975) - 24 July 1975
                            378 (1975) - 23 October 1975
                            396 (1976) - 22 October 1976
                            416 (1977) - 21 October 1977
                            438 (1978) - 23 October 1978

Mandated Functions: To supervise the cease-fire between Egyptian and Israeli forces
                    and, following the conclusion of agreements of 18 January 1974 and
                    4 September 1975, to supervise the redeployment of Egyptian and
                    Israeli forces and to man and control the buffer zones established
                    under those agreements.

Location: Suez Canal sector and later the Sinai Peninsula.

Headquarters: Ismailia

Duration: 25 October 1973 - 24 July 1979

Maximum strength: 6,973 (February 1974)

Strength at
withdrawal: 4,031 (July 1979)

Fatalities: 52, including 30 from various accidents, 13 from other causes, and
                    9 killed in a UNEF aircraft crash in Syria, as a result of anti-
                    aircraft fire, during a flight in support of UNDOF on August 9,
                    1974.

Financial costs: From inception to end of mission: $446,487,000.

Commanders: Major-Gen. Ensio Siilasvuo (Finland)
                        Interim Commander   25 Oct. 1973 - 11 Nov. 1973
                    Lt. Gen. Ensio Siilasvuo (Finland)
                        Commander   12 Nov. 1973-19 Aug. 1975
                    Lt. Gen. Bengt Liljestrand (Sweden) 20 Aug. 1975-30 Nov. 1976
                    Major-Gen. Rais Abin (Indonesia)   1 Dec. 1976-6 Sept. 1979

Troop contributors: Duration   Contribution

                    Australia   July 1976-Oct. 1979   Air unit (helicopters and
                                                          personnel)
                    Austria   26 Oct. 1973-3 June 1974 Infantry
                    Canada   10 Nov. 1973-30 Oct. 1979 Logistics: Signals, air,
                                                          and service units
                    Finland   26 Oct. 1973-August 1979 Infantry
                    Ghana   22 Jan. 1974-Sept. 1979   Infantry
                    Indonesia   21 Dec. 1973-Sept. 1979   Infantry
                    Ireland   30 Oct. 1973-22 May 1974 Infantry
                    Nepal   3 Feb. 1974-4 Sept. 1974 Infantry
                    Panama   11 Dec. 1973-25 Nov. 1974 Infantry
                    Peru   25 Nov. 1973-3 June 1974 Infantry

Poland	15 Nov. 1973–20 Jan. 1980	Logistics: engineering, medical, and transport units
Senegal	18 Jan. 1974–June 1976	Infantry
Sweden	26 Oct. 1973–30 April 1980	Infantry
UNTSO	26 Oct. 1973–Dec. 1975	Military observers for staff positions
	Dec. 1975–Mar. 1980	Military observers (Observer Group Sinai assisted in special tasks, entrusted to the Force, under the operational control of UNEF Force Commander.)

Other contributions - (free of all costs to UN)

Australia	Feb. 1974	Airlift: Nepalese troops Calcutta-Cairo
Canada	Nov. 1973	Airlift: Canadian troops
Germany, Fed. Rep.	Jan. 1974	Airlift: Ghanian and Senegalese troops
Japan	Feb. 1974	Cash contribution for airlift of Nepalese troops Kathmandu-Calcutta, and transport of its equipment to UNEF
Norway	Oct. 1973	Airlift: Swedish troops – Sweden-UNEF
Poland	Nov. 1973	Airlift: Polish troops
Sweden	Oct. 1973	Airlift: Swedish troops
Switzerland		Aircraft placed at disposal of UNTSO was available to UNEF as req.
UK	Oct. 1973	Airlift: Austrian, Finnish, Irish, and Swedish troops and vehicles - Cyprus-UNEF
USSR	Nov. 1973	Airlift: Austrian troops-Austria-UNEF, Finnish troops and heavy equipment-Finland-UNEF
United States	Nov. 1973	Airlift: Irish troops – Ireland-UNEF
	Nov. 1973	Airlift: Finnish troops – Finland-UNEF
	Nov. 1973	Airlift: Peruvian troops – Peru-UNEF
	Dec. 1973	Austrian troops – Austria-UNEF
	Dec. 1973	Indonesian troops – Indonesia-UNEF
	Dec. 1973	Panamanian troops – Panama-UNEF
	Oct. 1976	$10 million in goods and services.

UNITED NATIONS DISENGAGEMENT OBSERVER FORCE - UNDOF

Resolutions: S/RES/350 (1974) - 31 May 1974   470 (1980) - 30 May 1980
                          363 (1974) - 29 November 1974   481 (1980) - 26 Nov. 1980
                          369 (1975) - 28 May 1975   485 (1981) - 22 May 1981
                          381 (1975) - 30 November 1975   493 (1981) - 23 Nov. 1981
                          390 (1976) - 28 May 1976   506 (1982) - 26 May 1982
                          398 (1976) - 30 November 1976
                          408 (1977) - 26 May 1977
                          420 (1977) - 30 November 1977
                          429 (1978) - 31 May 1978
                          441 (1978) - 30 November 1978
                          449 (1979) - 30 May 1979
                          456 (1979) - 30 November 1979

Mandated Functions: To maintain the cease-fire between Israel and Syria; to supervise
                    the redeployment of Syrian and Israeli forces; and to establish a
                    buffer zone, as provided in the Agreement on Disengagement be-
                    tween Israeli and Syrian forces of 31 May 1974.

Location: Golan Heights (Syria)

Headquarters: Damascus

Duration: 3 June 1974 to date

Maximum strength: 1,289 (23 May 1980)

Strength at
1 July 1982:   1,279

Fatalities: 19, including 14 from various accidents and 5 from other causes.

Financial costs: From inception of mission to 31 May 1982: $121,355,321.

Commanders: Brig. Gen. Gonzalo Briceno Zevallos (Peru)
                          Interim Commander   3 June 1974 - 14 Dec. 1974
                    Col. Hannes Philipp (Austria)
                          Officer-in-charge   15 Dec. 1974 - 7 July 1975
                    Major-Gen. Hannes Philipp (Austria)
                          Commander   8 July 1975 - 21 April 1979
                    Col. Guenther G. Greindl (Austria)
                          Officer-in-Charge   22 April 1979 - 30 Nov. 1979
                    Major-Gen. Guenther G. Greindl (Austria)
                          Commander   1 Dec. 1979 - Feb. 1981
                    Major-Gen. Erkri R. Kaira (Finland) Feb. 1981 - May 1982
                    Major-Gen. Carl-Gustav Stahl (Sweden) June 1982 to date.

Troop contributors: Duration   Contribution

                    Austria   3 June 1974 to date   Infantry
                    Canada   5 June 1974 to date   Logistics: signals, supply,
                                                        and transport units
                    Finland   16 Mar. 1979 to date   Infantry
                    Iran   26 Aug. 1975-15 Mar. 1979 Infantry
                    Peru   3 June 1974-10 July 1975 Infantry
                    Poland   5 June 1974 to date   Logistics: engineers and
                                                        some transport service
                    UNTSO   3 June 1974 to date   Military observers as an
                                                        integral part of the Force.

UNITED NATIONS INTERIM FORCE IN LEBANON - UNIFIL

Resolutions:	S/RES/425 (1978) - 19 March 1978	483 (1980) - 17 Dec. 1980
	426 (1978) - 19 March 1978	488 (1981) - 19 June 1981
	434 (1978) - 18 September 1978	501 (1982) - 2 Feb. 1982
	444 (1979) - 19 January 1979	(increased force by 1,000
	450 (1979) - 14 June 1979	men)
	459 (1979) - 19 December 1979	511 (1982) - 18 June 1982
	474 (1980) - 17 June 1980	

Mandated Functions: To confirm the withdrawal of Israeli forces from south Lebanon, to restore international peace and security, and to assist the government of Lebanon in ensuring the return of its effective authority in the area.

Location: South Lebanon

Headquarters: Naqoura

Duration: 19 March 1978 to date

Maximum strength: 6,942 (3 June 1982)

Strength as of 1 July 1982: 6,942

Fatalities: 78, to 1 July 1982, including 67 killed in action and various accidents and 11 from other causes.

Financial costs: From inception of mission to 18 June 1982: $449,889,727.

Commanders: Major-Gen. Emmanuel A. Erskine (Ghana)

Interim Commander	19 Mar. 1978–11 April 1978
Commander	12 April 1978–Feb. 1981
Lt. Gen. William Callaghan (Ireland)	Feb. 1982 to date.

Troop contributors:

	Duration	Contribution
Canada	22 Mar. 1978–7 Oct. 1978	Signal, movement control, and communications units
Fiji	3 June 1978 to date	Infantry
France	23 Mar. 1978–15 Mar. 1979/ May 1982 to date;	Infantry
	23 Mar. 1978 to date.	Logistics: engineering, supply, transport and maintenance units.
Ghana	7 Sept. 1979 to date	Infantry
Iran	22 Mar. 1978–Mar. 1979;	Infantry
	1 April 1978–31 May 1978.	Falcon jet aircraft and crew
Ireland	24 May 1978 to date	Infantry
Italy	26 July 1979 to date	Air unit: helicopters and crews
Nepal	14 Apr. 1978– 20 May 1980	Infantry
Netherlands	27 Feb. 1979 to date	Infantry
Nigeria	30 Apr. 1978 to date	Infantry

Norway	28 Mar. 1978 - July 1979	Logistics: air unit,
	28 Mar. 1978 - Aug. 1980	medical unit maintenance
	28 Mar. 1978 to date	movement control unit
	28 Mar. 1978 to date	
	28 Mar. 1978 to date	Infantry
Senegal	27 Apr. 1978 to date	Infantry
Sweden	23 Mar. 1978 - 17 May 1978	Infantry
	21 Aug. 1980 to date	Logistics: medical unit
UNTSO	20 Mar. 1978 to date	Military observers
		(Observer Group Lebanon)
		assist in special tasks
		under the operational
		control of UNIFIL Force
		Commander.

Since April 1979, a Lebanese national army battalion of 500 all ranks has been deployed in the UNIFIL area of operation. This unit is under the operational control of the UNIFIL Force Commander; its members patrol and man observation posts and checkpoints jointly with UNIFIL soldiers.

Other contributions - (free of all costs to UN)

Australia	June 1978	Arms and ammunition for Fijian contingent.
Germany,	March 1978	Airlift: Norwegian troops.
Fed. Rep.	April 1978	Provided substantial part of vehicles and equipment for Nepalese contingent.
UK	June 1978	Airlift: Fijian troops.
United States	March 1978-June 1978	Airlift: Norwegian, Nepalese, Senegalese, and Irish troops.
		Airlift: equipment for Fijian troops.

Index

About the Editors and Contributors

THE EDITOR

DR. HENRY WISEMAN - Professor, University of Guelph's Department of Political Studies. He is the former Director of Peacekeeping Programs, International Peace Academy and was an official observer for the Academy in Rhodesia for the period of the cease-fire and elections in February - March 1980. He has published numerous articles and monographs on international peacekeeping, and coauthored with Dr. Alastair Taylor the process of the final self-determination of the people of Zimbabwe, From Rhodesia to Zimbabwe: The Politics of Transition.

THE CONTRIBUTORS

BRIG. GEN. CLAYTON E. BEATTIE, CMM, CD - Consultant, former Director General, Policy Planning, National Defence Headquarters, Canada; Commander, Canadian Forces, Northern Region; Chief of Staff, UNFICYP; and Commander, Canadian Contingent, UNFICYP.

DR. ROD B. BYERS - Director, York University Research Programme in Strategic Studies and Associate Professor of Political Science. Dr. Byers has published widely in the field of Canadian foreign and defence policy and strategic studies.

H.E. DR. MICHAEL COMAY - Research Fellow of the Leonard Davis Institute for International Relations, Hebrew University, Jerusalem. He has served as Israel's Assistant Director General of the Ministry of Foreign Affairs, Ambassador to Canada, Permanent Representative to the United Nations, Political Adviser to the Foreign Minister and Ambassador-at-Large, and Ambassador to the Court of St. James.

PROFESSOR DAVID COX - Department of Political Studies, Queen's University, Canada. Teaches and writes on the subjects of peacekeeping, Canadian foreign and defense policy, and Canadian-American relations.

H.E. DR. NABIL A. ELARABY - Ambassador from the Arab Republic of Egypt to India; former Deputy Permanent Representative of the Arab Republic of Egypt to the UN; was Legal Adviser, Camp David Middle East peace talks in 1978, and Legal Adviser to the Ministry of Foregin Affairs, Cairo.

COL. J.D. MURRAY - Base Commander, Canadian Forces Base Moncton and Commanding Officer, 5 Canadian Forces Supply Depot; former Chief Logistics Officer, UNDOF; Assistant Chief Logistis Officers, UNEF II; and Movement Control Detachment Commander, Port Said, UNEF I.

H.E. DR. EDGARDO PAZ-BARNICA - Minister of Foreign Affairs, Honduras; formerly with Secretary-General Department of the Organization of American States, Washington, D.C.

H.E. MR. GEOFFREY A.H. PEARSON - Ambassador from Canada to the U.S.S.R.; former Adviser on Disarmament and Arms Control Affairs, Department of External Affairs, Canada.

PROF. N.A. PELCOVITS - Former Director of UN Policy Planning, U.S. State Department, teaches at the Johns Hopkins School of Advanced International Studies in Washington, D.C. He has written extensively on problems of international peacekeeping.

DR. K. VENKATA RAMAN - Professor of Law, Queen's University, Canada; former Senior Fellow, United Nations Institute for Training and Research; and author of numerous works including The Ways of the Peacemaker.

MAJ. GEN. INDAR JIT RIKHYE - President, International Peace Academy; former Military Adviser to Secretaries-General Hammarskjold and Thant, and Commander, UNEF I. He is author of The Sinai Blunder and co-author of The Thin Blue Line.

COL. WILLIAM M. STOKES, III - Office, Chairman, Joint Chiefs of Staff, U.S. Department of Defense. Member, Task Force on Technology and Peacekeeping, International Peace Academy.

DR. ALASTAIR M. TAYLOR - Professor, Queen's University, Kingston, Ontario. He served with the National Film Board of Canada and the Secretariats of UN Relief and Rehabilitation Administration and the United Nations. Among his many published works are: From Rhodesia to Zimbabwe: the Politics of Transition (co-authored with Dr. Henry Wiseman); Peace-keeping, International Challenge and Canadian Response; Indonesian Independence and the UN; and Civilization - Past and Present.

MR. BRIAN E. URQUHART - Under-Secretary-General for Special Political Affairs, United Nations. He took an active part in the organization and direction of the first UNEF in the Middle East and all subsequent UN peacekeeping operations; he is also one of the principal political advisors of the secretary-general. He is the author of Hammarskjöld.